FROMMER'S EasyGuide TO BEIJING, SHANGHAI & XI'AN

By

Graham Bond

Easy Guides are • **Quick To Read** • **Light To Carry** • **For Expert Advice** • **In All Price Ranges**

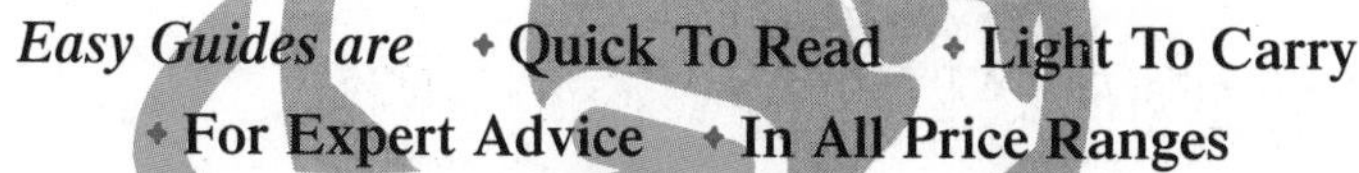

FrommerMedia LLC

Published by
FROMMER MEDIA LLC

ISBN 978-1-62887-170-8 (paper), 978-1-62887-171-5 (e-book)

Editorial Director: Pauline Frommer
Editor: Karen Fitzpatrick
Production Editor: Dika Lam
Cartographer: Elizabeth Puhl
Cover Design: Howard Grossman

For information on our other products or services, see www.frommers.com.

Frommer Media LLC also publishes its books in a variety of electronic formats. Some content that appears in print may not be available in electronic formats.

Manufactured in the United States of America

5 4 3 2 1

FROMMER'S STAR RATINGS SYSTEM

Every hotel, restaurant and attraction listed in this guide has been ranked for quality and value. Here's what the stars mean:

★ Recommended
★★ Highly Recommended
★★★ A must! Don't miss!

AN IMPORTANT NOTE

The world is a dynamic place. Hotels change ownership, restaurants hike their prices, museums alter their opening hours, and busses and trains change their routings. And all of this can occur in the several months after our authors have visited, inspected, and written about, these hotels, restaurants, museums and transportation services. Though we have made valiant efforts to keep all our information fresh and up-to-date, some few changes can inevitably occur in the periods before a revised edition of this guidebook is published. So please bear with us if a tiny number of the details in this book have changed. Please also note that we have no responsibility or liability for any inaccuracy or errors or omissions, or for inconvenience, loss, damage, or expenses suffered by anyone as a result of assertions in this guide.

CONTENTS

1 THE BEST OF CHINA 1

2 SUGGESTED CHINA ITINERARIES 7

3 CHINA IN CONTEXT 27

4 BEIJING 55

Essentials 56
Neighborhoods in Brief 59
Getting Around 60
Fast Facts: Beijing 63
Exploring Beijing 65
Where to Stay 96
Where to Eat 109
Shopping 118
Nightlife 121
Beijing for Kids 129

5 DAY TRIPS FROM BEIJING 131

6 XI'AN 142

Essentials 143
Neighborhoods in Brief 145
Getting Around 146
Fact Facts: Xi'an 150
Exploring Xi'an 150
Where to Stay 162
Where to Eat 168
Shopping 173
Nightlife 176

7 DAY TRIPS FROM XI'AN 179

8 SHANGHAI 191

Essentials 192
Neighborhoods in Brief 197
Getting Around 198
Fast Facts: Shanghai 201
Exploring Shanghai 202
Where to Stay 226
Where to Eat 238
Shopping 246
Nightlife 250
Shanghai for Kids 254

9 DAY TRIPS FROM SHANGHAI 257

10 PLANNING YOUR TRIP TO CHINA 279

11 THE CHINESE LANGUAGE 300

INDEX 308

ABOUT THE AUTHOR

Graham Bond has spent more than a decade writing about China. He lived in mainland China for 5 years, working on the editorial desks of the Shanghai-based travel magazine "Asia and Away" and Beijing's "China Daily," and contributing to a number of international publications, including "The Times," the "South China Morning Post," and "The Australian." Graham currently lives in Hampshire, England, where he has recently completed a doctorate in Chinese communications. He is the author of several guidebooks, including Frommer's Day by Day guides to Shanghai and Hong Kong.

ABOUT THE FROMMER'S TRAVEL GUIDES

For most of the past 50 years, Frommer's has been the leading series of travel guides in North America, accounting for as many as 24% of all guidebooks sold. I think I know why.

Although we hope our books are entertaining, we nevertheless deal with travel in a serious fashion. Our guidebooks have never looked on such journeys as a mere recreation, but as a far more important human function, a time of learning and introspection, an essential part of a civilized life. We stress the culture, lifestyle, history, and beliefs of the destinations we cover and urge our readers to seek out people and new ideas as the chief rewards of travel.

We have never shied from controversy. We have, from the beginning, encouraged our authors to be intensely judgmental, critical—both pro and con—in their comments, and wholly independent. Our only clients are our readers, and we have triggered the ire of countless prominent sorts, from a tourist newspaper we called "practically worthless" (it unsuccessfully sued us) to the many rip-offs we've condemned.

And because we believe that travel should be available to everyone regardless of their incomes, we have always been cost-conscious at every level of expenditure. Although we have broadened our recommendations beyond the budget category, we insist that every lodging we include be sensibly priced. We use every form of media to assist our readers and are particularly proud of our feisty daily website, the award-winning Frommers.com.

I have high hopes for the future of Frommer's. May these guidebooks, in all the years ahead, continue to reflect the joy of travel and the freedom that travel represents. May they always pursue a cost-conscious path, so that people of all incomes can enjoy the rewards of travel. And may they create, for both the traveler and the persons among whom we travel, a community of friends, where all human beings live in harmony and peace.

Arthur Frommer

THE BEST OF CHINA

1

China is a continent-size colossus that swats away those who to try to pin it down with platitudes. It's the font of an ancient, unyielding culture, sure, but it's also as modern and fearless as a joyriding teen. It's deeply traditional, no doubt, but remains oddly calm in the face of relentless change. It's a communist country, in name at least, but run by technocrats whose financial scheming would put even Wall Street to shame. If there's one thing that can be said with reasonable confidence, it's that China rarely stays still for long. The three cities at the heart of this book are rightly renowned, not only for being jam-packed with world-beating tourist sights but also for capturing the different sides of these beguiling contradictions.

Beijing is fast becoming a full-on megacity, dynamic and diverse with pockets of imperial grandeur and low-rise charm. Xi'an is the original melting pot—the New York City of the first millennium—and reels off its ancient hotspots like tomorrow never actually came. Shanghai's swagger is of the modern, moneyed variety, but the city tells a seductive tale of former colonial glory and soaring modern ambition. Amid this abundant tourist treasure, hidden dangers lurk: Pollution has become a serious problem for both residents and visitors, navigating what are increasingly large and crowded cities isn't always easy, and the startling rise of domestic tourism has transformed some of the best-known sights into overpriced circuses. Fortunately for every problem in the People's Republic, there is generally a clever solution. You just have to know the secret. That's what this book is all about. As an entrée to the very best that China has to offer, follow the lists overleaf.

CHINA'S best AUTHENTIC EXPERIENCES

- **Walking on the Great Wall** (Beijing) Seeing the Great Wall for the first time is sure to get the spine tingling, but for the full blood-pumping experience, you need to clamber up and walk. The section near Jinshanling is still in a pleasingly varied state of repair, some areas freshly restored, others thoroughly crumbling. It runs over steep peaks, through patches of astonishing wilderness, and is a worthy introduction to this magnificent monument. See p. 131.
- **Exploring Shanghai's French Concession** This is the most well preserved of Shanghai's former colonial enclaves, with roads lined with plane trees imported from Paris and gorgeous villas from the 1920s and 1930s, the heyday of swinging Shanghai. Art Deco gems abound, hidden behind years of grime and beneath webs of laundry poles—so keep your head up as you wander. See p. 213.
- **Cycling the City Wall in Xi'an** The largest city walls in China have been much pierced for modern needs but can at least be tackled by modern means with a breezy, traffic-free ride above the rooftops on rented bicycles and tandems. Behold views of the vernacular architecture and busy avenues on the inside of the wall, and an ever-thickening forest of skyscrapers on the outside. See p. 154.
- **Dining Like a Local** "A revolution is not a dinner party," said modern China's founding father Mao Zedong. However, a Chinese dinner party can sometimes feel a little like a revolution. Gathering over a meal is China's most popular and occasionally raucous leisure activity. Forget about chicken, beef, or pig's trotters. The essential ingredients are steaming plates, sweaty brows, loud conversation, and frenzied waiting staff. It won't be making the Michelin guide anytime soon, but for old-time dining fun, try Shanghai's **Bao Luo.** See p. 241.

THE most OVERRATED EXPERIENCES

- **Terracotta Warriors** (Xi'an) Qin Shihuang's funerary army remains wondrous on several levels, but it's worth moderating expectations. Problems include the remote location, the bloated commercial circus leading up to the entrance, the crowds, and the fact that years of exposure to beautiful "National Geographic" photography and clever camerawork may leave you underwhelmed. Don't even think about *not* going, but be prepared to dream a little to make the magic work. See p. 150.
- **Tian'anmen Square** (Beijing) To this day, the name conjures memories of the drama and tragedy of 1989. But the words James Fenton wrote then are as true today as ever: "Tian'anmen is broad and clean, and you can't tell

where the dead have been." It's worth remembering, especially for travelers of a more morbid or earnest persuasion. The world's largest patio is designed to a big, bombastic, but basically boring Stalinist spec. Wander around to say you've been but don't expect the memories to linger. See p. 73.

- **Oriental Pearl TV Tower** (Shanghai) There perhaps aren't that many who would "rate" this architectural abomination, but in case you are drawn toward the pink baubles of Shanghai's most iconic building, be warned: It's nearly as silly on the inside as it is on the outside (with the caveat that the separately run basement museum is pretty great). Get your cloud-level kicks instead at one of the three nearby skyscrapers. See p. 225.

THE best RESTAURANTS

- **Temple Restaurant Beijing (TRB)** Tucked away within a central Beijing *hutong* alley, TRB offers sumptuous fine dining within a charming back-street location that five-star hotel rivals can only dream of. It really doesn't matter that there's little authentically "Beijing" about the starchy table-cloths, debonair waiting staff, and snappy suits. It's a world-class restaurant, plain and simple. See p. 112.
- **Di Shui Dong** (Shanghai) This Hunanese restaurant has cornered the market in Shanghai for home-style chili-powered dishes. It's seriously unflashy, with the ruddy-cheeked waitresses observing few airs and graces. But for its mouthwatering—and occasionally face-numbing—peasant dishes and enduring ability to pull in a mixed foreign–Chinese crowd, it deserves its many plaudits. See p. 242.
- **Mr & Mrs Bund** (Shanghai) For a local take on the foamy food alchemy beloved in posh Western restaurants, this chic Bund restaurant is *the* destination. Head chef Paul Pairet has been tickling the taste buds of Shanghai high society for more than a decade, and on the menu are dishes that have attained semi-legendary status, such as the steamed lobster in a citrus jar and the reconstituted lemon tart. A true culinary romp. See p. 239.
- **Lost Heaven** (Beijing and Shanghai) Authentic ethnic cuisine without the fuss and mess of the street stalls in which it's usually served. From its perch just off Tian'anmen Square, Lost Heaven transports its customers to China's tropical Southeast Asian fringe with dreamy decor, sensuous lighting, and dishes of vivid color. For those who miss their moment of culinary romance in Beijing, check out the original Shanghai outpost. See p. 113.

THE best HOTELS

- **Park Hyatt Shanghai** Located in the upper reaches of the Shanghai World Financial Center, the Park Hyatt exists, literally, on a plane of its own. With its minimalist Zen-like interiors and lofty views, this is a hotel that seems to float above the fray and is complemented by some stunning facilities, like the 85th-floor infinity pool and tai chi courtyard. Having your head in the clouds is apparently no bad thing. Exclusive, and expensive, but worth every penny. See p. 237.

- **The Puli** (Shanghai) Styled as an urban resort, the Puli is the hipster's choice and a perfect tonic for China's relentless intensity. Rooms are spa sanctums in miniature and afford twinkling city views from the window-side bathtubs. The real spa downstairs is like a gleaming space pod, complete with sliding doors. And with its extraordinary long bar and cobbled floor, the lobby is perhaps Shanghai's finest. See p. 233.
- **The Peninsula Shanghai** Housed in a Bund new-build—the first major building to go up on Shanghai's famed riverside strip since the 1940s—the Peninsula does old colonial charm better than the *real* heritage hotels that surround it. Art Deco flourishes abound and, as with its world-famous sister hotel in Hong Kong, afternoon tea in the lobby comes with a string quartet. The spa, service, restaurants, and location all contribute to a hotel of near perfection. See p. 228.

THE best UNDISCOVERED EXPERIENCES

- **Beijing's Waterways** Beijing's clamorous streets have become increasingly hazardous for those seeking to explore the capital on foot. The solution is a wander around the metropolis just below pavement level—on its manmade waterways. The network is a combination of ancient canals, historic moats, and modern water diversions. The mostly excellent pedestrian access guides hikers past gleaming skyscrapers and ramshackle hovels and beneath giant intersections. See p. 84.
- **Jing'an's Shikumen** (Shanghai) Most visitors' experience of Shanghai's wonderful East-meets-West *shikumen* architecture begins and ends with the boutiques of Xintiandi. There's a better way. The wonderful stone gates and lintels on show in the Jing'an District may be slightly grimier but are all the more authentic for it. You'll also witness Shanghai's vibrant neighborhood street life, a far cry from the sometimes sterile main thoroughfares. See p. 219.
- **Xi'an's Central Mosques** Xi'an's famous Great Mosque is pretty great until you factor in the entrance ticket and tour-group hordes. A few hundred yards away are two other mosques, slightly smaller but nearly identical in their exquisite courtyard design and with a far greater sense of spiritual repose. They're also free. See p. 156.
- **Workers' Cultural Palace** (Beijing) This is a beautiful slice of imperial architecture that's rarely busy, despite being located right next to the Forbidden City—probably the country's busiest tourist attraction. It enjoys much of the same architecture, grandeur, and historic gravitas of its famous neighbor, yet hardly anybody bothers to stop by on the dash for the big ticket. Don't be put off by the rather dour name. Rather, thank the Maoist moniker for putting off the masses. See p. 72.

THE best FOR FAMILIES

- **Shichahai Skating** (Beijing) The collective name for the network of three lakes that run north of the Forbidden City, Shichahai is pleasant year-round but essential if you visit Beijing from December to February, when Houhai—the southernmost lake—turns into a fabulous natural skate rink. Kids need no skating skills to enjoy the funky chair sleds for hire. See p. 129.
- **The Maglev** (Shanghai) It was built to be a dazzlingly modern piece of Shanghai's transport network, but it takes almost no parental effort to repackage this for the kids as a chance to go faster than a racecar. Even those who hate rollercoasters will be able to enjoy the 431kmph (268 mph) top speeds from the security of the bullet carriages. See p. 193.
- **Shanghai Ocean Aquarium** China's waters may be shockingly murky, but the curators of this excellent aquarium have expanded their horizons, from the Amazon to the Antarctic. The spectacular underwater tunnel that twists and turns over 155m (509 ft.) is the highlight, though the twice-daily shark, penguin, and seal feedings will also intrigue, or appall, younger members of the clan. See p. 255.
- **Biking in Hangzhou** Flanked by misty mountains and studded with pagodas, Hangzhou's West Lake is China's most serene body of water. The oldest metropolitan bike-sharing network in China also happens to be the largest in the world and has made it a cinch to explore the watery jewel in Hangzhou's crown. The way is flat, so older kids can pedal themselves, but some of the 66,000 bikes also have child seats. See p. 26.
- **ERA: Intersection of Time** China is full of acrobatic shows, most of which are impressive in artistry but lacking in presentation. Not so at ERA, Shanghai's long-running spectacular. The creators were all schooled in Cirque du Soleil wizardry, and the result is a beautifully presented show of near unbelievable bravado. Assuming they can bear to look, the kids will love it. See p. 253.

THE best FREE THINGS TO DO

- **Chairman Mao's Mausoleum** (Beijing) After Mao Zedong died in 1976, the Communist Party, which he had molded in his image, ignored his wish to be cremated and instead embalmed his body for permanent display. Mao's crystal coffin is raised from its underground refrigeration unit each morning and there is a guaranteed line of devotees outside ready to pay their respects. Whatever your feelings about the Great Helmsman, it's a worthy cultural experience. See p. 74.
- **The Museums** China's major museums always charged their guests, up until the time of the 2008 Beijing Olympics, when "soft power" became the big new thing. Promoting the nation's cultural treasures is now part of a coordinated global strategy, generating pride at home and awe abroad. The net result is that overseas visitors need only their passports to enjoy the very

best of the cultural bounty on display at the **National Museum of China** (see p. 76), the **Shaanxi History Museum** (see p. 160), and the **Shanghai Museum** (see p. 208), among others.

- **The Wild Wall** (Beijing) Slithering over the undulating landscapes of northern China like some kind of mythical dragon, the Great Wall is unquestionably one of the wonders of the world. It's not always possible to appreciate the magic amid the hawkers, cable cars, and tourist mobs at the easily accessible sections north of the city. Those who relish an adventure and a chance to get away from the crowd should consider a trip to the undeveloped areas where entrance gates have not yet gone up. See p. 134.

THE best MUSEUMS

- **The National Museum of China** (Beijing) After a mammoth restoration effort that cost nearly $400 million, the National Museum—three times the size of the Louvre in Paris—impresses with its trove of more than one million cultural relics from China's lengthy history. Don't miss the exhibit on Ancient China, which covers in exhaustive detail the prehistoric era through China's final dynasty, the Qing. See p. 76.
- **Shaanxi History Museum** (Xi'an) Shaanxi may only be a humble province, but it's a province with serious historical pedigree. This compelling museum is compact and concise enough to get around in a couple of hours, and has an unrivaled collection of Silk Road relics. Oh, and then there's the small matter of the Terracotta Warriors, a handful of which are on display and can be seen from a closer vantage point here than at Qin Shihuang's fabled tomb itself. See p. 160.
- **Shanghai Municipal History Museum** (Shanghai) It's not free, but this superb museum paints a vivid picture of Shanghai's short-but-swashbuckling history. Where most Chinese museums major on statues and bronze work—exhibits that require a little background knowledge to appreciate—this place tells its tale using dioramas, sound effects, and colorful waxworks. It's a museum that even a history newbie can appreciate. See p. 225.

SUGGESTED CHINA ITINERARIES

2

Traveling independently in China looks a lot more straightforward than it did a decade ago, thanks to rapid advances in the transportation system. High-speed rail has given visitors an alternative to the already extensive airport network, and within major cities, new subway routes are being tunneled all the time. In theory, getting around has never been easier. The truth is a bit less rosy. There are now many more people on the move than there were even a few years back, and it shows. Hailing cabs is much harder than it ever was, and the subway can be an almighty squeeze. Advance planning on *when* and *how* to travel will pay steep dividends on the ground. Likewise, visiting sights at the right time is critical if you want to avoid delays and frustration.

This book is structured around a trinity of cities: Beijing and its cornucopia of imperial sights, Xi'an's ancient treasures, and the bustling contrasts of Shanghai and the surrounding water towns. All of the destinations mentioned are served by tour companies (p. 279), but you can also make arrangements yourself thanks to improvements in booking. Flights are now nearly all ticketless, and train tickets can be bought online up to 60 days in advance (p. 284).

With distances being so vast, it pays to avoid having to link the triangle at the end of your trip. This can be easily done by asking your agent to book a flight *into* either Shanghai or Beijing, and *out of* the other. Such a plan should present no problem, as both cities have extensive links to all major international destinations.

If at all possible, avoid being in China for the 2 weeks on either side of Chinese New Year. Dates for the holiday vary each year but, as a rule of thumb, late January and February are lousy times to visit. Not only is the weather frigid in northern China, all forms of transportation are booked solid, prices can rise steeply, and popular destinations become swamped. The weeklong National Day holiday, at the beginning of October, is also worth avoiding for similar reasons.

Finally, be prepared to be flexible around the pollution. These tours recommend long rambles around evocative lanes, through temples and palaces, and even across mountain peaks. Hopefully the skies will be clear, but realistically, they probably won't. The number of days when being outside is positively hazardous for your health is on the increase. In such circumstances, be prepared to swap schedules for days that focus more on indoor attractions. Or just join the locals and buy a face mask (see p. 52).

SHANGHAI & BEIJING IN 1 WEEK

Getting between cities is easier than ever, but no amount of high-speed tech changes the fact that China is big, lines tend to be long, and it just *takes time* to move between destinations. Because of this, cramming all three of the showcase destinations in this book into a single week is not recommended. It could be done, but you would certainly return home feeling more frazzled than inspired. Rather, we're going to use high-speed rail to our advantage around Shanghai, and we'll save time by booking a flight *into* Shanghai and *out of* Beijing to avoid wasting half a day in transit.

This weeklong itinerary takes in the obvious sights in the starkly contrasting but highly international cities of Shanghai and Beijing, and throws some of the *shanshui* (mountain and water) scenery of beautiful Jiangnan into the deal. Visiting this area used to require at least a weekend from Shanghai, transportation included, but rail links have made things simpler. This tour recommends staying over in Hangzhou, as the onward ride to Beijing takes roughly the same time from both cities. However, for those who prefer to change hotel only once, Hangzhou can be seen in a day from Shanghai. If jet-lag is really biting, Hangzhou can be skipped altogether. **Qibao** (p. 265), in the Shanghai suburbs, gives at least a taste of Jiangnan scenery without impacting the overall plan.

The tour assumes you arrive fresh as a daisy and ready to hit the road from sunrise on Day 1. If you've flown overnight, or have a shortened first day, Day 2 is the more relaxed of the two spent in Shanghai, so consider switching. Finally, ensure the two train rides are booked online a few days before you depart and the tickets delivered to your Shanghai hotel (see p. 285 for more on how this might work). Getting seats isn't the problem—there are plenty of trains—rather, the key is getting tickets on the very fastest trains and having them in your hand before you set out to avoid stress at what are huge, busy and sometimes confusing stations. It's also possible, and only marginally more expensive, to fly from Hangzhou to Beijing, though you'll obviously see less of the country. The eastern train routes have little wow factor in terms of natural scenery, but viewing the country up close from the train remains a wonderful experience.

Shanghai & Beijing in 1 Week

MONGOLIA
INNER MONGOLIA
Hohhot
HEBEI
Shenyang
LIAONING
NORTH KOREA
Pyongyang
Huang R.
Datong
Beijing
5 6 7
Tianjin
Yellow R.
HEBEI
Shijiazhuang
Taiyuan
SHAANXI
SHANXI
Weifang
Jinan
Qingdao
Tai Shan
SHANDONG
4
Qufu
Yellow Sea
GANSU
Luoyang
Kaifeng
Zhengzhou
JIANGSU
Xi'an
Huashan
Songshan
HENAN
ANHUI
Nanjing
Hefei
Suzhou
Shanghai
1 2
Tongli
HUBEI
Yangzi R.
Jiuhua Shan
Wuhan
3
Hangzhou
Huang Shan
Lu Shan
ZHEJIANG
Chongqing
CHONGQING
Nanchang
Changsha
HUNAN
JIANGXI
East China Sea
GUIZHOU
Heng Shan
Fuzhou
Guiyang
FUJIAN
Taipei
Guilin
Xiamen
TAIWAN
Yangshuo
GUANGDONG
Guangzhou
GUANGXI
Nanning
Hong Kong
South China Sea
Days 1 & 2 Shanghai
Day 3 Train to Hangzhou
Day 4 Hangzhou to Beijing
Days 5, 6 & 7 Beijing
0 200 mi
0 200 km
PHILIPPINES

Days 1 & 2: Shanghai

Though it doesn't have the world-famous tourist attractions of more historic locales, Shanghai is the most international, and compact, of China's cities, making it the easiest launch pad for your trip. If you're only here for a week, you'll need to minimize the time spent in culture shock as much as possible—the top hotels, excellent restaurants, extensive subway system, and superior English-language base will ease this process.

On Day 1, limit yourself to the 2.4km/1½-mile corridor between the financial district of Lujiazui and **People's Park** (p. 208), the closest thing Shanghai has to a geographic center. Start with a coffee in the 87th-floor lobby of the **Park Hyatt Shanghai** (p. 237), where you can get your bearings from a height usually reserved for helicopter passengers. For a more tactile introduction, head down to the nearby **Shanghai History Museum** (p. 225). With these orientations complete, cross the river via the tourist tunnel—silly, overpriced but nonetheless convenient—to the **Bund** (p. 203). Take a stroll south on the elevated waterside promenade, and back north on the pavement next to the neoclassical buildings, peering in to one or two as you go. Head west along **Nanjing Dong Lu** (p. 207), Shanghai's most famous shopping strip. Upon emerging into People's Park, culture vultures will want to make a beeline for the excellent **Shanghai Museum** (p. 208), while art lovers have the choice between the classical **Shanghai Art Museum** (p. 208) or the trendy **Museum of Contemporary Art** (p. 208). There's probably time for only one before sundown. After closing time, explore the leafy parts of the park, grab a happy-hour cocktail at lakeside restaurant **Barbarossa** (p. 251), then jump on the subway back to Lujiazui for dinner at **Jade on 36** (p. 252). If jet-lag allows, enjoy a nightcap at nearby **Flair** (p. 252), currently the highest bar in China (though probably usurped by the time you read this). The view is astonishing.

Start Day 2 in the leafy **French Concession** (p. 213). Wander slowly east from Changshu Road subway station to get to **Tianzifang** (p. 216) for lunch. Ride the subway to Laoximen and spend the afternoon exploring the **Old City** (p. 198), aiming to reach **Yu Yuan** (p. 209) garden for the final hour of opening, when the crowds should have thinned. The surrounding bazaar is great to shop after dark, and try to find time for a spot of tea in the **Huxinting Teahouse.** Street-food stalls are plenty, so after a quick bite, head up to the Shanghai Circus World on the subway for the evening performance of **ERA: Intersection of Time** (p. 253), still the best acrobatics show in town. For late drinks, head back down to **Xintiandi** (p. 216).

Day 3: Train to Hangzhou

Hangzhou is renowned for its serene beauty and was labeled by Marco Polo as the most beautiful city in the world when he (allegedly) dropped by in the 13th century. It still does a roaring trade in silk and tea, but West Lake, encircled by pagodas and misty mountains, is the real draw.

The 110-mile ride takes as little as 45 minutes on the bullet train. Aim to arrive by midmorning to maximize your time. On arrival, head for your hotel, ideally near West Lake, via Line 1 of the subway. After a restorative drink or an early lunch, stroll along to **Hefang Jie,** Hangzhou's attractive, if slightly Disneyfied, culture street. Wander west until you get to the landscaped gardens beside Hangzhou Museum. Skip the museum and instead apply for a bicycle rental at the counter beside the entrance to Wushan Square (see p. 268) to begin exploring properly on two wheels. Ride west to reach **West Lake** (p. 268), the most fabled body of water in China, thanks to its glassy tranquility and mountainous backdrop. Mini-attractions are spread around its 8-mile circumference. Take the southerly route through the beautifully cultivated parkland that buffers the bottom half of the lake. Pass the eye-catching **Leifeng Pagoda** and cross to the northern side of the lake via the long and scenic Su Di causeway. Ditch the bike here and have an early dinner (before 5pm) at **Lou Wai Lou** (p. 271) before the crowds arrive and while there is still light to enjoy the lake views. After dinner, and with tickets purchased in advance, walk to the touristy-but-lovely **Impression West Lake** (p. 272), a showcase of dazzling choreography and seductive lighting amid the pretty lakeside scenery.

Day 4: Hangzhou to Beijing

Make sure a ticket is in your hand before you set out (see p. 284 for more on the need to avoid station queues) and take the fast train (5–5½ hr.) for the 800-mile trip from Hangzhou East to Beijing South. Though a flight takes a little over 2 hours, time is made up both on the speedier check-in and the relative ease of transportation to and from the station compared to the airport. Overall, the train may still take an hour or so longer, door to door, but it's worth the sacrifice for the ground-level views of the Chinese hinterland. Aim to arrive by midafternoon and head downtown via the subway to reach your hotel. The late-afternoon and evening plan will depend *entirely* on where you are staying; Beijing is not a city where one gets anywhere fast. If you are staying centrally, take a dusk-wander around **Tian'anmen Square** (p. 73) and the **Legation Quarter** (p. 75). For those staying north of the Forbidden City, catch the sunset from **Jingshan Park** (p. 71). If you are on either side of the Forbidden City, ask at reception for the nearest *hutong* complex (you may well be staying *in* one) and take a stroll. For those farther east in Chaoyang—Beijing's social center—check out the night scene around the Central Business District (CBD) and **Sanlitun** (p. 60).

Days 5, 6 & 7: Beijing

Start early at the **Temple of Heaven** (p. 83). The temple itself is a must-see but the surrounding parkland is worth exploring in itself, especially at dawn when you'll find locals practicing tai chi, calligraphy, or morning exercises. Ride the subway north to **Qianmen** (p. 120) and walk north across **Tian'anmen Square** (p. 73), finding time to stop by **Chairman Mao's Mausoleum** (p. 74). At the top of the square, climb **Tian'anmen** (p. 71)—the Gate of Heavenly Peace—before walking north, beneath Mao's iconic portrait, into the **Forbidden City** (p. 65). Plan to spend the entire afternoon here. Emerge at the northern gate and head into **Jingshan Park** (p. 71) for a wonderful sunset view back down the length of the palace—pollution permitting. From here, it's not too far to walk to the spectacular **Temple Restaurant Beijing** (p. 112), though it's the kind of place where you might want to head home for a shower and a change of clothes first.

On your second day in town, focus farther north. Begin near where you left off yesterday at beautiful **Beihai Park** (p. 85). Continue the stroll alongside **Qianhai Lake** (p. 128). Cross to the north side of the lakes via the bridge where Qianhai Lake and Houhai Lake connect, and head along the touristy-but-fun **Tobacco Alley** (p. 97). It's a short stroll to the twin **Drum and Bell Towers** (p. 79). Finally, ride the subway to the **Lama Temple** (p. 82).

Your final day is all about the **Great Wall** (p. 131). Even the closest sections are sufficiently far from downtown and demand most of the day. **Mutianyu** (p. 132) is the best option if time is short. It's less crass than Badaling but still has a cable car to help make climbing the wall as brisk as you need it to be. A trip out to the **Summer Palace** (p. 94) is an alternative final-day excursion, but the mood is similar to Hangzhou's West Lake. If you've already seen Hangzhou, you're safe to skip it. Later, head back downtown via the subway before going to the airport for (ideally) a late flight home.

BEIJING, XI'AN & SHANGHAI IN 2 WEEKS

If you have booked a regular return flight into and out of the same city, 2 weeks is the least you'll need for a full circuit of the three showcase cities. This said, the last thing you'll want after 2 busy weeks on the road in urban China, and before a long flight home, is a half-day transit between Beijing and Shanghai, so try to avoid this if possible.

As the king of Chinese tourism, Beijing stands at the head of proceedings, and this 2-week tour allows for the 4 days needed to do it any kind of justice. The ride out to Xi'an will give visitors both a great sense of China's ancient pedigree as well as a taste of the stark differences in life between the suave eastern metropolises and the inland cities. It's also close to lovely Huashan mountain. Shanghai began the last tour but ends this one. Its air of global sophistication helps visitors ease into Chinese ways, but it's equally a great place for some R&R after the historic but austere sights of Beijing and Xi'an. There's also time to explore the area around Shanghai in a little more depth. Transportation between cities is a mixture of train and plane. While Beijing is

Beijing, Xi'an & Shanghai in 2 Weeks

MONGOLIA
INNER MONGOLIA
Hohhot
HEBEI
LIAONING
Shenyang
NORTH KOREA
Pyongyang
Huang R.
Datong
Beijing
Tianjin
HEBEI
Yellow R.
Shijiazhuang
Taiyuan
SHAANXI
SHANXI
Weifang
Jinan
Qingdao
Tai Shan
SHANDONG
Yellow Sea
Qufu
GANSU
Luoyang
Kaifeng
Zhengzhou
JIANGSU
Xi'an
Huashan
Songshan
HENAN
ANHUI
Nanjing
Hefei
Suzhou
Shanghai
Tongli
Yangzi R.
HUBEI
Wuhan
Jiuhua Shan
Huang Shan
Hangzhou
Chongqing
CHONGQING
Lu Shan
ZHEJIANG
Nanchang
Changsha
HUNAN
JIANGXI
East China Sea
GUIZHOU
Heng Shan
Fuzhou
Guiyang
FUJIAN
Taipei
Guilin
GUANGXI
Xiamen
TAIWAN
GUANGDONG
Guangzhou
Hong Kong
South China Sea
0 200 mi
0 200 km
PHILIPPINES
Days 1, 2, 3 & 4 Beijing
Day 5 The Great Wall at Jinshanling
Day 6 Train to Xi'an
Days 7 & 8 Xi'an
Day 9 Huashan
Day 10 Fly to Shanghai
Days 11 & 12 Shanghai
Day 13 Tongli
Day 14 Suzhou

linked with both Xi'an and Shanghai by high-speed rail, at the time of writing, it is a lengthier journey than by plane. For this trip, traveling by plane makes more sense, especially as it allows easy access to Emperor Jingdi's Mausoleum, one of the city's best sights. Alternatively, try an overnight sleeper train; they can be great fun. Finally, because of the extra time at the start of the trip, it means it's possible to wait until you reach Beijing to book onward transportation. This will allow for flexibility should the Beijing smog hit and you want to move on more quickly. Book online 3 days in advance, and it should be no problem to have tickets couriered to your concierge.

Days 1, 2, 3 & 4: Beijing

Begin your China adventure at the political heart of the Chinese universe. In terms of its attractions, Beijing is by far China's most tourist-friendly city and thus the most obvious point of departure for visitors. However, it's worth steeling yourself in advance, as Beijing is not for the faint-hearted. It's a sprawling city where, much like the country at large, distances are vast. Even the walk between subway interchanges can take the best part of 15 minutes. What this means for visitors is that you must decide which area to explore on any given day and stick to the plan, traveling on foot or by bicycle wherever possible. On Day 1, focus on south central Beijing, starting early at the **Temple of Heaven** (p. 83), moving north through the bustling outdoor *hutong* alleys and shopping streets near **Dazhalan** (p. 87) and the Communist bombast on and around **Tian'anmen Square** (p. 73). Get your shot of Mao's iconic portrait today because you'll enter the Forbidden City via a different route tomorrow. Spend the afternoon laying foundations for the rest of the trip at the first-rate **National Museum of China** (p. 76). Wander around the **Legation Quarter** (p. 75) toward dark, where there are a few wonderful bars and restaurants.

Day 2 begins at the entrance to the **Workers' Cultural Palace** (p. 72) on Nanchizi Dajie. Enjoy the stunning imperial surrounds in near solitude, and when you're ready, exit by the west gate and join the crowds streaming into the **Forbidden City** (p. 65). Begin the mandated south-to-north walk-through, exploring the side streams as you go. Plan to spend the entire morning here. After leaving, cross the road and wander up to **Jingshan Park** (p. 71) for views back across the imperial compound. Make the journey north to the **Drum and Bell Towers** (p. 79) by meandering through **Beihai Park** (p. 85) and north to the *hutong* to the west of **Qianhai Lake** (p. 128). Walk north to meet **Houhai** (p. 59) and make the pleasant stroll around the circumference of the lake to hit the **Drum and Bell Towers** (p. 79) by late afternoon. When sated, walk east toward the throng along **Nan Luogu Xiang** (p. 83), and peel off to quieter side streets for dinner and drinks.

Begin Day 3 with morning rituals at **Lama Temple** (p. 82). When the crowds begin pouring in, head over the road to the quieter but scarcely less lovely **Confucius Temple** (p. 79). Then it's a subway ride out east to Chaoyang, the center of non-tourist Beijing. Have lunch and enjoy early-afternoon shopping and people-watching around **Sanlitun Village** (p. 120). After that, head south by taxi or subway toward the noise and clamor of the **Panjiayuan** (p. 121) antiques market. It's back up to Guomao on the subway for drinks and dinner in the **Central Business District** (p. 66).

Day 4 is consumed by the ride out into the western suburbs to see the sublime **Summer Palace.** By the time you read this, it should be possible to get all the way there by subway.

Day 5: The Great Wall at Jinshanling

If you're trying to squeeze a Great Wall trip into half a day or less, your options are limited: It's probably **Badaling** (p. 132) or bust. Give over a full day, dawn until dusk, and suddenly the stunning mountains north of Beijing open up their treasure. Though it's about as far as you can get from downtown without leaving Beijing, Jinshanling is magnificent. It's no longer possible to walk all the way to nearby Simatai because of recent redevelopment. Book a tour through a hotel or hostel, ensuring that you get at least 4 hours on the wall—equaling the time you'll spend in transit. A trip to **Mutianyu** (p. 132) is easier, though more touristy. Just avoid Badaling, the least lovable of all the Great Wall options.

Day 6: Train to Xi'an

Take the morning fast train from Beijing West Station to Xi'an. It's a 5½-hour ride that runs down to Zhengzhou in Henan province, and across in Shaanxi, getting you into Xi'an for midafternoon. Station taxis change shift at this time, so take the subway to reach the city center instead. After checking in to your hotel, head out to **Beiyuanmen** (p. 156). It's a riot after dark. Follow the crowds into the first alley on the left, signposted "Great Mosque," into a continuation of the bazaar. At the end, turn right and right again into **Dapiyuan**, a great spot to settle down in a steamy restaurant while avoiding the mostly underwhelming and touristy food options on Beiyuanmen itself.

Days 7 & 8: Xi'an

Two days is more than sufficient to see Xi'an's premier sights. The **Terracotta Warriors** (p. 150) remain the big-ticket draw, so don't delay. It's farther out of town than you may think, so plan to spend the best part of the day here. Fast forward through the commercial nonsense outside the main gate by hiring one of the golf carts. Return to the city by late afternoon and enjoy an evening bicycle circuit of Xi'an's impressive **City Walls** (p. 154) at dusk. It'll take 2 hours at a leisurely pace, but bikes can be returned up until 8pm. Afterward, descend at the South Gate and head into one of the craft-beer bars alongside the south wall (see p. 176). Begin Day 2 at the **Small Wild Goose Pagoda** (p. 157) before wending south by taxi or subway to the city's main museum attraction and must-see, the **Shaanxi History Museum** (p. 160). Spend the afternoon in Qujiang, a short cab ride away (or walkable in 20 minutes). It's home to the **Great Wild Goose Pagoda** (p. 158) and surrounding parks and malls. As evening approaches, head into the nearby **Tang Paradise** (p. 161) theme park. The park is fairly dull during the day but sparkles at night, especially at the 7:45pm water show. After, head to the nearby **Xinlehui** (p. 174) mall, where there is a good selection of modern restaurants and bars.

Day 9: Huashan

Take Line 2 subway to Xi'an North Railway Station and ride an early bullet train to **Huashan** (p. 179), a precipitous and holy granite peak located half an hour east of the city. Ascend the mountain from the **West Peak cable car** and spend 3 or 4 hours walking the loop between the four 2,000m-plus (6,562-ft.) peaks before making the heart-pounding walk back down across the **Green Dragon Ridge** to the lower North Peak, where you can descend again, either by cable car or by the thigh-aching climb of the steep staircase. Grab a taxi back to the station and return to Xi'an in time for another supper in the **Muslim Quarter** (p. 156).

Day 10: Fly to Shanghai

Arrange a taxi collection early from your hotel and head out to Xi'an's rather distant airport. En route, depart the airport expressway for a short detour to the **Han Yang Ling Mausoleum** (p. 161). This is a pithier, and arguably better-presented, variation on Qin Shihuang's famed Terracotta Warriors—though the funereal guardians are considerably smaller. It's a 90-minute stop, but well worth it. Your flight should get you into Shanghai by early evening. Once in town, head to **the Bund** (p. 203) for a casual evening waterside stroll and the city's finest wining and dining.

Days 11 & 12: Shanghai

Follow the advice given in the 2-day trip to Shanghai sketched out in the previous itinerary. The 2 days can be done in either order, though begin, if possible, with the skyscraper views of **Lujiazui** (p. 252) and the **Shanghai History Museum** (p. 225). Both offer important context to what comes later.

Day 13: Tongli

Shanghai is bang in the middle of the Yangtze River Delta, and it only takes a short ride out of the asphalt jungle to understand that this is a megalopolis with decidedly watery foundations. While Shanghai is forever battling that sinking feeling, other parts of the region revel in their delta roots, not least the canal towns that dot the landscape between Shanghai, Suzhou, and Hangzhou. These come in various shapes and sizes but are consistent in their lovely canals, photogenic stone bridges, and waterside cafes. The big guns are **Wuzhen** and **Zhouzhuang,** but they attract the largest crowds and are hard to recommend. **Tongli, Xitang,** and **Nanxun** are smaller, and worthy alternatives. They'll still get packed on weekends—avoid visiting at these times at all costs, even if it means switching the schedule around—but can be pleasant on weekdays. For those moving on to Suzhou, **Tongli** (p. 263) is the obvious choice, not least because it combines lovely scenery with the fascinating **China Sex Culture Museum** (p. 263), assuming it has reopened. Visit as a day trip from Shanghai, stay over in a waterside guesthouse, or take a late bus or taxi onto Suzhou for the next stop. Stopping for the night is highly recommended. The night scenes around the canals are marvelous, and you avoid the crush for the last bus back to town.

Day 14: Suzhou

Take an early bus to Suzhou South Passenger Bus Station and head north to enter the ancient city, identified by the moat that surrounds it. Suzhou can tend to be seen as a slightly backward little brother by Shanghai and her more sophisticated residents. The truth is that Shanghai is the modern pretender to Suzhou's historic title of Jewel of the East. The ancient city admittedly now lies amid a very modern sprawl but contains some charming cobbled streets, meandering canals, and genteel gardens. Begin just east of Lindun Lu subway station and walk north on the canal side of **Pingjiang Lu** (p. 261). Near where the canal diverts at a T-junction is the **Humble Administrator's Garden** (p. 260), the largest of Suzhou's several classical gardens. Try to get here for midday, when many of the tour groups get dragged off for their lunch. The superb **Suzhou Museum** (p. 262) is just around the corner and has 30,000 cultural relics and archaeological finds from across the nation. Take the subway over to **Shangtang Jie** (p. 261) and take a canal-boat ride around sundown before heading up to Suzhou Railway Station on the subway and taking the train back to Shanghai.

Day 15: Fly Home

To finish your explorations of Shanghai, it's well worth heading back to **Xintiandi** (p. 216) if you didn't make it on your previous visit. Stop by the **Shikumen Open House Museum** (p. 217) and surrounding boutiques and restaurants. Or for a real *shikumen* experience, wander along the shopping street of Nanjing Xi Lu to meet **Taixing Lu** (p. 219). The residential lanes here are among the city's most attractive. Fly back home, either connecting in Beijing, or ideally, directly from Shanghai.

CHINA FOR FAMILIES IN 10 DAYS

First the bad news: China is not a particularly easy family destination. The drawbacks range from the pollution, which can tend to upset young lungs—especially those who may suffer from asthma—to the severe city congestion, which means pushing strollers or keeping hold of a small hand is that much more challenging. Conditions at dependable child-friendly options—zoos, fun parks, and swimming centers—are generally poor and they're not recommended. All told, the tiring intercity trips and reduced patience thresholds that most kids exhibit means 10 days is about your max. Now the good news: It's hard to imagine a place where children attract more ambient fondness than China. Travel with young kids on the subway and, regardless of your Mandarin levels, you're almost certain to fall into mimed dialogue with fellow passengers. They'll also take the edge off the hawking and hard-selling around major attractions. Best of all—for the kids at least—**Shanghai Disneyland** (p. 255) is scheduled to open by spring 2016. Because your visit to the Middle Kingdom's Magic Kingdom can be used as bait in the event of the kids becoming unruly, it's being scheduled right at the end of the trip. A multiday pass to the park could bring the vacation back up to the more traditional 2-week mark.

Days 1, 2, 3 & 4: Beijing

Beijing's sprawl makes it vital to plan carefully when traveling independently in the capital with youngsters. When it comes to waiting for cabs and walking between subway stations, adults have a hard-enough time with the whining and moaning. Children may fare even worse.

The kids won't necessarily be enthralled by the capital's history-heavy tourist sites, but that's no reason to skip them altogether. Start with the cool echo wall at the **Temple of Heaven** (p. 83). Close to the East Gate is the **Hongqiao Toy Market** (p. 121), which might provide a useful carrot to dangle if the kids get restless. Head north to **Tian'anmen Square** (p. 73), where kids will certainly enjoy the sense of space. Freedom to run in Beijing is rare; enjoy it. Next, head beneath Mao's giant portrait into the **Forbidden City** (p. 65). With kids, it's probably best to just do the straight walk-through, which takes about an hour. Head into **Jingshan Park** (p. 71) and enjoy sunset from the peak. Day 2 should begin with kite-flying in **Beihai Park** (p. 85). The Three Stones Kite store (25 Di'anmen Xi Dajie; ✆ **010/8404-4505**) is a short walk east of the park's north entrance (see p. 81). Emerging from the park via the same entrance, strike a deal with one of the rickshaw drivers who offer tours around the *hutong* close to the Shichahai lakes. Ask to stop for ice cream, if necessary. Return back to the southernmost lake, **Qianhai** (p. 128), where a lakeside ramble can be punctuated with a pedal-boat ride. Sell the young ones the idea of visiting the nearby **Drum and Bell Towers** (p. 79) on the basis of the noisy displays of drumming and ringing.

Begin Day 3 with morning rituals at **Lama Temple** (p. 82). Though temples rarely get the kids excited, the sheer color and vibrancy of Tibetan clothing, rituals, and architecture should hold the attention for a time. Take the subway east to Chaoyang. **Sanlitun Village** (p. 120) has shops and cafes to appeal to all tastes, and makes for great people-watching. Nearby is the rambling **Chaoyang Park** (p. 129), which

China for Families in 10 Days

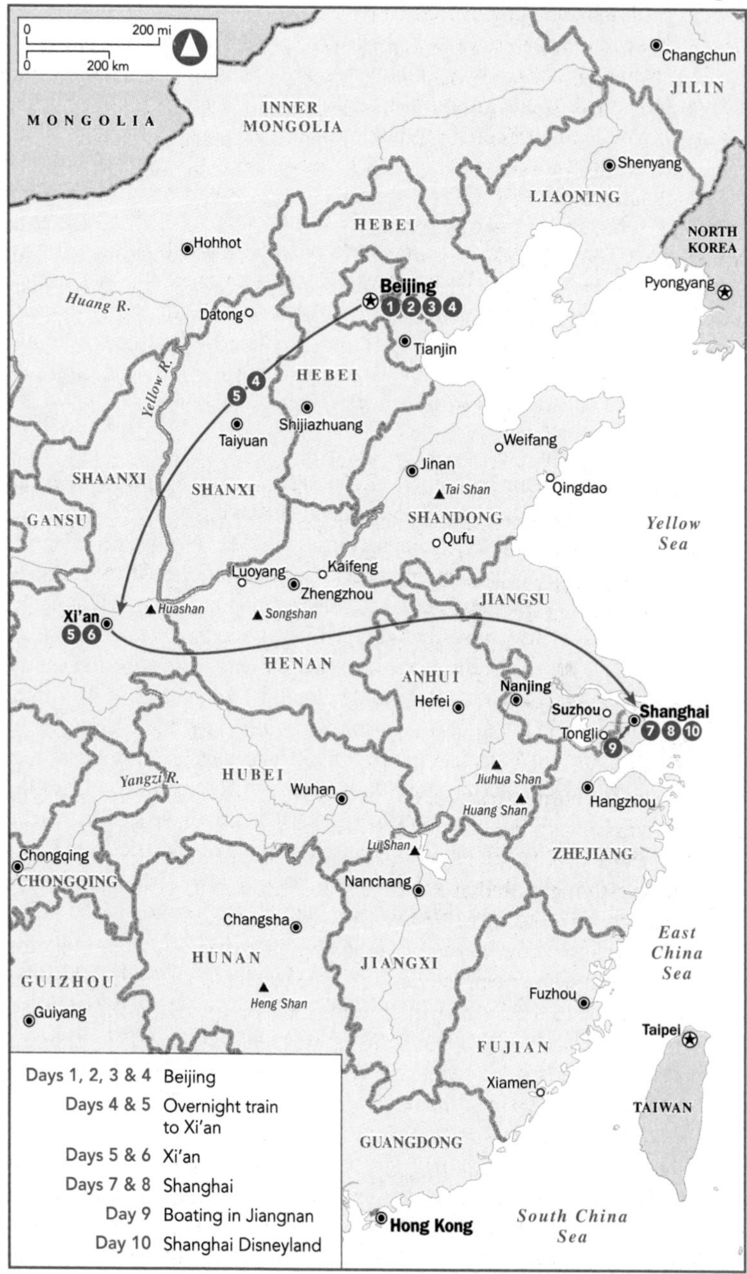

Days 1, 2, 3 & 4	Beijing
Days 4 & 5	Overnight train to Xi'an
Days 5 & 6	Xi'an
Days 7 & 8	Shanghai
Day 9	Boating in Jiangnan
Day 10	Shanghai Disneyland

comes complete with a swimming area and zip line. Come evening, kids will appreciate the daring displays at the **Chaoyang Theater Acrobatics** (p. 127) performance.

On Day 4, it's time to get out of the big city. Head for the **Mutianyu** (p. 132) section of the Great Wall. It's the only option if youngsters are in tow. They will love the cable-car ride up, while the trip down is achieved via the fun toboggan ride. It may look scary, but you're able to travel as fast or as slow as you want, and parents can ride with kids.

Days 4 & 5: Overnight Train to Xi'an

A bullet train or plane is the most obvious way to reach Xi'an, but overnight sleepers will make a fantastic adventure for adults and kids. A family of four can book an entire "soft-sleeper" berth, which is partitioned from the public corridor. Trains departing Beijing West after dinner will arrive in Xi'an at breakfast, meaning the kids can enjoy the adventure of the bunks without having time to get bored.

Days 5 & 6: Xi'an

The schedule from the previous itinerary can be followed in Xi'an, though switching the days is recommended: staying in the city on Day 5 and heading out to the Terracotta Warriors on Day 6. This will give you much-needed time to plan appropriate transportation, with the help of your concierge. On Day 5, kids will love ringing the giant bell at picturesque **Small Wild Goose Pagoda** (p. 157), while the Great Wild Goose Pagoda can be skipped in favor of a ride on Qujiang's **elevated monorail.** There are loads of child-friendly comfort-food options in the nearby **Xinlehui** (p. 174) mall development. Kids will enjoy the evening ambience at the **Tang Paradise** (p. 161) park. The stage performances may not appeal hugely, but the after-dark water display certainly will. When you reach the **Terracotta Warriors** (p. 150) on Day 6, be sure to skip the commercial frenzy around the entrance by taking an electric cart. This is a must if kids are part of the equation. Back in town, head up onto the **City Walls** (p. 154) and rent a tandem bike or two. The top of the wall is wider than many major roads, and there is no motorized traffic at all. You might not want to do the entire 8.5-mile circuit. Opt instead to ride back and forth along the southern section. At night, head to **Beiyuanmen** (p. 156). This raucous, neon-soaked lane is great for a short stroll, and there's a fabulous ice-cream shop at the far north end of the street, **Shanxi Thirteen** (p. 173).

Days 7 & 8: Shanghai

Book one of the many flights from Xi'an that arrive at Shanghai's Pudong airport. This will give you the chance to experience the **Maglev** train (p. 193), a surefire fave for young ones thanks to the 431kmph (268-mph) top speed. After check-in, there'll likely only be a few hours of daylight left. Most kids love a good skyscraper, and Lujiazui doesn't disappoint. Do the skywalk at the **Shanghai World Financial Center** (p. 226), secure enough not to be too scary, but scary enough to perk the kids up. Take a walk around the Lujiazui **river promenade** before heading to the evening performance of **ERA: Intersection of Time** (p. 253), a thrilling spectacle for old and young. Book tickets in advance. On your second day, begin with a walk in **People's Park** (p. 208). The kids will enjoy the giant model of "Future Shanghai" in the **Urban Planning Exhibition Center** (p. 209), while the **Museum of Contemporary Art** (p. 208) often has wacky installations that may appeal to youngsters. Experience the razzmatazz of the shopping street, **Nanjing Dong Lu** (p. 207), as you wander toward the river. There's a dinky tourist train if you need to ease leg strain. At the **Bund** (p. 203), take a stroll south to the **Shiliupu Ferry Port** (p. 223), where cruise ships depart. There are plenty of short options that do not stray too far from port, easily the most visually exciting part of the river. Try to book a ride that allows you to hop off on the other side of the river and spend the remainder of the afternoon in the fun **Shanghai Aquarium** (p. 255) or the adjacent **Natural Wild Insect Kingdom** (p. 255). Dinner can be enjoyed at one of the nearby sky-high hotel-buffet restaurants, such as **100 Century Avenue** in the Park Hyatt hotel (p. 226). These have the wow factor of the view, minus the excessively exclusive feel that is likely to make the kids uncomfortable.

Day 9: Boating in Jiangnan

Head out of the big city and spend a day in one of the canal towns of Jiangnan. These offer moderate appeal to young kids, principally for the gondola opportunities and the touristy atmosphere, which sees most visitors wandering the lanes and alleys with snacks and ice creams permanently in their hands. **Tongli** (p. 263) is pleasant, but the ride may be too far for little ones. The best option is to take the tourist bus (30 min.) to **Zhujiajiao** (p. 265), which lies within Shanghai city limits. Unlike other spots, there's no entrance fee to the town itself.

Day 10: Shanghai Disneyland

It's not yet open, and even detailed plans have not been released at the time of writing. However, **Shanghai Disneyland** (p. 255) is definitely taking shape, and barring development hiccups, will be open in the spring of 2016. Though it's not possible to make promises on details, Disney's track record in appealing to youngsters is sound, to say the least, and this Disneyland is likely to be the most high-tech yet.

Day 11: The Fast Track Home

You may want to extend your time in Shanghai, depending on the family's general affection for Disneyland. When it comes time to leave, make the journey back out to Pudong via the **Maglev** (p. 193), warning the kids all the while that the flight back home may not be quite so brisk.

CHINA FOR NATURE-LOVERS IN 2 WEEKS

It's inevitable that the civilization that gave the world Taoism retains a robust respect for nature. China's ancient religion-cum-philosophy took the natural flows of wind and water to serve up a recipe for good living that has echoed down the ages. Anyone who has seen the BBC-CCTV documentary "Wild China" might be salivating at the prospect of the Middle Kingdom's misty peaks and terraced paddies. However, it's important to know that nature worship has hit a couple of major roadblocks of late. Thirty years of Communist experimentation and 35 more of near-unbridled capitalism have left this land deeply scarred—if socialist and free-market doctrines share one thing, it's the attitude that the earth is ripe for exploitation. Much of the Chinese mainland now chokes under a thick cloud of pollution, many waterways are treated as giant garbage cans, and the soil has become alarmingly toxic in places. But within this bleak picture, there are still pockets of serenity and stunning beauty. The most picturesque parts of China are undoubtedly in its sparsely populated far west, but for those who want to combine the essential sights of the crowded eastern seaboard with a taste of China's natural bounty, this tour is for you. You'll probably need to book the train journey from Gongyi to Hangzhou in advance (either online, or through an agent in Xi'an or Luoyang) and be prepared for lots of hiking and hard work on the second half of the tour. Clean air, sadly, is not guaranteed.

Days 1, 2 & 3: Beijing

Start with the serene parkland around the **Temple of Heaven** (p. 83). Get here early to find the spirit of Taoism alive in the tai chi moves and kite-flying. Head north and take a stroll across **Tian'anmen Square** (p. 73) before climbing **Tian'anmen** (p. 71)—the Gate of Heavenly Peace—at the head of the square. Plan to spend the entire afternoon in the adjacent **Forbidden City** (p. 65) but be sure to emerge at the northern gate in good time for sunset. This can be enjoyed in the lovely **Jingshan Park** (p. 71), which has a surprisingly rich birdlife through warmer months, and colorful tulips and peonies in the spring.

On Day 2, cling to the parks and waterways northwest of the Forbidden City. Start at **Beihai Park** (p. 85) and continue along **Qianhai** and **Houhai Lakes** (p. 128). You can hire a chauffeured rickshaw or opt to explore this busy but beautiful area by bike, venturing away from the water, south of Houhai, to enjoy some of the best surviving *hutong*. After lunch, ride the subway across to the Tibetan **Lama Temple** (p. 82) and the nearby **Confucius Temple** (p. 79), both serene in subtly different ways.

Day 3 should be spent out in the western suburbs (there should be a new subway line to take you there by the time you read this). Spend the first half of the day exploring the **Summer Palace** (p. 94), a cluster of historic halls and temples surrounding a delightful central lake, then

China for Nature-Lovers in 2 Weeks

Days 1, 2 & 3	Beijing	Day 10	Huashan to Luoyang
Days 4 & 5	The Great Wall	Day 11	Songshan
Day 6	Train to Xi'an	Day 12	Hangzhou
Days 7 & 8	Xi'an	Day 13	Hangzhou to Shanghai
Day 9	Huashan	Day 14	Shanghai

jump back on the train to reach the **Fragrant Hills** (p. 93) and enjoy the best suburban hiking in Beijing.

Days 4 & 5: The Great Wall

It's hard to get the best of the Great Wall when you're rushing for the bus back to town. Hikers in particular will find it well worth giving over 2 entire days to the **Jinshanling** (p. 132) section of the Great Wall. Staying locally allows you to enjoy a sunset hike after you arrive, and another in the morning. It's possible to book a tour, but the adventurous can take a bus to Jinshanling and stay in a nearby campsite, though you'll need your own tent and sleeping bag. Back in Beijing, stay in one of the capital's restful *hutong* courtyard hotels before your first long train ride the following day.

Day 6: Train to Xi'an

Take the morning fast train from Beijing West Station to Xi'an. It's a 5½-hour ride and gets you into Xi'an for midafternoon. Pick a city-center hotel and visit the **Muslim Quarter** (p. 156) after check-in, contrasting the clamor of the shopping streets of Huajue Alley or Xiyangshi with the quiet calm in one of central Xi'an's **mosques** (see p. 156). **Beiyuanmen** (p. 156) is particularly fun after dark.

Days 7 & 8: Xi'an

Visit the **Terracotta Warriors** (p. 150) during your first full day in Xi'an and return to the city in late afternoon to take a dusk ride around Xi'an's magnificent **City Walls** (p. 154). Though you are surrounded by skyscrapers (on the outside of the wall) and crumbling tenements (inside), there is something wonderfully peaceful about being atop this ancient Ming structure.

On your second day in town, visit the **Small Wild Goose Pagoda** (p. 157), which, thanks to the partly damaged tower and the thick vegetation in the surrounding parkland, evokes a little of the jungle spirit of Angkor Wat, before visiting the **Shaanxi History Museum** (p. 160). Wander into the **Tang Paradise** (p. 161) theme park midafternoon and enjoy a lakeside ramble amid (newly built) Tang-era pagodas. The park has a wonderful 7:45pm water show, or you can head to the 8pm fountain at the public square just north of the **Great Wild Goose Pagoda** (p. 158).

Day 9: Huashan

Ride the bullet train to **Huashan** (p. 179), a holy mountain east of the city. Ascend the mountain from the **West Peak cable car** and spend the entire day attempting to scale each of the four 2,000m-plus (6,562-ft.) peaks. Stay in one of the simple mountain lodges.

Day 10: Huashan to Luoyang

After seeing sunrise from the East Peak, make the thrilling walk across the **Green Dragon Ridge** and descend Huashan. Back at the station, take a G-class (fastest) bullet train to Luoyang. Spend what remains of the day at the riverside **Longmen Grottoes** (p. 184). After dark, negotiate a taxi ride to Dengfeng, basecamp for the Songshan mountains (p. 187). If this proves difficult, stay in Luoyang for the night (where accommodation options are plentiful) and bargain a taxi ride out to Dengfeng early the next morning.

Day 11: Songshan

Rise early for a long day of hiking in the Songshan mountains (p. 188). **Shaolin Temple** (p. 188) is across the way. Stop in if you have time, but the crowds will be so big that you'll probably feel like you're back in the big city. To max out the nature vibe, spend the entire day tramping the wild and remote peaks. Aim to return to Dengfeng by 7pm and find somewhere to take a shower before grabbing a taxi to nearby Gongyi, where you can pick up the 9:14pm sleeper train to Hangzhou (this *must* be booked in advance unless you want to risk ending up in a seat for the 17-hour ride).

Day 12: Hangzhou

The ride to Hangzhou is a long one, but after your exertions, you'll hopefully be sleeping like a baby on the train for most of the journey. It's an early-afternoon arrival in Hangzhou. After check-in at your hotel, spend what remains of the day making a bicycle circuit of **West Lake** (p. 268). Try to grab an evening ticket for the **Impression West Lake** (p. 272) lakeside show.

Day 13: Hangzhou to Shanghai

Take a bus into the beautiful Lingyin Valley overlooking West Lake and stop for a vegetarian lunch at the **Lingyin Temple** (p. 271). In the afternoon, take one of the regular bullet trains to Shanghai. What you do now that you're back in the big city will depend on time. Look at the recommendations for Day 1 and Day 2 of the "1 week" tour for ideas. If possible, try to get to the Huangpu riverside around sunset and take a stroll past the neoclassical buildings of **the Bund** (p. 203). If you have the energy, head across to **Xintiandi** (p. 216) in the **French Concession** for some evening wining and dining.

Day 14: Shanghai

Generally speaking, Shanghai is no place for nature-lovers, though there are attractions aplenty within leafy **People's Park** (p. 208). Drop by the **Shanghai History Museum** (p. 225) and the **Shanghai Art Museum** (p. 208) while taking a stroll around the lakeside paths. There are some great views through the trees to the towering Art Deco buildings on the north fringe of the park. Take lunch on the rooftop restaurant of the **Museum of Contemporary Art** (p. 208), which looks out across the treetops. To end your trip, walk among the throngs on **Nanjing Dong Lu**

(p. 207), if only to remind yourself of what the rest of China has been doing during your wild adventure (answer: they were shopping). If you have time, ride the subway over to **Lujiazui** (p. 252) and take a cocktail at one of the high-rise hotel bars within either the Grand Hyatt, Park Hyatt, or Ritz-Carlton Pudong, contrasting your memories of mountains and lakes with one of *the* great man-made vistas. Finally, head out to the airport via the **Maglev** (p. 193) for your (late) flight home.

CHINA IN CONTEXT

3

Communism has a lot to answer for. Not only did Mao's efforts to rebuild society result in famine and cultural devastation at home, they also transformed views of the Middle Kingdom abroad. Rather than the dynamic, innovative, and cosmopolitan society it had been for much of its history, "Communist China" became an austere, secretive, and foreboding land. This Cold War mentality is still widely held today, but mainly by those who have never been. Visitors tend to have their preconceptions crushed pretty quickly.

In some ways, this has become part of the fun. Yes, there's the Great Wall (pretty great), the Forbidden City (not so forbidden), the one-child policy (boo, hiss), and a distinct lack of democracy. But there is also freedom, and lots of it. Just ask the architects building some of the planet's most fantastical (and sometimes absurd) buildings, the scientists pushing at the fringes of their fields, or the officials who, unlike counterparts back home, don't need to worry so much about rules and regulations. Yes, it helps if you have money and power—and many millions do not—but this is a land where dreams of the "possible" still rule, even for those who haven't yet cut a break. For now, at least, China is a land where little people think big. It's the East's Wild West.

CHINA TODAY

Be not afraid of growing slowly; be only afraid of standing still.

—Chinese proverb

If the above jars too much with what you might have heard about China, let's get some things straight. Media censorship still takes place, there's an absence of religious freedom, widespread repression exists in the frontier regions of Tibet and Xinjiang, and thousands of dissidents remain locked up for what they have written or said. The 2010 Nobel Peace Prize winner, Liu Xiaobo, still languishes in a Chinese jail and will likely remain there until 2019.

But these apparent violations don't tell the whole story. China's media suffers routine political interference, yes, but it's also surprisingly dynamic, vocal, and commercial. You can't start up a religion too easily in China, true, but tens of millions of Christians and Muslims still worship openly. Tibet and Xinjiang *are* both effectively colonized by Han Chinese, but the economic boom *has* benefited many ethnic Tibetans and Uighurs and improved living conditions. And though Liu Xiaobo fought with words, not weapons, he didn't just *write* an anti-Party online petition. He tried to *organize*.

Herein lays the key point when it comes to the puzzle around repression and freedom in modern China. If you have the money and the means, you can do pretty much what you want, so long as you don't attempt to *organize*, not on ethnic grounds, not on religious grounds, and certainly not on political grounds. You can go to China and bash the Communist Party as loudly and openly as you like. Just be careful about asking anyone else to join your Party-bashing cause.

There are problems away from politics too. China's great success in economic development has come at a massive environmental cost. Choking pollution has become a fact of life for hundreds of millions of Chinese. It was once treated with a stoic shrug, but the sheer number of face masks on the streets of major cities is testament to a growing awareness of long-term consequences. One prominent Chinese academic was even quoted (by state media) in 2014 as saying Beijing was "no longer livable for human beings." In addition to the air pollution, increasingly frequent dust storms blast through the north of the country, reducing the amount of arable land available to feed China's burgeoning population, while in many cities, rivers run black and groundwater is toxic. There are efforts to forestall disaster. China has agreed to tentative carbon-reduction targets on the international stage, and there are smaller-scale measures like the Green Great Wall (which aims to counteract soil erosion in the northwest of the country) and seawater–flushing toilets. However, nothing can disguise the fact that China is a land under enormous strain.

The challenges for the long-suffering Party do not end there. Runaway development has exacerbated many of the country's pre-existing problems, and created some new headaches. Overcrowding, gender imbalances, and territorial disputes were a live issue in Mao's day and have become only more acute as the years have passed. Add to this the rapidly aging population, caused by both the one-child policy and low urban birth rates, the creaking and corrupt health system, and the alarming debt-piles in the economy, and you can almost begin to sympathize with Party bosses.

And then there's the inequality. China does not have the desperate slums of other developing nations, but the wealth contrast can feel even more stomach-churning here because of the way the "haves" lord it over the "have-nots." Spend any time in Shanghai or Beijing and you'll likely spot an absurdly expensive sports car dispersing the lowly middle classes (and cyclists) with a combination of engine revs and loud blasts on the horn. Often the cars are driven by designer-clad kids still in full-time school. These are the privileged sons and daughters of the winners in China's reform process, the so-called *fu er dai* (second-generation rich). To be properly wealthy in modern China, you usually need to have parents who belong to a certain social stratum—call it the "entrepreneur-official class." These are individuals who have used their political power to further business interests, be they in manufacturing, real-estate, or finance. Plenty of corruption still works at the level of crude back-handers. But deeper inequality exists in the way many millions of members of the Communist Party have become budding entrepreneurs, putting themselves, or their family members, at the front of the line to take on lucrative projects (which may or may not be desired by target populations). This process applies as much in the countryside as it does in the big cities. While it's still possible to find farmers wearing blue "Mao suits" while ploughing their fields, China's villages also have a coterie of men and women who sport gold Rolexes and wide grins as they speed their way to the next property deal.

In spite of programs that set out to redress the balance, inequality looks to be a fixture in the Chinese social landscape for the time being. This disparity has yet to evoke real dissatisfaction—puzzling an entire generation of pundits who have long assumed the lack of democracy and free media to be inevitable fire-starters. The fact is, the Communist Party is genuinely cherished by a very large number of people in China. This is supported by the work of propaganda officials at all levels of government, sure, but it's not an entirely manufactured feeling. The Party commands respect for its historical achievement in banishing the colonial powers. It gets plaudits at home and abroad for dragging hundreds of millions out of poverty. And most important of all, it is seen by the wealthy and freedom-loving as their best protection against the social instability that might threaten their gains. China has a fairly rich history of bloody revolution, as we'll see in the next section. It means that, while people in China may admit the endemic corruption of the Party, they may also wish for its continued rule. Call it "a contradiction without a contradiction" (a turn of phrase the Party would surely approve of).

Stability at home has paved the way for China's return to the world stage. "China is a sleeping giant. Let her sleep, for when she wakes, she will shake the world," said Napoleon Bonaparte. The comment couldn't seem any more pertinent than it does now. China is finally being recognized as *the* ascendant power, and there is more interest than ever from international-relations experts the world over. In spite of ongoing trade disputes, China continues to produce and prosper. Links have been forged with a number of African and South American nations to create a truly global trading base, while profits are funneled to buy up property and businesses in the United States and Europe. Critics may voice concerns over China's "no conditions" investments in troubled countries like Sudan and Zimbabwe, or their purchase of high-end apartments in Manhattan, but these tend to be drowned out by those who see in China salvation for the world economy (and perhaps their own bank balances).

China has reemerged and will doubtless become an increasingly significant international player. But in many respects, it is still a developing country, and the economic, environmental, political, and social problems it faces will continue to test the leadership for years to come. To paraphrase Napoleon's metaphor, the slumbering Chinese dragon has awoken, but it remains to be seen whether it can fly.

A TRINITY OF teachings

Myth, religion, and philosophy are so intertwined in China that it can be difficult to separate the three. Likewise, the three principal "religions" known as the **Three Teachings** (Buddhism, Confucianism, and Taoism) are inextricably linked, and you will often find elements of all three in a single temple. Under Mao, the doctrine of the day was undoubtedly socialism, but these days, cynics claim that capitalism and the pursuit of money are the new religion.

Confucianism, based on the life of **Confucius** (Kongzi; 551–479 B.C.), is arguably a philosophy rather than a religion, but to visit a Confucian temple and see believers worshipping, you'd never know the difference. Kongzi lived as the Warring States Period was getting underway. This was a fractious, uncertain time, and thus it is unsurprising that his belief system focuses on social order. The **Five Confucian Virtues** (benevolence, propriety, righteousness, trustworthiness, and wisdom) form the pillars of the philosophy, and such was the importance attributed to his body of work that the Confucian texts remained the standard for imperial civil exams until early in the 20th century.

Taoism, China's other native religion, developed in the same time period as Confucianism under the semi-mythical **Laozi,** but could not be more different. Understanding Taoism is complicated by its focus on the highly abstract notion of the **Tao** (or "the Way") and its advocacy of **Wu Wei** (doing nothing). Better known are the Taoist notions of harmony between soft flowing *yin* and hard male *yang*.

China's third major religion, **Buddhism,** came from India originally but gradually found a new homeland in China; its popularity was aided by its willingness to incorporate pre-existing local deities, a factor that hindered the advancement of the less adaptive Christianity and Islam. Buddhism is based on the life of Siddhartha Gautama, a Nepali prince who relinquished his worldly possessions in search of a higher calling. After spending time as an ascetic wandering the plains of India, the former prince realized that asceticism wasn't the way, and finally, in Bodhgaya in northern India, he achieved nirvana (enlightenment) under the Bodhi Tree. Reborn as **Sakyamuni** (the Enlightened One), he spent the rest of his days traveling the Indian plains, giving sermons. When Buddhism first reached China in A.D. 67, its form was little different from that practiced in India, but, over time, like so many ideologies before it, it was Sinicized (made Chinese). This transformation is evidenced by the gradual change in appearance of Buddhist iconography in China; early examples featuring slim, Indian-looking deities can still be seen in cave art along the Silk Road, but by the Tang dynasty, more rounded, Chinese-looking gods were gracing temples. These changes are particularly well sketched at the Shaanxi History Museum (p. 160). As well as the assimilation of local gods into the Buddhist pantheon, there was a fundamental belief shift, replacing the individualist Theravada school developed in India with **Mahayana Buddhism,** a concept far more in keeping with the conformist group-nature of Chinese society. In Tibet, Buddhism was fused with aspects of the native shamanist Bon religion to produce Tibetan Buddhism.

The Three Teachings aren't the only religions to be found in China, though. There are huge numbers of **Christians** and **Muslims,** although it's difficult to ascertain exact figures because only officially recognized versions are tolerated, meaning that millions practice in secret.

LOOKING BACK AT CHINA

A journey of a thousand miles begins with a single step.

—Laozi

Given a timeline that fades into mythical beginnings, and a cast of emperors, scholars, and powerbrokers that runs into the thousands, it's fair to say Chinese history is complex. This short run-through covers the major periods while keeping things as simple as possible.

Prehistory

The 1926 discovery of skull remains in Zhoukoudian, near Beijing, showed that *homo erectus* was using fire and basic stone tools in China 600,000 years ago. The earliest signs of settlement by modern humans date to 5000 B.C., when farming communities around the Yellow River were already crafting ceramic and jade wares. This precursor to Chinese civilization has been called **Yangshao Culture,** and the best preserved examples can be found at the **Banpo Neolithic Village** (p. 161) and burial ground, out in the Xi'an suburbs.

China's current government often trumpets its "5,000 years" of uninterrupted history; they're not the first to take a few liberties with the hard historical record. Archaeology dates the earliest large-scale, literate civilization emerging around 1600 B.C. Before this lies a swirl of myth and legend, much of which can be attributed to the ancient historian **Sima Qian,** whose account of the fabled **Yellow Emperor** gave rise to an enduring cult. With cosmic grace, the Yellow Emperor is supposed to have ruled for 100 unbroken years sometime in the 3rd-century B.C., inventing the calendar, astronomy, and calligraphy, among other things. Whether this is a real historical person or not, the tale holds among modern Han Chinese, who claim him as a shared ancestor and the first great unifier of the scattered tribes of the central plains.

The Dynastic Age

Most of China's documented history follows a dynastic cycle. This should be thought of as a quasi-religious system of governance where emperors enjoyed a **heavenly mandate** to rule, passed down through bloodlines. The emperor, or **Son of Heaven,** was seen as the link between the heavenly and earthly realms and enjoyed absolute power. However, this mandate was conditional on his ability to keep the peace and occupy the throne. The very fact of his removal from power, be it through a natural disaster or a peasant rebellion, could be taken as evidence of the fact that he had lost his celestial mantle. Thus, without needing to justify a revolution or invent a new foundation myth, a new dynasty could emerge. This wasn't a seamless system, but it resulted in a pattern of alternating periods of stability, development, and expansion, invariably followed by tumultuous times of conflict and uncertainty.

The first dynasty for which there is anything like a consistent historical account is the **Shang dynasty** (1600–1046 B.C.). The earliest-known written Chinese can be found on oracle bones from the 13th century B.C. The Shang was followed by the long-lived, though often-fractious, **Zhou dynasty** (1046–256 B.C.), from which there is a rich archaeological heritage. Stunning bronze work from this period can be seen at all major Chinese museums. More important than the physical legacy is the Zhou's cultural legacy. Confucius, the founding father of Chinese moral philosophy, was born around 551 B.C. Like Jesus and John Locke rolled into one, Confucius has shaped Chinese society and politics ever since.

FOUNDING THE NATION: THE QIN & THE HAN

The latter part of the Zhou dynasty was known as the **Warring States Period.** This ended in 221 B.C., when the most infamous figure in Chinese history burst onto the scene. If the Yellow Emperor only has legend to back up his "Father of the Nation" claims, **Qin Shihuang** was the first unambiguously *real* person to unify China. Over an 8-year period, the six rival "warring" states were defeated and the **Qin dynasty** (221–206 B.C.) established. Qin Shihuang moved quickly to expand his territory down to the South China Sea and up toward modern-day Korea to form the first China-wide empire. Victory was won brutally and maintained with equal ferocity. According to **Sima Qian,** this was a time of mass execution, slave labor, and book-burning, though the account may have been exaggerated somewhat, given Sima Qian was working for the very people who usurped the Qin. Look beyond the hype, and facts begin to speak for themselves: Qin Shihuang established a legal system, built the first Great Wall, laid a countrywide road network, and standardized weights, measures, and currency. And that's all before you get on to *that* mausoleum. Whether the famous army of Terracotta Warriors, created to protect Qin Shihuang in the afterlife, worked or not is a moot point. His tomb *did* remain secret for most of China's modern history, but the empire he left behind collapsed within months of his death.

The **Han dynasty** (206 B.C.–A.D. 220), which still lends its name to China's dominant ethnic group, was a time of consolidation and expansion. The civil service was formalized, and exams, based on Confucian texts, were introduced as a means of assessing candidates, the first example of a meritocratic bureaucracy to which most modern governments still aspire. There were also great advances in agriculture, textiles, papermaking, and weaponry. The crossbow developed during this time was more accurate and had a longer range than any to date. This military superiority facilitated the Chinese army's progress as far south as Vietnam. To the west, the Silk Road developed as a trade artery that enabled passage from the capital at **Xianyang** (part of the Xi'an suburbs today) to Central Asia. The historian **Sima Qian** lived during the Han dynasty, and his work is the primary source for most ancient Chinese history. This research, so precious today, couldn't help the Han dynasty itself from repeating the errors of the past, and when it finally came to a close, China was vast but the imperial coffers were empty. A fractious four-century period known as the **Three Kingdoms** (220–581 A.D.) followed, and it wasn't until the **Sui dynasty** (581–618 A.D.) that China was reunited as a country. The Sui may have been short-lived, but this didn't stop them from completing one of humanity's greatest engineering projects, the 1,770km (1,100-mile) **Grand Canal,** which can still be seen close to Suzhou (p. 257) and Hangzhou (p. 267).

THE AGE OF ART: THE TANG & THE SONG

The **Tang dynasty** (618–907 A.D.) is regarded as China's greatest dynasty, and with good reason. The reconsolidation under the Sui was definitely progress, but it by no means ensured the reunification of north and south. The Tang took on, and then finished, the job, after three centuries of conflict and uncertainty. The importance of peace was signified by the choice of **Chang'an** (meaning Eternal Peace) as the name for the Tang capital (present-day Xi'an), and the resultant stability soon brought prosperity. This was boosted by the Tang's open-door approach. A Silk Road of sorts had long existed, but under the Tang, it became a secure and defended artery for commerce, culture, and religion, most notably Buddhism, which became embedded in Chinese society during this period. This early stab at globalization generated huge wealth for at least a part of Tang society, and many invested their time and money into developing ancient crafts such as painting, poetry, and pottery. Imperial and private patronage called into being some of China's most incredible cultural treasures, including the stunning Buddhist grottoes at Luoyang (see p. 183). It wasn't all about wishy-washy bohemians, though. Territorial expansion was fundamental to the Tang's success, and at its peak, Chinese control extended from Korea to Afghanistan. However, a catastrophic military defeat against the Arabs in 751 and a devastating internal rebellion a few years later turned the Tang inward, and a slow decline set in.

Another dark period followed where no one leader was able to consolidate control, and warring was common. This began to wane with the establishment of the **Song dynasty** (960–1279). The first Song emperor, Taizu, consolidated from the new capital in Kaifeng, and before long, the country was united once more. Once again the arts flourished, and the Song dynasty is remembered for landscape painting, poetry, and pottery. It was also a time of great innovation, though inventions such as the magnetic compass and gunpowder failed to save the Song in the end.

NORTHERN INVADERS: THE JIN & THE YUAN

In 1126, the Song court was ousted from Kaifeng by the Manchurian Jurchen tribe, who founded their own dynasty, the **Jin** (1115–1234). The Song relocated to Hangzhou and though the arts continued to develop, the Southern Song, as it became known, was hampered and humiliated by hefty payments to the Jin until its demise. Genghis Khan had been busy carving out a huge chunk of Central Asia, and his descendants followed suit, making incursions farther and farther into China. In 1279, Genghis's grandson, **Kublai Khan,** swept south and founded the **Yuan dynasty** (1279–1368), establishing Beijing as the capital. It wasn't too long before the nomadic Mongols adopted the imperial lifestyle and quickly lost the military might that had driven their success. Losses in both Japan and Southeast Asia contributed to their demise, but ultimately it was trouble on the home front that sealed the Yuan's fate. By segregating the Chinese into different social classes and giving Muslims and Tibetans favored treatment, the Yuan dynasty emperors alienated a huge portion of the populace, and a number of secret societies formed with the aim of ousting the outsiders. After a series of foiled plots, eventually a full-blown revolt headed by the rebel leader, Zhu Yuanzhang, installed a new dynasty in 1368.

THE MING DYNASTY (1368–1644)

The first Ming emperor, **Hongwu,** established his capital in Nanjing (you can still see the Ming city wall there to this day; see p. 154) and reestablished centralized rule. His successor, **Yongle,** moved the imperial seat back to Beijing and began construction of the **Forbidden City** (p. 65). Yongle also sent huge Chinese fleets to explore the world under **Admiral Zheng He.** In seven epic voyages, the Muslim eunuch admiral took the Chinese navy as far as West Africa, and trading routes were established to Malacca (Malaysia) and India's Malabar Coast. Records of the journeys were destroyed following an inauspicious lightning strike on the Forbidden City, and the Ming dynasty suddenly focused inward, going so far as to completely ban maritime activity. It was to prove a historic mistake. Protection against the increasingly powerful northern tribes became a priority, and significant improvements were made to the Great Wall under the Ming; most of the brick sections you'll see today (as at Badaling, Mutianyu, and Simatai; p. 132) date from this period. The threat from the south was less obvious but arguably more significant. This was the period in which the Chinese first encountered "Westerners" in the sense we might understand it today. Portuguese sailors first made contact with the Ming in the early part of the 16th century, later renting the tiny southern peninsula of Macau. It was through Macau that the Jesuit priest **Matteo Ricci** first entered China. Ricci spent nearly two decades living in China, translating texts, sharing scientific knowledge, and building a bridge that paved the way for mass commerce and then colonization. Ricci created the first world map in Chinese, as well as the first system of transcribing Chinese characters in Roman form. He was the first Westerner to set foot inside the Forbidden City in 1601 and became a treasured court insider. Ultimately though, the new international perspective he offered could not save the Ming. The dynasty ended in a revolt, and the last emperor, Chongzhen, fled the Forbidden City and hanged himself in **Jingshan Park** (p. 71).

THE QING DYNASTY (1644–1911)

The chaos at the end of the Ming dynasty presented the opportunity the increasingly powerful Manchurians had been waiting for. These were outsiders—non-ethnic Han—who swept in from the northeast, seizing Beijing and establishing it as the new Qing capital. The early years of the dynasty are celebrated as a golden age in Chinese history, heralded by the leadership of **Kangxi** (1661–1722), **Yongzheng** (1722–35), and **Qianlong** (1735–95). Kangxi crushed rebellions and expanded the empire to include Mongolia,

Tibet, Nepal, and parts of Central Asia, doubling its former size. Closer links with the Tibetan world also led to the construction of the **Lama Temple** in Beijing (p. 82), while the Manchurians' yearning for the simpler outdoor life of their homeland resulted in the building of the **Mountain Retreat** in Chengde (p. 137).

Foreign interest in the wealthy but militarily backward Middle Kingdom grew, and a trickle of traders made their way to China looking for a slice of the pie. In 1793, Lord Macartney, envoy to the British king George III, and representative of the **British East India Company,** sought a trade agreement with the Manchu court. The seeds for future conflict were laid by his infamous refusal to bow to the Qianlong emperor when they met at Chengde. The Qianlong emperor could see no use for foreign goods and refused the British request for an envoy in Beijing, but the East India Company wasn't about to give up and began importing Indian opium into China rather than silver. Before long a significant percentage of the Chinese population was hooked on the drug, demand rose, and the British had the trading leverage to get as much silk and tea as they wanted. This did not sit well with the Qing rulers, and they tried to ban the opium trade, but to little avail. When Lin Zexu, a southern commander, destroyed 20,000 chests of opium in south China, he was seen as a hero, but the British were incensed, and the **First Opium War** (1839–42) ensued. Defeat at British hands led to the signing of the humiliating **Treaty of Nanjing,** which forced indemnity payments and gave the British trading rights in Guangzhou, Xiamen, Fuzhou, Ningbo, and Shanghai. It also ceded the small and seemingly insignificant island of Hong Kong. In 1856 the Chinese made another stand, which ended with further humiliation 4 years later. This time, they had to cede land to the British, French, Germans, Russians, Japanese, and Americans.

Anti-Manchu sentiment, always there, but hidden below the surface, began to reemerge. The most destructive of all the anti-Qing revolts was the quasi-Christian **Taiping Rebellion** (1850–64). The name implies a little local trouble, but this "rebellion" was all-out civil war. By body count, some reckon this to be one of the bloodiest conflicts in human history, with a death toll of at least 20 to 30 million, with estimates of up to 100 million, over a 14-year period. For a time, large parts of the Chinese hinterland were under the control of Hong Xiuquan, who claimed to be Jesus' younger brother. His ambitions for total victory were ended only when the British moved to support the Qing to protect their increasingly imperiled assets. Thirty years later, in 1899, dissatisfaction with foreign influence once again boiled over in the **Boxer Rebellion.** This began as an anti-colonial movement and was hesitantly supported by the ruling **Empress Dowager Cixi** (1835–1908). When foreign powers moved in once more, the dowager and her puppet emperor fled to Xi'an, leaving imperial ministers to negotiate yet another peace settlement. Although Cixi held on to the throne until her death in 1908, the Qing had proven time and again unable to deal with incursions by Western powers. Despite desperate late efforts to reform, the Qing finally fell in 1911 when a dispute over a foreign-owned railway line provoked a seemingly innocuous revolt in Wuhan, central China. This rapidly spread, and the last emperor—5-year-old **Puyi**—was powerless to stop it. In 1912, the provisional Republic of China was founded in **Nanjing.**

Modern China

REVOLUTION & THE BATTLE OF IDEOLOGIES

Celebrations surrounding the end of imperial rule were short-lived. After only a few weeks at the helm, **Dr. Sun Yat-sen** (1866–1925) handed the presidency to **Yuan Shikai,** a Qing general, in the hope of creating stability during the democratic transition. Elections were held and power shared between Sun's Nationalist Party, the **Kuomintang (KMT),** and the Yuan-supporting **Republican Party,** but mutual suspicion soon soured relations. By 1913, the two were in armed conflict. Sun was eventually banished to Japan, and by 1915, Yuan Shikai had announced the new "Empire of China," with himself as emperor. Yuan died in 1919, but the **Warlord Era** was already underway, with the country disintegrating into regional blocks headed by military strongmen. One of them, in the far south, was led by the returning Sun Yat-sen—now a "Grand Marshal"—and his revived KMT party.

Despite the political chaos, this was a time of great optimism, born of the new ideas and influences that were flooding the country. At the heart of this **New Culture Movement** was a determination to see China regain its rightful place at the top table of nations. Nationalism was everywhere, particularly after the 1919 Treaty of Versailles, which saw colonial powers further carve up the country. It was an odd kind of nationalism, as it rejected traditional Confucian ways and saw the seeds of success in following new ideas borrowed from the West. Sun had already dabbled with **representative democracy,** while radical theories of **feminism** and **anarchism** were openly discussed in elite circles. **Modernist literature** by writers like Lu Xun emphasized ordinary speech rather than fusty classical prose, and modern, evidence-based **science** was hailed as the means of self-strengthening and advancement, particularly in military development.

Another European ideology that made huge headway was **communism.** The **Chinese Communist Party (CCP)** was founded in Shanghai in 1921 and counted **Zhou Enlai** and **Mao Zedong** among its earliest members. Following Russian advice and financial support, the CCP and the KMT united in 1923 with the aim of defeating northern warlords. By this time, Sun was ailing, and he nominated **Chiang Kai-shek** (1888–1975) as his successor. He passed away in 1925, heralded by both sides of the alliance as the "father of modern China," a label that still sticks today on both sides of the Taiwan Strait. However, in 1927, with Sun gone, Chiang ordered a mass purge of the CCP leadership. Those who survived, including Mao, fled to the mountains of Jiangxi. KMT troops encircled their base in 1934, and it looked like the end for the Communists. But Mao rallied and led 100,000 troops on a 9,656km (6,000-mile) trek that became known as the **Long March.** Only 10,000 made it all the way to Yan'an in Shaanxi, but the march demonstrated Mao's determination and cemented his position as the CCP's visionary leader.

The 1919 Treaty of Versailles had handed German territories in northeast China to the Japanese, and they had been eyeing up a larger slice of the country ever since. With the Communists and nationalists preoccupied, the Japanese seized the moment, capturing Manchuria in 1931, renaming it Manchukuo, and inaugurating the last Qing emperor, Puyi, as its puppet ruler. But Manchuria was just a staging post on the way to full-scale invasion, and in 1937, the Japanese swept into northern China. In spite of another short-lived CCP-KMT alliance, by 1939, the Japanese had captured much of the east coast, and the Chinese government was forced to relocate to central Chongqing. By the following year, the Japanese controlled Beijing, Shanghai, Nanjing, and Guangzhou, and the CCP-KMT alliance crumbled. As many as 20 million Chinese lost their lives during the Japanese invasion, and horrific atrocities were committed, not least during the infamous 1937 **Rape of Nanjing** (p. 277). The period of Japanese rule was brought to an abrupt halt by the Allied victory in World War II, and control of the nation was once again up for grabs. Though the KMT enjoyed U.S. support and control of the cities, it was the Communists who had captured the hearts and minds of the rural masses, which helped catapult them to victory. Chiang and the remnants of the KMT fled to Taiwan, along with much of the imperial treasure from the Forbidden City. In Taiwan, Chiang founded the **Republic of China (ROC),** from which he planned to eventually retake the mainland.

THE PEOPLE'S REPUBLIC OF CHINA

On October 1, 1949, Mao Zedong declared the foundation of the People's Republic of China, the world's most populous communist state. The nation was in tatters, but there was hope, and the new government set about instituting land redistribution and nationalization. The **Korean War** (1950–53) occupied precious time and funds, but the way in which the **People's Liberation Army (PLA)** pushed back U.S. troops bolstered belief in the fledgling government. From the beginning, the party gave the impression of wanting to involve the people in the rule of the country, and Mao's 1957 slogan, "Let a hundred flowers bloom, let a hundred schools of thought contend," was meant to encourage intellectual criticism of the bureaucracy. However, it resulted instead in a torrent of attacks on the communist system itself. Mao responded with an anti-rightist campaign that branded intellectuals as enemies of socialism and saw half a million people persecuted, sent to labor camps, and worse. Whether the campaign was a genuine move for freer governance or intended as a trap is still contested. Mao's next grand initiative, the 1958 **Great Leap Forward,** aimed to increase both agricultural and industrial productivity with a goal of matching British steel output within 15 years. But the crass plan was flawed from the beginning; the peasantry had only just been granted land, and were far from happy about collectivizing. The panic caused by over-ambitious quotas led to overplanting. The real focus was on industry, though, and farms were neglected. Crops failed 2 years running, and the resulting famine left millions dead. This was exacerbated by the quota system, which stripped food away from farms whose people were already starving. At the same time, following Khrushchev's historic summit with U.S. President Eisenhower, Sino-Soviet relations faltered, and the resulting withdrawal of Russian aid left the economy in ruins. Deng Xiaoping helped get the country back on track, but held fundamentally different views about the direction the country's development should take. Deng sought to open up the economy and encourage private enterprise. Mao's reaction was the 1966 **Great Proletarian Cultural Revolution,** which was designed to purge the country of "the four olds"—old culture, customs, habits, and ideas. In Beijing, Mao rallied students to form a radical militia, the **Red Guards,** armed them with his "Little Red Book" of thoughts, and set them loose on the country with instructions to destroy all evidence of the four olds. Books, buildings, and businesses were burned, and many of China's greatest treasures were lost forever. Over 1.5 million people died during the Cultural Revolution, and millions more were traumatized. Families and whole communities were torn apart as quotas were established for the reporting and "reeducation" of dissidents. In spite of this, the Cultural Revolution cemented Mao's cult status at home and made him a household name worldwide.

The Cultural Revolution lost its intensity but rolled on for a decade. In later years, Mao was little seen, and his third wife, **Jiang Qing,** often appeared in his place supported by her radical entourage, who became known as the **Gang of Four.** Following the mysterious death of his closest ally, Lin Biao, Mao sought new friends and, while Hua Guofeng was groomed as his successor, the exiled Deng Xiaoping returned to office. There were also some improvements on the international front. Zhou Enlai, who had been limiting the worst excesses of Mao's policies since the beginning, helped China gain a U.N. seat in 1971 and establish trade links with the United States after Nixon's 1972 visit. Zhou Enlai died in 1976, and a riot was sparked when radicals took away commemorative wreaths placed on the Heroes Monument in Beijing. The **Tian'anmen Incident,** as it became known, was blamed on Deng Xiaoping, and once again, he was deposed from office. With the sudden demise of the moderates, the radicals gained ground, but this was to be short-lived. Two months after a devastating earthquake hit Tangshan, Hebei province, Chairman Mao died, and the Gang of Four lost their leader. Shortly after Mao's death, the Gang of Four was arrested, but it wasn't until 1981 that they were tried and sentenced to 20 years in prison apiece. Jiang Qing killed herself, and the others died in jail. The Gang of Four was ostensibly blamed for the worst extremes of the Cultural Revolution, a factor that helped to keep the Mao cult alive long after his death. Ultimately, the legacy of "Mao the myth" triumphed over "Mao the man," and even today his image can be found adorning many living rooms and looming over public spaces.

THE REFORM ERA

Following Mao's death, Deng Xiaoping finally ascended, and his **Four Transformations** (agriculture, industry, defense, and science) presented the platform for China's economic modernization. Deng's policies were based on economic liberalization in order to encourage foreign investment and internal entrepreneurship. Agricultural collectives were disbanded, and farmers were freed to sell any surplus on the open market. Focus shifted away from traditional heavy industry, and many state-owned businesses were privatized. **Special Economic Zones,** such as Shenzhen (p. 138), were established and quickly attracted overseas investment. These measures, combined with China's huge population and low wages, provided the springboard for China's launch onto the world trade scene, and it quickly became the factory of the world.

THE STUDENT PROTESTS OF 1989

Economic reform and social reform did not go hand in hand, though. While the 1980s outwardly presented a more liberal face as shown by the appointment of moderate Hu Yaobang as general secretary, his forced resignation and the party's response to the 1989 Tian'anmen Square protests answered any question there may have been about how much freedom of speech the government would tolerate.

Following Hu Yaobang's death in April 1989, protests erupted in Tian'anmen Square and in other cities around China. In spite of the imposition of martial law, by June 1989, over a million people had gathered in Beijing alone. The crowd was predominantly composed of students protesting for social reform, but there were also urban workers, angry at the corruption and privatization that had seen many of them lose their jobs. When their demands went unanswered, more than a thousand students went on hunger strike. Tens of thousands of PLA soldiers were sent to Beijing, and between dusk on June 3 and dawn on June 4, they moved decisively to clear the protest camps. The details of what happened next remain mired in controversy. What is agreed is that at least 200 civilians died, though some say it was a thousand or more. Whether the deaths were caused by fighting or in self-defense, in the night or on following days, in clearing the square or in localized combat, is disputed. The consensus opinion is that most of the killing took place as the tanks and troops broke through barricades on their way to the square, and there is no evidence of "mowing down" of protesters in Tian'anmen Square itself. What can be said for sure is that a military solution was used for a civil problem, and a huge amount of blood was spilled. Abroad, the killings provoked international condemnation, economic sanctions, and an arms embargo. At home, the incident served to highlight a gaping divide between the moderates, who sympathized with the protesters, and the Party hardliners, who favored using force. Even now, *liu si* ("June 4th") is rarely talked about publicly in China, though private discussions, if handled sensitively, are unlikely to cause problems.

THE NEW GUARD: THIRD-, FOURTH- & FIFTH-GENERATION CHINESE COMMUNISM

Jiang Zemin, the former mayor of Shanghai, and untainted by the Beijing crackdown, moved up the party ranks to become general secretary of the CCP. Three years later, he was appointed president, and he fully took the reins of

DATELINE: CHINESE HISTORY AT A GLANCE

Era	Date	Significant Events & People
Prehistory	600,000 B.C.	Peking Man
Yangshao Culture	5000–3000 B.C.	
Zhou Dynasty	1046–221 B.C.	Confucius & Laozi
Qin	221–206 B.C.	Emperor Qin Shihuang, Great Wall built
Han	206 B.C.–A.D. 220	Territorial expansion
Three Kingdoms	A.D. 220–581	
Sui	581–618	Grand Canal
Tang	618–907	Printing begins, Buddhism established
Song	960–1279	Poet Su Dongpo
Yuan	1279–1368	Marco Polo visits China
Ming	1368–1644	Forbidden City built, Zheng He's voyages
Qing	1644–1911	Opium Wars, Taiping & Boxer Rebellions
Republican Period	1911–1949	Dr. Sun Yat-sen, CCP founded, Long March Japanese invasion & Rape of Nanjing
People's Republic	1949	Mao Zedong founds PRC
	1911	Chiang Kai-shek founds ROC (Taiwan)
	1956–57	Hundred Flowers Campaign
	1958–61	Great Leap Forward
	1966–1976	Cultural Revolution
	1976	Mao Zedong dies
Reform Era	1976–present	Deng Xiaoping heads PRC, Economic liberalization, China reopens to foreign visitors
	1980	One-Child Policy begins nationwide
	1989	Tian'anmen Square protest
	1992	Jiang Zemin ascends to power
	1997	Deng Xiaoping dies, Hong Kong returned
	1999	Portuguese return of Macau
	2001	China joins World Trade Organization
	2002	Hu Jintao & Wen Jiabao head CCP
	2008	Beijing hosts Summer Olympics Sichuan earthquake, Tibet protests
	2009	Xinjiang riots
	2010	World Expo in Shanghai
	2012	Xi Jinping & Li Keqiang head CCP
	2013	Corruption crackdown begins
	2014	Google services blocked in China Former security head Zhou Yongkang arrested
	2015	Economic growth falls to lowest level in 20 years

power when Deng died in 1997. Jiang oversaw the **1997 British return of Hong Kong** and the **1999 Portuguese return of Macau.** He continued the economic liberalization started by Deng and, under Jiang, the benefits of 20 years of economic reform began to be seen, especially when sanctions started to be rescinded. Internationally, everyone wanted a piece of the Chinese economic pie, though relations with Western powers, particularly the United States, were tested by continued arms embargoes and allegations of nuclear espionage. In 2001, a U.S. spy plane collided with a Chinese fighter jet and crash-landed on Hainan Island, China's most southerly province. Although none of the U.S. crew was seriously injured, the Chinese pilot died. The incident came at a crucial time, when the Bush administration was deciding whether or not to supply Taiwan with arms, a sensitive-enough subject in itself. Tensions were further heightened following the NATO bombing of the Chinese Embassy in Belgrade during the Kosovo Crisis. The United States claimed this was an "accident," but thousands of Chinese protesters disagreed. In the end, economics prevailed, and late in 2001, China was eventually admitted to the **World Trade Organization.** The following year, Vice President **Hu Jintao** was promoted to the position of president, and the fourth generation of Communist leadership began.

The following 10 years were marked by rapid advances in economic growth, the rise of the Internet, and a burgeoning international reputation. This was clinched by a successful Olympic Games in 2008, celebrated wildly as a coming-out party for the nation. But it was also a decade of widening inequality and worsening corruption, leading to a sharp increase in protest and a corresponding increase in police budgets. The slogan most associated with the second half of the Hu-Wen era was "harmonious development"—barely an editorial or major political speech would pass without mentioning it—but beneath the surface, disharmony was brewing.

This became clear shortly after the most recent succession took place, late in 2012. Incoming General Secretary **Xi Jinping** moved quickly to declare that corruption presented a threat to the Party's very existence and launched a campaign that has continued ever since. This has ensnared thousands of officials, both powerful "tigers" and lowly "flies," to use Xi's favorite slogan, including one of the most important leaders of the previous administration, Zhou Yongkang. Critics suggest the campaign is more about eliminating powerful enemies than ridding the Party of graft—indeed, the provinces where Xi built his career are surprisingly corruption-free—but the campaign has been longer and deeper than anyone expected. The crackdown has gone hand in hand with restrictions on openness in the media and on the Internet—reports of the fabulous wealth of Xi's own family were quickly quashed—and a recentralization of power, making Xi, on paper at least, the most powerful leader since Mao.

It's probably no coincidence that these changes are taking place at the same time that the "growth miracle" is fading. For most of the last 35 years, the people of China could assume that, regardless of how poor they were, next year would be better than the last. Year after year, they were proven right. But over-development and a massive debt buildup have begun to cause China's leaders sleepless nights. Officially, GDP growth is at its lowest level in 20 years, but even that number is boosted mainly by financial, not real, engineering.

Though exponentially richer than it was in the 1980s, the China of the mid-2010s is not satisfied with the gains it already has. This is a nation on a historic mission to *reclaim* the mantle of "superpower," one which it has held for much of its history. As the economic engine begins to sputter, the nationalist engine is beginning to rev. A strongman is at the helm, and China is at a crossroads. These are interesting times.

THE ARTS IN CHINA

China's history is so long, the country so big, and its cultural range so wide that getting a hold on "the arts" in China isn't straightforward. The following passages concentrate on bronzes, ceramics, calligraphy, literature, poetry, and painting, but whole careers have been spent studying other artistic forms such as jade and lacquerwork. Examples of all the art listed below can be seen today across the country, but many of the best pieces are to be found in Beijing's **National Museum of China** (p. 76), the **Shanghai Museum** (p. 225), and the **Shaanxi History Museum** (p. 160).

Bronzes & Ceramics

After cave paintings, the earliest form of artistic expression in China was the decorating of household items and funerary objects. As settled communities began to have more time, and techniques improved through the ages, the objects themselves were elevated to the point where they became art, and Chinese bronzes and ceramics were admired the world over. Bronzes first emerged in the **Shang dynasty** (1600–1046 B.C.), and ceramics can be traced back to roughly the same time, but it wasn't until more effective glazing techniques were established in the **Han dynasty** (221 B.C.–A.D. 220) that they were prized as artistic creations rather than ceremonial objects. The stability of the **Tang dynasty** (A.D. 618–907) afforded the time, effort, and expertise to further refine techniques, and it was during this period that the famous tricolor glaze, which can still be seen in emporiums around the country, was established. China's iconic blue-white porcelain dates from the **Ming dynasty** (1368–1644), but the cobalt underglaze was actually pioneered in the previous **Yuan dynasty** (1279–1368).

Calligraphy, Poetry & Prose

The tones, rhythms, and ideographic forms of the written Chinese language all lend themselves to the arts. Calligraphy remains popular throughout the country, from the streets to store showrooms. As an art form, calligraphy is like music; though it's possible to learn "correct" forms, the real beauty is in the way those standards are interpreted. Calligraphers' tools are the brush, the ink, and the paper, all of which can be manipulated to change the overall effect. Then there's the style, which can vary in levels of expressionism, from highly cursive scripts, which can look like random flicks of the wrist, to tight, controlled shapes in the regular *kaishu* script. Calligraphy traditionally went hand in hand with poetry, and the latter was a favored mode of expression for the educated elite. The words of China's most prominent poets, figures such as **Li Bai** (701–762) and **Su Dongpo** (1037–1101), still pepper speeches, adorn sculptures, and even sneak their way into popular advertisements.

Early Chinese literature is rich and enduring, but mainly bound up with the twin pillars of ancient Chinese culture, Confucianism and Taoism. Among the "Four Books and Five Classics" of traditional Confucian culture is the poetry of the **"Book of Songs"** *(Shi Jing)*, the semi-mystical divination manual that is the **"Book of Changes"** *(Yi Jing),* and the famous **"Analects"** *(Lun Yu),* a summary of Confucius's pithy observations on life, the universe, and everything (and the source of "Confucius Say" jokes). The most important book in the Taoist canon is Laozi's **"The Book of Tao and Virtue"** *(Dao De Jing).* Written about the same time was Sun Tzu's **"The Art of War"** (*Sunzi Bingfa*), now dished out by Western CEOs to success-hungry senior managers. About a century before Christ, Chinese literature branched out into history, thanks to Sima Qian's surprisingly lively **"Records of the Grand Historian"** *(Shi Ji)*, which remains a key historical source today. In the Ming dynasty (1368–1644), writers began harking back to the formative glory years of China, constructing epic tales such as **"Journey to the West"** and **"Romance of the Three Kingdoms,"** which remain as touchstones of Chinese culture today. However, books were not made for the masses until the end of the 19th century, when the vernacular writing style of **Lu Xun** (1881–1936), and later, **Shen Congwen** (1903–86), opened up the printed word to ordinary people. However, once the Communists emerged victorious, literature was labeled as a "propaganda tool," and literary freedom disappeared. Restrictions eased slightly during the 1980s, but major publishing houses still endured strict political oversight, and risqué literature often attracted accusations of causing "spiritual pollution." This pushed some to seek freedom overseas; Nobel Prize winner **Gao Xingjian** is one of many authors who settled in the West after promising early careers in China. Censorship continues to this day, though removal of state subsidies has led to literature being commercialized and writers becoming more adventurous in topic and style, though highly political works remain rare. **Mo Yan** became the first mainland-based writer to win the Nobel Prize for Literature in 2012, despite working within the establishment. Outside the major publishing houses, modern Chinese literature is surprisingly dynamic, thanks almost entirely to online publishing. Many have turned online blogging success into lucrative mainstream careers, although those who continue to write political work after they hit the big time tend to have their wings clipped. One of the most celebrated young writers of recent years, **Han Han,** gained a huge audience with his provocative online essays through the 2000s. However, his attempts to self-publish were blocked, and his current online work is not particularly outspoken. Being allowed to write in modern China remains a privilege, not a right.

Painting

Aside from cave paintings and calligraphy, painting in China didn't really develop until the Tang dynasty (A.D. 618–907). Tang paintings were mostly portraits of the imperial family and courtesans, and it wasn't until the Song dynasty (960–1279) that things got interesting with the development of **landscape painting.** Mountains were considered the abode of the gods, and this led to paintings that focused exclusively on the natural world, centuries before anything comparable emerged in Europe. Song-dynasty artists wanted to convey the endless expanse of the Chinese landscape, and to this end, they left large blank spaces on the canvas. In the Yuan (1279–1368) and Ming dynasties (1368–1644), the focus on the natural world continued, but rather than whole landscapes, detailed pictures of plants, flowers, and animals became the subjects of choice. During the Qing dynasty (1644–1911), increasing foreign influence in China also made its way onto the canvas, but the bold brushstrokes and traditional subjects chosen by artists like **Xu Peiheng** (1893–1953), who had studied in Europe, illustrated that Chinese artists hadn't completely abandoned their roots. Under Mao, artistic creativity in all shapes and forms was suppressed and many prior works were destroyed, but the big, bold **Red Art** that was churned out as just another part of the party propaganda machine is now enjoying a postmodern revival.

Since economic liberalization, contemporary **modern art** has moved in manifold directions, heavily inspired by outside influences, albeit often paying homage to old-time traditions and subjects. **Wang Qingsong**'s photographic parody of the 10th-century "Night Revels" is a prime example. Despite of, or perhaps *because of*, repression at home, **Ai Weiwei** is the poster boy for modern Chinese art overseas, and his work sells for millions. However, he is only one of many Chinese artists who command sky-high price tags in Western auction houses. Good places to get a feel for China's modern arts scene in China itself are Beijing's **Factory 798** (p. 88) and its less-celebrated Shanghai equivalent, **M50** (p. 220), as well as the **Shanghai Museum of Contemporary Art** (p. 208).

ARCHITECTURE IN CHINA

Lest any readers take their expectations of Chinese architecture from "Kung Fu Panda," here's the most pertinent fact about Chinese cities: They're ugly. What invasion, civil war, and simple carelessness couldn't wreck before 1949, grim Soviet planning and the Cultural Revolution finished off after it. Rapid modernization did promise a cure, but it's ended up being part of the disease. Where Mao's Red Guards took sledgehammers to landmark temples and palaces, modern developers have taken the wrecking ball to many of Beijing's lovely *hutong* alleys (p. 97) or Shanghai's charming *shikumen* lanes (p. 219). The new high-rise apartment blocks that have gone up in their place have

KNOWING YOUR dragons FROM YOUR PHOENIXES

As Chinese culture becomes more accessible around the world, there are many symbols that are instantly identifiable with the Middle Kingdom, and traveling around China, you'll see them cropping up again and again. But what do they mean? A **pair of lions** standing outside the entrance of a palace, temple, or even a bank represents status and natural order, and if you look carefully, you'll see that the female has a cub beneath her paw, while the male has the world at his feet. **Dragon** and **phoenix** motifs represent the emperor and empress, respectively. **Yellow** is the color of the emperor, and **red** symbolizes luck and prosperity. The number of **stone animals** on roof eaves indicates how important a temple or palace is. The rotund, **laughing Buddha** seen in the entrance halls to many temples is Maitreya, a Chinese interpretation of the (skinny) Indian god who has come to represent prosperity.

made bits of Shanghai and Beijing look a little tidier, and wealthier, but the charm has been vanquished. As in the Cultural Revolution, the higher-uppers may now be belatedly realizing their mistake. While big-ticket sights such as the **Forbidden City** (p. 65) and **Temple of Heaven** (p. 83) have obvious tourist value, smaller, less obvious buildings and neighborhoods are being protected by municipal governments for heritage reasons alone. However, the system remains creaky and subject to corruption, and in most cases, it's simply too little, too late. In China, it is always worth asking whether you are looking at an original building or a rebuilt version of the original building. It's likely the latter.

When coming across any surviving traditional architecture, it's important to have a basic understanding of feng shui (literally, "wind and water") concepts. Feng shui is a philosophy that tries to explain how energy flows most efficiently and harmoniously in any given space. This has become a critical part of architectural design in China and can operate on the scale of a single room, an apartment, a palace, or even an entire city. Some of the most basic feng shui principles are that the north should be protected (thus Jingshan Park protects the back of the Forbidden City), and there should be water flowing toward the front (to bring prosperity). Small mirrors, which you'll often see above doorways to people's houses, are put there to reflect evil spirits.

Foreign influences have also been important to the history of architecture in China, and many can be seen today. **Xi'an's Great Mosque** (p. 156) is a fascinating combination of traditional Islamic design fused with Chinese architectural features. Foreign influence in China was not always welcome in the latter part of the Qing dynasty (1644–1911), but the architecture left behind still adds diversity and character to cities like Shanghai and Beijing, which have interesting colonial features. It's Shanghai where the foreign factor is most obvious. The **Bund** (p. 203), for example, looks like a little chunk of Victorian London, or Liverpool, airlifted to the Orient. The city's **Art Deco** buildings are also a marvel, and hotels like the Broadway Mansions and the Fairmont Peace (p. 227) are worth visiting for fans of architecture, even if you don't stay there.

Foreign influence continued to be felt once the PRC was founded, and grand Soviet-style monoliths, like **Beijing's Great Hall of the People** (p. 74), became the norm. Since economic reforms in the 1980s, China has followed Hong Kong's model of reaching for the sky, and skyscrapers now dominate many city centers. In the most competitive and richest arenas, standing out from the crowd has become increasingly difficult. Even Shanghai's ersatz **Oriental Pearl TV Tower** (the one with the silly pink baubles, see p. 225) is cowed beside the **Jinmao Tower** (p. 224), the **Shanghai World Financial Center** (p. 226), and the new **Shanghai Tower** (p. 224), which have been constructed, one after the other, in an apparent (and probably doomed) effort to be *the* defining Shanghai skyscraper. Most of these buildings were built with private capital, but the 2008 Olympics allowed the state to get in on the architectural act too. It signed off on the **Bird's Nest** stadium and the **Water Cube** swimming complex in Beijing (p. 91). Though dazzling, only time will tell if they will be celebrated or demolished in years to come. What seems clear is that China's buildings will continue to move remorselessly toward the heavens. The question remains: Will the designers of these buildings remember a little more of the heritage they left behind (and possibly destroyed) back at ground level?

EATING & DRINKING IN CHINA

Eating

You can tell a lot about a country from the way its people greet one another. In the United States, it might be a cheery "How are you doing?" In the UK, it's normally a comment about the weather. And in China? Well, when the standard greeting between friends is *"Ni chi le ma?"* or "Have you eaten yet?", you know you are in a place where food is seriously important to the general flow of life.

In China, eating is a tool of business, a social lubricant, a reason to travel, and a rhythm of life. Bugs and illnesses are cured with food and drink, not medicine, while specific dishes perform symbolic functions during ceremonies. Where Western friends might meet in the bar or coffee shop, the restaurant is the stage for most social interactions in China. Lunch break for schools and state-run businesses are up to 3 hours long, and slow dining is sacred.

This might all sound very promising, especially if you are one of the many who visit China looking forward to 2 weeks of glorified takeout. Beware. Chinese food is far different, and far more varied, than what is on offer from the local Chinese restaurant back home. Things have diversified in recent years, but most Chinese restaurants in the West have their roots in Hong Kong and Guangdong province, where Cantonese language, culture, and cuisine reign supreme. Ignoring for a moment the huge differences between Western

Cantonese food and authentic Cantonese food, Cantonese cuisine is only one of the four great "schools" of Chinese cooking and just a fraction of its culinary heritage. Move into other parts of the country, and there's barely a "chicken chow mein" in sight. Arm yourself with a phrasebook and a curious palate, and you'll never run short of new things to try.

Places to eat Chinese food range from opulent banquet halls to hole-in-the-wall canteens and street stalls. Generally, the focus is on the food rather than the decor, and strip lighting and Formica tables are often the norm. Don't let this deter you; if a place is busy, chances are it's worth pulling up a chair. So rid yourself of preconceptions of what Chinese food tastes like at home and dig in.

CUISINE TYPES

Traditionally, cuisine was defined by the produce available locally, and thus the wheat-yielding north of the country made bread and wheat noodles, while rice was the staple in the warmer, wetter south. This division exists to this day, but with improved transportation and refrigeration, culinary variety from around the country is available in all of the major cities. In terms of the best food, though, the lower the carbon miles of the ingredients, the better your meal is likely to be.

CANTONESE (GUANGDONG CAI) Cantonese food is the most widely exported and thus most familiar of all the Chinese cuisines, though real Cantonese food, even if eaten in the northern cities of this book, is very different from what you'll find back home. The Cantonese are proud of their desire to try anything and everything. Those who enjoy snakes, snails, and every form of innards will likely love genuine Cantonese food. Other, more foreigner-friendly characteristics include superfresh seafood and the light, fragrant sauces that are rarely heavy on spice. Dim sum (*dian xin* in Mandarin) is a Cantonese breakfast or lunch favorite featuring a huge selection of miniature buns, spring rolls, and dumplings served from trolleys that are pushed around the restaurant. Not only is dim sum delicious, it also affords non-Chinese-speakers an easy way to have a look at what's on offer before committing.

QUICK STICKS: a chopstick primer

The main character in the Chinese word for chopsticks, ***kuaizi,*** blends the words "bamboo" and "fast." This points to both the original material used to make chopsticks, and also the fact that they are regarded, quite simply, as the quickest and most efficient way of eating. Techniques do vary, though the classical method has the bottom stick remaining immobile while the upper one is held like a pen, between thumb and two forefingers, to position the food. Sticking your chopsticks vertically into your bowl or passing food with chopsticks should both be avoided, as these actions are associated with funerary rites. When you've finished eating, place both sticks horizontally across the rim of the bowl.

SHOCKING orders

There are almost as many sayings about what the southern Chinese will eat as there are Cantonese dishes, but the gist is basically the same: "Cantonese people will eat anything on four legs that isn't a table, and anything in the air that isn't an airplane." Southern markets can be a riot, and restaurants often have live animals on display for customers' delectation. Because of the colder weather and more conservative eating culture, Cantonese restaurants in the northern cities of Beijing, Xi'an, and Shanghai tend to omit bat, cat, dog, frog, rat, scorpion, snake, and their like from the menu, and live animals are rare. The astonishing diversity in Cantonese food is mainly bound up with traditional Chinese medicinal beliefs, which state that certain foods are beneficial for particular parts of the body. Dining on dog is purported to keep you warm in the winter, while eating snake is supposed to increase virility.

NORTHERN (BEIFANG CAI) Northern cuisine is typified by the use of salt, garlic, ginger, and onion, and hearty staples of steamed buns *(mantou)*, noodles *(mian)*, pancakes *(bing)*, and numerous varieties of dumplings *(jiaozi)* for which **Xi'an** is particularly famous. The highest form of Northern cuisine is the opulent Mandarin style, the food of emperors, and **Beijing Duck** is deservedly its most famous dish.

EASTERN (HUAIYANG CAI) Eastern dishes are often considered the least appealing to foreigners, but get beyond the sometimes-strange sweetness and occasional oiliness and you'll find a host of fresh flavors and dishes that feature bamboo shoots, mushrooms, seafood, and river fish. **Shanghainese** *(shanghai cai)* cuisine is at the refined end of the eastern scale and offers lightly cooked minuscule treats akin to dim sum, including delicious **steamed pork dumplings** *(xiaolongbao)*.

SICHUAN (CHUAN CAI) Spicy Sichuan dishes typify western cuisine and pack a punch to rival any Indian or Mexican meal. In Sichuan cooking, the meat, fish, or tofu sometimes feel like a mere vehicle to carry the chilies and peppercorns to your palate. At the heart of Sichuan cuisine is the concept of **manifold flavoring,** and the aim is to detect the subtler tastes that emerge from beneath the initial chili hit, though this can be near impossible when your mouth feels like it's on fire. Use of fragrant Sichuan peppercorns *(huajiao)* is also common and sends a disarming numbness racing around your mouth. Some of the best known and tastiest Sichuan dishes are chicken with chili and peanuts, referred to as *kung pao* chicken in the West *(gongbao jiding)*, fish-flavored pork *(yuxiang rousi)*, spicy tofu *(mapo doufu)*, and the ubiquitous spicy hotpot *(huoguo)*. People from Hunan province like to think their cuisine is even spicier than Sichuan's, so expect a similar experience if dining out in a Hunanese restaurant.

WESTERN & VEGETARIAN FOOD

If you tire of Chinese food, Western-style burger joints and coffee shops serve sandwiches in most towns of any size, and in the culinary capitals of Beijing, Shanghai, and Hong Kong, you can take your pick of almost any cuisine in the world. For vegetarians, while there are seemingly countless dishes on many menus, you may well find that your egg fried rice has the odd shrimp or pieces of pork in it, and many dishes are cooked in animal-based fats. The bigger cities have vegetarian restaurants, but in smaller places, your best bet will be to head to the local Buddhist temple restaurant, where vegetarian food is guaranteed, or failing that, try saying *"wo shi fojiao tu"* ("I'm a Buddhist") when you order.

The flavor enhancer **monosodium glutamate (MSG)** is commonly used in Chinese cooking, and some people can have an adverse reaction to this. It's best to say, *"Wo bu yao weijing"* ("I don't want MSG") when you order.

Drinking

Summers are long and hot in most of China, and it's vital that you keep hydrated. Bottled water is sold everywhere and is often very cheap. While perfectly safe, most consist of double- or triple-filtered tap water rather than the spring waters they purport to be. Be sure not to drink directly from the tap.

Green tea *(lu cha)* has 2,000 years of history in China and, despite coffee's recent inroads, it is still the drink of choice for most Chinese. Almost all travelers and office workers have their own personal thermoses that they regularly refill and clutch for warmth in the winter months. Hundreds of different varieties of tea are found across the country, some of the most famous being *longjing cha* (Dragon Well Tea) from Hangzhou (p. 270) and *tie guanyin* (Iron Goddess Tea) from Fujian. Flower teas, such as jasmine *(molihua cha),* are also common and particularly refreshing.

Beer *(pijiu)* is also very popular, and thanks to Germany's early 20th-century incursions into Shandong province, the local pilsner varieties on sale around the country are pretty decent. Belgian and German wheat beers have enjoyed a spectacular rise in the last few years, as have U.S.-style craft beers. Sadly, what the Germans did for beer in China, the French could not do for **red wine** (*hong putao jiu*) or **white wine** (*bai putao jiu*) during their own colonial escapades. Good restaurants and supermarkets have an increasing number of imported wines on offer, albeit at much higher prices than you'll find back home, but domestic wine—Dynasty and Great Wall being the biggest brands—remains fairly awful. This said, China's taste for wine is growing, and there are a handful of domestic wineries making some high-end stuff.

Baijiu**,** a strong, sorghum-based spirit, is often drunk with food and comes in a dizzying variety of flavors and grades of quality. It can be great fun to try while eating out but, to avoid a killer hangover, ensure you take it with plenty of food. **Rice wine** *(mijiu)* makes for a similar experience but is a little easier on both the liver and the palate.

WHEN TO GO

There are three critical factors in deciding when to visit. The first—**weather**—is the easy one. It's saggingly hot in summer and can be numbingly cold in winter. The other two factors relate to the peculiarities of modern China. **Pollution** has gone from being a potential inconvenience a decade ago to posing a threat to an entire vacation. If you're staying for 2 weeks or more, you'll almost certainly be smothered in muck at some point. The two great natural pollution-flushes—wind and rain—may arrive to save you, but not necessarily. There are times of the year when the pollution tends to be worse and times when it tends to be better. These guidelines, given below, are less reliable than weather predictions, but well worth bearing in mind nonetheless. Finally, there is the real story of our times: the rise of the Chinese middle class. In 1990, the number of **domestic tourism** visits was 280 million; by 2007, it was 1.6 billion, and in 2015, it was around 3.3 billion. This gives a clear idea of how crowded many of the "must-see" spots have become, and you should expect to mingle with plenty of domestic travelers wherever, and whenever, you travel. When this wider phenomenon intersects with official holidays, you have the recipe for good old-fashioned travel chaos.

Official holidays are complicated, and dates change year to year, partly because most are based on lunar calendar calculations. The three most predictable holidays—and definite times to avoid—occur in January or February, for Chinese New Year, the first part of May, for the Labor Day holiday, and the first week of October, for National Day.

In the case of Chinese New Year (usually referred to in Chinese as **Spring Festival,** or *chun jie*) and **National Day,** 3 days' paid vacation is given, with the dates arranged so that workers in Chinese companies have 7 continuous days of vacation time, having to work during another weekend to make up the deficit. This affords migrant workers the time to make the often long trip home. During these so-called "golden week" holidays, Chinese tourists take to the road in the tens or even hundreds of millions, crowding all forms of transportation, booking up hotels, and turning tourist sights into seas of humanity. In May, it's only a 1-day official holiday, arranged around the weekend to make for a 3-day break. Other single-day holidays fall in April, for the grave-sweeping **Qingming Festival;** in June for the **Dragon Boat Festival;** and in September (occasionally October) for the **Mid-Autumn Festival.** January 1 is also a 1-day holiday.

Peak Travel Seasons

CHINESE NEW YEAR (SPRING FESTIVAL) Like many Chinese festivals, this one operates on the lunar calendar. Solar equivalents for the next 3 years will be February 8, 2016, January 28, 2017, and February 16, 2018. The effects of this holiday are felt from 3 weeks before the date until 3 weeks after, when anyone who's away from home attempts to get back, including an estimated 150 million migrant workers. Although tens of thousands of extra bus and train services are added, tickets for land transportation are still at a premium. Rules requiring tickets to be marked with the passenger's name and ID number have dampened the once-rampant black market, but long lines at stations remain a feature of the winter months. Air tickets are usually more obtainable, but increased demand means prices are usually high. In the few days immediately around the New Year, traffic on long-distance rail and bus services can suddenly become light, but local services may dry up altogether. Most tourist sights stay open, although some shut on the holiday itself or have limited opening hours.

NATIONAL DAY & MAY DAY In a policy known as "holiday economics," the October 1 holiday—marking the founding of the People's Republic of China—and the Labor Day holiday on May 1 were expanded to 7 days in 1999, primarily as a means of stirring domestic tourism. Suffice it to say it worked. The official label of "golden week" quickly took on a bitter irony among those fed up with being forced to vacation at the same time as half the country and deal with the resulting transportation crush and artificially inflated prices. Partly because of these concerns, the May "golden week" was cut back to 3 days in 2008, with the single-day holidays redistributed to several other important cultural occasions. These are the grave-sweeping **Qingming Festival** in April, the **Dragon Boat Festival** in June or July, and the **Mid-Autumn Festival** in September or October.

SCHOOL & UNIVERSITY HOLIDAYS Exact term dates vary, but train tickets become more difficult to obtain when the student population moves between home and college. University semesters generally run for 18 weeks with 2 weeks of exams, from the end of August to just before Spring Festival, and from just after Spring Festival to the end of June. School holidays run through most of July and August. As in the West, despite the sweltering temperatures, this is the time for families to take vacation, and crowds are common.

Climate

China is the third- or fourth-biggest country in the world (the United States and China are almost exactly the same size and both claim bronze position). China is a continent-size landmass, containing some of the lowest inland depressions in the world as well as its highest peaks. Whereas the northeast shares the same weather patterns as Siberia, the southwest has roughly the same subtropical climate as northern Thailand.

The destinations of this book are concentrated in **central** and **northern** China. In the north, early spring and late fall are the most pleasant, both offering warm, dry days and cool, dry evenings. In **Beijing,** winds in March and April sometimes bring sand and topsoil from high ground to the northeast. The sky can at times turn a vivid yellow. Winters here can be very cold, while summer is hot and sweaty, with occasional thundery downpours. **Xi'an** is very similar, though suffers fewer sandstorms and isn't quite so bitter in winter.

Coastal **Shanghai** is actually fairly moderate compared to other spots in central China, which have bitter winters and searing summers. Winters here tend to be gray and dreary, but it's rarely cold enough for snow. Summers are scorching hot, but thanks to the proximity to the sea, not quite as furnace-like as inland cities such as Nanjing.

Average Temperatures (°F/°C)

	JAN	FEB	MAR	APR	MAY	JUNE	JULY	AUG	SEPT	OCT	NOV	DEC
BEIJING	26/-3	32/0	43/6	57/14	68/20	76/24	79/26	77/25	69/21	57/14	41/5	30/-1
SHANGHAI	40/4	42/6	48/9	59/15	68/20	75/24	83/28	82/28	75/24	66/19	55/13	44/7
XI'AN	32/0	35/2	48/9	57/14	66/19	77/25	80/27	77/25	66/19	57/14	44/7	33/1

Average Precipitation (Inches)

	JAN	FEB	MAR	APR	MAY	JUNE	JULY	AUG	SEPT	OCT	NOV	DEC
BEIJING	0.2	0.2	0.3	0.7	1.3	3.1	8.8	6.7	2.3	0.7	0.4	0.1
SHANGHAI	1.8	2.4	3.3	3.7	4.1	6.8	5.7	5.4	5.4	2.7	2.1	1.5
XI'AN	0.3	0.4	0.9	1.8	2.4	2.1	3.8	3.4	4.2	2.3	1	0.2

Pollution

With many of China's most iconic attractions being open-air affairs, the state of the skies can make or break a visit. China's air quality has been poor for a long time, but it's only in the last 5 years that it's become a major story, both at home and abroad. The subject was semi-sensitive in domestic media until recently, but facing a looming environmental disaster, central government is now fairly frank about the severity and impact of air pollution. It disseminates information itself and also permits, and sometimes even encourages, discussion in traditional media and on various online platforms. Extreme measures have been attempted to ease the pressure. Cloud-seeding was widely touted—though never formally admitted—in the run-up to the 2008 Beijing Games. Another policy at that time has become a permanent feature of life in Beijing, with most cars being banned from the road on alternate days, depending on their plates. Factories are sometimes forcibly closed down for short periods by local governments in the event of an important event or VIP visit.

Most urbanites have live pollution apps on their smartphones, indicating whether they'll need to take the face mask on their commute to work. Many obsess over the current PM2.5 reading, which measures the concentration of toxic airborne particulates fine enough to be absorbed directly into the bloodstream. However, most apps focus on general AQI (Air Quality Index) readings, which synthesize a number of different pollutants, PM2.5 included, to offer a single figure to represent the overall quality of the air. In the West, an API of more than 50 would be regarded as fairly mucky. In much of China, a 50 reading would be reason to dance a jig. For Beijingers, anything under 100 is a pretty good day, and it's not uncommon to see readings upward of 200. At 300, one can begin to taste the air while walking in the open. When it's 400 or more (not as rare an occurrence as you'd hope), symptoms tend to be immediate, from sore throats to dizziness to heavy legs.

Pollution problems are at their most acute across the dry plains of northern China, particularly away from the coast. Beijing and Xi'an both get it bad. Shanghai generally has the better air, but pollution appears to be on the increase, even here. Summer is generally fresher than other seasons, mainly thanks to the increased rains, though pollution feels all the more intense when it is combined with searing temperatures and humidity. As the chart below shows, September is normally one of the better months across all three cities. March and April tend to be windier in northern China. Though they bring in Beijing's infamous sandstorms, they can equally flush out the pollution. March can also be a good time to be in Beijing, as this is when China's parliament holds its major annual meeting. Year after year, the air miraculously improves for 2 weeks or so.

Average AQI Reading

	JAN	FEB	MAR	APR	MAY	JUNE	JULY	AUG	SEPT	OCT	NOV	DEC
BEIJING	124	185	127	131	102	92	132	100	96	155	121	115
SHANGHAI	103	75	84	78	95	68	70	60	62	69	76	161
XI'AN	185	218	140	104	103	77	74	75	63	114	120	219

Holidays

Offices generally close on weekends, but stores, restaurants, post offices, transportation, sights, and in some areas, banks, all operate the same services 7 days a week. Most sights, shops, and restaurants are open on public holidays, but those in government offices take as much time off as they can.

China Calendar of Events

China's festivals follow the traditional lunar calendar, and to increase confusion, some minority calendars operate according to different traditions. Dates change year to year but are flagged well in advance.

JAN/FEB

Spring Festival (*Chun Jie*), Chinese New Year, nationwide While Chinatowns worldwide put on lion dances and other colorful festivities, China itself celebrates in more modest, homey fashion. This is a time for feasting with family and gathering around the TV. New Year's Eve, ironically not part of the official weeklong holiday, is perhaps the most important date for families to be united. Fireworks and firecrackers were banned for a while, but are making a reappearance, making it a loud, smoky, and sometimes dangerous time to be wandering the streets. Spring Festival is on the day of the first new moon after January 21, and can be no later than February 20.

FEB/MAR

Lantern Festival (*Yuanxiao Jie*), nationwide This festival perhaps reached its peak in the late Qing dynasty, when temples, stores, and other public places were hung with fantastically shaped and decorated lanterns, some with figures animated by ingenious mechanisms involving the flow of sand. People paraded through the streets with lightweight lanterns in the shapes of fish, sheep, and so on, and hung lanterns outside their houses, often decorated with riddles. The festival has undergone a revival on the mainland in recent years with increasingly elaborate designs featured in cities across the country. The festival always falls on the New Year's first full moon, 15 days after Spring Festival.

APR

Formula One Racing, Shanghai Motorsport fans can catch Formula One drivers zooming around a state-of-the-art track in the Shanghai suburb of Anting. Dates vary, but races are generally held in the middle of the month.

Tomb-Sweeping Festival (*Qingming*), nationwide Another festival frequently observed in Chinese communities overseas, and celebrated in more rural areas of China, tomb-sweeping is a day to honor ancestors by visiting and tidying their graves and making offerings of snacks and alcohol. April 4 or April 5 annually.

MAY

Labor Day (*Laodong Jie*), nationwide The local iteration of this international holiday is understandably a big deal in communist China. There are few public events, but everyone gets a holiday, and shops, parks, and tourist attractions are packed in the first week of May. May 1–3.

JUNE

Dragon Boat Festival (*Duanwu Jie*), nationwide Dragon boat races are held at events across the nation to mark this historic festival, which commemorates the watery death of 4th century B.C. Mandarin Qu Yuan. Legend has him drowning himself in a Hunan river to protest government corruption. His faithful followers, wishing to recover his body, raced out into the river in boats, beating their paddles on the surface of the water and throwing rice to prevent the fish from feasting on his body. This is now an official nationwide holiday, when it's traditional to eat *zongzi*, a sticky rice dish served in wrapped leaves. Fifth day of the fifth lunar month (usually around mid-June).

JULY

Eid al-Fitr (*Kaizhai Jie*), predominantly Muslim regions The biggest festival in the Islamic world, Eid al-Fitr marks the end of the month-long Fast of Ramadan and is celebrated with serious feasting. Presents are exchanged, and alms are given to the poor. Xi'an has a small but important Muslim population, and rituals can be observed in and around the city center's many mosques. The festival is held for 4 days after the first sighting of the new moon in the 10th month (Shawwal) of the Islamic calendar. July 8, 2016, moving backward by about 11 days each year.

SEPT

Mid-Autumn Festival (*Zhongqiu Jie*), nationwide This is probably the most pleasant of Chinese public holidays, marked with the giving and eating of moon cakes (*yuebing*), circular pies with sweet and extremely fattening fillings. Traditionally it's a time to read poetry under the full moon. Friends may skip the readings but still head out into the parks and feast together under the full moon, pollution willing. The 15th day of the 8th lunar month (usually September).

OCT

National Day (*Guoqing Jie*), nationwide A day spent in commemoration and celebration of Mao Zedong's historic proclamation on the steps of Tian'anmen in 1949, announcing the birth of the People's Republic of China. The displays of military might have been toned down, but there's often a patriotic fervor in the air, and on the airwaves, as well as a distinct commercial fervor associated with the weeklong holiday. October 1–7.

BEIJING

If China's vast landmass looks a little like a giant rooster, it's perfectly appropriate that Beijing sits right at the jugular. The roll-call of invaders and usurpers over the past seven centuries have looked to make their mark here, from Mongol marauder Kublai Khan all the way to guerrilla upstart Mao Zedong, with the Ming, the Manchurians, and the ransacking British crashing the party in between. This is the nerve center of Chinese civilization, anchored by foreboding temples and palaces, strafed by huge boulevards, and ordered by the concentric circles of its ring roads. But between these mighty surges of people and traffic, Beijing retains pockets of pedestrian charm. Get caught in the fast lane, and there's nowhere more intense. Hang out in the gaps, where kites fly, tai chi flows, and old-timers chat, and Beijing can feel almost provincial.

From an emperor's-eye view, Beijing is a strange vantage point from which to lord it over the nation. It lies on a sandblasted plain, more than 4,500km (2,796 miles) from the nation's farthest borders, and has neither major river nor coastline. This is a clue to the fact that the city developed from the drawing board rather than by an organic progress. The planned grid pattern was first laid down in the 13th century and labeled Khanbalik ("Dadu" in Mandarin), new capital of the Yuan dynasty (1279–1368). It was razed, rebuilt, and renamed Beijing—"northern capital"—by the Han Chinese rulers of the subsequent Ming dynasty (1368–1644). They added most of the city's most impressive surviving structures, the Forbidden City among them. The Manchurian Qing (1636–1912) chose to repurpose the city, rather than start afresh, and layered on new landmarks like the Summer Palace.

Some of the greatest damage to Beijing has occurred in the last 170 years. Invasion, rebellion, and civil war all altered the face of the city. Revolution too. In the first decade of the People's Republic, a distinctly Soviet-style grandeur was imposed. The ancient city walls and old Imperial Way were both leveled and paved over in a gesture of socialist modernity.

Present-day Beijing is vast. Unconstrained by natural obstructions, the city has grown into a seemingly endless sprawl, and it can take hours to get from one side to the other. It has also become a magnet for migrants from around the country, and the population is now more than 22 million. Roads that once swarmed with bicycles are now choked with traffic.

The 2008 Olympics may feel distant, but their legacy in changing the face of Beijing cannot be underestimated. The development-scramble added tidiness, even a little glamour in parts, but took its toll on Beijing's most charming aspect, the *hutong*. The city was once a giant warren of these narrow residential lanes, which twisted and turned for miles on end. Many survive, but they have been sliced and diced by development.

Beijing has a dry, still climate, searing in summer and bitter in winter. When the northern breeze blows from the Mongolian steppe, the skies are a rich, cerulean blue. But without the movement of wind or rain, the pollution can build to apocalyptic proportions. When it's nice, it's *really* nice. When it's bad, it's horrid.

It all adds up to a city that requires both time and patience, but offers rich rewards. And for those seeking China's essence, it's unbeatable. Whether you're after the upturned eaves and imperial palaces of "ancient" China, the pomp and power of "communist" China, or the malls, jackhammers, and gridlock of "rising" China, Beijing serves all needs.

ESSENTIALS

Arriving

BY PLANE Beijing Capital International Airport (Beijing Shoudu Guoji Jichang) (✆ **010/96158** for information and ticket inquiries) is 25km (16 miles) northeast of the city center. The wonderfully modern Terminal 3 (T3) is Air China's home base but also serves the majority of international passengers, while Terminal 1 (T1) and Terminal 2 (T2) largely cater to domestic flights. Free 24-hour shuttle buses connect all three terminals.

Taxis line up outside the international arrivals gate at T2 and T3 and take 30 minutes to an hour to reach the city center, depending on Beijing's (often horrendous) traffic. The fare should be around RMB80 to RMB100 (20% higher after 11pm), not counting the RMB15 toll. Bypass any drivers who approach you inside the airport, and head for the taxi stand instead. Insist on using the meter.

The cheapest way to get into the city is on the air-conditioned **airport shuttle buses.** Of the 16 lines, the busiest depart between approximately 7am and midnight. They run approximately every 30 minutes, and tickets cost between RMB15 and RMB30, depending on the route. Of the three most useful routes, Line 1 connects with Guomao in the Central Business District, Line 2 skirts just north of the city center on its way to Xidan, while Line 3 goes via Chaoyangmen on its way to Beijing Railway Station.

The **Airport Express** line connects T2 and T3 with Sanyuanqiao (Line 10) and Dongzhimen (Lines 2 and 13) on the Beijing subway. Trains run from T3 between 6:20am and 10:50pm, and for RMB25, you'll get yourself to downtown Beijing in about 30 minutes. You can use regular subway cards (see "Getting Around," below) for the journey. Unfortunately, many Beijing subway stations, including Dongzhimen, connect to street-level via stairs, meaning the Airport Express is not ideal for those hauling heavy luggage. It can also be very difficult to find an onward taxi, especially near busy central stations like Dongzhimen.

BY TRAIN The advent of high-speed rail may have speeded up journey times, but it's pushed passengers arriving in Beijing to the fringes. Whereas the oldest station, **Beijing Railway Station** (Beijing Zhan), is just southeast of Tian'anmen Square, the newer stations, which serve most incoming and outgoing rail passengers, are located between the second and third ring roads. Most passengers will end up using the new, gleaming **Beijing South Railway Station** (Beijing Nan Zhan), which serves high-speed rail along the crowded eastern seaboard cities, or the older but equally huge **Beijing West Railway Station** (Beijing Xi Zhan). All three stations are connected to the subway network, and this is certainly the best way to get to your hotel, assuming you are traveling light. Such are the interchange distances, and the number of stairs on Beijing's subway network, however, that those with large bags may be better off waiting in line for a taxi. Taxi stands are clearly marked at the stations, but expect to queue. Also expect traffic. If you are looking to get anywhere fast, take the subway.

BY BUS Beijing does not have a central bus station, but rather a series of region-specific stations spread around the outskirts of the city. Given the distances involved, and the excellent conditions on trains and planes in China, bus travel is not recommended but may be useful for trips to nearby places like Chengde (p. 137). The **Dongzhimen Long Distance Bus Station** (Dongzhimen Changtu Qiche Zhan), just east of the Dongzhimen subway station, is probably the most useful terminal for readers of this book and has services to Chengde. The **Liuliqiao Long Distance Bus Station** (Liuliqiao Changtu Qiche Keyun Zhan) mainly serves points to the south and west of the city.

Visitor Information

For the most current information on life in Beijing, particularly nightlife and restaurants, see listings in the free English-language monthlies **"Time Out"** (www.timeoutbeijing.com), **"The Beijinger"** (www.thebeijinger.com), **"City Weekend"** (www.cityweekend.com.cn/beijing), and **"That's Beijing"** (http://online.thatsmags.com/city/beijing). They are scattered around many foreigner-friendly bars and restaurants in the tourist areas but can be hard to find. "City Weekend" and "The Beijinger" have useful Android and iOS apps that can be downloaded for free, while "That's Beijing" offers the magazine as a free PDF download from its website. "Time Out" can be read digitally on the desktop site.

The Beijing Municipal Commission of Tourist Development runs an English-language website (http://english.visitbeijing.com.cn) and maintains a

Beijing Orientation & Outlying Attractions

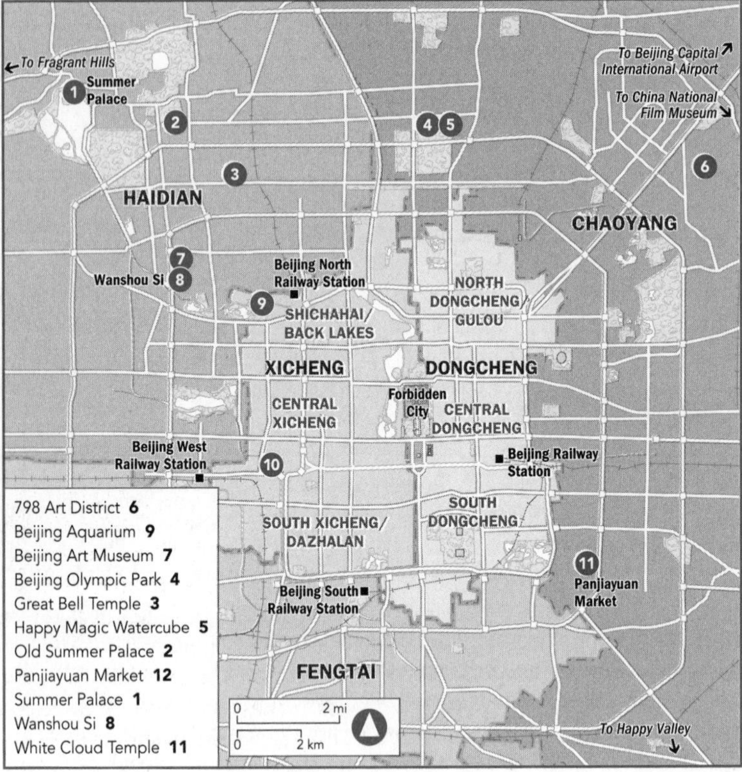

tourist information hot line (✆ **6513-0828,** dial 1 for English). It also oversees the network of **Beijing Tourist Information Centers (Beijing Shi Luyou Zixun Fuwu Zhongxin).** These are run more as private tour operators, linking with services provided by state-run agencies. While useful for grabbing a map or asking for help making a phone call, they should not be relied upon for impartial advice.

City Layout

Beijing is bordered to the north and west by mountains, the closest of which can be seen from elevated points on clear days. The city center, known to foreigners in the Qing period (1644–1911) as the Tartar City, was originally surrounded by a complex of walls and gates. These were destroyed in 1958 to make way for the **Second Ring Road (Er Huan).** Central Beijing is organized along a grid, with nearly all major streets running along compass axes. Ring roads two to six run concentrically, appearing to radiate outward from the city center. Technically, there is no "First Ring Road," though Di'anmen and Qianmen avenues, in the north and south, and Xisi and Dongsi avenues, in the east and west, form a square that is the assumed "First Ring Road" marking Beijing's city center. Appropriately enough, this boundary encloses **Tian'anmen Square** and **the Forbidden City.**

MAJOR STREETS

Beijing can be tricky to navigate for a host of reasons. One of them is the fact that a single road, running straight and true, can change names multiple times over its course. A little bit of knowledge about Chinese pinyin (see p. 300) can go a long, long way here. It is quite common in Chinese cities for main roads to be labeled by compass point, with a name changing between its north (*bei*), south (*nan*), east (*dong*), west (*xi*), or central (*zhong*) sections. To add to the headache, these direction markers can sometimes come *before*, sometimes *after* the main road name (for example, "**Dong** Chang'an Dajie" is "East Chang'an Avenue," while "Gulou **Dong** Dajie" is "Gulou East Avenue"). In Beijing, roads may be further divided by whether they are inside (*nei*) or outside (*wai*) the old imperial wall (now the Second Ring Road). Most confusing of all is that in Beijing, more than in most cities, the same road may change its basic name without any kind of deviation. A good example is the city's most important east-west artery. As it bisects Tian'anmen Square and the Forbidden City, this road is called **Chang'an Dajie.** However, beyond the boundaries of the implied First Ring Road (see p. 58), it abruptly becomes Jianguomen Nei Dajie, in the east, and Fuxingmen Nei Dajie, in the west. **Di'anmen Dajie** is a similar offender, and an equally important road. It runs across the back of Beihai Park and changes name four times within the space of the Second Ring Road. Among important north-south streets, **Wangfujing Dajie** (two blocks east of the Forbidden City) is the Beijing consumer equivalent of Chicago's Magnificent Mile or London's Oxford Street. **Qian Men Dajie** extends down from the southern end of Tian'anmen Square.

Neighborhoods in Brief

Beijing's neighborhoods can be divided according to the official administrative districts, as below, but need to be further sliced before they make sense as places that might be explored in one go. Because of recent development, they're not marked out by a specific architectural style, though the most central bits of Beijing—Dongcheng and Xicheng—are generally low-rise and contain the majority of the surviving *hutong*. Chaoyang and Haidian, by contrast, are large, sprawling, and modern.

Dongcheng Dongcheng ("East City") occupies the eastern half of the imperial city center. It's best to think of it in three sections. **Central Dongcheng** is as close to a "city center" as Beijing gets (though such a term is not used by locals). It contains Tian'anmen Square, the Forbidden City, and Wangfujing Dajie, as well as a cluster of *hutong* in its eastern section. The northern part of the district is often referred to informally as the **"Gulou Area,"** in a nod to the nearby Drum Tower (Gu Lou). It has *hutong* galore, the most famous of which is Nan Luogu Xiang, as well as the Lama Temple. **South Dongcheng** is mainly notable for the Temple of Heaven.

Xicheng District The western half of central Beijing, Xicheng, is less touristy than its eastern counterpart but does have some appeal. The northern section is known as **Shichahai** (or more informally as "Houhai," which translates as "rear lakes"). This is Beijing's Lake District and one of the most scenic places to wander, the watery vistas complemented by some lovely *hutong*. **Central Xicheng** is home to Zhongnanhai, the off-limits compound of the Chinese Communist Party's most senior leaders, which flows into Beihai Park immediately to the north. In the southern section are the emporiums of **Dazhalan,** as well as the narrow *hutong* of the nearby Muslim district.

Chaoyang District The wealthiest administrative district in Bejing takes in almost all things east of the Second Ring Road. Due east of the city center is the **Central Business District (CBD),** stuffed with fine hotels and glitzy office towers like the iconic CCTV Building. A couple of miles north is **Sanlitun.** This used to be primarily associated with its sleazy bar strip, but development here has been rapid, and this is now the capital's premier shopping and nightlife hub. Alongside the CBD, it also contains Beijing's most expensive apartment complexes. In the northwest of the district is the Olympic Park, home to the 2008 Games, while in the far northeast is the Factory 798 Arts District.

Haidian District Occupying a large swath of northwest Beijing, Haidian is home to most of the capital's universities as well as its blossoming high-tech enterprises. Farther out, beyond the Fourth Ring Road, are the tourist spots of the Summer Palace and Yuanmingyuan (the Old Summer Palace), while there's hiking in the even more distant Fragrant Hills.

GETTING AROUND

By Subway

At the time of writing, Beijing had 17 subway lines and more than 515km (320 miles) of track, making it the second-largest network in the world (after Shanghai). By the time you read this, there will almost certainly be more lines, and more track. Given the traffic up at ground level and the difficulty in finding taxis, it is the easiest, quickest, and most reliable way to get to where you need to go. The most important lines are: **Line 1,** which runs east-west past Tian'anmen Square and the Forbidden City; **Line 2,** or the Loop Line, which follows the path of the Second Ring Road; **Line 4,** which takes arrivals at Beijing South Railway Station north into the city and on up to the Summer Palace; **Line 6,** which runs east-west and passes the northern entrance to Beihai Park and Nan Luogu Xiang; **Line 8,** which runs north from Shichahai towards the former Olympic Village; and **Line 10,** which traces the North and East Third Ring Road and is helpful for navigating to and from the CBD. The **Airport Express** runs regularly from Dongzhimen (Lines 2 and 13) and Sanyuanqiao (Line 10), while the **Western Suburban Line** (unfinished at the time of writing) heads out from Bagou, on Line 10, toward the Fragrant Hills, via the Summer Palace.

Signs on platforms tell you which station is the next in each direction, and English announcements are made on trains. However, trains heading in opposite directions sometimes depart from separate platforms. To get to the right place the first time, it helps to know the next station (in whichever direction you are going), as this is used to point passengers to the right platform.

NAVIGATING THE SUBWAY Tickets cost between RMB3 and RMB7, calculated by distance (most city-center rides will cost RMB3 to RMB4).

Buying a subway card, officially known as the "Municipal Government Transportation Card" (*Shizheng Jiaotong Yikatong*, or *Yikatong* for short) is highly recommended. This costs RMB40, which includes RMB20 of stored value and RMB20 for a refundable deposit. You can buy and return cards at any station. It's possible to buy single-ride tickets at the electronic ticket machines (which have an English language service), but there are usually lines, and the machines often have problems taking low-value notes. Tickets are also available from cashiers. To avoid language issues, try to work out how much your ride will cost using the price guides around ticket desks and gesture the amount to the cashier. (See the subway map on the inside back cover.)

DRAWBACKS There are significant drawbacks to be aware of. Due to Beijing's heightened terrorism fears, all bags, even handbags, now need to pass through airport-style scanners. This is a quick process, but lines can form merely to *enter* the station, especially at peak hours. You'll be slowed down even further by the lengthy walk between interchanges, especially where the two older lines (Lines 1 and 2) intersect with newer lines. Finding your station in the first place can be an issue, as entrances are hidden away and not always clearly marked. Some exits have no escalator to street level. While platform-level elevators have been installed in most stations, it's not guaranteed, so those with severe mobility issues should choose to travel by car wherever possible. Finally, and most importantly for anyone wanting to enjoy Beijing's excellent nightlife, trains stop running ludicrously early for a major capital city. Trains begin around 5am, but the final train departs central stations around 11pm. If you know you'll need to change trains en route, aim to get to your departure station no later than 10:20pm. Make it even earlier if you need to change twice.

By Taxi

Taxis cost RMB13 for the first 3km (2 miles), then RMB2.3 per kilometer thereafter. Rates per kilometer jump by 50% after 15km (9 miles), and both base fare and the journey price rise by around 20% after 11pm. Insist on the drivers using the meter ("*da biao*") and get out if they refuse. The one exception is for lengthy out-of-town journeys (to the Great Wall, for example), when a price should be agreed beforehand. Write down the amount to avoid any possible misunderstandings and withhold payment until you return to the city. Tips are not expected.

Few drivers speak any English, and the names of familiar attractions are often completely different between languages (the Forbidden City has neither the Chinese word for "Forbidden," nor the word "City" in its original name, Gu Gong), so try to have your destination written down for you in advance. Carry your hotel's business card at all times.

Beijing suffers many of the taxi ills described in Chapter 10 (see p. 286), and it can be very hard to find a cab at certain times, particularly around busy areas like Gulou and Sanlitun.

By Bus

Despite the subway expansion, bus is still the most popular means to move about for the city's residents. Buses can be very crowded and are not recommended for visitors. Route information is usually only in Chinese script, and you will be very fortunate to find anybody who speaks English. City buses and trolleys (nos. less than 124) charge a flat fare of RMB2 (RMB1 with a travel card), and this is often collected by a conductor rather than the driver. Most buses run between 5am and 11pm (specific times are posted at the stops).

By Bicycle

On a good traffic day, a bike is the best way to experience the flow of the city between sights. On a bad traffic day, it's a fantastic way to bypass the gridlock. Cycling down narrow *hutong* is one of Beijing's most alluring experiences, but on the main roads, things can be treacherous. Pay attention to cars and other riders, both of which pose risks to the unwary. The municipal government has introduced a "free" network of around 120 public bicycle stations. These are dotted around, but if in doubt, head for the nearest subway station. Before you can use them, you'll need to get a public transportation card (*yikatong*), available at most subway stations. Ensure you have at least RMB30 of stored value, then take it along to one of the city-center offices to activate bike rental. You'll need to fork over RMB400 (most of which acts as a deposit) and show your passport. The most convenient offices are at Temple of Heaven East Gate subway (Line 5, near Exit A2), Dongzhimen (Lines 2 & 13, near Exit A), and Chaoyangmen (Lines 2 & 6, near Exit A), though office hours are short and open only Monday to Friday. After swiping the activated *yikatong*, a lock is released and you'll be able to pedal off. The first hour of rental is free, with a small fee if you go beyond this time. Alternatively, bikes are often available for rent at a number of hotels. Expect to pay a deposit of several hundred renminbi and between RMB30 and RMB50 per day. If you're taking a three-wheel pedicab or rickshaw, make sure to bargain before you hop on, as rates vary wildly and are usually exorbitant. Pay no more than RMB30 for short distances.

On Foot

By and large, Beijing is no friend of the pedestrian. The city's sights are scattered, and most of its roads are broad rivers with few channels for safe crossing (use pedestrian underpasses and footbridges wherever available). This said, exploring on foot is sometimes essential due to the difficulties in hailing cabs and the nature of sights like the Forbidden City and Tian'anmen Square, both of which can *only* be seen on foot. ***Warning:*** Traffic turning right at lights does not give way to pedestrians, nor does any other traffic unless forced to do so by large groups of people bunching up to cross the road. The only parts of the city where walking is enjoyable are the few remaining *hutong* neighborhoods. Otherwise, use a vehicle.

[FastFACTS] BEIJING

Banks, Foreign Exchange & ATMs

ATMs belonging to the **Bank of China,** the **Industrial and Commercial Bank of China (ICBC), China Construction Bank,** and the **Agricultural Bank of China** will permit money to be drawn directly from your overseas account, and converted into RMB at the point of withdrawal, though this depends on your home account and card (see p. 292 for more on this). Though fees will likely be levied, ATM withdrawals can actually be a surprisingly efficient way of obtaining renminbi in cash. There are dozens of branches across the city center, though the most central Bank of China branch is located at the bottom of Wangfujing Dajie, next to the Oriental Plaza, with foreign-exchange and credit-card cash advances handled at windows 5 to 11 (until 5pm). Other useful branches include those at 410 Fuchengmen Nei Dajie; on Jianguomen Wai Dajie, west of the Scitech Building; in the Lufthansa Center, next to the Kempinski Hotel; and in Tower 1 of the China World Trade Center. One other bank that offers forex is the **CITIC Industrial Bank,** with a major branch located inside the CITIC building (Guoji Dasha) on Jianguomen Wai Dajie. There are also several ATMs at the airport that accept international cards. Look out for the banking brands listed above.

Doctors & Dentists

Even a brief consultation with an English-speaking doctor or dentist at one of the private centers below can cost more than US$100, so ensure you have the necessary insurance before you travel. For comprehensive care, the best choice is **Beijing United Family Hospital (Hemujia Yiyuan;** **✆ 010/5927-7000**) at Jiangtai Lu, Chaoyang District. It is open 24 hours, staffed with foreign-trained doctors, and has a pharmacy, dental clinic, inpatient and outpatient care, and ambulance service. Other reputable health-service providers, both with 24-hour ambulance services, are the **International Medical Center** (**✆ 010/ 6462-2079**), inside the Lufthansa Center, 50 Liangmaqiao Lu, Chaoyang District; and the **International SOS Clinic** (**✆ 010/ 6462-9100**), in the Kunsha Building, 16 Xinyuanli, Chaoyang District.

Embassies

Beijing has two main embassy areas—one surrounding Ritan Park, north of Jianguomen Wai Dajie, and another in Sanlitun north of Gongti Bei Lu. Embassies are typically open Monday through Friday from 9am to between 4 and 5pm, with a lunch break from noon to 1:30pm. The **U.S. Embassy** is at 55 Anjialou Lu (**✆ 010/8531-3000**). The **Canadian Embassy** is at 19 Dongzhimen Wai Dajie 19 (**✆ 010/5139-4000**). The **British Embassy** is at 11 Guanghua Lu (**✆ 010/5192-4000**). The **Australian Embassy** is in Sanlitun at 21 Dongzhimen Wai Dajie (**✆ 010/5140-4111**). The **New Zealand Embassy** is 3 Sanlitun Dong Sanjie (**✆ 010/8531-2700**).

Emergencies

For medical emergencies and ambulance service 24 hours a day, call the **United Family Health Center** emergency number at **✆ 010/5927-7000** or the **International SOS Clinic** (**✆ 010/ 6462-9100**).

Internet Access

Free public Wi-Fi is offered in many busy central locations, Wangfujing and Sanlitun included. This requires a registration code to be sent to your phone, so you'll need to buy a local China SIM card in order to take advantage. Free Wi-Fi has become the norm in both bars and restaurants, though you'll often need to ask for the password. Hotels generally offer free Wi-Fi only to guests, but some also offer universal access in the lobby areas. Bear in mind that many popular Western websites, among them Facebook, Twitter, and all sites run by Google (YouTube and Gmail included) are blocked in China. To access them, you'll need to have a VPN installed on your phone, tablet, or computer (see p. 295).

Maps & Books Ordinarily, owning a smartphone would render the need to carry a map redundant. However, as explained above, Google Maps is blocked in China, and its equivalent, Baidu Maps, has little English. Old-fashioned maps with Chinese characters, English, and/or Pinyin can be purchased cheaply for around RMB5 from vendors near major sights and in hotel lobbies and bookstores. A good selection can be found inside the **Wangfujing Bookstore** (9:30am–9pm) at 218 Wangfujing Dajie, north of the Oriental Plaza's west entrance. The rise of online publishing has meant that it's increasingly rare to find a good selection of foreign newspapers in China, even at top-end hotels. The English-language "China Daily" is *always* available and is more readable than it used to be.

The best selection of English-language books in Beijing can be found at the **Foreign Languages Bookstore** (9:30am–9:30pm) at 235 Wangfujing Dajie, opposite the Xin Dong'an Plaza. Look on the left side of the first floor for China-related nonfiction, glossy *hutong* photo books, cookbooks, and the full range of Asiapac's cartoon renditions of Chinese classics. Cheap paperback versions of popular English-language classics, as well as a number of contemporary works, are sold upstairs. A more daring collection of fiction is carried by **The Bookworm** (p. 119).

Pharmacies Simple Western remedies can be found at branches of **Watson's,** a reliable Hong Kong pharmacy brand that has made huge headway in China in recent years. Central shops include the first floor of Full Link Plaza at 19 Chaoyangmen Wai Dajie; in the basement of the Oriental Plaza at the bottom of 1 Wangfujing Dajie; and in the basement of Sanlitun Village, Sanlitun Bei Lu. They are a good place to get hold of an anti-pollution face mask. For more specific drugs, try the pharmacies in the Beijing United Family Hospital or the International SOS Clinic (see "Doctors & Dentists" above).

Post Office Numerous post offices are scattered across the city, including one a long block north of the Jianguomen subway station on the east side of Jianguomen Bei Dajie (8am–6:30pm), one next to the Friendship Store on Jianguomen Wai Dajie, and one on Gongti Bei Lu (opposite the Workers' Stadium). For international shipping of vacation purchases, opt for one of the international carriers. There are eight **FedEx** offices (✆ **800/988-1888** toll-free from a land line, or ✆ **400/889-1888** from cell phone with local call charges). There's a useful branch in the Lonsdale Center, 5 Wanhong Lu, Chaoyang District. **DHL** has more than a dozen branches, including in the China World Trade Center and the Lufthansa Plaza, while **UPS** also has a useful branch in the China World Trade Center.

Visa Extensions One-time extensions of single-entry tourist visas can usually be obtained, though visas are routinely politicized by both the U.S. and China, meaning rules and regulations can often change suddenly for U.S. citizens. Make inquiries before setting out. Extensions are granted at the **PSB** office (✆ **010/8402-0101**) at 2 Andingmen Dong Dajie, Dongcheng District, just east of Lama Temple (Yonghegong) subway stop (Mon–Sat 8:30am–4:30pm). You will need a Registration Form of Temporary Residence (your hotel should be able to give you a copy, upon request) and it's possible you'll be asked for evidence of an ability to fund your continued stay (bank statements showing a balance of the equivalent of RMB21,000 should suffice). Ensure you bring your passport and a passport photo. You must visit at least 7 days before your visa expires, as it will take approximately 5 days to process the application and make a decision. Extension fees vary by nationality but expect the price to be roughly the same as your original visa.

Weather Both the Google Play Store and the Apple App Store offer a selection of free China weather apps (though note the former is blocked in China, so download any Android apps before you travel). In Beijing, it's also useful to have an app to give you an indication of the pollution. If the AQI is 150 or above, you should be wearing a face mask if you plan to spend any serious time outside (see "Pharmacies" above for advice on where to buy masks). The **Beijing Air Quality** app is a good option (see p. 282 for information about other useful apps). More traditional weather information can be found in the "China Daily" newspaper or on CCTV 9, China Central Television's English channel (broadcast in most hotels).

EXPLORING BEIJING

No other city in China offers so many must-see attractions. It is possible to see the big names—the Forbidden City, the Temple of Heaven, and the Summer Palace—in a couple of days, with an extra day spent making a trip out to the equally essential Great Wall (see chapter 5), but you'll probably need a week or more to begin to get a feel for the city.

The key to touring in Beijing is advance-planning. Regardless of whether you choose to get around by taxi, subway, bus, bike, or foot, plan each day to see sights that are close together. Do *not* plan to see too many sights that are far apart unless you want your memories of the capital to consist of staring helplessly out of a taxicab window. Scale back your ambitions, focus on one area at a time, and walk wherever possible.

The list of attractions below uses the neighborhood division given above. However, because Dongcheng is so large, and packed with sights, it's divided into central, northern, and southern sections.

Note: Most major sights now charge admission according to the season. The summer high season officially runs from April 1 to October 31, and the winter low season from November 1 to March 31.

Central Dongcheng

THE FORBIDDEN CITY & SURROUNDINGS

The Forbidden City (Gu Gong) ★★★ PALACE A 720,000-sq.-m (7.75-million-sq.-ft.) complex of red-walled pavilions and halls topped by a sea of glazed vermilion tile, the Forbidden City is the largest palace in the world. It receives more visitors than any other attraction in the country (more than nine million a year, according to the Chinese government) and has been eulogized in Western literature ever since the first Europeans laid eyes on it in the early 1600s. Despite the flood of superlatives, it is impervious to an excess of hype and is large and compelling enough to draw repeat visits from even the most jaded travelers.

Sourcing of materials for the original palace buildings began in 1406, during the reign of the Yongle emperor, and construction was completed in 1420. Much of it was designed by a eunuch from what is now Vietnam, Nguyen An. Without improvements to the Grand Canal, construction would have been impossible—timber came from as far away as Sichuan, and logs took up to 4 years to reach the capital. The Yuan dynasty palace was demolished to make way for the Forbidden City, but the lakes excavated during the Jin

Central Beijing

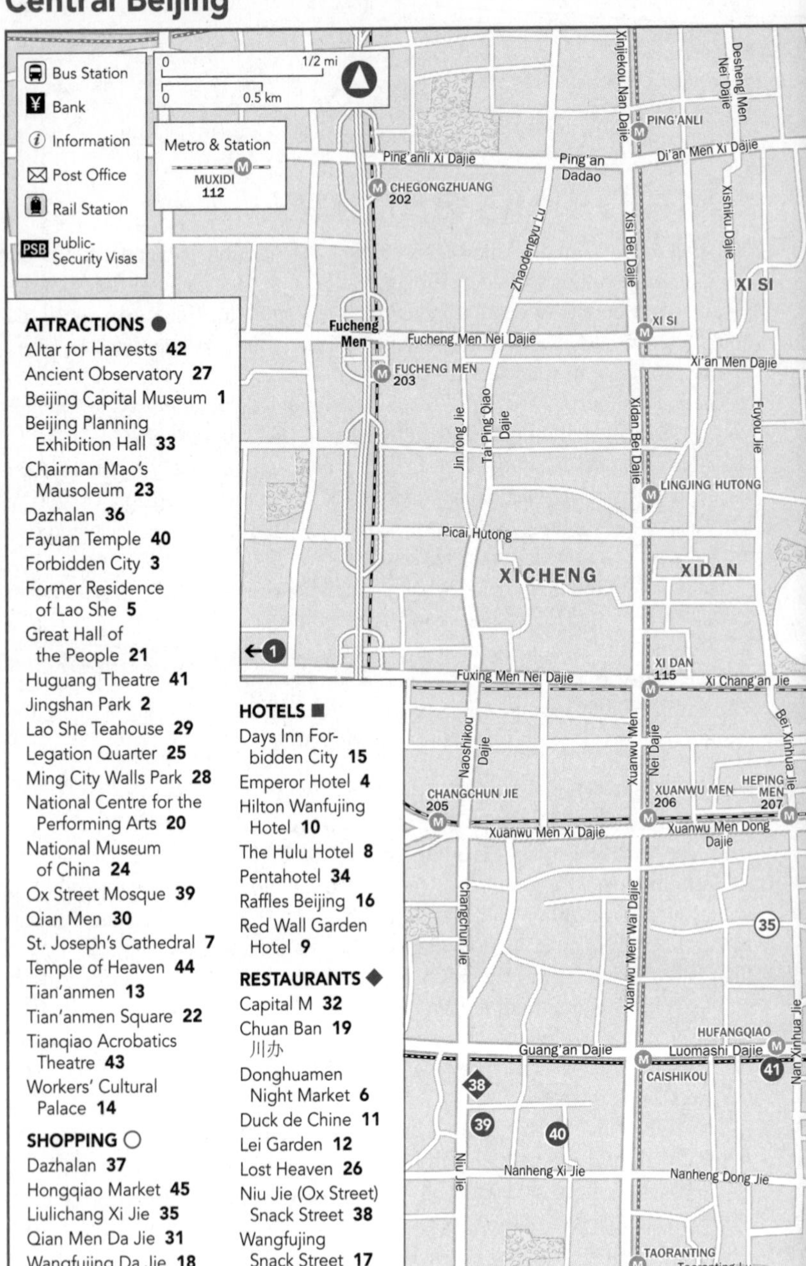

Bus Station
Bank
Information
Post Office
Rail Station
PSB Public-Security Visas
0 1/2 mi
0 0.5 km
Metro & Station
MUXIDI 112
ATTRACTIONS
Altar for Harvests 42
Ancient Observatory 27
Beijing Capital Museum 1
Beijing Planning Exhibition Hall 33
Chairman Mao's Mausoleum 23
Dazhalan 36
Fayuan Temple 40
Forbidden City 3
Former Residence of Lao She 5
Great Hall of the People 21
Huguang Theatre 41
Jingshan Park 2
Lao She Teahouse 29
Legation Quarter 25
Ming City Walls Park 28
National Centre for the Performing Arts 20
National Museum of China 24
Ox Street Mosque 39
Qian Men 30
St. Joseph's Cathedral 7
Temple of Heaven 44
Tian'anmen 13
Tian'anmen Square 22
Tianqiao Acrobatics Theatre 43
Workers' Cultural Palace 14
SHOPPING
Dazhalan 37
Hongqiao Market 45
Liulichang Xi Jie 35
Qian Men Da Jie 31
Wangfujing Da Jie 18
HOTELS
Days Inn Forbidden City 15
Emperor Hotel 4
Hilton Wanfujing Hotel 10
The Hulu Hotel 8
Pentahotel 34
Raffles Beijing 16
Red Wall Garden Hotel 9
RESTAURANTS
Capital M 32
Chuan Ban 19 川办
Donghuamen Night Market 6
Duck de Chine 11
Lei Garden 12
Lost Heaven 26
Niu Jie (Ox Street) Snack Street 38
Wangfujing Snack Street 17
Xinjiekou Nan Dajie
Desheng Men Nei Dajie
PING'ANLI
Ping'anli Xi Dajie
Ping'an Dadao
Di'an Men Xi Dajie
CHEGONGZHUANG 202
Zhaodengyu Lu
Xisi Bei Dajie
Xishiku Dajie
XI SI
Fucheng Men
Fucheng Men Nei Dajie
XI SI
Xi'an Men Dajie
FUCHENG MEN 203
Jin rong Jie
Tai Ping Qiao Dajie
Xidan Bei Dajie
Fuyou Jie
LINGJING HUTONG
Picai Hutong
XICHENG
XIDAN
XI DAN 115
Fuxing Men Nei Dajie
Xi Chang'an Jie
Naoshikou Dajie
Xuanwu Men Nei Dajie
Bei Xinhua Jie
CHANGCHUN JIE 205
XUANWU MEN 206
HEPING MEN 207
Xuanwu Men Xi Dajie
Xuanwu Men Dong Dajie
Changchun Jie
Xuanwu Men Wai Dajie
HUFANGQIAO
Guang'an Dajie
Luomashi Dajie
CAISHIKOU
Nan Xinhua Jie
Niu Jie
Nanheng Xi Jie
Nanheng Dong Jie
TAORANTING
Taoranting Lu
Baizhifang Dong Jie

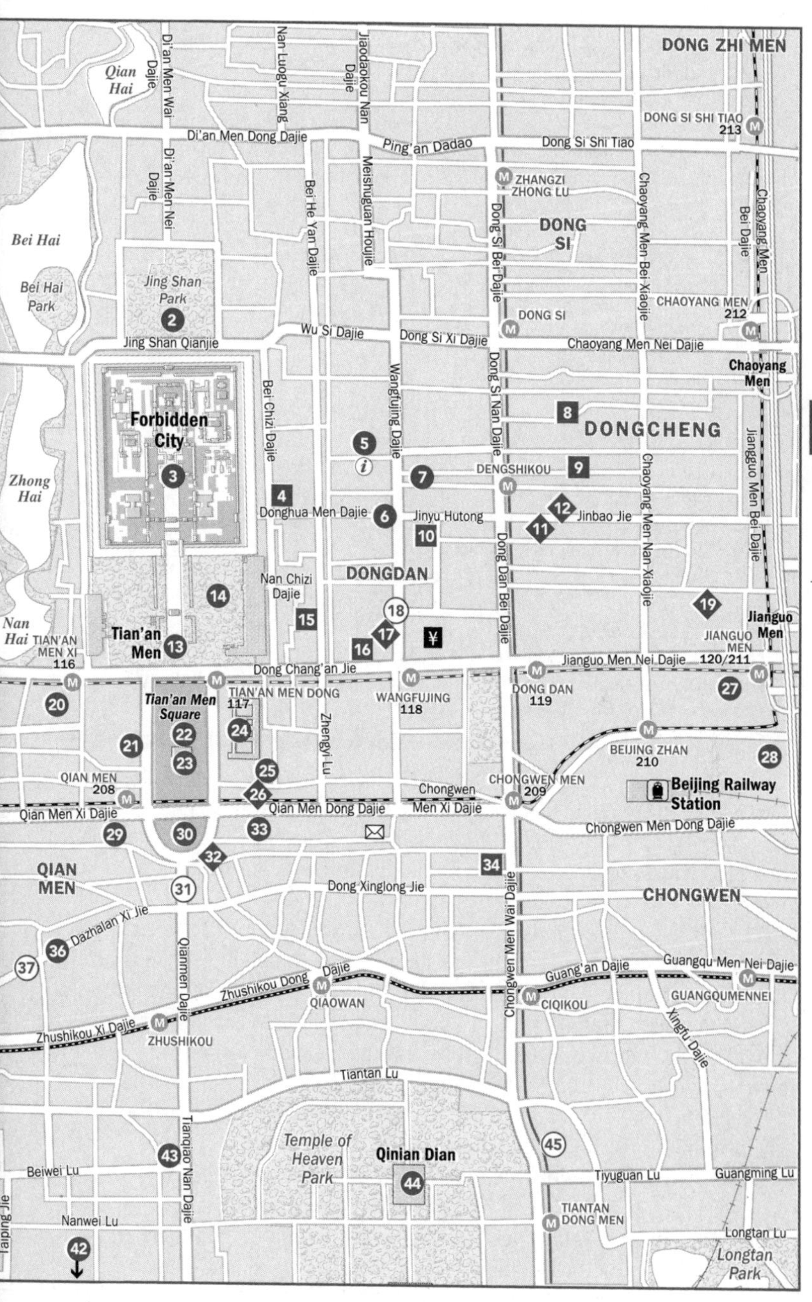

DONG ZHI MEN
Qian Hai
Di'an Men Wai Dajie
Nan Luogu Xiang
Jiaodaokou Nan Dajie
DONG SI SHI TIAO 213
Di'an Men Dong Dajie
Ping'an Dadao
Dong Si Shi Tiao
Di'an Men Nei Dajie
Bei He Yan Dajie
Meishuguan Houjie
ZHANGZI ZHONG LU
Dong Si Bei Dajie
DONG SI
Chaoyang Men Bei Xiaojie
Bei Dajie
Chaoyang Men
Bei Hai
Bei Hai Park
Jing Shan Park
CHAOYANG MEN 212
DONG SI
Jing Shan Qianjie
Wu Si Dajie
Dong Si Xi Dajie
Chaoyang Men Nei Dajie
Chaoyang Men
Forbidden City
Bei Chizi Dajie
Wangfujing Dajie
Dong Si Nan Dajie
DONGCHENG
Jianguo Men Bei Dajie
Zhong Hai
DENGSHIKOU
Donghua Men Dajie
Jinyu Hutong
Jinbao Jie
Chaoyang Men Nan Xiaojie
Dong Dan Bei Dajie
DONGDAN
Nan Chizi Dajie
Nan Hai
TIAN'AN MEN XI 116
Tian'an Men
Jianguo Men
JIANGUO MEN 120/211
Dong Chang'an Jie
Jianguo Men Nei Dajie
TIAN'AN MEN DONG 117
WANGFUJING 118
DONG DAN 119
Tian'an Men Square
Zhengyi Lu
BEIJING ZHAN 210
QIAN MEN 208
CHONGWEN MEN 209
Chongwen Men Xi Dajie
Beijing Railway Station
Qian Men Xi Dajie
Qian Men Dong Dajie
Chongwen Men Dong Dajie
QIAN MEN
Dong Xinglong Jie
CHONGWEN
Dazhalan Xi Jie
Chongwen Men Wai Dajie
Zhushikou Dong Dajie
Guang'an Dajie
Guangqu Men Nei Dajie
QIAOWAN
CIQIKOU
GUANGQUMENNEI
Qianmen Dajie
Zhushikou Xi Dajie
ZHUSHIKOU
Xingfu Dajie
Tiantan Lu
Temple of Heaven Park
Qinian Dian
Tianqiao Nan Dajie
Beiwei Lu
Tiyuguan Lu
Guangming Lu
TIANTAN DONG MEN
Taiping Jie
Nanwei Lu
Longtan Lu
Longtan Park
2
3
4
5
6
7
8
9
10
11
12
13
14
15
16
17
18
19
20
21
22
23
24
25
26
27
28
29
30
31
32
33
34
36
37
42
43
44
45

THE BIG makeover

An immense **US$75-million renovation of the Forbidden City** has been going on for more than a decade now and is hoped to be finally completed by 2020, increasing the total number of areas open to public gaze from the current 50% to around 70%. This has been undertaken on a hall-by-hall basis. A flurry of work on the halls and pavilions along the central axis ahead of the Beijing Games in 2008 came in for criticism, with accusations that columns were repainted with contemporary acrylic paint and that ancient tiles were lost or stolen and simply replaced with contemporary ceramics. This was an era when Starbucks was permitted to open a branch within the Palace compound, and rumors about elite private clubs opening up within remote nooks of the museum regularly made the rounds.

Recent restoration appears to have been carried out with greater care. Experts from the World Monuments Fund and the World Cultural Heritage Foundation have been called upon in what is slow and painstaking work. If anything, the pendulum has swung heavily in the opposite direction. One of the most interesting restorations of recent years has been **Juanqinzhai,** an elaborately constructed private opera house within the Complete Palace of Peace and Longevity (Ningshou Quan Gong) in the northeast section of the palace. Qianlong commissioned the European Jesuit painters in his employ to create large-scale trompe l'oeil paintings, which were displayed here as well as in the Old Summer Palace (Yuanmingyuan; p. 94). Juanqinzhai has the best remaining examples of these paintings, including a stunning image of a wisteria trellis, almost certainly painted by Italian master Castiglione. Sadly, it's only accessible by first submitting to a screening process. Applicants must apply to the palace authorities at least a month in advance of their visit, and there's no guarantee of success. To try your luck, email the palace at gugong@dpm.org.cn.

(1122–1215) were retained and expanded. Between 1420 and 1923, the palace was home to 24 emperors of the Ming and Qing dynasties. The last was Aisin-Gioro Puyi, who abdicated in 1912 but carried on living in the palace until 1924.

The palace has been ransacked and parts destroyed by fire several times over the centuries, so most of the existing 800 or so buildings date from the Qing rather than the Ming. Many of the roofs are trimmed in blue or green tile, which some scholars think was designed to stir unconscious memories of the wide skies and sweeping grasslands of the far northeast, a land the Manchu Qing called home before their rise to power.

The Forbidden City is arranged along the compass points, with most major halls opening to the south (the direction associated with imperial rule). In the southern section is the **Outer Court (Qian Chao),** used exclusively for ceremonial events and dominated by a series of imposing halls. Beyond, in the north, is the **Inner Court (Nei Ting),** a series of smaller buildings and gardens where the emperor and his entourage lived, worked, and played day-to-day. Indeed, most of the palace greats spent the vast majority of their lives cocooned here in a consummately landscaped, highly refined bubble.

Outer Court The intimidating **Meridian Gate (Wu Men),** built in 1420 and last restored in 1801, marks the historic entrance to the Forbidden City and is where all tourist visitors must enter the compound. The emperor would come here to receive prisoners of war, issue proclamations, and supervise the punishment of troublesome officials. Beyond the gate, across a vast stone-paved courtyard bisected by the balustraded Golden River (Jin Shui), is the **Gate of Supreme Harmony (Taihe Men),** which marks the official beginning of the Outer Court.

Elevated on a marble terrace amid a forest of balustrades are "Three Great Halls" (San Da Dian). The recently restored **Hall of Supreme Harmony (Taihe Dian)** ★★ is the first of these you'll come to. It's the largest wooden hall in China, and the most elaborate and prestigious of the palace's throne halls. Inside is the imposing and lavishly decorated **Dragon Throne (Long Yi).** It was used only rarely, heightening its impact on those fortunate (or perhaps unfortunate) enough to bear witness. As the emperor sat in resplendent glory, all would kowtow before him, touching their heads to the floor nine times in solemn deference.

Immediately behind it is the **Hall of Perfect Harmony (Zhonghe Dian),** where the emperor would rehearse speeches and make last-minute preparations ahead of a bombastic entrance. Inside are two sedan chairs, the emperor's primary mode of transportation around his palace. Farther north is the **Hall of Preserving Harmony (Baohe Dian).** This last hall, supported by only a few columns, is where the highest levels of imperial examinations were held. At the rear of the hall is a carved marble slab weighing over 200 tons; twenty-thousand men supposedly spent 28 days dragging it to this position from a mountain roughly 50km (31 miles) away.

Inner Court Only the emperor, his family, his concubines, and the palace eunuchs (who numbered 1,500 at the end of the Qing dynasty) were allowed in this section, sometimes described as the *truly* "forbidden" city. It begins with the **Gate of Heavenly Purity (Qianqing Men),** directly north of the Hall of Preserving Harmony, beyond which are three palaces designed to mirror the three halls of the outer court.

The first of these is the **Palace of Heavenly Purity (Qianqing Gong),** where the emperors lived until Yongzheng decided to move to another part of the palace in the 1720s. Beyond are the rather boring **Hall of Union (Jiaotai Dian),** containing the throne of the empress, and the rather more interesting **Palace of Earthly Tranquillity (Kunning Gong),** a Manchu-style bedchamber where a trembling 16-year-old Puyi (China's last emperor) was forced to spend his wedding night (Puyi eventually had five wives, none of whom bore children).

At the rear of the inner court is the elaborate **Imperial Garden (Yu Huayuan)** ★, a marvelous scattering of ancient conifers, rock gardens, and pavilions said to be largely unchanged since it was built in the Ming dynasty. Puyi's famous British tutor, Reginald Fleming Johnston, lived in the **Yangxin Zhai,** the first building on the west side of the garden (now a tea shop).

From behind the mountain, you can exit the palace through the **Gate of Martial Spirit (Shenwu Men)** and continue on to Jingshan Park and/or Beihai Park. Those with time to spare, however, should explore less-visited sections on either side of the central path.

Western Axis Most of this area is in a state of heavy disrepair, but a few buildings have been restored and are open to visitors. These are primarily in the north of the complex and should be visited as you explore the Inner Court. Just southwest of the Imperial Garden is the **Hall of Mental Cultivation (Yangxin Dian) ★★**. The reviled Empress Dowager Cixi, who ruled China for much of the late Qing period, made decisions on behalf of her infant nephew Guangxu from behind a screen in the east room. This is also where emperors lived after Yongzheng moved out of the Qianqing Gong. The **Palace of Gathered Elegance (Chuxiu Gong)** has a series of fascinating photographs of Puyi from his early days as child sovereign.

Eastern Axis This side of the palace tends to be peaceful even when other sections are teeming. It also has a greater number of areas open to the public. Turn right at the Gate of Heavenly Purity to get to the **Hall for Ancestral Worship (Fengxian Dian)** and the first of the highlights. Pay the RMB10 entrance to enter the wonderful **Hall of Clocks (Zhongbiao Guan) ★★**, a collection of elaborate timepieces, many of them gifts to the emperors from European envoys. Several of the clocks chime in semi-orchestral fashion at 11am and 2pm.

Slightly east again is the **Nine Dragon Screen (Jiulong Bi) ★**, a 3.5m-high (12-ft.) wall covered in striking glazed-tile dragons depicted frolicking above a frothing sea. Just north is the entrance to the **Complete Palace of Peace and Longevity (Ningshou Quan Gong),** a palace-within-a-palace. The Qing dynasty Qianlong emperor (reign 1736–95) abdicated at the age of 85, and this section was built for his retirement, although he never really moved in. He continued to "mentor" his son while living in the Hall of Mental Cultivation, a practice later adopted by Empress Dowager Cixi, who also partially took up residence here in 1894. Entrance to the **Treasure Gallery (Zhenbao Guan)** at the heart of this complex costs RMB10 and allows for visits to a number of small exhibition halls. One of the highlights here is the secluded **Palace of Peace and Longevity Garden (Ningshou Gong Huayuan) ★**. The Qianlong emperor composed poems and drank from cups of wine he floated in a snake-like, water-filled trough carved in the floor of the main pavilion. Qianlong's personal compendium of verse ran to a modest 50,000 poems; he was seldom short of words. East of the garden is the **Pavilion of Cheerful Melodies (Changyin Ge) ★★**, sometimes called "Cixi's Theater," an elaborate three-tiered performance pagoda with trapdoors and hidden passageways to allow movement between stages. In the far northeastern corner is the **Well of the Pearl Concubine (Zhenfei Jing),** a narrow hole covered by a large circle of stone, slightly askance. The Pearl Concubine, one of the Guangxu emperor's favorites, was 25 when Cixi had her stuffed down the well as they were fleeing in the aftermath of the Boxer Rebellion. According to most accounts, Cixi was miffed at the girl's insistence that Guangxu stay and take responsibility for the imperial family's support of the Boxers.

In addition to the major attractions listed here, the Palace Museum puts on many temporary exhibitions. Before you come, it's well worth visiting the palace website (www.dpm.org.cn) to see what's on. Unusually for Chinese attractions, its English-language service is pretty decent.

The palace is on the north side of Tian'anmen Square across Chang'an Dajie. It is best approached on foot or via subway (Tian'anmen East), as taxis are not allowed to stop in front. All visitors must enter through the Meridian Gate (Wu Men), a short walk north of Chang'an Dajie, but can exit from any of the four gates. Ticket counters are clearly marked on either side as you approach. **Audio tours** in several languages, including English (RMB40, plus RMB500 deposit), are available at the gate itself, through the door to the right. Those looking to spend more money can hire **tour guides** with varying degrees of English fluency on the other side of the gate (RMB200 for a 1-hr. tour, RMB300 for 1.5-hr., RMB400 for 2.5-hr.). The tour-guide booth also rents **wheelchairs** and **strollers** free of charge, with a RMB500 deposit, though only the central walkthrough of the palace is easily accessible for those using wheelchairs or strollers.

Tip: If you have a little more time, it is highly recommended that you approach the Meridian Gate via the Workers' Cultural Palace (see p. 72) to the east, avoiding the gauntlet of touts and souvenir stalls.

North of Tian'anmen; ticket office beside the Meridian Gate (*Wu Men*). www.dpm.org.cn. ✆ **010/8500-7421.** Admission RMB60 Apr–Oct, RMB40 Nov–Mar, some halls and gardens inside the palace charge additional RMB10. Open 8:30am–5pm May–Sept, 8:30am–4:30pm Oct–Apr, last tickets sold 1 hr. before doors close. Subway: Tian'anmen East, Tian'anmen West.

Jingshan Park (Jingshan Gongyuan) ★★★ PARK If you want a clear aerial view of the Forbidden City, you'll find it here. The park's central hill was created using earth left over from the digging of the imperial moat and was the highest point in the city during the Ming dynasty. It was designed to enhance the feng shui of the Forbidden City by blocking the harsh northern wind and by burying a Mongol Yuan dynasty pavilion (the Yanchun Ge). In something of a riposte to the Chinese Ming dynasty, the Manchu Qianlong emperor built a tower by the same name (albeit in a very different style) within the Forbidden City. A tree on the east side of the hill marks the spot where the last Ming emperor, Chongzhen, supposedly hanged himself in 1644, just before Manchu and rebel armies overran the city. The original tree, derided as the "guilty sophora" during the Qing, was hacked down by Red Guards who failed to recognize a fellow anti-imperialist.

1 Jingshan Qian Jie (opposite Forbidden City north gate). ✆ **010/6404-4071.** Admission RMB2. Jan–Mar and Nov–Dec 6:30am–8pm; Apr–May and Sept–Oct 6am–9pm; June–Aug 6am–10pm. Bus: no. 812 from Dongdan subway station (exit A) to Gu Gong.

Tian'anmen (Gate of Heavenly Peace) ★★ MONUMENT This gate is the largest in what was once known as the Imperial City and the most emblematic of Chinese state grandeur. Above the central door, once reserved for the emperor, now hangs the famous portrait of Mao, flanked by inscriptions that read: LONG LIVE THE PEOPLE'S REPUBLIC OF CHINA (left) and LONG LIVE THE GREAT UNITY OF THE PEOPLES OF THE WORLD (right). Mao declared the founding of the People's Republic from atop the gate on October 1, 1949. There is no charge to walk through, but tickets are required if you want to ascend to the upper platform for worthwhile views of Tian'anmen Square. You might imagine yourself as the Great Helmsman addressing a sea of Red Guards, all struggling to understand your thick Hunan accent while waving their little red books. Note the pair of *huabiao* (ornamental columns) topped with lions, wreathed in dragons and clouds, and facing the square. In their original form, *huabiao* were wooden posts in the shapes of battle-axes, upon which subjects would attach petitions or scrawl their grievances to the king. Over time, their function was reversed. Turned to stone and wreathed in the ultimate symbol of the emperor's mandate—the dragon—they became a warning to the ruled to keep out. ***Tip:*** If you're traveling in a group of two or more, split up and have one person line up to buy tickets and the other line up to check bags; you'll save yourselves both time and frustration.

North of Tian'anmen Square; ticket office to left as you pass through the gate. Admission RMB15. 8am–5pm, last ticket sold at 4:30pm. Mandatory bag storage for RMB2–RMB6 behind and to left of ticket booth; cameras allowed.

Workers' Cultural Palace (Laodong Renmin Wenhua Gong) ★★

PARK/PALACE Opened in 1420 as the Imperial Ancestral Temple, this large complex to the northeast of Tian'anmen combines ancient landscaped gardens (more than 700 trees are classified as "ancient") with a Forbidden City in miniature. Beyond the **Halberd Gate (Ji Men),** untouched since it was constructed in 1420, the three main buildings are lined up on a central axis within a walled compound. These were used for ritualistic displays of filial piety by the emperors of the early Ming dynasty. The largest is the **Sacrificial Hall (Xiang Dian).** This is only one of four buildings in Beijing to stand on a three-tiered marble plinth, a hint that it was once among the most sacred sites. Just north is the **Resting Hall (Qin Dian)** and north again, within its own walled mini-compound, is the **Ancestral Shrine (Tiao Miao),** the only example of an imperial ancestral hall (*zu miao*) remaining in China. It's the only one of the three halls open for exploration (RMB10) and, though the ceiling carvings are particularly beautiful, there's no need to pony up for a ticket if you are going into the Forbidden City itself. Mao renamed the temple the "Workers' Cultural Palace," and the effect seems to have put off the tourist hordes. If you're finding it hard to enjoy the Forbidden City proper amid the crowds, or frustrated by the masses walking across your photographs, try this as an option. It's not as large as Gu Gong and shouldn't stand in as a *replacement* for the real thing, but it's perfect for quiet enjoyment of the imperial architecture and ambience. Try entering from the eastern gate at Nanchizi

Dajie and leaving by the northwest exit of the park, where you'll find yourself instantly amid the throng heading into the Forbidden City.

Northeast of Tian'anmen; ticket office to left as you pass through the gate. Admission: RMB2. Daily 6:30am–7:30pm. Subway: Tian'anmen East.

TIAN'ANMEN SQUARE & SURROUNDINGS

Tian'anmen Square (Tian'anmen Guangchang) ★ PUBLIC SQUARE

The world's largest public square is the size of 90 American football fields (40 hectares/99 acres), with standing room for 300,000. It is surrounded by **Tian'anmen** (the "Gate of Heavenly Peace") to the north, the **Great Hall of the People** to the west, the **National Museum of China** to the east, and **Qianmen** ("Front Gate") to the south. In the center of the square stands the **Monument to the People's Heroes (Renmin Yingxiong Jinian Bei),** a 37m (124-ft.) granite obelisk engraved with scenes from famous uprisings and bearing a central inscription (in Mao's handwriting): THE PEOPLE'S HEROES ARE IMMORTAL.

The area on which the obelisk stands was originally occupied by the **Imperial Way**—a central road that stretched from Tian'anmen to Qianmen, the still extant main entrance to the Tartar City (see below). This road, lined on either side with imperial government ministries, was the site of the pivotal May Fourth movement (1919), in which thousands of university students gathered to protest the weakness and corruption of China's then-Republican government. Mao ordered destruction of the old ministries and paved over the rubble in 1959, replacing them with the vast **Great Hall of the People** to the west and a series of equally vast **museums** to the east, as part of a spate of construction to celebrate 10 years of Communist rule. But the site has remained a magnet for politically charged assemblies. Historically, the most significant of these was probably in 1976 when a mass rally drove a wedge between the Maoist old guard and modernizers like Deng Xiaoping, one that was to prove lasting. By far the most famous gathering was the **student prodemocracy protesters** in the spring of 1989. That movement, and the government's violent suppression of it, still defines the square in the minds of most foreign visitors, though the square itself was not where the blood was shed on the morning of June 4, 1989. All physical traces of the crackdown disappeared long before the square received an official face-lift in 1999, just in time to celebrate the 50th anniversary of the founding of the People's Republic. However, it has remained a focal point for activists/extremists (delete according to your personal politics). Falun Gong's silent staged protest around Tian'anmen in 1999 came as such a shock to leaders in nearby Zhongnanhai that the group was swiftly outlawed and exiled. And in 2013, a 4x4 was driven into barriers close to Mao's famous Tian'anmen portrait, bursting into flames and killing five people. Police described the event as a "suicide attack" by Islamic extremists, and there is a continued nervousness in the stiff-backed soldiers, video cameras, and now permanent security cordon that surrounds the square. Expect to have your bag scanned on your way through the underpass leading to the square. If you look like you might come from China's restive province of Xinjiang, you'll probably be frisked too.

There isn't much to do in the square, but early risers can line up in front of Tian'anmen at sunrise to watch the **flag-raising ceremony,** performed by a troop of PLA soldiers who goose-step out of Tian'anmen at dawn to hoist the flag, and return at sunset to draw it down. Times vary, so ask at your hotel to get an idea of when you might need to arrive. And beware: It gets crowded.

Beijing Planning Exhibition Hall (Beijing Guihua Bowyuguan) ★★ MUSEUM Seeing the enormity of Beijing sprawled at your feet is quite a sight. At this surprisingly fun and interactive museum, the history of the capital comes to life. Children and adults alike will be astounded by the museum's centerpiece—a complete scale model of this city of 22 million, composed of aerial photographs lit up from beneath. Another highlight is an electronic scroll painting that gives a view of the city's central north-south axis during the 1930s and 1940s, from Yongdingmen Gate in the south to the Drum and Bell Towers to the north. A number of short and entertaining films about Beijing's past, present, and future are offered. A 3-D movie tells the history of the city's development, while the so-called 4-D movie offers the sensation of a roller-coaster ride through a tour of future subway lines. It's easy to spend a full morning or afternoon here.

20 Qianmen Dong Lu (southeast corner of Tiananmen Square). www.bjghzl.com.cn. ✆ **010/6702-4559.** Admission RMB30; RMB10 for movies. Tues–Sun 9am–5pm. Subway: Qian Men.

Chairman Mao's Mausoleum (Mao Zhuxi Jinian Guan) ★ TOMB A trip here is one of the eeriest experiences in Beijing. The decision to preserve Mao's body was made hours after his death in 1976. Panicked and inexperienced, his doctors reportedly pumped him so full of formaldehyde that his face and body swelled almost beyond recognition. They drained the corpse and managed to get it back into acceptable shape, but they also created a wax model of the Great Helmsman just in case. There's no telling which version is on display at any given time. The mausoleum itself was built in 1977, near the center of Tian'anmen Square. However much Mao may be mocked outside his tomb (earnest arguments about whether he was 70% right or 60% right are perhaps the biggest joke), he still commands a terrifying sort of respect inside it. This is not quite the kitsch experience some expect. The tour is free and fast, with no stopping or photos, and no bags allowed inside. ***Note:*** The line to enter the mausoleum grows *very* long as soon as 9am, so get there early to secure your spot.

South end of Tian'anmen Square. ✆ **010/6513-2277.** Free admission. Tues–Sun 8am–noon. Bag storage across the street, directly west, RMB14. Subway: Qian Men.

Great Hall of the People (Renmin Dahui Tang) ★ HISTORIC BUILDING The Forbidden City may be a "palace" in name, but it's the Great Hall of the People that looks more the part, at least as seen through modern eyes. Built in 1959 using an obviously Soviet architectural blueprint, it's big, bulky, and, frankly, a little scary-looking. It's now the home of the National People's Congress (NPC), China's rubber-stamp parliament, though former occupants of this hallowed space in central Beijing include the *Jinyiwei*, the Ming's feared secret-police force. It's possible to take a tour of the Great Hall, where you'll see the banquet room where Richard Nixon carried on his Ping-Pong diplomacy in 1972 and the impressive 10,000-seat central auditorium where Party policy is debated before being inevitably signed into law. It meets for around two weeks every March, during which time tours temporarily halt. The ticket office is on the south side of the building.

Renda Huitang Xi Lu (west of Tian'anmen Sq.). Admission: RMB30. Mandatory bag storage for RMB2–RMB5. Daily 8:30am–3pm. Tour times vary. Subway: Tian'anmen West.

Legation Quarter (Dongjiaomin Xiang) ★ NEIGHBORHOOD The capital's answer to Shanghai's French Concession, the Legation Quarter is where Beijing's unwelcome colonial powers established homes, churches, schools, banks, and embassies after the Second Opium War (1856–60). It was subject to a three-month siege during the Boxer Rebellion (1900), prompting eight nations—Germany, Japan, the United States, and the U.K. among them—to send an armed expedition to the capital. It was to prove one of the Qing's final military humiliations at the hands of their colonial tormentors. The area once ran all the way to Beijing Railway Station, but the best of the atmosphere and architecture can be enjoyed in the two blocks immediately east of Tian'anmen. Here, along the lane of Dongjiaomin Xiang, you'll find the **Beijing Police Museum (Beijing Jingcha Bowuguan)** at 36 Dongjiaomin Xiang (✆ **010/8522-5018;** RMB20; Tues–Sun 9am–4pm), which has some fascinating displays on law-and-order (including the occasional lack of it) in 20th-century Beijing. You even get to do some shooting practice with a laser gun. **Zhengyi Lu** is lined with plane trees like a transplanted Parisian boulevard. Farther east on Dongjiaomin Xiang is the distinctive **Former French Post Office** building, now a restaurant, and at the road's junction with **Taijichang Dajie,** the spires of St. Michael's Church can be seen off to the left. Access Dongjiaomin Xiang up a flight of steps from Guangchang Dong Ce Lu, to the east side of Tian'anmen Square. If you're visiting *from* the square, you'll need to first cross at the underpass in the southeast corner before walking north slightly.

Dongjiaomin Xiang. Subway: Qian Men, or Tian'anmen East.

National Centre for the Performing Arts (Guojia Da Juyuan) ★ THEATER Designed by Frenchman Paul Andreu with apparent disregard for its austere surroundings, the NCPA is an eye-catching titanium-and-glass dome housing the capital's premier musical, theatrical, and operatic stages. The building, which rises surreally from an artificial lake, attracted much criticism for the stark break it made with its neighbors' architectural style. It is sited opposite the east side of the concrete monolith that is the Great Hall of the People, and within a stone's throw of the glazed tiles and upturned eaves of the Forbidden City. Since its opening in 2007, Beijingers have become gradually accustomed to the juxtaposition as similarly dazzling buildings have sprung up around the city. Judge for yourself whether you think it works by taking a tour, which sees visitors descend on escalators "through" the waters of the lake, and visit the three separate auditoriums.

2 Xi Chang'an Jie (west of the Great Hall of the People). www.chncpa.org. ✆ **010/6655-0000.** Admission RMB40. Daily 9am–5pm. Subway: Tian'anmen West.

National Museum of China ★★ MUSEUM The largest museum in the world was formed when two already-huge buildings just to the east of Tian'anmen Square—the National Museum of Chinese History and the National Museum of Chinese Revolution—merged back in 2003. Like everyone else in Beijing, museum administrators began a renovation ahead of the 2008 Olympic Games. Unlike everyone else, it casually remained closed throughout the festival, finally reemerging with a gleaming new look in 2011. This is a colossal space, with corridors like airport waiting lounges and spacious galleries arranged in clusters across two distant wings. Either accept you'll be here for the better part of the day (there's a cafe on the ground floor if you do take this option) or grab a map at the entrance and plot a route through the galleries that sound of most interest. Picking out the "best" exhibits from six floors' worth of treasure is futile. The **Ancient China** exhibition on the basement floor is excellent, beautifully presenting its wares in spacious and low-lit halls, but can probably be skipped if you've already spent hours at either the Shanghai Museum or the Shaanxi History Museum in Xi'an. The awkwardly named **Road of Rejuvenation** on Levels 2 and 3 offers a great insight into the sense of manifest destiny at work in modern China. After 19th-century tragedy, humiliation, and division, there was a stirring 20th-century comeback led by the Party's unifying force. It's not as overdone as you might expect, and there are even fleeting references to the Party's 20th-century mistakes, but it gives a great insight into the psychology of China's leaders and many of its people. China is less a "new" superpower, as is sometimes claimed in Western media, than a "recovering" superpower. This said, some of the nationalistic symbolism in the smaller exhibits—the gold medal of China's first Olympic gold medalist, Xu Haifeng, for example, or the gavel used to announce China's accession to the World Trade Organization—suggest a nation trying quite hard to *prove* it belongs at the head table. The more ancient stuff does a much better job of making the case.

16 Dong Chang'an Jie (east side of Tian'anmen Square). http://en.chnmuseum.cn. ✆ **010/6511-6400.** Admission free, RMB10 special exhibits, RMB30 audio guides (all visitors need to show their passport at the ticket office to get the free tickets). Tues–Sun 9am–5pm. Subway: Tian'anmen East.

Qian Men ★ MONUMENT The term Qian Men (Front Gate) is actually a reference to two separate towers on the south side of the square that together formed the main entrance to the Tartar (or Inner) City. The southernmost Arrow Tower (Jian Lou) is no longer open to the public. You can, however, still climb the interior of the rear building, the **Zhengyang Gate (Zhengyang**

new museum NEW HISTORY

In opening a revamped National Museum that was, on floor space, three times the size of the Louvre in Paris, China made a statement about its reemergence as an international power. The new museum measures a staggering 192,000 sq. m (2,066,671 sq. ft.) and boasts more than a million cultural relics. Yet for all its historical treasure, critics say the new museum has failed to measure up because it doesn't confront controversial aspects of China's tumultuous 20th-century history. Instead, the exhibits paint a Communist Party–approved version of the country's more recent economic-powered triumphs, from recent space flights to its hosting of the 2008 Olympic Games. Pigtailed female guides in gray Mao uniforms give sanitized history lessons, *sans* death and destruction. The result is less an examination of China's past than a revisionist spin by a Communist government determined to mold its version of truth. Then again, as Beijing authorities would no doubt point out, there's hardly a museum in the world that doesn't whitewash the past, at least a little. Look in the British Museum for a detailed account of how many of the exhibits found their way into the tender care of the curators and expect to be disappointed.

Men), where a photo exhibition depicts life in Beijing's pre-1949 markets, temples, and *hutong*.

Tian'anmen Square. ✆ **010/6511-8101.** Admission RMB20. 8:30am–4pm. Subway: Qian Men.

Around Central Dongcheng

Ancient Observatory (Gu Guanxiang Tai) ★ OBSERVATORY Built in 1442 during the Ming dynasty, and later expanded in the Qing dynasty, this observatory is among the world's oldest. Housed within the battlements of a Ming city-wall watchtower, this observatory was where Matteo Ricci and his Jesuit scholar colleagues worked in the 17th century in one of the earliest examples of the now-extensive "knowledge transfer" between China and the West. Several of the huge original bronze instruments are up on the roof of the tower, while others, including sundials, can be found on the expansive observatory grounds. The astronomical devices are beautifully embellished with clouds, dragons, and other mythical creatures. Inside the quiet exhibition rooms, don't miss the impressive replica of a gold-foil map of the constellations used during the Ming dynasty. This museum is a pleasant spot to spend an hour or two.

2 Dong Biaobei Hutong (southwest side of Jianguomen intersection). ✆ **010/6512-8923.** Admission RMB20. Tues–Sun 9:30am–4:30pm. Subway: Jianguomen.

Former Residence of Lao She (Lao She Jinian Guan) ★ HISTORIC BUILDING Lao She (1899–1966) was one of China's greatest 20th-century writers, lauded by early Communists for his use of satire in novels like "Teahouse" and "Rickshaw Boy" and persecuted for the same books during the Cultural Revolution. The rooms here contain photos, copies of his books, and his own library (works by Hemingway, Dickens, and Graham Greene among the titles).

Start in Hall 3, to the right, which records Lao She's early years in London, the United States, and Shandong Province. Hall 2 is an attempt to recreate the mood of his original study and sitting room, with his personal library untouched and his desk calendar left open at the day of his disappearance—August 24, 1966. While the date of his death is certain, the details are murky. The official line has him committing a poetic suicide in nearby Taiping Lake (pictured in Hall 1) after enduring a "struggle session" at Confucius Temple. It's possible that he was simply murdered by Red Guards.

19 Fengfu Hutong (from Wangfujing Dajie, turn left at the Crowne Plaza along Dengshikou Xi Jie to the 2nd hutong alley on your right). ✆ **010/6514-2612.** Free admission. 9am–4:30pm. Subway: Wangfujing.

Ming City Wall Park (Ming Chengqiang Gongyuan) ★ PARK/GARDEN The section of wall presented here, running a mile east-to-west from Dongbianmen to Chongwenmen, was originally built in the Yuan dynasty (1279–1368) and reconstructed in the mid-1500s by the Ming. Modern restoration work on the section began in 2002 and is still in progress, using bricks from the original Ming reconstruction collected from nearby residents (some of whom employed them to build toilets after the wall was demolished in the 1950s). A pleasant park runs east along the length of the wall to the dramatic Southeast Corner Tower (Dongnan Jianlou), open daily 9am to 5pm, RMB10, with its dozens of arrow slots; a contemporary art gallery and interesting exhibition on the history of Chongwen can be found inside.

✆ **010/6527-0574.** Subway: Chongwen Men. 24-hr.

St. Joseph's Cathedral (Dong Tang) ★ RELIGIOUS BUILDING This gray Gothic structure has endured a torrid history. Built on ground donated by the Shunzhi emperor in 1655, this Jesuit church was toppled by an earthquake in 1720, then gutted by fire in 1812, after which it was leveled by an increasingly antiforeign regime. It was rebuilt after foreigners forced their way into Beijing in 1860 and was razed again during the Boxer Rebellion of 1900. Chinese Christians were the first targets of the xenophobic Boxers, who disparagingly referred to them as "lesser hairy ones." Local converts were slaughtered in the hundreds before the Boxers (who also murdered women with unbound feet) worked up the courage to kill a real foreigner. Yet they are usually portrayed as a "patriotic" movement in China's history books. After a major renovation in 2000, Dong Tang is notable for its wide, tree-lined forecourt, a favorite spot for Beijing's skateboarders. Its counterpart in the south of town, Nan Tang (South Church), is just northeast of the Xuanwu Men subway stop and has services in English (✆ **010/6603-7139** to check times). Note: Catholic churches in Beijing are not recognized by the Roman Catholic Church.

74 Wangfujing Dajie. ✆ **010/6524-0634.** Sat services in Latin at 6:30 and Chinese at 7am. Subway: Wangfujing.

North Dongcheng (Gulou Area)

The northern part of Dongcheng may only have a handful of standout sights, but this is perhaps *the* nicest part of Beijing to wander for an afternoon. It has one of the greatest concentrations of surviving *hutong*, heaps of great restaurants, bars, and cafes, while the back lakes of Shichahai (see Xicheng section) are only a short walk west.

Confucius Temple & Imperial College (Kong Miao & Guozijian) ★★ TEMPLE Buried down a tree-shaded street west of the Lama Temple, **Confucius Temple (Kong Miao),** China's second-largest Confucian temple, is on the right, and Imperial College (Guozijian) is on the left; both were originally built in 1306. Two steles at the front instruct you to park your horse in six different languages. The front courtyard of the temple contains 198 steles inscribed with the names of successful candidates in the *jinshi* (highest-level) imperial examinations during the Yuan, Ming, and Qing dynasties. Staff admit they see few local visitors, except during the weekend before the university entrance examinations, when students and their parents descend in droves to ask for the Great Sage's assistance. The main hall, Dacheng Dian, is the focus for students, who must throw their incense on the shrine rather than burn it, because of fire regulations. Ancient musical instruments, which Confucius saw as essential to self-cultivation, are the main point of interest. Behind the hall and to the left are 189 steles, which contain the 630,000 characters that make up the Thirteen Confucian Classics—incredibly, copied by one man over a 12-year period. The attendant enhances the mood of antiquity by earnestly reciting old texts.

Success in the imperial examination was the key to social advancement, so educators at the **Imperial College** wielded immense power. It was originally joined to Confucius Temple by the Chijing Gate (Chijing Men), to the right as you enter. They will be reunited when the Ministry of Culture (housed in the Imperial College) and the Ministry of Cultural Relics (housed in the Confucius Temple) can sort out their differences. A striking yellow glazed-tile *pailou* (gate) with elaborately carved stone arches leads to a square wooden hall encircled by a moat (Bi Yong Dadian). The emperor would deliver a lecture on the classics here at the start of his reign, although the irrepressible Qianlong visited three times—after assuming the throne, after renovations were completed to mark the 50th anniversary of his reign, and when handing the throne over to his son, the Jiaqing emperor. He even wrote poems to decorate the sandalwood screen behind the throne. Ministers and the royal family were permitted inside, while three criers (to the west, south, and east) would repeat the emperor's words to students and minor officials kneeling outside.

13 Guozijian Jie (walk south from station along west side of Lama Temple, turn right onto street marked with arch). ✆ **010/8401-1977.** Admission RMB30 to both. Confucius Temple daily 8:30am–5:30pm; Imperial College daily 9am–5pm. Subway: Yonghegong.

Drum & Bell Towers (Gu Lou/Zhong Lou) ★★ MONUMENT Facing each other across a paved courtyard, the Drum and Bell Towers lie on

The Gulou District & Back Lakes

Bus Station
Bank
Information
Post Office
Rail Station
PSB Public-Security Visas
Metro & Station
MUXIDI 112
0 1/2 mi
0 0.5 km
Beijing North Railway Station
Desheng Men
Desheng Men
JISHUITAN 218
Xi Hai
Gulou
Hou Hai
Hou Hai
Liuyin
Gaoling Qiao Xiejie
Desheng MenXi Dajie
XI ZHI MEN 201
Xi Zhi Men Nei Dajie
Xi Zhi Men Wai Dajie
XINJIEKOU
Xinjiekou Bei Dajie
Xinjiekou Nan Dajie
Desheng Men Nei Dajie
XI ZHI MEN
Chegongzhuang Dajie
CHEGONGZHUANG WEST
Ping'anli Xi Dajie
CHEGONGZHUANG 202
Ping'an Dadao
Di'an Men Xi Dajie
PING'ANLI
Xishiku Dajie
Zhanlanguan Lu
Zhaodengyu Lu
Xisi Bei Dajie
XI SI
XI SI
Fucheng Men Wai Dajie
Fucheng Men
Fucheng Men Nei Dajie
FUCHENG MEN 203
Xi'an Men Dajie
Jin rong Jie
Tai Ping Qiao Dajie
Xidan Bei Dajie
Fuyou Jie
LINGJING HUTONG
Picai Hutong
XICHENG
XIDAN
Fuxing Men Nei Dajie
XI DAN 115
Xi Chang'an Jie
Naoshikou Dajie
Xuanwu Men Nei Dajie
Bei Xinhua Jie
XUANWU MEN 206
HEPING MEN 207
Xuanwu Men Xi Dajie
Xuanwu Men Dong Dajie
Changchun Jie
Xuanwu Men Wai Dajie
Nan Xinhua Jie
ATTRACTIONS ●
Ancient Coins Exhibition Hall 2
Confucius Temple and Imperial College 27
Drum and Bell Towers 7
Lama Temple 29
Mei Lanfang Grand Theatre 5
Nan Luogu Xiang 15
Prince Gong's Mansion 4
Teahouse of Prince Gong's Mansion 4
White Dagoba Temple 30
HOTELS ■
Bamboo Garden Hotel 6
Courtyard 7 12
Double Happiness Courtyard Hotel 34
Du Ge Hotel 21
Han's Royal Garden 22
The Orchid 9
Peking International Youth Hostel 16
Red Lantern House 1
RESTAURANTS & NIGHTLIFE ◆
Amilal 19
Black Sesame Kitchen 13
Café Zarah 20
Crescent Moon 35
Dali Courtyard 18
El Nido 23
Great Leap Brewing 11
Jiumen Snack Street 3
King's Joy 28
Mai Bar 14
MAO Livehouse 17
Mr Shi's Dumplings 10
The Star Live 26
Susu 32
Temple Restaurant Beijing 31
Temple Bar 8
Wudaoying Hutong 25
Yugong Yishan 33
SHOPPING ○
Wudaoying Hutong 24

Ande Lu
Anding Men
Anding Men Xi Dajie
Dong Dajie
Anding Men Dong Dajie
GULOU DAJIE 217
ANDING MEN 216
YONGHE GONG 215
PSB
Xi Dajie
Hou Hai Bei Yan
Nan Yan
Jiu Gulou Dajie
Bei Luogu Xiang
Anding Men Nei Dajie
Yonghe Gong Dajie
Dong Zhi Men Bei Xiaojie
DONG ZHI MEN 214/1316
Gulou Dong Dajie
Jiaodaokou Dong Dajie
Dong Zhi Men Nei Dajie
Dong Zhi Men
BEI XIN QIAO
DONG ZHI MEN
SHICHAHAI
Nan Luogu Xiang
Jiaodaokou Nan Dajie
Qian Hai
Di'an Men Wai Dajie
BEIHAI NORTH
Di'an Men Xi Dajie
Di'an Men Dong Dajie
Ping'an Dadao
DONG SI SHITIAO 213
Dong Si Shi Tiao
NANLUOGUXIANG
ZHANGZI ZHONG LU
Bei Hai Park
Bei Hai
Di'an Men Nei Dajie
Bei He Yan Dajie
Meishuguan Houjie
Dong Si Bei Dajie
DONG SI
Chaoyang Men Bei Xiaojie
Chaoyang Men Bei Dajie
Jing Shan Park
CHAOYANGMEN 212
Jing Shan Qianjie
Wu Si Dajie
Dong Si Xi Dajie
DONG SI
Chaoyang Men Nei Dajie
Chaoyang Men
Forbidden City
Bei Chizi Dajie
Wangfujing Dajie
Dong Si Nan Dajie
DONGCHENG
Jianguo Men Bei Dajie
Zhong Hai
DENGSHIKOU
Chaoyang Men Nan Xiaojie
Donghua Men Dajie
Jinyu Hutong
Jinbao Jie
DONGDAN
Nan Chizi Dajie
Dong Dan Bei Dajie
Jianguo Men
Nan Hai
TIAN'AN MEN XI 116
Tian'an Men
JIANGUO MEN 120/211
Jianguo Men Nei Dajie
Dong Chang'an Jie
TIAN'AN MEN DONG 117
WANGFUJING 118
DONG DAN 119
Tian'an Men Square
Zhengyi Lu
BEIJING ZHAN 210
QIAN MEN 208
Beijing Railway Station
Qian Men Xi Dajie
Qian Men Dong Dajie
Chongwen Men Xi Dajie
CHONGWEN MEN 209
Chongwen Men Dong Dajie
QIAN MEN
Dong Xinglong Jie
CHONGWEN
Dazhalan Xi Jie
Qianmen Dajie
Chongwen Men Wai Dajie
Guangqu Men Nei Dajie
Guang'an Dajie
Zhushikou Dong Dajie
QIAOWAN
CIQIKOU
GUANGQUMENNEI

the north-south axis that runs down through the Forbidden City. The Drum Tower clearly takes its design inspiration from its imperial cousin to the south, painted in resplendent red and decked with green tiles. You can climb the steep interior staircase for fantastic views back south toward the dynastic heart of Beijing. The Bell Tower, to the north, looks more in keeping with its Yuan dynasty roots and, again, can be climbed for the 360-degree views. Within an interior exhibition room there is an extraordinary 63-ton bell. Note this, like all the other bells, lacks a clanger. Chinese bells were made to be hit from the outside rather than rung from within. Both towers were originally built in 1272 and sat at the heart of the Mongol empire, performing ceremonial timekeeping duties. The towers were both damaged during later turbulence and rebuilt in the 18th century. If possible, time your visit with one of the percussive performances at the Drum Tower. These take place hourly from 9:30am to 3:30pm (except 12:30pm), with a final performance at 4:45pm. It's also worth whiling away half an hour in the central square. It's a place where locals, rather than tourists, hang out and is great for people-watching.

Off Gulou Dong Dajie. Admission RMB30 for combined ticket (RMB20 individual tickets). Daily 9am–5pm. Subway: Shichahai.

Lama Temple (Yonghegong) ★★★ TEMPLE The most important hub for Tibetan Buddhism outside of Tibet itself, *Yonghegong* offers a wonderful introduction to the beguiling arts and rituals of the Land of Snows. Lama Temple was built in 1694 and originally belonged to the Qing prince who would become the Yongzheng emperor. As was the custom, the complex was converted to a temple after Yongzheng's move to the Forbidden City in 1744. The site took on a vital diplomatic importance in 1792 when the Qianlong emperor was forced to quell an uprising in Tibet. The Lama Temple became the place where the Panchen Lama was anointed, giving Qing emperors tighter control over their minority subjects. The temple comprises a series of progressively larger buildings topped with ornate yellow-tiled roofs. It's also home to several beautiful **incense burners,** including a particularly ornate one in the second courtyard that dates from 1746. The **Hall of the Wheel of Law (Falun Dian),** second to last of the major buildings, contains a 6m-tall (20-ft.) bronze statue of Tsongkapa (1357–1419), the first Dalai Lama and founder of the now-dominant Yellow Hat sect of Tibetan Buddhism. He's easily recognized by his pointed cap with long earflaps. The final of the five central halls, the **Tower of Ten Thousand Happinesses (Wanfu Ge),** houses the temple's prize possession—an ominous Tibetan-style **statue of Maitreya** (the future Buddha), 18m (60 ft.) tall, carved from a single piece of white sandalwood. Once something of a circus, Lama Temple is slowly starting to feel like a place of worship, as there are now many Chinese devotees of Tibetan Buddhism. If you visit only one temple after the Temple of Heaven, this should be it.

12 Yonghe Gong Dajie, south of the N. Second Ring Rd. (entrance on the south end of the complex). ✆ **010/8419-1919.** Admission RMB25; audio tours in English additional RMB50. Summer 9am–4:30pm, winter until 4pm. Subway: Yonghegong.

Nan Luogu Xiang ★ HUTONG After a revamp in 2006, Nan Luogu Xiang (literally "South Gong and Drum Alley") went from being a hip, bohemian hangout to a veritable tourist highway. This is now Beijing's most renowned *hutong*, and though it's hard to pick out the best of the cafes, bars, and souvenir shops through the pulsing crowd, it's a fun stroll nonetheless. Be sure to explore the many *hutong* that branch off east and west from the main walk-through. These contain some of Beijing's nicest bars and restaurants.

Nan Luogu Xiang, north of Di'anmen Dong Dajie. Cafes and shops 10am–10pm, approx. Subway: Nan Luogu Xiang.

South Dongcheng

The Temple of Heaven (Tian Tan) ★★★ PARK/TEMPLE At the same time Yongle built the Forbidden City, he also oversaw construction of this enormous park and altar to heaven to the south. Each winter solstice, the Ming and Qing emperors would lead a procession here to perform rites and make sacrifices designed to promote the next year's crops and curry favor from heaven for the general health of the empire. The park is square (symbolizing Earth) in the south and rounded (Heaven) in the north.

The best approach into the park is from the **Zhaoheng Gate (Zhaoheng Men),** the entrance the emperor himself would have used. The first structure you'll come across from this direction is the **Circular Altar (Yuan Qiu).** This three-tiered marble terrace was built in 1530 and enlarged in 1749, with all of its stones and balustrades organized in multiples of nine (considered a lucky number by northern Chinese). North again is the **Imperial Vault of Heaven (Huang Qiong Yu).** This smaller version of the Hall of Prayer was built to store ceremonial stone tablets. The vault is surrounded by the circular **Echo Wall (Huiyin Bi).** In years past, when crowds were smaller and before the railing was installed, it was possible for two people on opposite sides of the enclosure to send whispered messages to each other along the wall with remarkable clarity. The highlight of any visit is the stunning **Hall of Prayer for Good Harvests (Qi'nian Dian) ★★**. This circular wooden hall, with its triple-eaved cylindrical blue-tiled roof, is perhaps the most recognizable emblem of Chinese imperial architecture outside the Forbidden City. Completed in 1420, the original hall burned to the ground in 1889, but this near-perfect replica was built the following year. It stands 38m (125 ft.) high and is 29m (98 ft.) in diameter, and is constructed without a single nail. The 28 massive pillars inside, made of fir imported from Oregon, are arranged to symbolize divisions of time: The central four represent the seasons, the next 12 represent the months of the year, and the outer 12 represent traditional divisions of a single day. The hall's most striking feature is its ceiling, a kaleidoscope of intricate painted brackets and gilded panels.

Near the west gate is the **Fasting Palace (Zhai Gong),** an east-facing, double-moated compound containing several buildings. Emperors would fast and pray for 5 days, spending their final night in the **Resting Hall (Qin Dian)** at the rear. Note the rare swastika emblems, a symbol of longevity in China, on the door piers.

WALKING BEIJING'S waterways

Beijing was not a city that just *sprang up*. When Kublai Khan decided on the site, then known as "Dadu," for his glorious new capital in 1272, it looked an unlikely choice. There was no major river, no coastline, and the nearest sections of the Grand Canal, built over the preceding six centuries, were 18km (11 miles) east of the city. Dadu had scraped by for the previous two millennia on a series of small lakes and lotus ponds for its water, but Khan knew that fixing this was the key to success. Not only did he need a means of bringing in supplies from the Grand Canal, he also needed moats to defend the new city walls. Khan employed Guo Shoujing, a renowned engineer, who discovered a spring in the hills to the northwest. He channeled this freshwater down into the city via Kunming Lake (now an integral part of the Summer Palace, see p. 94) and fused it with new trenches, hacked from the earth by tens of thousands of laborers, which linked up with the Grand Canal in the east. As the waters flowed, so did Dadu's security and prosperity.

The closest brush tourists usually get with these waterways is a boat ride out to the Summer Palace (see p. 94). However, this is but one small section of what is a vast network. If the sun is shining and you have half a day to spare, strike out for **Gongzhufen** subway station. From here, walk north and wander along the north side of the lake in **Yuyuantan Park.** Continue along the Yongding River to meet the **16th-century city moat** near the Muxidi subway station. This loops down and then east, passing **Taoranting Park,** all the way to the **Temple of Heaven,** passing close to its south entrance. This 15km (11 mile) route will take 3 to 4 hours, but there's little better way of getting a sense of the *real* Beijing. You'll skirt leafy parks, pass gleaming new apartment blocks, head beneath colossal spaghetti junctions, and come upon random *tan'r* market stalls spread out across the pavements. The walkways are not always perfect; rather than being created by local government, many of them have been paved by real-estate developers looking to give buyers extra inducement by selling a swanky "riverside lifestyle." There are few shops along the way, too, so pack some snacks and water. Take a map (or your phone if you have Internet access), as occasionally you'll need to temporarily come away from the water, onto the street, before returning. The moat loops back up, and it's possible to walk all the way to Beijing Railway Station. For the really hardy, you can continue way out to Chaoyang, though this would make for a dawn-to-dusk hike.

The two-tier, green-tile roof of the **Animal Killing Compound (Zaisheng Ting)** is distinctive in the east of the park. Here, deer, oxen, and sheep, among others, were prepared for ritual sacrifice.

The **Temple of Heaven Park (Tian Tan Gongyuan)** surrounds the main imperial thoroughfare. There are entrances to the park from all four compass points. It's popular with tai chi practitioners in the mornings and is large enough for an hour's stroll amid the tangled cypress trees, some of which are 800 years old. Just to the west of the central walkway is a delightful rose garden.

East gate off Tiantan Dong Lu. ✆ **010/6702-8866.** Admission: all-inclusive tickets *(lian piao)* Apr–Oct RMB35, Nov–Mar RMB30. Simple park admission RMB15 summer, RMB10 winter. Apr–Oct daily 8am–6pm; Nov–Mar 8am–5pm. Last ticket sold an hour before closing. Subway: Tiantan Dong Men.

Xicheng

BACK LAKES

Ancient Coin Exhibition Hall (Gudai Qianbi Zhanlanguan) ★

MUSEUM Housed in the Deshengmen Gatehouse, this museum is an interesting spot for a quick visit by travelers who are into ancient currency. Packed into three rooms are the various coins, shells, and paper used as money over China's 5,000 years of history. Those with kids might find it a fun visit, since the imposing gatehouse that houses it is a bit castle-like, with its many dark nooks and crannies. Outside are stalls where vendors show how easy it is to actually mint money nowadays, with examples available for purchase as souvenirs.

Deshengmen Jianlou, Bei Erhuan Zhong Lu. ✆ **010/6201-8073.** Tickets RMB10. Tues–Sun 9am–4pm. Subway: Jishuitan.

Beihai Park (Beihai Gongyuan) ★★ PARK An imperial playground dating back to the Tartar Jin dynasty (1115–1234), Beihai ("North Lake") lies to the north of Zhonghai ("Middle Lake") and Nanhai ("South Lake"). All three were opened to the public in 1925, a year after "last emperor" Puyi was stripped of his imperial title and belatedly ejected from the Forbidden City. In the best "Animal Farm" tradition, Communist leaders created their own "Forbidden City" around two of the lakes and named it Zhongnanhai, and it has been off-limits to the public ever since. Beihai, in contrast, has remained open to the masses. Although it's a convenient way to combine a morning visit to the Forbidden City with a more relaxing afternoon in the Back Lakes area, most visitors have a quick peek at the southern half and then disappear. Unfortunately, they miss the north side of the park, which is more interesting.

Entering from the south, you come to **Round City (Tuan Cheng),** a small citadel on a raised platform on which the most notable structure, **Chengguang Hall (Chengguang Dian),** houses a 1.5m-tall (5-ft.) statue of a feminine-looking Buddha, crafted from Burmese white jade. Crossing the Yong'an Bridge to the **Jade Islet (Qiong Dao),** you soon reach **Yong'an Temple (Yong'an Si),** where the founder of the prominent Geluk sect of Tibetan Buddhism, Tsongkapa, was the focus of devotion. He is now portrayed as a Chinese reformer of corrupted minority faith on the grounds that he was born in Qinghai rather than "autonomous" Tibet. From here, boats run to the north side of the park for RMB5, or you can walk around the east side, passing calligraphers wielding enormous sponge-tipped brushes to compose rapidly evaporating poems on the flagstones.

Boats pull in to the east of **Five Dragon Pavilion (Wu Long Ting),** where aspiring singers treat the public to revolutionary airs popular in the 1950s. Off to the left is an impressive green-tile *pailou* (memorial arch; the green tiles signify a religious purpose, in contrast to the yellow imperial tiles of the Forbidden City and Imperial College). Continue on to the square-shaped Jile Shijie Dian, encircled by a dry moat. Built by the Qianlong emperor to honor his mother, the sandalwood structure is exquisite, topped with a priceless gold dome (apparently too high for either foreign troops or local warlords to reach). To the west stands an impressive **Nine Dragon Screen (Jiulong Bi),** which guarded the entrance to a now-vanished temple. Farther east is the **Dacizhenru Hall (Dacizhenru Bao Dian),** an atmospheric Buddhist hall built during the late Ming from unpainted cedar. Topped with a black roof (to protect the precious wood from fire), it has a cool slate floor. Continue east to the northern exit onto Ping'an Dadao, which marks the southern end of the Shichahai (Back Lakes) area.

1 Wenjin Jie (north entrance off Dian'anmen Xi Dajie, south entrance is just west of the north gate of the Forbidden City; east entrance is opposite the west entrance of Jingshan Park). ✆ **010/6403-3225.** Park admission Apr–Oct RMB10; Nov–Mar RMB5; through-ticket RMB20 (inc. Round City and Jade Islet). Daily 6am–10pm (earlier closing in winter). Subway: Beihai North (for north entrance).

Prince Gong's Mansion (Gong Wangfu Huayuan) ★ HISTORIC BUILDING This splendid imperial residence belonged to several people, including the sixth son of the Guangxu emperor (Prince Gong) who, at the age of 27, was left to sign the Convention of Peking in 1860, after the Qing royal family took an early summer holiday when British and French forces advanced on the capital. The convention (which ratified the ill-enforced Treaty of Tianjin) is reproduced in an exhibition hall. But other than one picture, there's little information concerning the original owner, Heshen (1750–99), the infamously corrupt Manchu official. Thought to have been the Qianlong emperor's lover, he ruled China for his own gain when Qianlong abdicated in 1796, embezzling funds earmarked for suppressing the White Lotus rebellion. After Qianlong's death, Heshen's demise was swift. While he was mourning in the Forbidden City, officials were dispatched to this mansion. Though the extent of his graft was widely known, officials were shocked by the piles of gold-and-silver ingots uncovered. His remaining friends at court managed to persuade the Qianlong emperor's son to spare him from "death by a thousand cuts," but he was soon hanged. The labyrinthine combination of rock gardens and pavilions here offers plenty, but you're seeing only half of the mansion, and it's often overrun by tour groups. Short but sweet performances of opera and acrobatics are served up in the three-story "Grand Opera House."

17 Liuyin Jie (signposted in English at top of Qianhai Xi Dajie, running north off Ping'an Dadao, opposite north gate of Beihai Park; turn left at sign and follow alley past large parking lot; entrance marked with huge red lanterns). ✆ **010/8328-1758.** Admission RMB40; RMB70 including guide and opera performance. 7:30am–4:30pm. Subway: Beihai North.

White Dagoba Temple (Baita Si) ★ RELIGIOUS SITE Seemingly continuously under renovation, this Liao dynasty temple features the largest Tibetan pagoda (also called *chorten, dagoba, or stupa*) in China, towering over the neighborhood at 51m (167 ft.) tall. A Nepali architect built it over 700 years ago (completed 1279) by order of Kublai Khan, one of the first Mongols to convert to Tibetan Buddhism. The temple has undergone numerous reconstructions, usually as a result of fire. The Hall of the Great Enlightened Ones (*Dajue Dian*), the first building, contains thousands of little Buddhas in glass cases set into the columns. An earthquake in 1976 turned up numerous artifacts, some of which are now on display in the museum. You'll find Buddhist statuary demonstrating ritualistic hand positions (*mudra*) and vivid *thangka* (silk hangings depicting Buddhist images).

171 Fuchengmen Nei Dajie. ✆ **010/6616-0211.** Admission RMB20. Daily 9am–4:30pm. Subway: Fuchengmen.

DAZHALAN AREA

Altar for Harvests (Xiannong Tan) ★★ MUSEUM Sited a short distance west of the Temple of Heaven, this recently refurbished and ravishingly attractive temple complex was once a key stop on the emperor's ritual tour. It was here during the spring equinox that he would ask for heaven's blessings for the coming harvest amid ceremony and sacrifice. The site is rarely visited but well worthwhile for the **Ancient Architecture Museum (Gudai Jianzhu Bowuguan) ★★**, which lies within the Hall of Jupiter (Taisui Dian). There are miniature reproductions of all the significant buildings in Beijing so that travelers can preview what they want to visit later, as well as fragments of buildings that have fallen by the wayside in the drive for development, all complemented by surprisingly comprehensible English captions. A highlight is the scale model of the old walled city.

21 Dongjing Lu. ✆ **010/6304-5608.** Admission RMB15. Daily 9am–4pm. Subway: Taoranting.

Capital Museum (Shoudu Bowuguan) ★ MUSEUM Focusing on traditional Chinese arts, this museum houses a large collection of ancient porcelain, bronze, calligraphy, and painting. The building itself is sleek and modern, with clever references to traditional Chinese architecture. Exhibits tell the story of Beijing's history and culture—a significant part of the collection of 200,000 relics was unearthed in the capital. Some (though not much) English explanation is included. Highlights include a section on *hutong* and Chinese courtyard architecture and an area dedicated to Beijing opera, complete with costumes and staging. Bring your passport for free entry.

16 Fuxingmenwai Dajie. www.capitalmuseum.org.cn. ✆ **010/6339-3339.** Free admission. Subway: Muxidi. Tues–Sun 9am–4pm.

Dazhalan ★ HUTONG Alternatively known as Dashilar, this ancient market street has, like its neighbor Qianme Dajie, come in for a Disneyish revamp over the last decade. You'll now find McDonalds amid the silk-hawkers and purveyors of fragrant herbal remedies, but it's still fun for a wander. Dazhalan Xi Jie, to the west, has heaps of street-food vendors. Head off the main drag here to explore some lovely old *hutong* to the north and south.

Dazhalan Jie & Dazhalan Xi Jie (east of Qianmen Dajie). All day. Subway: Qianmen.

Fayuan Temple (Fayuan Si) ★ TEMPLE Despite guides boasting of a long and glorious history, most of Beijing's sights are relatively new, dating from within the past 600 years. This temple, constructed in 645 in what was then the southeast corner of town, retains both an air of antiquity and the feel of a genuine Buddhist monastery. Orange-robed monks, housed in the adjacent Buddhist college, go about their business in earnest, and the visitors are asked to "respect religious ceremonies: Do not interfere with religious activities." The ancient *hutong* immediately surrounding the temple are "protected" and worth exploring on foot. Lanman Hutong, just to the east, was formerly a moat that marked the boundary of the old town during the Tang dynasty.

7 Fayuan Si Qian Jie. Admission RMB5. Thu–Tues 8:30–11am and 1:30–4pm. Subway: Caishikou or Taoranting.

Ox Street Mosque (Niu Jie Qingzhen Si) ★ TEMPLE This is Beijing's largest mosque and the spiritual center for the city's estimated 200,000 Muslims. Built in 996, the complex looks more "Eastern" than Middle Eastern, with sloping tile roofs similar to those found in Buddhist temples. Halls are noticeably free of idols, however, as dictated by Islamic tradition. A small courtyard on the south side contains the tombs and original gravestones of two Arab imams who lived here in the late 13th century. The main prayer hall is ghostly quiet except on Friday, the traditional day of worship.

88 Niu Jie (on east side of street). ✆ **010/6353-2564.** Admission RMB10 for non-Muslims. All day. Subway: Caishikou or Taoranting.

Chaoyang

798 Art Zone (Qijiuba Yishuqu) ★ Optimistically billed as Beijing's SoHo, this East German–designed factory district is a grungy hub for local art and fashion. It's gone from being edgy and barely tolerated by local authorities to being a full-on commercial jamboree, taking away some of its former charm. The site is still fascinating to explore, replete with chimney stacks, industrial fittings, and communist slogans, and some of the more cavernous private exhibition halls and galleries have worthwhile displays. From entrance no. 4 (Jiuxian Qiao Lu 4), you'll soon arrive at the impressive **UCCA** (admission RMB15; closed Mon), a nonprofit, spacious gallery that often hosts intriguing and buzzworthy exhibitions that merge the international and Chinese modern art worlds. Keeping west, hang right, and on your left is the remarkable Bauhaus-inspired **798 Space,** still daubed with slogans offering praise to Mao. The most consistently interesting exhibitions are held by **798 Photo,** immediately opposite. Turn right and right again as you emerge from the building to find the first gallery to open in Factory 798, **Beijing Tokyo Art Projects** (www.tokyo-gallery.com), which has a formidable stable of local and international artists. Turn left and duck down a narrow lane to emerge at the Gao Brothers' cuddly **Beijing New Art Projects** (✆ **010/8456-6660**). Those with an interest in socialist kitsch will appreciate the trip, but anyone with a genuinely artistic bent may want to explore **Songzhuang** instead, a village to the east of town (www.artistvillagegallery.com) where many of the

Chaoyang District

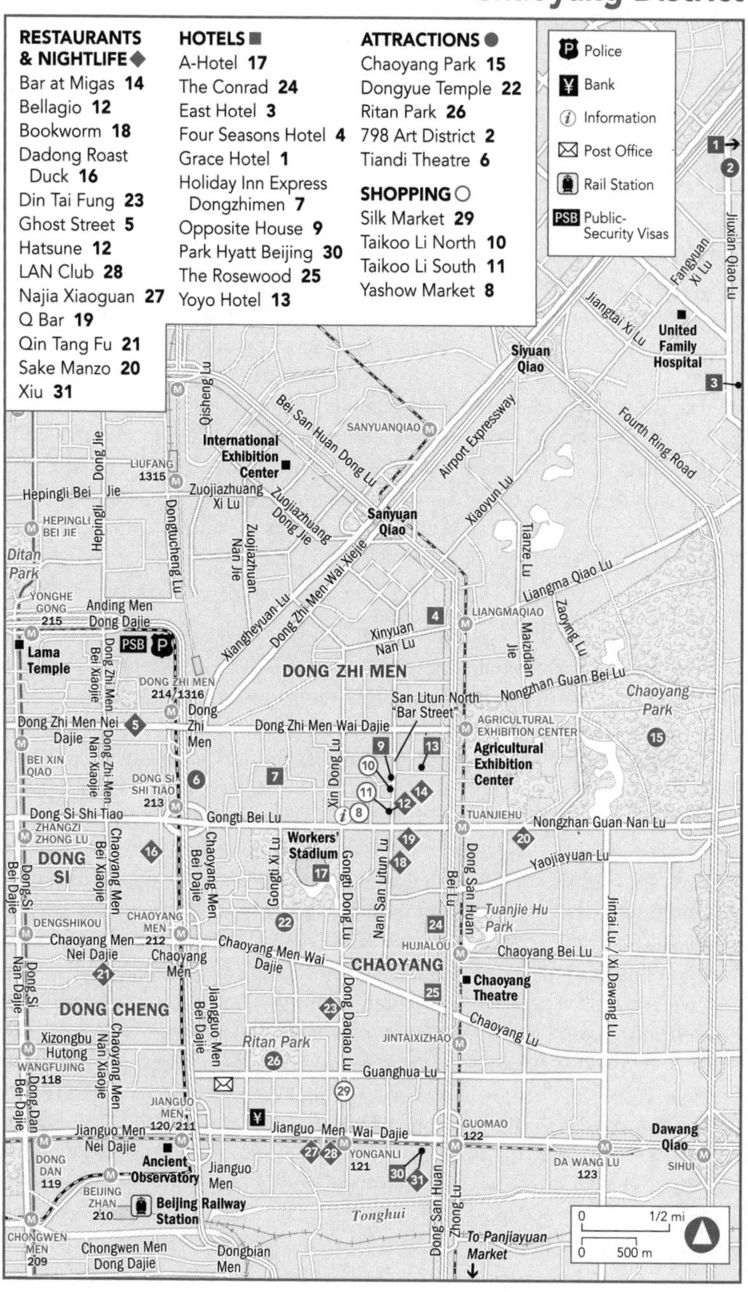

avant-garde artists forced out of 798 by spiraling rents have relocated. Unfortunately, 798 is not particularly accessible from downtown—it's safe to skip it if time is short.

Jnc. Jiuxianqiao Lu & Jiuxianqiao Bei Lu. Daily 10:30am–7:30pm approx., some galleries closed Mon. Bus: 813 east from Chaoyangmen subway to Wangye Fen, or subway to Wangjing, then 15-min. walk southeast.

China National Film Museum (Zhongguo Dianying Bowuguan) ★ MUSEUM If you love Chinese movies, you can easily spend a few hours here. The exterior of this modern black-and-white complex was loosely designed to look like a giant screen and movie clapperboard. The central atrium has a constantly changing light fixture that bathes the hall in cool colors, along with a wide ramp leading to the upper floors. Exhibits show off black-and-white stills and old camera equipment among other movie memorabilia. There's even a special-effects section where photos can be taken against different blue-screen backgrounds, letting visitors make a virtual escape from a dinosaur or float over the Temple of Heaven. There's little English here, so if you don't read Chinese, you're out of luck. The Museum also houses one of the few IMAX theaters in town. The big drawback is the location, far outside central Beijing, although a visit here could easily be combined with a trip to the nearby 798 art district.

20 Nanying Lu. ✆ **010/6431-9548.** Free admission. Tues–Sun 9am–4:30pm. No Subway, 40-min. taxi ride from the city center.

Dongyue Temple (Dongyue Miao) ★ TEMPLE Reopened to the public in 1999, one of Beijing's most captivating Taoist temples stands largely disregarded. Founded in 1322 by the devotees of the Zhengyi sect, the temple is dedicated to the god Dongyue, who resides in the sacred mountain of Tai Shan. Aside from coping with the hordes of tourists who now visit his abode, Dongyue is charged with supervising the 18 layers of hell and the 76 departments. The garishly represented emissaries of these departments may be found in the 72 halls that ring the main courtyard of the temple. Worshipers present themselves at the relevant hall with offerings of money, incense, and red tokens inscribed with their names (*fupai*). With 76 departments (some are forced to share a cubicle), there are emissaries for every conceivable wish, and if viewed as a straw poll of China's preoccupations, the results are not encouraging. The Department for Accumulating Wealth ("justifiable" is added in the translation) is busy, while the Department of Pity and Sympathy, depicting beggars, awaits its first petition. There are an alarming number of donations for the Department for Implementing 15 Kinds of Violent Death. This may or may not be related to the ongoing popularity of the Department of Official Morality, which rails against corrupt government. A glassed-in stele at the northeast corner of the courtyard is written in the fine hand of Zhao Mengfu, recording the building of the temple and the life of its founder, Zhang Liusun, who died soon after purchasing the land. At the north of the complex stands the two-story Minsu Bowuguan (Folk Museum). This hosts exhibitions to remind Beijingers of their marvelous but largely forgotten traditions.

141 Chaoyangmen Wai Dajie (10-min. walk east of Chaoyangmen Subway on the north side). ✆ **010/6551-0151.** Admission RMB10; free during festivals. Tues–Sun 8:30am–4:30pm. Subway: Chaoyangmen.

Olympic Park (Aolinpike Gongyuan) ★ PARK You might have heard of China's so-called "Ghost Towns," cities built at great expense in the absence of any obvious sign that anyone wants to live there. The Olympic Park is Beijing's variation on the theme. Of course, back in 2008, people *did* want to come to this fairly remote corner of north Beijing, and those who were there will probably never forget it. However, times have moved on, and the **Olympic Green,** covering an area roughly three times the size of New York's Central Park, now feels strangely out of time. It's not totally deserted; tour groups often breeze through, and there are roaming souvenir sellers and snack vendors. But given the size of the park, and the lack of atmosphere, it's probably only worth coming if you are looking for architecture shots or need to get *away from* the crowds.

Electric trolleys with tours in Chinese will take you around the green for RMB20 round-trip. The biggest draw remains the **Beijing National Stadium,** dubbed "the Bird's Nest" because of its oblong shape and interlocking steel grids closely resembling the twigs and branches of, well, a bird's nest. It was designed by architecture darlings Jacques Herzog and Pierre de Meuron, costing roughly US$400 million, and can hold 91,000 spectators. It hosted the opening and closing ceremonies, as well as athletic events and football. The RMB50 entrance fee (ticket booths are at the north end of the nest) gets you into the stadium, where you can walk right onto the field and have your picture taken with the Olympic torch for RMB15. An on-site post office sells commemorative stamps, and a few other stores sell Olympic kitsch inside. A healthy stone's throw away from the Bird's Nest is the **National Aquatics Center,** also known as "the Water Cube" (it's actually a rectangle, but "Water Rectangle" didn't have the same ring), which was recently converted into the **Happy Magic Watercube Waterpark** (p. 130). North of the Water Cube is the **National Indoor Stadium,** which hosted gymnastics and handball events. Its design plays on the theme of a traditional Chinese folding fan. Unlike its neighbors, it doesn't have a cutesy nickname.

Behind the Olympic Green is the **Olympic Forest Park.** During the Olympics, the park hosted tennis, archery, and hockey events. This spacious bit of greenery includes **Main Mountain,** a man-made pile of 3.98 million cubic m. (141 million cubic ft.) of earth, and **Main Lake,** a 110-hectare (272-acre, roughly 205 football fields) body of water shaped like the Olympic torch. While this is Beijing's largest city park at 640 hectares (1,581 acres) and makes for a pleasant stroll, there's nothing terribly interesting in store at ground level. However, at the time of writing, a huge new **Olympic Park Observation Tower** was on the verge of opening close to the south gate of the Forest Park. This is one of the tallest buildings in the city, rising to 246.8m

(810 ft.) in height, and each of the five circular platforms at its peak has an observation deck with stunning views. Prices were not yet confirmed, but it looks like it could well be a reason to visit.

Beichen Dong Lu. ✆ **010/8437-3017.** Free admission to the Olympic Green. Open 24 hr. Admission to National Stadium RMB50; RMB25 for children under 1.2m/4 ft. and seniors. National Aquatics Center: Admission RMB30, free for children under 1.5m/5 ft. and seniors 65–69. 9am–5:30pm. Opening times for both stadiums will vary in the case of sporting or entertainment events. Swimming at National Aquatics Center RMB50 for 2 hr. Weekdays 1–9pm, weekends 9am–9pm. Free admission to Olympic Forest Park. Mar 15–Nov 15 6am–8pm; Nov 16–Mar 14 8am–6pm. Subway: Olympic Sports Centre (for Olympic Green sights), South Gate of Forest Park (for Olympic Forest Park and observation deck).

Ritan Park (Ritan Gongyuan) ★ PARK Built in 1530, Ritan is a pleasant park with a delightful outdoor **teahouse** and a **rock-climbing wall.** Fishponds, a pedal-powered monorail, kites, and a bonsai market also keep the locals amused. The **Temple of the Sun (Ritan)** served as an altar where the emperor conducted annual rites. The other imperial altars are located in similar city parks, roughly marking the five points of the Chinese compass. To the north is **Temple of Earth (Ditan Gongyuan),** just north of the Lama Temple; to the west is **Temple of the Moon (Yuetan Gongyuan),** and the much grander **Temple of Heaven** (see p. 83) marks the southern point. **Altar of Land and Grain (Shejitan)** in Zhongshan Gongyuan, southwest of the Forbidden City, predates them all by several centuries and marks that peculiarly Chinese compass point, the center.

6 Ritan Lu. ✆ **010/8561-1389.** Free admission. Daily 6am–9:30pm (6:30am–9pm in winter). Subway: Yong'an Li.

Haidian

Beijing Art Museum (Wanshou Si) ★★ MUSEUM Wanshou Si, otherwise known as Longevity Temple, was built by a eunuch in the 16th century to house Buddhist scripture. It became a favorite rest stop for the Qianlong Emperor and his successors as they made their way to the Summer Palace by boat. This beautiful temple now houses the Beijing Art Museum. A long row of restored halls houses an eclectic mix of exhibits on everything from ceramics to copperware to lacquer. Among the more interesting pieces are examples of Chinese calligraphy, painting, weaving, and embroidery from the Ming and Qing dynasties. Also on display are some modern Chinese and Japanese paintings. The nice rock garden in back was reportedly a favorite spot of the Dowager Empress Cixi. A visit here is a pleasant way to spend an hour or two.

18 Xi Sanhuan Bei Lu. ✆ **010/6841-3380.** Tickets RMB20; RMB60 includes a cup of tea. Daily 9am–4:30pm. Subway: National Library, plus 10-min. taxi ride.

Great Bell Temple (Da Zhong Si) ★ RELIGIOUS SITE An attraction to bring out the hunchback in anyone, this Qing temple now houses the **Ancient Bell Museum (Gu Zhong Bowuguan),** best visited on the way to the Summer Palace. The temple was known as Juesheng Si ("Awakened Life

BEIJING futurism

Tourist brochures still often have China as an unchanging landscape of pristine paddies, misty mountain temples, and dynastic grandeur, but this is a nation that seems far more interested in where it is going than where it has been. Nowhere is this more obvious than in Beijing; just look at the buildings. The pinup for Beijing's headlong leap into the future is the new **CCTV Building** in Chaoyang, headquarters of the state broadcaster and labeled the "giant underpants" (*da kucha*) for reasons that scarcely need explaining (suffice it to say Rem Koolhaas didn't see the comparison when he designed it). This one's not open to the public, but others are: The **Olympic Park Observation Tower,** opened in 2014, seems to be dicing with a lawsuit from the *Jetsons* creators. The **National Centre for Performing Arts** (see p. 75) is a shimmering teardrop that fell amid the socialist bombast and imperial flummery in the middle of town. Back out in Chaoyang, the office and commercial complex of **Galaxy Soho** looks like a giant ocean-liner after it's been through a particle accelerator. Nearby **Opposite House** hotel (see p. 105) seems to have been designed by a kid playing Minecraft. Then there's **Parkview Green,** a glass pyramid with its own internal microclimate, the **Phoenix International Media Center,** which looks like it belongs in a book of optical illusions, and—perhaps weirdest of all—Kempinski's **Yanqi Lake Hotel,** which was modeled on "the rising sun" and appears as a giant UFO dropping beside a serene lake north of Beijing. The much-hyped **National "Bird's Nest" Stadium** is positively old-fashioned by comparison. Shanghai used to be where architects went wild—the ridiculous Oriental Pearl TV Tower a case in point—but the city feels positively *repressed* now compared to Beijing. Eccentrics rejoice!

Temple"). But the 47-ton bell transported here on ice sleds in 1743 clearly took center stage, hence the temple's current moniker. The third hall on the right houses clangers garnered from around Beijing. Some were donated by eunuchs wishing the relevant emperor long life, with hundreds of donors' names scrawled on their sides. But frustratingly, none of this is fleshed out. The main attraction is housed in the rear hall, carved inside and out with 230,000 Chinese and Sanskrit characters. The big bell tolls but once a year, on New Year's Eve. Visitors rub the handles of Qianlong's old washbasin and scramble up narrow steps to make a wish while throwing coins through a hole in the top of the monster. But it is no longer the "King of Bells"—that honor now goes to the 50-ton bell housed in the **Altar to the Century (Zhonghua Shiji Tan),** constructed in 1999 to prove that China could waste money on the millennium too.

31A Bei Sanhuan Xi Lu. ✆ **010/6255-0819.** Admission RMB10; extra RMB2 to climb the bell tower; Free admission for the first 200 visitors on Wed. Tues–Sun 8:30am-4:30pm. Subway: Da Zhong Si.

Fragrant Hills Park (Xiangshan Gongyuan) ★ PARK Like Beijing's two summer palaces (below), the Fragrant Hills Park began life as a villa retreat for Qing dynasty royalty. And like Yuanmingyuan, it suffered during assaults by colonial forces, first in 1860 and again in 1900, leading to the loss of much original architecture. The park does, however, contain a number of temples and exhibition halls that survived the sack, notably the Tibetan **Temple of Brilliance (Zhao Miao)** and the **Azure Clouds Temple (Biyun Si),** admission RMB10, which was originally built in the Yuan dynasty. The park's name derives not from the occasionally piquant maple, cypress, and persimmon trees, but rather Incense Burner Peak (Xianglu Feng), so named for the two stones at the top, which resemble a pair of incense sticks. Temples aside, this is a great spot for forest hiking. The 557m (1,827 ft.) peak can be climbed, with a chairlift (RMB30) easing the strain if needed.

Admission RMB10 Apr–Oct; RMB5 Nov–Mar (extra for certain temples and chairlift). Daily 6am–7:30pm. Subway: Fragrant Hills (Western Suburban Line).

Old Summer Palace (Yuanmingyuan) ★★ RUINS An amalgamation of three separate imperial gardens, these ruins create a ghostly and oddly enjoyable scene. Established by the Kangxi emperor in 1707 as an imperial retreat, Yuanmingyuan is a more recent construction than the New Summer Palace to the west, but it is misleadingly translated as the "Old Summer Palace" because it was never rebuilt after troops looted and razed it at the culmination of the Second Opium War in 1860. The troops who carried out the desecration made no distinction between the buildings they targeted, but ironically, those that survive were built by two of their European predecessors, Italian painter Castiglione and French scientist Benoist. The Jesuit priests were commissioned by Qianlong to design the 30-hectare (75-acre) **Western Mansions (Xiyang Lou)** in the northeast section of the park. The buildings were made from hard stone (thus difficult to burn) and later filled with furnishings and art carried from Europe. Inaccurate models suggest that the structures in Yuanmingyuan were entirely European in style, but they were curious hybrids, featuring imperial-style vermilion walls and yellow-tiled roofs. A few restorations have begun, starting with the **10,000 Flowers Maze (Wanhua Zhen),** a nicely reconstructed labyrinth in the Garden of Eternal Spring **(Changchun Yuan).** This is a large area, great for rambling and picnics, so expect to spend a few hours.

28 Qinghua Xi Lu (north of Peking University). ✆ **010/6262-8501.** Admission RMB10; RMB25 for through ticket including the Western Mansions. 7am–7pm (to 5:30pm in winter). Subway: Yuanmingyuan.

Summer Palace (Yiheyuan) ★★★ PARK/PALACE This expanse of elaborate Qing-style pavilions, bridges, walkways, and gardens, scattered along the shores of immense Kunming Lake, is the grandest imperial playground in China; it was constructed from 1749 to 1764. Between 1860 and 1903, it was twice leveled by foreign armies and then rebuilt. The palace is most often associated with the Empress Dowager Cixi, who made it her full-time residence.

The park covers roughly 290 hectares (716 acres), with **Kunming Lake (Kunming Hu)** in the south and **Longevity Hill (Wanshou Shan)** in the north. The lake's northern shore has most of the buildings and other attractions and is the most popular area for strolls, although it is more pleasant to walk around the smaller lakes behind Longevity Hill. The hill itself offers fabulous views back across the entire complex, and has a number of temples as well as the **Precious Clouds Pavilion (Baoyun Ge),** one of the few structures in the palace to escape destruction by foreign forces. Dozens of pavilions and a number of bridges are on all sides of the lake, enough to make a full day of exploration if you so choose.

The most remarkable sight in all of the palace is the **Long Corridor (Chang Lang) ★**, a covered wooden promenade that stretches 700m (2,297 ft.) along the northern shore of Kunming Lake. Each crossbeam, ceiling, and pillar is painted with a different scene taken from Chinese history, literature, myth, and geography. There are roughly 10,000 in all. Docked at the end of the Long Corridor is the infamous **Marble Boat (Shi Fang).** Those Chinese who blame the Empress Dowager for China's decline during the Qing dynasty cite this above all else as the symbol of China's demise. Cixi funded a general restoration of her increasingly precious Summer Palace using money intended for the Chinese navy, and the (completely frivolous) boat is said to be Cixi's backhanded reference to the source of the funds. Shortly after the restoration was completed in 1888, China's paltry fleet was destroyed in a skirmish with Japan, glaring evidence of China's weakness in the modern era.

From here, it's easy to walk upward into Longevity Hill. However, if you are in the mood to walk, strike out toward the **Western Causeway (Xi Di)** and do a (lengthy) loop around Kunming Lake. It's a pleasant stroll amid willow and mulberry trees.

Back at the eastern shore, you'll find the **Seventeen Arch Bridge (Shiqi Kong Qiao) ★**, a 150m-long (490-ft.) marble bridge that connects to South Lake Island **(Nan Hu Dao).** There is a rather striking life-size bronze ox near the eastern foot of the bridge. Located directly across the courtyard from the east gate entrance is **the palace's main ceremonial hall,** the **Hall of Benevolence and Longevity (Renshou Dian).** This is where the empress dowager received members of the court, first from behind a screen and later, controversially, from the Dragon Throne itself, which traditionally was only ever used by the emperor. North of the hall is Cixi's private theater, now a museum that contains an old Mercedes-Benz—the first car imported into China.

The **Summer Palace** is located 12km (7 miles) northwest of the city center in Haidian. You can get to the eastern and northern sections of the palace on Line 4, exiting at Xiyuan and Beigongmen stations respectively. By the time you read this, you should be able to get to the southern and western entrances on the subway too, taking the soon-to-open Western Suburban Line. A more unusual way to access the palace is to travel here by **boat** along the renovated canal system. Slightly rusty "imperial yachts" leave from the Beizhan Houhu Matou (✆ **010/8836-3576**) behind the Beijing Exhibition Center just south of the Beijing Aquarium (10am–4pm hourly, or every 30 min. during student summer holidays; 50-min. trip; RMB40 one-way; RMB70 round-trip; RMB100 includes round-trip travel and the entrance ticket). These dock at Nan Ruyi Men in the south of the park.

Go early and allow at least four hours for touring on your own. Overpriced **imperial-style food** in a pleasant setting is available at the Tingli Guan Restaurant, near the East Palace Gate (Dong Gong Men). Spots around the lake are perfect for picnics, so consider bringing your own food.

East gate off Tongqing Jie. ✆ **010/6288-1144.** Admission: RMB60 Apr–Oct, RMB50 Nov–Mar for all-inclusive ticket (*lian piao*), reduced by RMB30 for entry to grounds only. Apr–Oct 6:30am–6pm, Nov–Mar 7am–5pm. Subway: Xiyuan, Beigongmen, Summer Palace South Gate, or Summer Palace West Gate.

White Cloud Temple (Baiyun Guan) ★ TEMPLE If the incense here somehow smells more authentic, it's because this sprawling complex, said to have been built in 739, is the most active of Beijing's Taoist temples. Chinese visitors seem intent on actual worship rather than smug tourism, and the blue-frocked monks wear their hair in the rarely seen traditional manner—long and tied in a bun at the top of the head. The temple acts as headquarters for the Chinese Taoist Association. Although the texts of Taoism (China's only native religion) decry the pursuit of wealth and honors as empty, the gods of wealth attract the most devotees. One notable structure is the **Laolu Tang,** a large cushion-filled hall in the third courtyard originally built in 1228, now used for teaching and ceremonies.

On Baiyun Guan Lu, east of the intersection with Baiyun Lu (1st right north of Baiyun Qiao, directly across from Baiyun Guan bus stop). ✆ **010/6346-3531.** Admission RMB10. 8:30am–4:30pm. Subway: Muxidi, then bus 727.

WHERE TO STAY

Beijing has emerged from its Communist era of drab government-owned hotels and motels characterized by horrendous service, dim lighting, and rock-hard beds. In the old days, hotel attendants let you in and out of your room, keeping control over your keys. Toilets were smelly. The breakfast buffet consisted of leftovers from last night's stir-fries and fake Wonder bread.

Nowadays, booking a room in the capital has never been easier, and a glut of new privately owned guesthouses and hotels—spurred by development for the 2008 Olympics—means that options exist for every budget. Five-star hotels come in various shapes and sizes: gleaming skyscrapers, colonial mansions, and eccentric design hotels. Creative types will be drawn to the plentiful boutique hotels, decorated with antique Chinese furniture and contemporary art, while those seeking a quieter side of Beijing can plump for one of the many small *hutong* hotels that have sprung up. Even simple two-star hotels are generally clean and efficiently run. In Beijing, more than in most major cities, finding a place to stay is never a problem.

Indeed, with tourism numbers now declining after years of runaway growth and breakneck hotel construction, Beijing is arguably oversupplied with guestrooms. It's probably one of the best-value cities in the world for a luxury hotel stay: In the off-season, you may be able to pay as low as RMB800 (US$129) for a sparkling new room at a top-brand hotel. How cheap this

the HUTONG

As distinct as Beijing's palaces, temples, and parks may be, it is the ***hutong*** that ultimately set the city apart. Prior to the 20th century when cars and the Communist love of grandeur made them impractical, these narrow and often winding lanes were the city's dominant passageways. Old maps of Beijing show the city to be an immense and intricate maze composed almost entirely of *hutong,* most no wider than 10m (30 ft.) and some as narrow as 50cm (20 in.).

Aside from their enduring sense of quietude and calm, one of the most interesting features of the *hutong* is the ***siheyuan*** courtyard homes that can be found within. *Hutong* close to the Forbidden City would historically have housed well-to-do artisans, and their dwellings were typically composed of four single-story rectangular buildings arranged around a central courtyard with a door at one corner (ideally facing south). The Communist revolution ended aristocratic associations and subdivided these prize homes to accommodate up to six separate families at a time. Until recently, as much as half of Beijing's population lived in some form of *siheyuan,* but large-scale bulldozing of the *hutong* has resulted in significant migration into modern apartment buildings. Foreign visitors, charmed by the quaintness of the old houses, often assume this migration is forced, and it often is. But many who move do so willingly, eager for central heat and indoor plumbing (both of which are rare in certain *hutong* neighborhoods).

The *hutong* have been leveled at a ferocious pace over the last 20 years, but there has been a recent swing toward preservation. Tourism has no doubt played its role. Rickshaw pedalers have long known how fond tourists are of roving through sleepy alleys around the **Back Lakes** (Shichahai) and in the Gulou area (especially north of the eastern and western sections of **Di'anmen Dajie**). Tobacco Alley is one of the oldest. In recent years, many courtyard homes in these areas have morphed into trendy (though often grungy) hotels and hostels.

The most well-known *hutong* is undoubtedly **Nan Luogu Xiang,** which has now been found by the Chinese tourist hordes after a precarious 10-year existence as a hipster hangout. It's dynamic, but with wall-to-wall commerce, it's not particularly representative of *hutong* life. Wander along the lanes east and west of here to get a better feel for things.

Pedicab tour companies offer to bike you around the areas listed above, and perhaps even take you inside a couple of courtyards, but they all charge absurd rates. It's much cheaper, and far more enjoyable, to walk around on your own and book a night or two in one of the courtyard hotels listed in the "Where to Stay" section.

actually feels will depend on exchange rates, which have moved in the wrong direction for most travelers over recent years.

Getting the very best rates may require some skills. It's easy to book independently through either a hotel's own site or an online aggregator such as **Booking.com** or **Ctrip.com** (smaller guesthouses and *hutong* hotels are best booked through aggregators, as the perennial discounts rarely show up on the smaller hotels' homepages). However, the very cheapest rates are available by bargaining directly with the hotel yourself—in Mandarin, preferably. If you don't speak Mandarin, try to find a friend to do the bargaining for you. Make sure to ask what the rate includes—if you're willing to forgo breakfast and airport transfer, you can often save a few hundred renminbi. Or you may want to bargain by asking for a room upgrade—many hotels in Beijing offer executive rooms, which come with lounge privileges that provide breakfast and free drinks. Most hotels are also willing to offer better rates for longer stays. When booking your room, make sure to specify if you want a double bed. Many hotels have nonsmoking floors or rooms as well.

While service has improved in Beijing, it still lags behind that of other international cities. With the competition fierce between hotels to retain quality staff, you may find that hotel employees don't speak English particularly fluently and that simple requests become easily complicated, even at the more expensive hotels. Try to be patient.

Also requiring patience are the heating systems at many Beijing hotels. Most large buildings run on a single boiler system and follow energy-efficiency guidelines mandated by the government. These say that heat should be pumped into rooms during the frigid winter months and the air-conditioning only engaged as the weather warms. It's unlikely you'll be left craving further heat in summer, so no problem there, but it's possible you might get a warm early spring or late autumn day when the only in-room option is more heat. This problem doesn't tend to apply to the newest hotels or the smaller courtyard hotels, which run individual air-conditioners on a room-by-room basis.

All establishments still need to report your presence to the local police station (a Communist procedure that still exists), so you'll need to show your passport at check-in. Passports can be safely left in your room—break-ins are rare—but using the safe is recommended. This said, if you are planning on visiting the **National Museum of China** (see p. 76), you'll need your passport to gain free entry.

City Center & South Dongcheng

EXPENSIVE

Hilton Beijing Wangfujing ★★ Occupying a fairly anonymous high-rise, the Hilton Beijing is 2 minutes' walk from the shopping delights of Wangfujing, 20 minutes' walk from Tian'anmen Square, and 7 minutes from the nearest subway station. The rooms here are unusually spacious and stylishly decked in clean, beige tones. A standard room is equipped with a 42-inch flatscreen TV embedded in the wood-paneled wall, with another TV in the marble bathroom, as well as an MP3 docking station. The glass-encased rooftop pool is a particular treat. Ask to book a room on the upper levels, as there's plenty of street-level traffic and an outdoor car park within the complex, which can create noise for those staying on lower floors. With a central location and reasonable room rates, this is a solid city-center five-star option.

8 Wangfujing Dong Jie. www.wangfujing.hilton.com. ✆ **010/5812-8888.** 255 units. RMB1,400 standard; RMB2,000–RMB2,700 suites. Subway: Dengshikou. **Amenities:** 4 restaurants; cafe; wine bar; babysitting; fitness center; library; indoor pool; room service; spa; Wi-Fi: RMB120 per day.

Choosing the Right Location

Because of Beijing's size and the problems in transportation described on previous pages, choosing a hotel with the right location is arguably more important in Beijing than in most major capital cities. Finding a room within walking distance of likely nighttime spots—the *hutong* of Dongcheng, or the Sanlitun strip, for example—is a great way of avoiding headaches over taxis or missing your late-night subway train home. In many ways, it's better to be lodging farther away from tourist sites, if it means being nearer bars and restaurants. For the best balance, I'd recommend the **Gulou area,** filled with *hutong* and close to the lakes of Shichahai. Here you'll find charming courtyard dwellings to suit most price ranges. The **city-center** area puts you within walking distance of the Forbidden City, Tian'anmen Square, and Wangfujing, and has a greater range of hotels. However, the most charming parts of Dongcheng are a long way north. The greatest luxury and highest standards of service can be found in **Chaoyang,** near the two main diplomatic areas just outside the East Second Ring Road. The **Central Business District** (CBD) is filled almost exclusively with high-end hotels and is the city's glitziest shopping area, but the area is not very walkable and you'll likely end up hanging around the hotel at night. North Chaoyang, meanwhile, has the dining and nightlife options of Sanlitun, but Chaoyang is sprawling and it could still be too far to walk to any of the sights. **Xicheng** and the **South Dongcheng** areas are the least desirable among city-center locations but offer convenient access to the major railway stations. Staying in **Haidian** is only to be recommended if you're planning on spending most of your time near the universities or the remote tourist sites (like the Summer Palace, the Olympic Green, or the Fragrant Hills).

Raffles Beijing ★★ Opened in 1917 as the Grand Hotel de Pekin, this grand dame of Beijing hospitality has witnessed the major upheavals of modern China. The Beaux Arts building was a haven for colonial high society in the swinging '20s and '30s, seized by the Japanese during wartime occupation, and saw the People's Republic of China signed into being by Mao Zedong in 1949 (be sure to beg, sneak, or bluff your way into the Golden Hall where this happened; it's not technically part of the hotel, but there's a connecting door that is sometimes left ajar). The Raffles chain took up management in 2006 and restored much of its former glory, with a marble lobby lit by sparkling chandeliers and interiors of stately elegance, especially in the Landmark Building overlooking Chang'an Dajie. The most expensive of the 171 rooms and suites occupy this front building—including the two-story Presidential Suite, a favorite of visiting monarchs and their entourages—while guestrooms in the newer 1980s block behind are slightly larger and geared up for business travelers. Afternoon tea can be taken in the Writers Bar, which has the same sprung wooden dance-floor where Mao Zedong danced with his mistresses. There are two excellent on-site restaurants, but other amenities are less exclusive, as they are shared with the adjacent Beijing Hotel. The location is superb for tourist sights (Tian'anmen Square, the Forbidden City, Wangfujing, and the National Museum of China are all just steps away), though nighttime attractions require a subway ride. Ask the concierge for a free transportation card.

33 Dong Chang'an Dajie, near Wangfujing. www.raffles.com/beijing. ✆ **010/6526-3388.** RMB1,500–RMB1,800 standard, RMB2,800–RMB3,150 suites, plus 15% service charge. Subway: Wangfujing. **Amenities:** 2 restaurants; bar; room service; free Wi-Fi.

MODERATE

Double Happiness Courtyard Hotel ★ Set deep inside a colorful, tree-lined *hutong* in central Beijing, this courtyard hotel provides simple but friendly accommodation. The long walk down the alley from the main road brings you past small fruit-and-vegetable markets, local noodle shops, and courtyards crammed with multiple families. This is a slice of lively and authentic Old Beijing. No two rooms in this hotel are the same, but try to get one with a private balcony. The pretty courtyard is surprisingly peaceful. Room decor is basic—expect Chinese-style wooden furniture and small bathrooms—but the friendly staff and lower prices make up for it. Both single travelers and adventurous families would feel welcome here. The small restaurant has a limited menu, but right outside the door are plenty of tasty local eateries.

37 Dongsi Sitiao, off Dongsi Bei Dajie. www.doublehappinesscourtyard.com. ✆ **010/6400-7762.** RMB680 rooms, RMB820 suites, breakfast included. Subway: Dongsi or Zhangzizhonglu. **Amenities:** Restaurant; bar; free Wi-Fi.

Pentahotel Beijing ★★ Though caught in something of a no-man's land between central Beijing's main sights, Pentahotel is a likable midmarket hotel with clean, comfy rooms and a bright and breezy lobby downstairs. Rooms are sparse but stylish, with light-wood floors and whitewashed walls hung with 37-inch flatscreens. Pentaplus rooms are newly refurbished and have larger windows, while the largest units come with a kitchenette and extra beds for family stays. The lobby lounge has a noodle bar, cafe, and a games room complete with pool table. The feel is of an upmarket hostel. Though Chongwenmen is home to some good malls and restaurants, it's kind of *between* sights. The Temple of Heaven and Tian'anmen Square are both around 30 minutes' walk away, but bicycles can be borrowed for free, and Chongwenmen subway station is just around the corner.

3–18 Chongwenmen Wai Dajie. ✆ **010/6708-1188.** 307 units. RMB500 standard rooms, RMB600 Pentaplus rooms, RMB1,000 family rooms. Subway: Chongwenmen. **Amenities:** Lounge bar and cafe; games zone; laundry service; free bicycle rental; fitness center.

Red Wall Garden Hotel ★ Set in a small, tree-lined *hutong* in central Beijing, this cozy and charming courtyard hotel features a huge garden at the center. The small lobby opens up into a popular lounge-bar that overlooks the wooden patio with lots of seating. The 40 deluxe wood-floored rooms are stylish and colorful, with lacquer cabinets and bright ethnic bedspreads. The property attracts travelers whom you suspect could probably afford a business hotel but went looking for extra character. Ensuite bathrooms and flatscreen TVs, along with complimentary Wi-Fi, keep things up to date in terms of modern conveniences. Friendly service along with a central location make this a popular spot. The hotel restaurant serves good, basic Chinese dishes, and guests can try Beijing street food as interpreted by the executive chef.

41 Shijia Hutong, off Dongsi Beidajie. www.redwallgardenhotel.com. ✆ **010/5169-2222.** 40 units. RMB970–RMB1,120 rooms, RMB1,570 suites, breakfast included. Subway: Dengshikou. **Amenities:** Restaurant; bar; free Wi-Fi.

The Emperor Beijing Forbidden City ★ It may look like an anonymous four-story motel, but the Emperor has hidden delights in its boutiquey decor and fabulous location beside the Forbidden City. It's a place built for modern Chinese tastes: The 55 rooms are like something out of an eccentric modern living magazine, all vivid pastel shades, smooth curves, and odd shapes. Some will find it excitingly futuristic, others a touch pretentious. The rooftop bar offers views over the adjacent Forbidden City, though height restrictions mean you are looking *across* rather than *into* the palace. This is a local hotel, appealing mainly to domestic tourists and run to domestic standards, which can lag behind those you'll find at the international brands. Levels of English are not particularly good and, annoyingly, there's no elevator. However, it will please those wanting to stay centrally at a good price. There's a sister hotel east of Qianmen that hasn't got the same location perks, so be sure to clarify upon booking.

33 Qihelou Jie. www.theemperor.com.cn. ✆ **010/6701-7990.** 55 units. RMB1,000–RMB1,500 superior/deluxe room. Subway: Tian'anmen East. **Amenities:** 2 restaurants; rooftop bar; health club; massage room; free Wi-Fi.

The Hulu Hotel ★ Located in a tangle of *hutong* just west of Dongsi Dajie, the Hulu is a quiet and compact courtyard hotel with a pleasing air of exclusivity. Part-owned by a Hong Kong designer, it's beautifully presented with restored moon gates and gray-slate bamboo groves. However, as with so many independently owned *hutong* hotels, there are quibbles over the room finishes and the service standards, which suggest a company still learning its craft. On the upside, there's a pleasant rooftop terrace and a great central lounge that feels like a modern living room. The alleys around the hotel are nice for a stroll, but the Forbidden City is a lengthy, 30-minute walk away, and you'll need to take a subway to other central attractions.

91 Yanyue Hutong, off Dongsi Nan Dajie. www.thehuluhotel.com. ✆ **010/8517-5200.** RMB700–RMB1,100 standard rooms, including breakfast. Subway: Dongsi. **Amenities:** Restaurant/cafe; rooftop terrace; free Wi-Fi.

INEXPENSIVE

Days Inn Forbidden City ★★ For those looking for a place to rest their heads while they max out central sights, Days Inn Forbidden City ticks all the boxes. There are now thousands of Days Inns across the nation, and standards can be inconsistent. This branch is one of the better offerings, with free Wi-Fi and morning newspaper, satellite TV, clean, bright bathrooms, and decent levels of English among staff (something almost unheard of in cheaper establishments). The main draw is the location, one short block from Wangfujing and two from the Forbidden City.

1 Nanwanzi Hutong, off Nanheyan Jie. www.daysinn.com. ✆ **010/6512-7788.** 164 units. RMB558–RMB1,800 standard to superior rooms. Subway: Tian'anmen East. **Amenities:** Restaurant; room service; smoke-free floors; free Wi-Fi.

North Dongcheng (Gulou Area)

EXPENSIVE

Du Ge Hotel ★ With its rich designer decor, Du Ge is one of many *hutong* hotels that claim "boutique" status, but one of few that deserve it. There are only six rooms and suites, set around a quiet courtyard, and each has a distinct theme. The two standard rooms—the "White House" and "Gold Lotus"—are self-consciously luxe (think sparkly wallpaper and Baccarat chandeliers), while the four suites offer brightly decorated but slightly more demure lodgings. The building was once home to a Qing-era Mandarin and lies on a quiet lane, a stone's throw from throbbing Nan Luogu Xiang. It's a top location, and for those who crave style and fashion, Du Ge is a solid choice. The main drawbacks are the unusually cramped floor plans (space-wise, the suites are more akin to what you would expect of a generously portioned standard room), and the "five-star"-level rack rates don't quite match the levels of service and amenities. Stay if you can bag a discount.

801 Qianyuan'ensi Hutong, off Nan Luogu Xiang. www.dugecourtyard.com. ✆ **010/6445-7463.** 6 units. RMB1,580 standard rooms, RMB2,180 suite. Subway: Shichahai, Nan Luogu Xiang. **Amenities:** Restaurant; bar; cigar lounge; teahouse; free Wi-Fi.

Han's Royal Garden ★ The former residence of a Chinese nobleman, this grand courtyard hotel offers all the modern comforts in a wonderfully restored space. There is a distinct ambience of classical Chinese grandeur here, complete with tranquil ponds filled with koi. Rooms are equipped with all the modern perks, including a TV above the tub in the huge marble bathrooms. From the two restaurants to the beautifully maintained grounds, amenities are top of the line, but so are the prices. Remarkably, this quiet spot is just steps away from bustling Nan Luogu Xiang, with its many bars, cafes, and shops.

20 Qinlao Hutong, off Jiaodaokou Nan Dajie. www.hansroyalgarden.com. ✆ **010/8402-5588.** RMB1,280–RMB1,580 doubles, RMB1,980 suites, rates include breakfast. Subway: Nan Luogu Xiang. **Amenities:** 2 restaurants; bar; free Wi-Fi.

MODERATE

Bamboo Garden Hotel (Zhu Yuan Binguan) ★ One of the oldest *hutong* hotels in Beijing, Bamboo Garden was once the former residence of Qing eunuch Li Lianying, the power behind the throne in the last years of the doomed dynasty. It's more sprawling than the average courtyard hotel, organized around three large compounds filled with koi ponds, bamboo groves, mature trees, and lawns. They make for picturesque views from rooms, though the overall feel is of a large three-star rather than a proper *hutong* hideaway. Rooms feel a little dated; interior fittings are tidy but basic, with bathrooms in need of modernization. Standard rooms are located in one of the two multistory buildings at either end of the complex. Houhai Lake is a short walk away, as is the Gulou Dajie subway stop.

24 Xiaoshiqiao Hutong, off Jiugulou Dajie, www.bbgh.com.cn. ✆ **010/5852-0088.** 60 units. RMB760–RMB880 standard room. Subway: Gulou Dajie. **Amenities:** 3 restaurants; bar; teahouse; free Wi-Fi.

Courtyard 7 ★★ Tucked away off busy Nan Luogu Xiang, Courtyard 7 is one of the few courtyard hotels where the old-world character hasn't been compromised by modernization. It's amazingly serene, despite its proximity to the tourist chaos nearby. Enter via a nondescript entrance, through a sliding door and a circular moon-gate, and into a quiet courtyard complex, decorated in grand imperial colors. Rooms are simple but beautifully decked out in traditional furniture, bathrooms are sparkling and spacious, and there are heated floors. Standard rooms are arranged motel-style along the back wall, while the superior and deluxe rooms are set around the central courtyard.

7 Qiangulouyuan, off Nan Luogu Xiang. www.courtyard7.com. ✆ **010/6406-0777.** 16 units. RMB700–RMB900 standard rooms, 1,200–1,500 deluxe. Rates include breakfast. Subway: Nan Luogu Xiang, Shichahai. **Amenities:** Restaurant, bar, free Wi-Fi.

The Orchid ★★ A cozy 10-room charmer, The Orchid is a favorite with travelers looking for character and comfort at reasonable rates. Restored wooden-beam ceilings, a small garden courtyard, and a cute bar are highlights. The decor is simple but stylish, with natural elements of wood and slate. Rooms with gorgeous wooden headboards offer all the modern comforts, including heated floors and on-demand movies. The view over neighboring rooftops of an older Beijing is a rare treat. Upper-floor rooms with private rooftop terraces or gardens are worth the higher price. This spot also has the added plus of being in one of the hippest *hutong* in the city, with cool bars and good restaurants just a few steps away.

65 Baochao Hutong, off Gulou Dong Dajie. www.theorchidbeijing.com. ✆ **010/8404-4818.** RMB735–RMB1,260 rooms, breakfast included. Subway: Shichahai or Nan Luogu Xiang. **Amenities:** Restaurant (breakfast and lunch only); free Wi-Fi.

INEXPENSIVE

Peking International Youth Hostel ★ This small and friendly hostel is set in the middle of the very lively Nan Luogu Xiang *hutong*. Fresh flowers and greenery abound in the small lobby, while the rooftop terrace is filled with bougainvillea and other plants. The attached cafe is popular, though its prices for coffee are on par with Starbucks. Overall, the rooms here are spartan but spotless; the pleasant public areas are where you'll want to spend your waking hours. The shared dorm rooms are rock-bottom-cheap, while doubles are generally available at a decent price. Friendly service makes for a standout stay.

113 Nan Luogu Xiang. www.peking.hostel.com. ✆ **010/6401-3961.** RMB110 dorms, RMB450 private rooms, breakfast not included. Subway: Nan Luogu Xiang. **Amenities:** Restaurant; bar; free Wi-Fi.

Chaoyang District

EXPENSIVE

Conrad Hotel ★★★ The Conrad Hotel's futuristic exterior, with its curved edges and membrane-like covering, is instantly visible above the flat cityscape of Beijing. The space-age architecture outside is matched by the ultramodern feel of the interiors. Rooms are spacious, decorated with subtle Asian touches like pale silk walls in a Chinese motif. Bathrooms are a sheer pleasure, with heated floors and television projected on the mirrors. Among the three different kinds of bath products offered is Shanghai Tang, the luxury Hong Kong brand. Other perks include Nespresso machines, 400-thread-count bed linens, flatscreen TVs with DVD players, and iPod docks. One welcome surprise: Blueair air-purifiers, along with humidifiers, are available on request—executive suites have them installed automatically. The Conrad stands out among Beijing's other five-star hotels with its attention to detail, especially the attentive service of the immaculately attired staff. The gorgeous Chapter restaurant, designed to look like a three-story library with a circular staircase, is a popular brunch spot. A two-story Cantonese restaurant, Lu Yu, has its own elevators for exclusive entry to the dining space and nine private rooms. The fifth-floor nightclub Vivid has all the sleek leather seating and flashy glitz of a Hollywood hotspot, with an appealing open-air terrace that draws big crowds when the weather is warm.

29 Dongsanhuan Beilu. http://conradhotels3.hilton.com. ✆ **010/6584-6000.** RMB1,500–RMB1,800 rooms, RMB2,100 suites. Subway: Tuanjiehu, plus 15-min. walk. **Amenities:** 3 restaurants; bar; fitness center; indoor swimming pool; spa; room service; free Wi-Fi.

Four Seasons ★★ Gorgeously elegant, the Beijing branch of this luxury chain stands up to the high standards of its brand. Interiors are stylish, with prominently displayed Chinese modern art and understated wooden furniture with Chinese motifs. The skylighted atrium is adorned with a vertical wall featuring metallic silver butterflies fluttering their way up. Spacious rooms

The Best Spas

The glut of luxury hotels also means that there's a glut of luxury hotel **spas** in Beijing. These feature state-of-the-art treatment-and-relaxation rooms and massage therapists who excel in Asian techniques. Prices tend to be on par with what you'd pay in other international cities. A particular favorite is the recently renovated **Tian** spa at the **Park Hyatt,** which offers a range of treatments based on traditional Chinese medicine, plus access to the hotel's gorgeous pool and gym. For a wonderfully sedate experience, visit the **Espa** at the **Peninsula,** where you'll first go to the sauna and steam room and de-stress in a plush reclining armchair before finally sinking into a heated massage bed in a darkened treatment room. If you're looking to get away from city stress, physically and figuratively, try the out-of-town **Aman Spa** inside the **Aman at Summer Palace** hotel.

In the Red Light District

Southwest of Qianmen, beyond the mercantile madness of Dazhalan, is where you'll find the remains of Beijing's once-thriving brothel district, **Ba Da Hutong** ("eight great lanes"). Prior to the Communists' "elimination" of prostitution in the 1950s (and its rapid reemergence since the 1980s), officials, diplomats, and other men of means would come here to pay for the pleasures of "clouds and rain." The transaction was not always lurid. The women were closer to courtesans, akin to Japanese geisha, and their customers often paid simply for conversation and cultured entertainment. Many old bordellos still stand, although most buildings were converted into apartments or stores. A few have come full circle and become cheap hotels, and while those who can afford it might prefer to stay in a more luxurious hotel farther north, travelers on a budget would be hard-pressed to find affordable accommodations with so much character. If you're hunting for a cheap room with a whiff of history, try **Shanxi Xiang,** a poorly marked lane that runs south from Dazhalan. A number of hotels line the way, and you can get a windowless room (nod-nod, wink-wink) with air-conditioning, a TV, and an ensuite bathroom for around RMB100 (US$16) per night.

exude luxury, while huge bathrooms are downright decadent with large tubs that provide city views. The chain's famously attentive service is on display, with staffers greeting guests by name. Facilities are top-notch, from the indoor pool (with more city views) to the world-class spa with an adjacent tea garden. Signature Italian restaurant Mio has won rave reviews for its food and splashy decor. Chinese restaurant Cai Yi Xuan offers impeccable Cantonese cuisine. Hospitality also extends to children, provided with everything from cribs and baby bathtubs to diapers and rubber-duck toys. Of course, this level of service doesn't come cheap, but if you can afford to splurge, this is a good spot to do it. The downside is the rather remote location, great for the airport but poor for central sights.

48 Liangmaqiao Lu. www.fourseasons.com/beijing. ✆ **010/5695-8888.** Rooms RMB1,700–RMB2,500, suites RMB2,900–RMB6,500. Subway: Liangmaqiao. **Amenities:** 3 restaurants, fitness center, swimming pool, spa, room service; smoke-free floors; free Wi-Fi.

Opposite House ★★★ With its dramatic green-and-yellow glass facade, the Opposite House is memorable from first glance. Designed by avant-garde Japanese architect Kengo Kuma, this chic 99-room spot is currently among Beijing's hippest addresses. Befitting a design-forward property, the lobby is a wide atrium filled with modern art installations. Rooms are airy, loft-style spaces; the blond wood and minimalist design are soothing. Hedonists can delight in the sumptuous bathrooms, which come with huge, Japanese-style wooden soaking tubs. Other unusual touches include the complimentary minibar, restocked daily, with goodies like jellybeans and local and imported beers. There's also a free in-room iPad. Located smack in the middle of the trendy Sanlitun neighborhood with bars, restaurants, and shops, this hotel, the first by Hong Kong developer Swire Hotels, offers the ultimate urban experience in Beijing. For globe-trotting creative types who want to be in the middle of the action, this is the place to be.

The Village, Building 1, 11 Sanlitun Lu. www.theoppositehouse.com. ✆ **010/6417-6688.** 99 units. RMB2,300–RMB3,100 standard, RMB4,300–RMB5,800 suite. Subway: Tuanjiehu. **Amenities:** 3 restaurants; 2 bars; fitness center; indoor pool; room service; smoke-free floors; complimentary culture tour; free Wi-Fi.

Park Hyatt Beijing ★★ Housed in the upper reaches of the 66-floor Yintai Center, in the heart of the CBD, the Park Hyatt is quietly luxurious without being as superexclusive as some of its sister hotels in Asia. Rooms are spacious and sleek, with blond wood and neutral colors, as well as a window-side sofa for enjoying the superb views. Bathrooms are a highlight, with enormous, deep-set limestone tubs, oversize rain showers, and heated floors. There's a recently refurbished gym and indoor pool toward the top of the building, plus a fabulous spa for those who want even more relaxation. Guests are treated to eye-popping four-way views of the city when checking in at the lobby on the 63rd floor. The hotel's China Grill bar and restaurant on the two top floors offers 360-degree views over downtown Beijing, including vistas of the iconic CCTV tower (which you can also enjoy if you opt for a north-facing room). The sixth-floor terrace bar, Xiu, brings in the crowds with live music that runs from jazz to rock.

2 Jianguomenwai St. http://beijing.park.hyatt.com. 246 units. ✆ **010/8567-1234.** RMB1,500–RMB2,200 rooms, RMB2,200–RMB3,100 suites. Subway: Guomao. **Amenities:** 3 restaurants; bar; airport limousine transfers; fitness center; pool; room service; spa; free Wi-Fi.

The Rosewood ★★★ Entering an already packed five-star marketplace in 2014, the luxurious Rosewood has won plaudits for its design-led luxury and superb service. Twin bronze dragons lead the way to a gorgeous lobby, festooned with sculptures and giant artwork. The dark-wood rooms are invitingly stylish, and giant 50-inch TVs, Blu-ray DVD players, imported Italian toiletries, and lush coffee-table books provide further inducement to lie low during your stay. The pool is a beauty, with natural light pouring in from overhead and lush vegetation clinching the feel of a spa retreat. Service levels are superb, something that even five-star status does not always guarantee in Beijing. The only downside is the location: Sanlitun, to the north, is just about walkable, but this part of the CBD has little to offer tourists. That said, there is a subway station a few minutes from the front entrance—and with interior comforts so lush, should the weather be bad outside, you might choose to spend your entire time indoors.

Jingguang Center, off Chaoyangmen Wai Dajie. www.rosewoodhotels.com/en/beijing. ✆ **010/6597-8888.** RMB2,000–RMB2,500 deluxe rooms, RMB3,500–RMB4,000 suites. Subway: Hujialou. **Amenities:** 5 restaurants; bar; sauna; fitness center; indoor pool; spa; yoga room; room service; free Wi-Fi.

MODERATE

A.hotel ★ One might expect a hotel housed within a major sports stadium to be boringly corporate, but A.hotel surprises with its modern, minimalist design efforts. Rooms are comfy and well maintained, with chic maroon accents here and there and monochrome photos on the walls. The location is good for Chaoyang's highlights; renovated Yashow Market and the sights of Sanlitun are both easily walkable, though it's 15 minutes to the nearest subway. Amenities are simple. Breakfast is served at the bar, and you shouldn't expect too much of the lobby staff, whose English skills are basic. Because the hotel is actually *in* the stadium complex, you may have to deal with security during soccer matches and concerts. During such times, head straight for the east gate, where there should be a member of staff to spirit you past the guards.

6/F, Workers' Stadium (east gate), off Gongren Tiyuchang Donglu. www.a-hotel.com.cn. ✆ **010/6586-5858.** 116 units. RMB550–RMB800 standard rooms. Subway: Tuanjiehu. **Amenities:** Bar/restaurant; Free Wi-Fi.

East Hotel ★ Billed as an unconventional business hotel, this is the second venture in Beijing by Hong Kong's Swire Hotels. Pale wood floors and a neutral palette give the guestrooms a minimalist feel, and smart amenities include a complimentary iPod touch and free Wi-Fi. The larger suites are worth the extra price, with tubs perched on raised platforms. Though not as artsy as sister hotel Opposite House, East Hotel makes the most of its proximity to the 798 Art District, which is a 5-minute cab ride away. Pieces by Chinese artists are displayed throughout the premises. The hip feel extends to the hotel's staff, who are garbed in gray sweatshirts, black pants, and black sneakers. The property is attached to Indigo Mall, one of Beijing's trendiest, so shopping is a breeze.

22 Jiuxianqiao Lu. www.east-beijing.com. ✆ **010/8426-0888.** RMB900–RMB1,350 standard, RMB1,500–RMB1,650 suite. Subway: Wangjing West plus 15-min. taxi ride. **Amenities:** 3 restaurants, fitness center, indoor swimming pool, business lounge, free Wi-Fi.

Grace Hotel ★ This artsy hotel is a perfect match for its surroundings amid the thriving 798 Art District. There's a definite funkiness, but as at 798, also something a little pretentious about the cold, self-consciously "designer" fittings. The use of bold colors throughout is striking, from tomato-red sofas to bright chartreuse cabinets. The 30 rooms and suites all include lofty ceilings and original Bauhaus-style windows, though the cheapest rooms in the east of the building are a bit of a squeeze, especially in the tiny bathrooms. The hotel restaurant, Yi House Bistro, serves up decent continental fare, and its two-course lunch set-menus are a bargain. Just outside the hotel are galleries and studios galore, so art lovers can wander to their heart's content. However, it is a long way back downtown, and transportation options are not great, so only stay if 798 is a major part of your itinerary.

2 Hao Yuan, Jiuxianqiao Lu. www.gracebeijing.com. ✆ **010/6436-1818.** RMB1,200–RMB1,300 rooms, RMB1,700–RMB2,000 suites, breakfast included. Subway: Wangjing, then 5-min. taxi ride.

Holiday Inn Express Beijing Dongzhimen ★★ This crisp budget hotel is located in its own private garden right in the middle of the Sanlitun shopping and entertainment district. Furnishings are all shiny and modern. The rooms have funky lime-green armchairs, flatscreen TVs, and coffeemakers. The helpful young staff, dressed in orange sweaters, is eager to please. The biggest plus is that the city's best nightlife and shopping are all within easy walking distance. This is a long way from being Beijing's flashiest hotel, and amenities are simple, but in terms of price, decor, and location, it's a superb choice for the midmarket traveler.

1 Chunxiu Lu, near Dongzhimenwai Dajie. www.hiexpress.com. ✆ **010/6416-9999.** Rooms RMB598, breakfast included. Kids eat free. Subway: Dongsishitiao. **Amenities:** Restaurant; free Wi-Fi.

INEXPENSIVE

Yoyo Hotel ★ If you're on a tight budget and plan to major on Salitun's shopping and nightlife scene, this quirky little hotel is a sound choice. The building, hidden away from the hustle of Sanlitun on a side street, has the feel of a public-housing project, but there's clearly an effort inside to distinguish the hotel from low-budget two- or three-stars. Rooms are decorated in tan tones, and the bathrooms, though small, are clad in marble and mosaic chips. There's not much in the way of amenities, but there are dining options galore around the corner on Sanlitun. The very cheapest rooms have no windows.

Middle Building 10, Dong Sanlitun Erjie. www.yoyohotel.cn. ✆ **010/6417-3388.** 52 units. RMB369–RMB399 standard room. Subway: Tuanjiehu. **Amenities:** Restaurant; free Wi-Fi.

Xicheng District

INEXPENSIVE

Red Lantern House ★ Offering a *hutong* experience without the expense of the chichi courtyard hotels, the Red Lantern House is a lively hostel with good access to the back lakes of Xicheng. The seriously cheap rooms attract both foreign and Chinese backpackers, and are dotted around this sprawling courtyard complex. The neighborhood has an authentic, ramshackle feel, away from most touristy areas. Rooms are decked in vintage wallpaper and dark-wood furniture. They vary in size, and the smallest are very cramped, so ask to see your room before check-in and bargain your way up if you're not happy. Ask for an ensuite bathroom on booking. Many rooms share the communal toilets, though new facilities have been added to ease the pressure. The central garden and dining area is lovely, though it can create noise later on, so pack your earplugs.

5 Zhengjue Hutong, near Xinjiekou Nan Dajie. www.redlanternhouse.com. ✆ **010/8328-3935.** 68 units. RMB200–RMB300 private rooms. No credit cards. Subway: Jishuitan or Ping'anli. **Amenities:** Restaurant; bar; free Wi-Fi; bike rentals.

Haidian District

EXPENSIVE

Aman at Summer Palace ★★ For those looking to get away from the chaotic urban feel of Beijing, Aman is the perfect retreat. Located on the city

Pants Are on Fire

The Mandarin Oriental Blaze

Images of fireballs engulfing the then-unopened Mandarin Oriental Beijing made international news in early 2009. The hotel, one of the most highly anticipated luxury property openings, was part of an iconic new development that included the Rem Koolhaas-designed CCTV Tower, labeled by locals as the "giant underpants" (*da kucha*), on account of it resembling a squatting pair of legs. The blaze resulted in one fatality and completely gutted the 44-floor building, causing billions in damages and acute embarrassment to the authorities. The blaze was apparently caused by an illegal New Year's fireworks display, organized by CCTV itself, and was seen by some as a chilling example of how powerful officials could bypass safety regulations on a whim. Initial denials and excuses were disputed online, where images, videos, and rumors about the blaze spread online even more quickly than the flames. Under online pressure, newspaper and TV journalists were soon allowed to report the full story, and 20 people were eventually jailed. The episode was the first in a short-lived era of "citizen journalism," where individuals used private blog and microblog accounts to challenge official explanations. It also led to a renewed bout of soul-searching around fireworks, which had been banned in Beijing up until a few years before the fire. The skyscraper has been successfully renovated around the original structure, but at the time of writing, there was still no official announcement about when the hotel might finally open.

outskirts, next to the stately grounds of the Summer Palace, where Chinese emperors relaxed, this latest outpost of the ultraluxe Aman chain gives a taste of imperial living in modern times. Beijing's priciest hotel is housed in a series of traditional pavilions—the whole complex was once used by guests awaiting an audience with the empress dowager. Rooms and courtyards reflect traditional Chinese architecture, with wood floors, high ceilings, and classic Ming-style furniture. There's a classy spa, a movie theater, and a Pilates studio among the facilities. Another key perk is the private back entrance to the Summer Palace. Dining options include a well-regarded steakhouse and a Japanese *kaiseki* restaurant, both featuring wine selections from the resident sommelier. The big drawback (or big positive, depending on your point of view) is that the hotel is about 45 minutes away from central Beijing.

1 Gongmenqian Jie. www.amanresorts.com/amanatsummerpalace/home.aspx. ✆ **010/5987-9999.** RMB4,600 rooms, RMB5,800–RMB8,000 suites. Subway: Beigongmen. **Amenities:** 4 restaurants, bar, library, fitness center, spa, indoor pool, squash courts, private cinema.

WHERE TO EAT

Too many of Beijing's restaurants open and close in any given month to offer an accurate count, but it is difficult to imagine a city with more eateries per square mile, or a more exhaustive variety of Chinese cuisines. The short life span of the average restaurant in Beijing can create headaches (for guidebook writers, in particular), but the upside is a dynamic culinary environment where establishments that manage to stick around have generally earned the right to exist.

Beijing has a few local dishes that are worth trying: **dumplings, hot pot,** and **Peking duck.** While these mainstays remain popular, it seems that every few years, a new, "hot" regional-cuisine trend sweeps the city. Once upon a time, it was Cultural Revolution nostalgia dishes, then yuppified minority food from Yunnan, and now fiery Sichuan dishes are served in upscale dining rooms. Each leaves its mark on the culinary landscape after it has passed, making it possible for visitors to sample authentic dishes from nearly every corner of the country.

Non-Chinese food is not neglected either. Vietnamese cuisine has become very trendy, along with upscale French cuisine, Spanish tapas, and Japanese sushi bars. And if you're feeling like a homesick American, there is always Subway, Sizzler, and even Outback Steakhouse (in addition to KFC, which actually does a pretty decent Peking duck wrap).

Main courses in almost every non-Western restaurant are placed in the middle of the table and shared between two or more people. The "meal for two" price estimates in this chapter include two individual bowls of rice and between two and four main dishes, depending on the size of the portions, which tends to decrease as prices rise. Generally speaking, a typical dinner for two at a nice restaurant costs under RMB200 (US$32), but prices can go much lower with little to no drop in quality.

Credit cards are generally accepted in most restaurants above the moderately priced level. Hotels frequently levy a 15% service charge, but freestanding restaurants seldom do. Tips are not necessary; waitresses will often come running out into the street to give your money back if you try to leave one.

You can buy basic **groceries** and Chinese-style **snacks** at local markets and at the ubiquitous convenience stores. Several fully stocked **supermarkets** and a handful of smaller grocers carry imported wine and cheese, junk food,

Airport Hotels

Plenty of hotels, all with free shuttle services, are located near the airport. The most pleasant choice is the **Hilton Hotel** (www.hilton.com; ✆ **010/6448-8888**), right next to Beijing's sparkling Terminal 3 Airport, where most international flights arrive and depart. The **CITIC Hotel Beijing Airport** (www.citichotel beijing.com; ✆ **010/6456-5588**) contains large rooms with two queen-size beds for around RMB850. It has a pleasant resort-style pool complex, and regular shuttles go to the airport (every 30 min. 6:15am–10:45pm) and downtown.

Also convenient for the airport are hotels around Liangmaqiao and Sanyuanqiao, both on the Third Ring Road. From here, it's a 20-minute drive to the airport, while the Airport Express runs direct from Sanyuanqiao. The **Four Seasons Beijing** (see.p. 104) is a luxury option, but the **Traders Upper East Hotel** (www.shangri-la.com; ✆ **010/5907-8888**), part of the well-respected Shangri-La hotel chain, is a solid choice for those on a budget. The hotel has a good restaurant, Wu Li Xiang, offering regional Chinese dishes.

Street Food in Beijing

Affordable Chinese food is everywhere in Beijing, indoors and out. In the warmer months, the capital's **snack streets** come into their own. Quality is sometimes variable; many of these places are rammed, especially after dark, and occasionally you'll feel like it's you being served up at the end of an industrial production line. No matter, they're guaranteed fun and should be experienced at least once. The easiest, if perhaps most touristy option, is the **Donghuamen Night Market,** located at the northern end of Wangfujing, stretching westward. You'll be able to find snacks from across the nation, including Xi'an's beloved *Rou Jia Mo* "burgers" (see p. 169) and scorpions. Stall-holders set up at 4pm daily and go until around 10pm. Ghost Street (Gui Jie), on Dongzhimen Nei Dajie **(between the Beixinqiao and Dongzhimen subway stations)**, is now much reduced from its former glory, but dozens of eateries still offer hot pot, *mala longxia* (spicy crayfish), and home-style fare through the lantern-lit night. **Wangfujing Snack Street** is a steamy network of alleys opposite the Oriental Plaza on the west side of Wangfujing Dajie. It's a riot of baying vendors, and insects seem to be sold at every second stall. Less adventurous diners can grab egg-fried *jianbing* pancakes, while noodles are served on plastic tables spread across the crowded lanes. **Jiumen Snack Street,** on Xiaoyou Hutong at the northernmost point of Houhai Lake, is the most picturesque of the snack streets and is busy day and night. The **Niujie (Ox Street) Snack Street,** south of Guang'anmen Nei Dajie in south Xicheng, is the best spot for sampling Uighur and Hui Muslim food, dominated by kebabs and fresh breads. There's little fear of food poisoning, but for those who worry about hygiene standards, there are always the **point-to-order food courts** on the top or bottom floor of almost every large shopping center (see "Shopping," p. 118).

Newcastle Brown Ale, and just about anything else you could want, albeit at prices above what you'll pay back home. Supermarkets include one in the basement of the Lufthansa Center, the CRC in the basement of the China World Trade Center, and Oriental Kenzo, above Dongzhimen subway. April Gourmet, north of Sanlitun bar street, has sliced meats, a decent cheese selection, and a full selection of familiar breakfast cereals; much the same can be found at Jenny Lou's, which has six branches in Beijing—the biggest one is near Chaoyang Park west gate.

For restaurant locations, see the map on p. 66.

Central Dongcheng

EXPENSIVE

Capital M ★ CONTINENTAL The sweeping views from an outdoor terrace overlooking Tian'anmen Square would be enough to ensure a steady flow of business at Capital M, but this glamorous space also has consistently good food. It's hearty rather than essentially gourmet, with the pared-back international menu majoring in Mediterranean and North African flavors, while throwing in a few more European favorites such as suckling pig and Icelandic halibut. The creative interior, with vibrant geometric parquet floors, a huge mural depicting seasons along a river, and elegant tableware, makes this 400-seat space always feel like a special occasion. Australian owner Michelle Garnaut, who also set up the legendary M on the Bund in Shanghai and M on the Fringe in Hong Kong, pulled out all the stops here. Make sure to save room for the famed pavlova dessert, which is a mouthwatering concoction of meringue, cream, and fruit. Reservations are recommended.

South of Tiananmen Square, 3/F, 2 Qianmen Pedestrian St. www.capital-m-beijing.com. ✆ **010/6702-2727.** Meal for two, RMB700–RMB1,200. Mon–Fri 11:30am–2:30pm, 6–10:30pm, Sat–Sun 11:30am–10:30pm. Subway: Qian Men.

Duck de Chine ★★ CHINESE Specializing in Beijing's most famous poultry dish, Duck de Chine serves its soft, succulent, red-skinned meat with a double serving of glamour. The restaurant is housed in a gorgeous, traditional-style courtyard, and the elegant decor, huge windows, and low lighting create a striking environment. The ambience is Asian luxe, with red lacquer pillars, ceramic tile floors, and red silk lamps overhead. Duck de Chine is where locals bring out-of-towners to be impressed. This is the second and larger location for the restaurant, which is just blocks away from the landmark Wangfujing pedestrian shopping street. If you want the duck, call ahead to order it in advance.

98 Jinbao Jie. ✆ **010/6521-2221.** Meal for two, RMB700–RMB800. Daily 11am–2:30pm, 5:30–10:30pm. Subway: Dengshikou.

Temple Restaurant Beijing ★★★ CONTINENTAL Hidden in a historic *hutong* neighborhood in central Beijing, the 600-year-old Tibetan Buddhist temple complex that houses this restaurant is one of the capital's most spectacular locations. Inside, a wall of windows allows diners to gaze into TRB's renovated courtyard. The bar/lounge area preserves an original stone archway, wooden beams, and painted ceiling panels. The fine-dining menu is inspired by French cuisine, and is simply spectacular. Specialties include pot-roasted lobster with smoked eggplant caviar, king crab ravioli, and confit of suckling pig. Desserts, from a white-chocolate-and-passion-fruit cheesecake to caramel mousse and coffee panna cotta, are capped with extra rounds of nibbles, including homemade marshmallows. Diners should arrive early to explore the temple grounds and have a drink at the bar, which offers homemade bitters and gourmet versions of rice wines. The main temple itself, with its original beams and red pillars, is located in the back and reserved for special events and functions. There's also a fabulous lunchtime set menu for as little as RMB135 (US$22), which allows those on a budget to enjoy Beijing's best fine-dining without blowing the entire vacation budget.

23 Shatan Bei Jie, off Wusi Dajie. www.trb-cn.com. ✆ **010/8400-2232.** Meal for two, 700RMB–RMB1,200. Daily 11:30am–2:30pm, 6–10pm. Subway: Dongsi, plus 30-min. walk.

MODERATE

Lei Garden ★★ CANTONESE For the best dim sum and authentic Cantonese in town, this branch of an acclaimed Hong Kong chain doesn't have much competition. The classic standards are done incredibly well. Shrimp dumplings are addictive translucent morsels, and small squares of crispy pork belly are sublime. Pan-fried turnip cakes and leaf-wrapped sticky rice are two other standouts. The egg tarts are a tasty mouthful of custard and flaky pastry. Prices are high, admittedly, but then again this is very upscale dim sum. The red-and-gold decor is stylish and bright, with comfy booth seating and windows all around. The only drawback is the restaurant's location in a bland office building. Weekends are packed, so make sure to call in advance for reservations.

3/F, Jinbao Tower, 89 Jinbao Jie (next to the Regent Hotel). www.leigarden.hk/tc/location/china.asp. ✆ **010/8522-1212.** Meal for two, RMB400–RMB500. Daily 11:30am–3pm, 6–11:30pm. Subway: Dengshikou.

Lost Heaven ★★★ YUNNANESE Lost Heaven is an exotically decorated and sensuously lit restaurant, tucked away in a neoclassical quadrangle in the south of the Legation Quarter. The restaurant specializes in tribal dishes from the southwestern province of Yunnan. However, the Dai people, who provide much of the culinary inspiration, are spread across Indochina, and the extensive menu blends into perhaps more familiar Thai dishes. Forest fungi are big in the lush southwest, and the stir-fried shrimp with jizong mushrooms is a chewy delight. The dining area is bedecked in colorful woven fabrics and splashes of vegetation. With frangipani plants on each table and heavy incense permeating the room, this is a deeply romantic spot for a meal. Come for lunch after morning explorations around Tian'anmen Square, or glam up for a nighttime visit.

23 Qianmen Dong Dajie. www.lostheaven.com.cn. ✆ **010/8516-2698.** Meal for two, RMB300–RMB500. Daily 11:30am–2pm, 5:30–10:30pm. Subway: Qian Men, then 5-min. walk east.

INEXPENSIVE

Chuan Ban (川办) ★★ SICHUAN If you're looking for old-school, burn-your-mouth, authentic Sichuan food, this is the place. This perpetually crowded restaurant has the plainest of decor and sometimes surly service, but it's the quality of the food that brings in the customers. The spicy *shui zhu yu* (fish stew), which comes with slices of tender fish floating atop bean sprouts in hot oil, is on virtually every table. The *mapo doufu* (tofu in chili sauce) is an intense mix of silky and spicy. The incredibly addictive *lazi ji* combines bits of fried chicken mixed into a huge plate of chili. The mouth-numbing flavor of the *huajiao* peppercorn, which gives Sichuan food its distinctive kick, is present in almost every dish. The restaurant is located at the headquarters of the Sichuan provincial government's representative office, so its reputation (and authenticity) is spoken for. Reservations aren't accepted, so it's best to come before 6pm or after 8pm. Otherwise, be prepared to wait 30 to 45 minutes.

Off Jianguomen Nei Dajie, 5 Gongyuan Toutiao. ✆ **010/6512-2277, ext. 6101.** Meal for two, RMB150–RMB250. Mon–Fri 11am–2pm, 5–9:30pm, Sat–Sun 11am–9:30pm. Subway: Jianguomen.

Crescent Moon ★ CHINESE This small but perennially popular spot offers the distinctive cumin-spiced lamb kebabs, crispy nan bread, homemade yogurt, and hand-pulled noodle specialties that come from China's far northwestern province, Xinjiang. The huge *dapanji* adds slow-cooked chicken on the bone to a savory broth of potatoes, veggies, and noodles. The *dan xian subing kaorou* is a crispy vegetable-and-egg pie with a huge mound of lamb and onions piled on top. The house's mint tea makes a refreshing change from the jasmine version. The green-and-gold decor outside, and the restaurant's name itself, hint at the Muslim faith of the Chinese proprietors.

Off Chaoyangmen Bei Xiaojie, 16 Dongsi Liutiao. ✆ **010/6400-5281.** Meal for two, RMB200–RMB300. Daily 10am–11:30pm. Subway: Zhangzizhonglu.

North Dongcheng (Gulou Area)

EXPENSIVE

King's Joy ★★ VEGETARIAN From the first steps through the courtyard's mist-covered entrance to the small grove of bamboo trees in the back, the focus at this elegant, upscale restaurant is on the bounty of nature. Vegetables reign supreme here. The "monkey's head" mushroom, cooked in a sweet-and-sour sauce, is satisfyingly chunky. The truffle-grilled crispy rice squares are a crunchy mouthful, while the braised spicy tofu leaves a kick with its Sichuan peppercorn flavoring. The wine list is lengthy, but the more interesting drinks are healthy infusions of hawberry juice, palm juice, or chilled papaya milk. Though there's a traditional courtyard on the outside, the restaurant's interior is a modern melding of natural elements like wood and stone. Dining spaces are separated by stacked wood panels that create a sense of privacy while maintaining an airy feel. Reserve seats in the tranquil outdoor courtyard when the weather is good.

2 Wudaoying Hutong (Across from Lama Temple). ✆ **010/8404-9191.** Meal for two, RMB700–RMB1,000. Daily 10am–10pm. Subway: Yonghegong.

MODERATE

Black Sesame Kitchen ★★ CHINESE This cooking school and private kitchen serves up one of the best communal dining experiences in town. The twice-weekly dinners, known as Wine & Dine events, offer a 10-course meal paired with free-flowing imported wine. Set in a renovated courtyard with an open kitchen and dining room, Black Sesame provides a front-row seat to Chinese cuisine, as the chefs prepare the meal before your eyes in the spacious kitchen. There's no menu, but signature dishes include pan-fried pork and pumpkin dumplings, fried shiitake mushrooms seasoned with bamboo shoots and coriander, and cashew kung pao chicken. Diners can inform the kitchen ahead of time if they have any dietary preferences or restrictions. The communal dinners seat up to 24 guests. Those who want to dive in more deeply can take the cooking classes on Tuesdays, Thursdays, and Saturdays. These events are highly popular, and reservations are essential. For those wanting to set up a private dinner, advance booking is available.

Off Nan Luogu Xiang, 3 Heizhima Hutong. www.blacksesamekitchen.com. ✆ **136/9147-4408.** Prix-fixe meal RMB300. Wed, Fri 7–10pm. Subway: Nan Luogu Xiang.

Dali Courtyard ★★ YUNNAN This cozy courtyard restaurant specializing in southwestern Yunnan cuisine was one of the first to be located inside the *hutong,* the historic neighborhoods of the capital. The restaurant charms with rustic wooden furnishings and a tree-covered outdoor space. Influenced by neighbors Burma and Vietnam, Yunnan province's food is light and sophisticated, making good use of the region's abundant mushrooms and unusual herbs. There is no menu; diners enjoy prix-fixe courses made from whatever the chef found freshest in the market that day. Favorites like the slightly salty fried goat cheese, spicy mint salad, and herb-encrusted fried fish make regular appearances. The place is a little tricky to find. Your taxi will drop you at the mouth of the alley; walk straight about 150 yards and look to your left for a red lantern down an even smaller alley.

67 Xiaojingchang Hutong (Off Gulou Dongdajie). ✆ **010/8404-2030.** Prix-fixe meal RMB100–RMB300. Daily noon–2pm, 6–10:30pm. Subway: Nan Luogu Xiang.

Susu ★★ VIETNAMESE Given its location, hidden away in a *hutong* to the east of the National Art Museum, just finding Susu brings a sense of satisfaction. Walk down West Alley No. 10 and turn the corner. There's no sign, but head through the red double doors at the end of the lane, and inside, you'll find an airy and stylish courtyard restaurant that offers up the most authentic Vietnamese food in Beijing. The food here is a testament to the skills of the head chef, who moved up from Ho Chi Minh City to take the helm of a kitchen known for its light and fresh flavors. Spring rolls mix an assortment of fresh herbs with traditional pork-and-shrimp filling, wrapped in translucent rice paper. The signature DIY *cha ca la vong* is a highlight, with turmeric-seasoned yellow fish fillets cooked in dill over a burner, to be assembled with fresh noodles, crumbled rice crackers, and a piquant peanut sauce. Lunch set-menus are a particularly good deal, with options like a classic pho beef noodle soup or crepe-like *banh xeo*. In summer and fall, be sure to snag a table outside under the shade of Susu's huge tree.

10 Qianliang Hutong (west of Dongsi Bei Dajie). www.susubeijing.com. ✆ **010/8400-2699.** Meal for two, RMB200–RMB400. Tues–Sun 11:30am–10pm. Subway: Dongsi.

INEXPENSIVE

Mr. Shi's Dumplings ★ CHINESE This modest hole-in-the-wall has some of the tastiest dumplings around. The traditional *jiaozi*, which are boiled, come with a variety of fillings: Pork, shrimp, and vegetarian options are mainstays. If you prefer the fried potstickers, known as *guotie*, the version here is delicious and a bit different than most, since they are not completely enclosed. The servings are large: Each order comes with 15 dumplings, so make sure you're hungry. The rest of the simple menu focuses on well-done basics like fried rice and stir-fried vegetables. The decor is a testament to the place's appeal among foreign visitors, with walls covered in international flags, colorful drawings, and appreciative comments by customers from around the world. The servers speak some English, unusual for such a local spot.

74 Baochao Hutong (north of Gulou Dongdajie). ✆ **010/8405-0399.** Meal for two, RMB50–RMB100. Daily 10:30am–10:30pm. Subway: Nan Luogu Xiang or Shichahai.

Chaoyang District (Around Sanlitun)

MODERATE

Bellagio ★★ TAIWANESE This bright and trendy chain specializing in Taiwanese food brings in the hipster crowds. There are multiple locations throughout town, and this newer branch in the Sanlitun shopping area is always bustling—probably because the food here is consistently tasty. The soft, silky cold tofu with preserved egg and peanuts is a great starter. The braised pork, *lurou*, where slices of pork belly meet soy gravy, is a moreish classic. Order the *sanbei ji* chicken, cooked in rice wine, sesame oil, and soy sauce, and you won't be disappointed. The enormous shaved ice desserts are also not to be missed—the peanut butter one is heaven! The waitstaff, mostly women with short, hip haircuts, provides service with a chipper attitude. The interiors are slick, with plush purple banquette seating, mirrored walls, and mosaic ceilings.

S2-31, 3/F, Sanlitun Taikoo Li, 19 Sanlitun Lu. www.bellagiocafe.com.cn. ✆ **010/6417-7040.** Meal for two, RMB150–RMB200. Daily 11am–10pm. Subway: Tuanjiehu.

Dadong Roast Duck (大董烤鸭店) ★★ CHINESE This popular institution is famed for its Beijing roast duck, and rightly so—it's done remarkably well here. The skin comes out crispy and the meat is moist. The accoutrements include a thin crepe-like wrapper, julienned green onion, and a tangy plum sauce. For an unexpected burst of flavor, dip the skin into the small platter of sugar provided—it makes for a sublime combination of sweet and salty. The birds, which come in whole or half orders, are known for being less greasy and fatty than other restaurants' versions. You can also order other duck dishes, including a flavorful soup, or a tasty fried rice with duck liver. The restaurant's decor is bright and modern: There are the obligatory round tables with lazy Susans, but the sleek white chairs and nice tableware create a more upscale feel than your typical duck restaurant. Bustling crowds keep the noise level at a low roar, making for a lively night out.

F1-2, Nanxincang International Mansion, A 22 Dongsishitiao. ✆ **010/5169-0329.** Meal for two, RMB300–RMB600. Subway: Dongsishitiao. Daily 11am–10pm.

Hatsune ★★ JAPANESE This cool California-style sushi restaurant is a mainstay on the Beijing restaurant scene for good reason. Hatsune's dozens of inventive, fusion-inspired sushi rolls are delicious. Check out the creatively named "Moto-Roll-Ah" (which has spicy tuna, snow crab, and avocado) and "Pimp My Roll" (a tasty mix of soft-shell crab and avocado). Sushi purists may not approve, but virtually everyone else will love the combination of attentive service, good food, and hip ambience. This branch in the Sanlitun Village shopping center is glitzier than the original. Enter through a waterfall glass door to two sushi bars and an outdoor terrace. The contemporary decor follows an underwater theme, with nice touches like the school-of-fish sculpture hanging from the ceiling.

3/F, Taikoo Li South, 19 Sanlitun Rd. www.hatsunesushi.com. ✆ **010/6415-3939.** Meal for two, RMB150–RMB300. Mon–Sun 11:30am–2pm, 5:30–10pm. Subway: Tuanjiehu.

Sake Manzo ★★ JAPANESE Part sake bar, part *izakaya*, this restaurant specializes in down-to-earth Japanese homestyle cooking. The house's delicious tofu is made fresh daily. Of course, the grilled food here is wonderful as well. Don't miss the grilled eel with rice. The beer-marinated fried chicken with vinegar sauce is addictive, as are the gingko nuts. Though not its main focus, the restaurant's sushi and sashimi are just as good as the hot dishes. Definitely spring for the small pots of sake, served hot or cold—there are more than 30 kinds to choose from. The bar's beautifully renovated space is large and airy, with clever touches like sake bottles for lighting. The vibe is every bit as chilled-out as the design would suggest.

8A Tuanjiehu Beisitiao. ✆ **010/6436-1608.** Meal for two, RMB200–RMB300. Daily 6pm–midnight. Subway: Tuanjiehu.

INEXPENSIVE

Qin Tang Fu (秦唐府) **★** SHAANXI From the framed paper cutouts to the handicrafts on the walls, colorful decor gives this bustling joint a charm not found in many local eateries. Customers come for the classics from the central Chinese province of Shaanxi—best known as home to the Terracotta Warriors. Top on the list is *Rou Jia Mo,* tasty pork patties cooked in an aromatic broth and served between rounds of unleavened bread (think of it as a Chinese version of a slider). Noodles are done particularly well, from wide green spinach noodles to chewy "long life" noodles made from yellow wheat flour. Qin Tang Fu also has some of the tastiest fried chicken this side of Colonel Sanders. Low tables and chairs, inexpensive prices, and a busy atmosphere make this a particularly fun stop for travelers with children.

69 Chaoyangmennei Nanxiaojie. ✆ **010/6559-8135.** Meal for two, RMB50–RMB100. Daily 9am–2:30pm, 5–10:30pm. Subway: Chaoyangmen, plus a 15-min. walk west.

Chaoyang District (Around the CBD)

MODERATE

Din Tai Fung ★★ CHINESE, DUMPLINGS This famed Taiwanese chain specializing in *xiaolongbao* (soup dumplings) lives up to its reputation at this sparkling outpost in Beijing. Biting into the delicately thin skin of the dumplings brings a sharp burst of flavorful broth and meaty filling. There's a variety of stuffings, but if you're lucky enough to be here during the right season, the hairy crab dumplings are stellar. If you like wonton soup, that's also well done here. This branch (there are multiple locations around town) is set in the basement of the splashy Parkview Green shopping mall, which showcases huge public art pieces. The decor is decidedly modern, with sleek wooden panels separating seating areas and whimsical, dumpling-shaped lights overhead. But it's the good service and yummy dumplings that keep loyal customers coming back. Families are especially welcome, with a play area set up for kids.

Basement level, Parkview Green mall, LG2-20, Parkview Green, 9 Dongdaqiao Lu. www.dintaifung.com.cn. ✆ **010/8562-6583.** Meal for two, RMB200–RMB300. Mon–Fri 11:30am–9:30pm, Sat–Sun 11am–10pm. Subway: Dongdaqiao.

Najia Xiaoguan (那家小馆) ★★ MANCHU A chain of restaurants that specialize in Qing-dynasty cuisine, Najia Xiaoguan combines beautiful decor and a certain regal grandeur with the low prices and slapdash service of a family-run street eatery. The best of their Beijing offerings is tucked away close to the Central Business District. Attendants will swing open the heavy wooden doors as you enter into a palatial two-story hall organized around a central courtyard festooned with lush vegetation. Elegant stringed pipa music plays as you tuck into Qing favorites, such as lamb on the bone, or sautéed chicken with walnut and garlic. The restaurant can be a nightmare to find, but it's worth the effort. Take the road south of Jianguomen Wai Dajie between the Bank of Beijing and Bank of Bangkok. You'll come to a cross street, Yong'an Xili. The restaurant is just to your right, identified by the wooden door and stone frame. There's no English on the signage, but perfectly respectable translations (and pictures) on the menu.

Yong'an Xili, behind the Xinhua Insurance Building, Jianguomen Wai Dajie (see access instructions above). ✆ **010/6567-3663.** Meal for two, RMB200–RMB300. Mon–Fri 11:30am–9:30pm. Subway: Yong'anli.

SHOPPING

Economists are fond of claiming that the thrifty Chinese save too much and need to consume more if the country has any hope of getting through the troubled waters ahead. Anyone who spends more than a day or two in Beijing would conclude that economists should probably get out a bit more. If you only had one word to describe the ideology of modern China, you'd have to plump for "consumerism." Shopping is the national sport. Spend, spend, and spend some more is the message drummed into China's willing citizens at every turn. Those who have done well in the country's recent economic boom (that is, almost everyone living in the major cities) seem more than happy to go along with the plan.

The capital's stores and markets sell everything from cashmere and silk to knockoff designer-label clothing to athletic wear, traditional art, cloisonné, lacquerware, furniture, Mao memorabilia, and enough miscellany to stuff Christmas stockings from now until eternity. Shopping in Beijing can be lots of fun. However, there are several caveats ("emptor" not least among them) that should be remembered. Firstly, it's now very, very hard to find anything that is genuinely antique; assuming you're not an oligarch or a hedge-fund manager, be skeptical of anyone who claims to be able to sell you a genuine piece for a price you can actually afford. Secondly, not all that is green and

Cafes & Coffee Shops

Cafe Zarah (46 Gulou Dong Dajie; www.cafezarah.com; ✆ **010/8403-9807**) is a well-established favorite among increasing numbers of indie cafes. It has the best iced lattes in the city, reliable free Wi-Fi, and a cozy space with exposed wood beams and rotating art exhibited on the walls. Curl up with a book at the spacious **Bookworm** (4 Sanlitun Nan Lu, behind Pacific Century shopping center, near The Loft; www.beijingbookworm.com; ✆ **010/6586-9507**). This Sanlitun fixture is popular among creative types, and though most of its book collection is a subscription-based lending library, it has a small shop with a decent selection of China- and Asia-focused books in the back. They also have free Wi-Fi and put on regular literary and cultural events. It would be churlish not to point out that **Starbucks** outlets are all over the city like a rash, though the shop that once occupied a prime piece of real estate *within* the Forbidden City has been evicted. There's one at the southernmost tip of Qianhai, which could be useful for post-stroll recuperation after a lake tour.

gleams in Beijing is jade. Indeed, the majority of it is colored glass. The same principle holds for pearls and most brand-name clothing. Lastly, despite China's "factory of the world" reputation, many products are nowhere near as cheap as you might expect. This is a result of the renminbi's relentless rise in value over the last decade and increasing costs faced by factory owners. It's also due to taxes, especially true toward the top end of the market. Luxury goods are significantly more expensive here than in the West (which also explains why most of the customers in your nearest luxury shopping street back home hail from China).

Finally, be wary of any English-speaking youngsters who claim to be **art students** and offer to take you to a special exhibit of their work. This is the oldest scam in the Beijing book (and there are a few) but it still catches the odd unsuspecting tourist out. The art, which you will be compelled to buy, almost always consists of assembly-line reproductions of famous (or not-so-famous) paintings offered at prices several dozen times higher than their actual value.

Top Shopping Areas

Any tale of Beijing's shopping districts must begin at **Wangfujing Dajie,** east of the Forbidden City. The street was overhauled in 1999, the south section turned into a pedestrian-only commercial avenue lined with shops, and it's still consumer central (two of Beijing's biggest malls—the **Beijing APM** and the **Oriental Plaza**—are here). Things are more pleasant, but scarcely less commercial, around **Nan Luogu Xiang** (p. 83). Gulou's most famous *hutong* is lined with boutiques but has become massively commercialized in recent years and doesn't necessarily deserve (or "fully deserve," depending on how ironic you're being) the huge crowds it attracts. The "new" Nan Luogu Xiang is arguably **Wudaoying Hutong,** near the Andingmen subway station. This has lots of indie craft shops, plus the excellent King's Joy restaurant (see p. 114) and a vampire-themed bar for good measure.

Wangfujing-style development has come to the famous old commercial district southwest of Tian'anmen Square. **Liulichang Xijie,** just east of Nanxinhua Jie, south of the Hepingmen subway station, is perhaps the nicest section of the **Liulichang** shopping district, filled with shops selling Buddhist bric-a-brac, traditional chops (stone ink-stamps), art, tea, and musty-looking "antiques." Nearby, running south from Qian Men, is **Qianmen Dajie.** It's one of the city's oldest commercial streets, originally built in 1436, but came in for a major overhaul ahead of the 2008 Games and is now a Disneyfied "Old Street," with architecture as "traditionally" Chinese as the Venetian architecture tends to be in Las Vegas. Running west from Qianmen Dajie is **Dazhalan Jie,** also known as "Dashilar," which has come in for similar treatment. This said, the vendors here at least tend to be the predevelopment shopkeepers, albeit operating out of new storefronts.

Probably the most dominant shopping development in Beijing is the complex formerly known as **Sanlitun Village.** It's grown tremendously in the years since it was built and is now divided into two areas: **Taikoo Li South (Taigu Li Nan Qu),** a generally middle-class shopping area with a mix of Western and Asian brands (including an Apple Store and the excellent Page One bookstore), and **Taikoo Li North (Taigu Li Bei Qu),** which has a heap of upmarket clothing brands and upscale restaurants. They face each other across a street lined with bars and knock-off DVD shops. Just to the west, on Gongren Tiyuchang Bei Lu, is **Yashow Market (Yaxiu Shichang),** formerly *the* place to buy all manner of fakes. It was closed at the time of writing but scheduled to reopen late in 2015 as *another* high-end mall. Ask your concierge if the counterfeiters have truly been chased from the temple.

Malls

Any attempt to list Beijing's major malls is, one, doomed to failure, and, two, probably pointless: For one thing, new malls are going up all the time; wherever you are (assuming you're staying in Dongcheng, Xicheng, or Chaoyang), you're unlikely to be more than one subway stop from a gleaming multistory altar to high commerce. For another, malls are unlikely to be places that overseas shoppers will want to visit. Most things you can take home will cost *more*, not less, in Beijing, and things that you *can't* get back home won't be sold in the local mall. Malls are super-useful for toilet facilities and food courts, but not much else, at least as far as the traveler is concerned. Beijing really comes into its own for knick-knacks, bric-a-brac, and knockoffs, and the listings below give an idea of where you can pick these up.

Markets

The three markets below are inexpensive, chaotic, and for the visitor, tremendously interesting. Payment is in cash, bargaining is universal, and pickpockets are plentiful.

Hongqiao Market (Hongqiao Jimao Shichang) & Toy City (Hongqiao Tianle Wanju Shichang) ★ Better known as the **Pearl Market,** Hongqiao Market lies just northeast of the Temple of Heaven. The way in is whiffy—there are seafood stalls and restaurants on the lower level—but head upstairs for the good stuff. Floors one and two have cheap silks, luggage, and Chinese curios, while the pearls can be found from the third floor up. The higher you climb, the more expensive (and theoretically better) they tend to be. Expect to bargain. If children are with you, don't miss the **Toy City** at the rear. It's packed with everything from PlayStation games to makeup dolls.

9 Tian Tan Lu. Daily 8:30am to 7pm. Subway: Tian Tan Dong Men.

Panjiayuan Flea Market (Panjiayuan Jiuhuo Shichang) ★★★ This is still sometimes referred to as the "Panjiayuan Antique Market," but those who favor truth over PR tend to go for the "flea" label instead. The lack of genuine antiques doesn't detract from the experience at all. It's a souvenir shopper's paradise, with serried ranks of traders selling calligraphy, jewelry, ceramics, teapots, ethnic clothing, Buddha statues, paper lanterns, Cultural Revolution memorabilia, PLA belts, little wooden boxes, Ming- and Qing-style furniture, pipes, opium scales, and the odd painted human skull. The market starts crazily early on Saturday and Sunday mornings, the best time to visit according to legend, while vendors tend to drift off after 4pm. Initial prices given to foreigners are always absurdly high—divide most opening gambits by at least 10.

South side of Panjiayuan Lu (inside southeast corner of Third Ring Road). Mon–Fri 8:30am–4:30pm, Sat–Sun 4:30am–4:30pm. Subway: Panjiayuan.

Silk Market (Xiushui Fuzhuang Shichang) ★★ Now that Yashow appears to have fallen by the wayside, the Silk Market is the place you'll need to go if you're keen on knockoffs. Forget about silk; rather, look for the tiny (but probably only tiny) imperfections in otherwise perfectly respectable "Louis Vuitton" handbags or "North Face" jackets. It seems that the fakers are being squeezed hard in Beijing these days, so it's not beyond the realm of possibility that these kinds of goods will be hidden away (or, heaven forbid, are in police hands). Under such circumstances, be assured knockoff sellers will find you before you find them. However, be wary about being led away from the building. This is a crowded, six-story maze of stalls with a large selection of shoes and clothing, and vendors can be fierce, so expect to battle hard.

14 Dongdaqiao Lu. Daily 9:30am–9pm. Subway: Yonganli.

NIGHTLIFE

If you measure a city's nightlife by the number of chances for debauchery it offers, then Beijing has never held (and probably will never hold) a candle to such neon-lit Babylons as Shanghai and Hong Kong. If, instead, you measure nightlife by its diversity, the Chinese capital rivals any major city in Asia.

Such was not always the case. As recently as a decade ago, Beijing's populace routinely tucked itself into bed under a blanket of Mao-inspired Puritanism shortly after nightfall, leaving visitors with one of two tourist-approved options: Attend Beijing opera and acrobatic performances in a sterile theater, or wander listlessly around the hotel in search of a drink to make sleep come faster.

Since then, the government has realized there is money to be made on both sides of the Earth's rotation. The resulting relaxation in nocturnal regulations, set against the backdrop of Beijing residents' historical affinity for cultural diversions, has helped remake the city's nightlife. Opera and acrobatics are still available, but now in more interesting venues, and to these have been added an impressive range of other worthwhile cultural events: teahouse theater, puppet shows, intimate traditional music concerts, live jazz, even the occasional subtitled film.

This diversity continues with Beijing's drinking and dance establishments, of which there are scores. Some are even beginning to rival Shanghai's for style and, unfortunately, price. With the opening of a few modern dance clubs, the city's cheesy old discos are thankfully no longer the only dance option, although the latter can still be tremendously entertaining for kitsch value. The same goes for karaoke, a favorite in China as it is in Japan. Foreigner-Chinese interaction in bars hasn't progressed much beyond the sexual exploitation rampant in the 1920s and 1930s, but this is by no means a necessary dynamic. The traveler not afraid to bumble through language barriers can often connect with local people over a bottle or two of beer.

Bars, Pubs & Clubs

Beijing's oldest drinking district is **Sanlitun.** The name comes from Sanlitun Lu, a north-south strip of drinking establishments east of the Workers' Stadium between the East Second and Third ring roads that at one time contained practically all of the city's bars. Though the official street sign reads Sanlitun Bei Lu, the strip is more commonly known as Bar Street (Sanlitun Jiuba Jie). It has been joined by other bars in the Xingfu Cun area to the west and scattered around the stadium area. Bars here are rowdy and raunchy, and are packed to overflowing on weekends.

A similar vibe exists around the **back lakes** of Qianhai and Houhai. Though a handful of these bars benefit from terraces next to the lake, they are designed primarily to appeal to Chinese revelers: Think generic bottled lager, plenty of chain-smoking, and entertainment provided by karaoke, dancing girls, or cover bands. Stop for a drink if you're out for a walk, by all means, but there should be no great rush to head back after dark, lovely views notwithstanding.

The **Wudaokou** area in Haidian is perhaps the cheapest and most genuinely mixed of Beijing's drinking districts. This is the city's student district, and dive bars and dance clubs congregate around the gates of several universities. Expect to meet as many foreigners majoring in Chinese as Chinese English-language majors, alongside the odd aspiring writer too.

By far the most salubrious spot for drinking is the **Gulou area,** where "artisan" bars dominate the scene. These are often tiny, convivial places, tucked away in obscure *hutong* and difficult to find if you're without directions. Many specialize along the lines of cocktail alchemy, single-malt whiskey, or home-brewed craft beer. The anti-hipster may find some of them flat-out pretentious—listen for the scoffs of derision directed at anyone naive enough to request a Tsingtao—but many combine warmth and friendliness with drinks that are genuinely different. The best are listed below.

Amilal ★★ BAR This beautifully laid-back Gulou bar is *the* spot for whiskey lovers and raconteurs. It's in a renovated courtyard dwelling that has been decorated with secondhand furniture and subdivided into a series of semi-secluded spaces, each fitting no more than a couple of tables. The owner is from Inner Mongolia, and as well as having an obvious penchant for imported single-malts (there's almost nothing else behind the tiny bar), there's an appreciation of folk music, with Mongolia and Kazakh bands performing occasional impromptu sets. It's nowhere near as rowdy as other bars in the area, but there's nowhere better for a quiet tipple.

48 Shoubi Hutong (south of 66 Gulou Dong Dajie). ✆ **010/8404-1416.** Whiskey RMB50 a glass. Subway: Andingmen, plus 15-min. walk.

Bar at Migas ★★ BAR/CLUB This hugely popular rooftop terrace and bar is attached to a Spanish restaurant, but it's best known for its rocking dance parties. A well-heeled crowd comes for an industrial-chic dance floor with a skyline view. Local and visiting DJs spin house, soul, disco, and funk. There's an extensive cocktail list. An additional bar has been opened downstairs, adjoining the restaurant, and it offers cozy nooks and crannies for grabbing seats throughout the spacious interior. This bar was built to resemble a beach shack, and its low-key vibe is a nice touch. But when the weather is good, the action is on the rooftop. Weekends bring in big crowds, although the scene stays relaxed.

On top of Migas restaurant, 6/F Nali Patio, 81 Sanlitun Lu. ✆ **010/5208-6061.** Bottled beers RMB30–RMB50, cocktails RMB50–RMB80. Subway: Tuanjiehu, plus 15-min. walk.

El Nido ★ BAR This local dive bar began with the simplest of ideas: Provide a wide selection of international beers and a few picnic tables and the customers will come. The formula has worked like magic. El Nido is the ultimate *hutong* drinking hole, with ample varieties of alcohol from around the world, beginning with reasonably priced French wine and moving on to imported beers from Belgium and Germany. There are even specialty drinks like absinthe. The location is just a few steps from the very hip Fangjia Hutong theater complex, and you'll find expatriates and trendy young Chinese here on any night of the week. Service is patchy, especially on busy nights, so just help yourself to the bottles on the shelves.

59 Fangjia Hutong (Off Dongsi Bei Dajie). ✆ **010/8402-9495.** Local Harbin beer RMB10 a bottle, German or Belgian beer RMB30–RMB35 a bottle. Subway: Beixinqiao or Yonghegong.

Great Leap Brewing ★★★ PUB Beer-lovers, rejoice! This microbrewery, which got its start in a tiny *hutong* space, has made a big splash with its roomy second location. Great Leap's expansion into the popular Sanlitun neighborhood brings in the crowds. The rowdy but convivial atmosphere is reflected in the decibel levels. Seating is casual, on simple but stylish wood tables and benches. Started in 2010, Great Leap gets credit for introducing craft brews to Beijing. Try the popular Honey Ma Gold (which has a slight whiff of Sichuan peppercorn), the smooth, amber-colored Cinnamon Rock Ale, or the malty and fragrant Banana Wheat. The food here is surprisingly tasty as well, with good old-fashioned cheeseburgers, beer-battered onion rings, fried chicken nuggets, and crispy chicken wings.

12B Xinzhong Jie. www.greatleapbrewing.com. ✆ **010/6416-6887.** Craft beers from RMB35–RMB50, cheeseburger with fries RMB50. Subway: Dongzhimen, plus a 15-min. walk.

LAN Club ★★ CLUB This opulently luxe bar and club was designed by French superstar Philippe Starck over a decade ago, but it still has its wow factor. The enormous interior is eclectic and wild: Think rhino heads, Chinese vases, gold-plated Kalashnikov lamps, Hindu icons, animal-print seats, and velvet chaises. Then there's the Renaissance-style paintings hung upside down from the ceiling. In addition to the bar and lounge, there's also a restaurant, a cigar room, and several dozen private VIP rooms. Everything here is over the top, including the toilets—don't miss the individual bathrooms that come with mirrored walls, a silver armchair, and swan-shaped faucets. The drink menu is enormous, of course, with a huge array of European and New World wines; the beverages are delivered by a rigorously trained staff. Food covers basic and fusion Chinese and sushi territory, and there are lounge acts and visiting DJs as entertainment, but the real fun here comes from ogling the surroundings.

4/F, LG Twin Towers, 12B Jianguomen Wai Dajie. www.lanclub.cc. ✆ **010/5109-6012.** Bottled beers RMB50, cocktails start at RMB80. Subway: Yong'anli.

Mai Bar ★★ BAR Despite the grungy surrounds, Mai Bar is renowned for serving up the kind of creative cocktails you'd normally expect in the city's five-star hotel lounges. Mojitos and martinis are dribbled over giant ice balls, and local ingredients such as Chinese dates, figs, or hawthorn apples are thrown into the mix. Beer lovers can get a better variety elsewhere (see "Great Leap Brewing," above), but there's still something quite nice about helping yourself to a bottle from the fridge. The bar has a tiny outdoor section, more "alley" than "patio," which creates a cozy behind-the-bike-sheds kind of camaraderie among the mostly young, non-Chinese revelers.

40 Bei Luogo Xiang (10-min. walk south from North 2nd Ring Rd., on the left). ✆ **138-1125-2641.** Bottled beers RMB30–RMB50, cocktails RMB50–RMB80. Subway: Andingmen, plus 15-min. walk.

Q Bar ★★ BAR This lounge bar set the original standard for mixed cocktails in the capital, and it remains ever-popular. Don't be put off by the shabby interior of the hotel that houses Q Bar. Once you emerge on the top floor, you're in an oasis of style, dim lighting, and good music. A long bar is set against windows with panoramic views. The expansive rooftop seating, with its comfy booths, is a huge draw during warmer months. DJs spin lounge and house music most nights. The crowd is a mix of Beijing's old-timers and young professionals. The excellent martinis (try the lychee-flavored one or the Q Bar Mintini) are joined by an extensive cocktail list. Prices are comparable to other top spots in town. The bar also stocks an extensive range of single malt Scotches as well as Irish and American whiskeys, for those who prefer their drinks straight up.

On top of Eastern Inn Hotel, 6 Baijiazhuang Lu (south end of Sanlitun Nanlu). ✆ **010/6595-9239.** Beers RMB30, cocktails RMB40–RMB90. Subway: Tuanjiehu, plus a 15-min. walk.

Temple Bar ★ BAR One of the hot spaces for live music in Beijing, this midsize bar on the second floor of a *hutong* courtyard near the historic Drum and Bell Towers draws on a loyal fan base. An unassuming entrance leads up to a large interior with a few sofas and tables and a low stage. The decor is minimal, but the vibe is lively. In the middle of the room is a retractable set of stairs that can be lowered from the ceiling, giving access to the terrace. The huge space there has an outdoor bar and offers stunning *hutong* views. Good local rock bands play here, with performances most nights of the week. With cheap drinks, friendly atmosphere, and good service, this dive pub is rightly popular. It stays open into the wee hours, still going strong after others leave off.

Door #202, Bldg. B, 206 Gulou Dong Dajie. www.templebarlivehouse.com. ✆ **131-6107-0713.** Beers on tap RMB20–RMB50, mixed drinks RMB40–RMB50. Subway: Shichahai.

Xiu ★★ COCKTAIL LOUNGE The very exclusive feel of the Park Hyatt's palatial indoor lounge and rooftop terrace bar has made Xiu a hotspot in Beijing's ultraluxe nightlife scene. Located on the sixth floor of the hotel, the interior design mixes traditional Chinese architecture and contemporary lines to stunning effect. But it's the outdoor terrace, designed like a traditional courtyard, with stellar views of the city, that's the real draw. Bartenders mix creative but pricey cocktails like lychee martinis, while live bands rally the dance floor. If you're not in a dancing mood, there's plenty of space to sit and gawk. This is where the city's beautiful people gather to see and be seen. Looking your best is par for the course: the door policy is tough, so if you fancy joining the young, fashionable crowd, be dressed to impress.

6/F, Park Hyatt Hotel, 2 Jianguomen Wai Dajie. ✆ **010/8567-1108.** Cocktails and wine by the glass start at RMB70, Moët & Chandon champagne RMB880. Subway: Guomao.

Performing Arts

BEIJING OPERA

A relatively young opera form dating from only 300 years to the early Qing dynasty, Beijing Opera (Jingju) dazzles as much as it grates. Performances are loud and long, with dialogue sung on a screeching five-note scale and accompanied by a cacophony of gongs, cymbals, drums, and strings. This leaves most first-timers exhausted, but the exquisite costumes, elaborate face paint, and martial-arts-inspired movements ultimately make it worthwhile. Several theaters now offer shortened programs more amenable to the foreign attention span, sometimes with English subtitles and plot summaries.

Most tourists on tours are taken to the bland, cinema-style **Liyuan Theater (Liyuan Juchang)** inside the Qianmen Hotel, where nightly performances at 7:30pm cost RMB80 to RMB480. The venues below offer essentially the same performances in much better traditional settings.

Huguang Guild Hall (Huguang Huiguan Xilou) ★ OPERA This combination museum-theater, housed in a complex of traditional buildings with gray tile roofs and bright red gables, has a connection with Beijing Opera dating back to 1830. To the right of the main entrance is a small museum filled with old opera robes and photos of famous performers (including the legendary Mei Lanfang), probably interesting only to aficionados. On the left is the expertly restored theater, a riot of color with a beautifully adorned traditional stage, paper lanterns hung from the high ceilings, and gallery seating on all three sides. Subtitles are in Chinese only, but brochures contain brief plot explanations in English. Performances take place nightly at 7:30pm.

3 Hufang Lu (at intersection with Luomashi Dajie; plaza out front contains colorful opera mask sculpture). ✆ **010/6352-9134.** Tickets RMB150–RMB580. Subway: Hepingmen, then 10-min. walk south.

Mei Lanfang Grand Theatre (Mei Lanfang Da Juyuan) ★ OPERA This brand-new, multistory theater was built specifically for Beijing Opera. The performance quality and times vary, so be sure to check the schedule ahead of time. If you don't want to chance sitting through a bad Beijing opera show, the ultramodern glass theater and the giant bust of Mei Lanfang in the foyer are worth viewing on their own.

32 Ping'anli Xi Dajie. ✆ **010/5833-1288.** RMB100–RMB880. Performances usually begin at 7:30pm but check ahead. Subway: Chegongzhuang, then walk south for 5 min.

Teahouse of Prince Gong's Mansion (Gong Wang Fu Chaguan) ★ OPERA Not a traditional opera venue, Prince Gong's teahouse is nevertheless picturesque, with a rare bamboo motif on the exterior beams and columns and an intimate interior outfitted with polished wood tables and pleasing tea paraphernalia. This is opera for tourists, kept short and sweet, with a guided tour of the surrounding gardens included in the price (see Prince Gong's Mansion). There are several performances daily until 4:30pm.

17 Liuyin Jie. ✆ **010/6616-8149.** Tickets RMB70, including entry to Prince Gong's Mansion. Signposted in English at top of Qianhai Xi Dajie (running north off Ping'an Dadao opposite north gate of Beihai Park; turn left at sign and follow alley past large parking lot. Entrance marked with huge red lanterns). Subway: Beihai North.

ACROBATICS

China's acrobats are justifiably famous, and probably just a little bit insane. This was the only traditional Chinese art form to receive Mao's explicit approval (back flips, apparently, don't count as counterrevolution). Not culturally stimulating, they're nevertheless highly recommended, especially if you haven't already seen the amazing **ERA: Intersection of Time** in Shanghai (see p. 253). Should you have seen acrobatics elsewhere, these three Beijing offerings can be skipped. Impressive though the artistry and razzmatazz are, the shows are fairly generic.

The most famous venue is probably the **Tianqiao Acrobatics Theatre (Tianqiao Zaiji Juchang),** at 95 Tianqiao Shichang Jie (✆ **010/6303-7449;** subway: Taoranting, then 5-min. taxi ride), located on the west side of the Temple of Heaven. The Beijing Acrobatics Troupe performs nightly shows here at 7pm. Tickets cost RMB180 to RMB580. The acrobats of **Chaoyang Theatre (Chaoyang Juchang),** at 36 Dong Sanhuan Bei Lu (✆ **010/6507-2421;** subway: Hujialou) perform twice nightly at 5:15pm and 7:15pm, with tickets costing RMB180 up to RMB880. The other option is the **Tiandi Theater** (10 Dongzhimen Nan Dajie; ✆ **135-5252-7373;** subway: Dongsi Shitiao), which has nightly shows at 7:15pm, with tickets going for RMB180 to RMB680. Take your pick, depending on where you are staying. Those in Dongcheng should go for the Tianqiao performance, while those in Chaoyang should pick between Chaoyang and Tiandi, depending on which is closer.

TEAHOUSE THEATER

Snippets of Beijing opera, cross-talk (stand-up) comedy, acrobatics, traditional music, singing, and dancing flow across the stage as you sip tea and nibble snacks. If you don't have time to see these kinds of performances individually, the teahouse is a perfect solution. Performances change nightly at **Lao She Teahouse (Lao She Chaguan),** at 3 Qianmen Xi Dajie, west of Qianmen on street's south side (✆ **010/6303-6830;** tickets RMB180–RMB380), a somewhat garishly decorated teahouse that always includes opera and acrobatics. It pays to buy the more expensive tickets, as rear views are obstructed. Nightly shows take place at 7:50pm.

LIVE MUSIC

Beijing has the best live-music scene in China. The midsize venues listed below are the main destinations for established local and international bands. However, there's heaps of singer-songwriter bohemian action in the Gulou area. The up-and-coming **Wudaoying Hutong,** running parallel to the Second Ring Road just east of the Yonghegong subway station, has several bars that host local bands and decent-quality open-mike nights. South of here is **Jianghu Bar** (7 Dongmianhua Hutong; RMB30 and up; subway: Nan Luogu Xiang), with performances every day other than Monday, including weekly jazz and blues jams. **Temple Bar** (Building B, 206 Gulou Dong Dajie; subway: Shichahai) is another dependable low-key option that runs out of a hard-to-find single room just off Gulou Dong Dajie. Walk beneath the archway beside no. 206 and head upstairs from an entrance next to the rear parking lot.

MAO Livehouse ★ LIVE MUSIC Tucked into one of the single-story storefronts in the historic Drum and Bell Towers neighborhood, MAO is a popular stop for Chinese bands and touring alternative acts. The unfinished, industrial interior feels more organic than a neon-flashing techno dance club. Rudimentary design notwithstanding, MAO Livehouse boasts a state-of-the-art sound system. There's a decent amount of space if you combine the dance floor, outlying walkways, and the small loft. Bands start around 8:30pm nightly. The ever-popular pedestrian shopping area Nan Luogu Xiang is just around the corner.

111 Gulou Dong Dajie. http://mao-music.com. ✆ **010/6402-5080.** Beers start at RMB10; cover charges vary, from free to RMB50–RMB250. Subway: Nan Luogu Xiang.

The Star Live ★ LIVE MUSIC The biggest and most secure of the venues listed here, Star Live attracts international bands too cool/unpopular to play the big stadium shows. When it's not doing rock music, it may well be hosting a dance party.

79 Hepingli Xi Jie. ✆ **010/6425-5677.** Entry costs depend on band but expect to pay RMB50 and up. Subway: Yonghegong.

Yugong Yishan ★★★ LIVE MUSIC This wonderful performance space is the best live-music venue in Beijing, period. The variety is astounding, with performances of everything from death metal to Mongolian throat-singers. As with MAO Livehouse (see above), the owners have been shunted from pillar to post over the years, so while you can be fairly sure the venue will still exist by the time you read this, it's well worth checking to see that it's still in the same spot.

West Courtyard, 3-2 Zhangzigong Lu. www.yugongyishan.com. ✆ **010/6404-2177.** Tickets from RMB50 and up. Subway: Zhangzigong Lu.

OTHER PERFORMING ARTS VENUES

Beijing hosts a growing number of international music and theater events every year, and its own increasingly respectable troupes—including the Beijing Symphony Orchestra—give frequent performances.

Among the most popular venues for this sort of thing is the **National Centre for Performing Arts** (see p. 75), the modern egg-shaped glass structure next to the Great Hall of the People, the **Forbidden City Concert Hall** inside Zhongshan Park (✆ **010/6559-8285**), and the **Beijing Concert Hall (Beijing Yinyue Ting)** at Bei Xinhua Jie in Xuanwu (✆ **010/6605-5812**). The **Poly Theater (Baoli Dasha Guoji Juyuan)**, in the Poly Plaza complex on the East Third Ring Road (northeast exit of Dongsi Shitiao subway station), also hosts many large-scale performances, including the occasional ballet (✆ **010/6506-5343**). For information on additional venues and the shows they're hosting, check one of the expat magazines (see p. 3).

BEIJING FOR KIDS

While Beijing's historical sights may be captivating for adults, kids are likely to lose interest after a short while. However, there's plenty to keep the little ones happy during a trip to the capital. **Qianhai** and **Houhai** have pedal boats and get even more exciting in winter when the lakes ice up and the Shichahai area turns into one giant ice rink (skates and sleds can be rented at various points around either lake). Elsewhere, Beihai Park and the Temple of Heaven both have **kite-flying** fun and provide great places to get out and run around. The **Toy City** (see p. 121) will appear far more heavenly to younger children than the real Temple of Heaven just to the west. And on clear days, the goliath new **Olympic Park Observation Tower,** at the south entrance to the Olympic Forest Park (see p. 91), may be worth visiting for the thrill factor alone. The specific attractions listed below offer more long-lasting diversions, and could easily take up half a day or more.

Beijing Aquarium (Beijing Haiyangguan) ★ZOO/AQUARIUM The world's largest (allegedly) inland aquarium attracted plenty of opposition from local environmental groups when it opened in 1999, and the logic of keeping countless marine animals so far from the sea is questionable. Efforts to compensate are obvious—an environmental message is laid on thickly in the Chinese captions. Introducing Chinese children to the concept that shrimp can exist somewhere other than in a sea of garlic sauce has to be commended, although descriptions of "horrible" sharks show there's a ways to go in its efforts. **Dolphin shows** at 11am and 3pm pack in the one-child families. **Beijing Zoo (Beijing Dongwuyuan)** lies to the south, and despite improvements to some areas—notably the **Panda House**—the zoo is more likely to traumatize your child than provide entertainment. It is possible to take a boat from the canal south of the aquarium to the Summer Palace.

18B Gaoliang Qiao Xie Jie. ✆ **010/6217-6655.** Admission RMB120 includes admission to Beijing Zoo; children RMB60; 2 children (under 1.2m/4 ft.) free with 1 paid adult ticket. Daily 7:30am–5pm. Subway: Beijing Zoo.

Chaoyang Park (Chaoyang Gongyuan) ★ PARK/MUSEUM Second only to the Olympic Forest Park (see p. 91) in size, Chaoyang Park is huge and rambling and makes for a pleasant stroll beside lakes and across boardwalks. Youngsters will enjoy the arcades, the "Happy Monkey Tree Top Adventure Park" (complete with zip lines) and "Water World," where there's a massive man-made beach (RMB120 weekends, RMB80 weekdays). Perhaps the main reason to visit is the ParkSony ExploraScience (Suoni Tan Meng) museum within. Kids of all ages will love the interactive displays, including highlights like robotic dogs, musical sculptures, soap-bubble rings blown out of a machine, and light-and-sound-distortion machines. The interior is futuristic and very high-tech. Add in live shows on science (in Chinese), and this becomes the closest thing to a modern children's museum in Beijing. Your "smart" card, provided on arrival, helps activate each hands-on science station (English translations are provided). This is a fun place for a family to spend a few hours, plus you can enjoy all the fresh air and green space of Chaoyang Park outside. Buy your tickets at the museum booth outside the park's south or east gates, and you won't have to buy park tickets as well.

Inside Chaoyang Park, 1 Chaoyang Gongyuan Nan Lu. ✆ **010/6501-8800.** Explora-Science tickets RMB30. Mon–Fri 9:30am–5:30pm, Sat–Sun 9:30am–6:30pm, closed second Mon and Tues of every month. Subway: Tuanjiehu, plus 10-min. taxi ride.

Happy Magic Watercube Waterpark ★★ SWIMMING Formerly the site of the swimming pool where Michael Phelps won all that gold during the 2008 Olympics, the National Aquatics Center has been converted into a new waterpark, which swarms with ecstatic children careering down waterslides and playing in the wave pool. The various rides, some of which pile up to four guests in giant inner tubes and are titled "Tornado" and "Bulletbowl," offer thrills for all ages. Adults can laze in the hot Jacuzzi pools. It's an ingenious use of a former Olympic space.

Beichen Lu, Olympic Green. ✆ **010/8437-2030.** Free admission for children under 1.2m (3¾ ft.); RMB180 for children between 1.2 and 1.4m (3¾–4½ ft.); RMB200 for adults and children over 1.4m (4½ ft.). Daily 10am–9:30pm. Subway: Olympic Green or Olympic Sports Center.

Happy Valley Amusement Park (Beijing Huanle Gu) ★ AMUSEMENT PARK Beijing's answer to Disneyland, this theme park features stomach-turning roller coasters and themed sections called Shangri-La Land, Mayan Aztec Village, and Greek Town. Lines for rides can be 3 hours long, so arrive early and avoid the weekends. Opened by overseas Chinese investors and designed with the help of Westerners, the roller coasters are state-of-the-art.

Xiaowuji Bei Lu (nr. southeast corner of Fourth Ring Rd.). ✆ **010/6738-9898.** Admission RMB160 adults, RMB80 for children between 1.2 and 1.4m (3¾–4½ ft.), free for kids under 1.2m (4 ft.). Apr 1-Nov 14 daily 9am–7:30pm (last ticket at 5:30pm); Nov 15–Mar 31 10am–5pm. Subway: Panjiayuan, then 10-min. taxi ride.

DAY TRIPS FROM BEIJING

The most essential day trip from Beijing scarcely needs mentioning. The mountains across which the Great Wall slithers are within city limits but far enough out of town to require an excursion. The most touristy section, Badaling, could possibly be seen in a whistle-stop half-day, but for the best experience, travel farther out and give over an entire day to the experience, more if you have time. Elsewhere within Beijing are the Ming Tombs, while the high-speed rail that hurtles into Hebei is the route to the royal retreat of Chengde.

5

THE GREAT WALL ★★★

Even after you dispense with the myths that it is a single continuous structure, or that it can be seen from space, China's best-known attraction is still a mind-boggling achievement. The easternmost section of the Great Wall (Chang Cheng) begins at Shanhaiguan on the Bohai Sea and continues, in fits and starts, all the way to the dusty fort of Jiayuguan on the edges of the Gobi Desert in China's far west. Its origins date from the Warring States Period (453–221 B.C.), when rival kingdoms began building defensive walls to thwart each other's armies. The king of Qin, who eventually conquered the other states to become the first emperor of a unified China, conscripted around 300,000 laborers to combine the walls into a more or less uninterrupted rampart. During the Han dynasty (206 B.C.–A.D. 220), the wall was extended farther west, with subsequent dynasties adding their own bits and branches. It's difficult to pin down the wall's exact length, but it's thought to stretch out for at least 6,690km (4,160 miles). Astonishingly, this figure is at the most *conservative* end of the various estimates.

Most sections of the Great Wall visible north of Beijing were reconstructed by the Ming dynasty (1368–1644) in an (ultimately vain) effort to defend against attack by Manchus and Mongols from the north. The three sections recommended, presented from easiest and most popular to less traversed and remote, are: **Mutianyu, Simatai,** and **Jiankou.**

The Great Wall will remain great, no matter what's thrown at it. However, hikers should note that more and more sites have begun to follow the path that **Badaling** charted way back in the 1950s. This involves a distinctly commercial strain of "development"—think huge motorcoach parking-lots, bustling shopping plazas, grand ticket halls, and ever-spiraling entrance charges, not to mention fencing off otherwise uninterrupted stretches of the wall that *belong* to this section, or that. Mutianyu has long had its ski-lift and toboggan rides, while Simatai now has an imitation water town surrounding its main gate and requires hikers to state their intentions a day in advance. **Badaling** remains the most crassly developed section, but expect tour groups elsewhere too.

The Great Wall is so vast that no one person, company, or government department can develop it all, and there are plenty of undiscovered and wild sections. However, it is getting harder and harder to find them independently, which is where a local guide can really come in handy (see box). If you want to do it all yourself, the best advice is to stick to these "known" sections of the wall and be prepared to walk as far away from the main entry point as possible.

Getting to the wall currently involves a fairly difficult public bus ride, bargaining a taxi, or joining an organized tour. These are best organized from hostels and hotels rather than with street-hawkers. If you opt to join a tour, be clear about what is involved. Ask: Is the trip *direct* to the Great Wall? How long will I get to spend on the wall itself? Are there any (normally unwanted) side trips? The tours that roaming agents offer around the Forbidden City and Tian'anmen Square are a great example of what you're looking to *avoid*. These are cheap (generally RMB100), but you'll be forced to travel *en masse* to Badaling, the most touristy and unpleasant section of the wall, and will have little freedom, either when you're on the wall, or in terms of being press-ganged into food-and-shopping side trips. Most Badaling tours pass by the Ming Tombs on the way back, but again, the stop will be brief and fairly pointless. Moreover, these buses leave only when they are full, giving a good idea of the cattle-truck mentality at work.

The lack of genuine mass transit has always been a double-edged sword for travelers. It makes getting to the best bits that much harder, or more expensive, but crowds tend to be thinner once you're there. The new Jingshen high-speed railway line, linking Beijing and Shenyang in Liaoning province, may change this. At press time, it was still a few years off completion, but stations are expected to be built near the satellite towns of Huairou and Miyun, both gateways to remote sections of the wall. While the railway may become an alternative way to get to the wall in the future, it may equally spur "development" which, as Badaling proves, can be a mixed blessing.

MUTIANYU ★

This wonderfully scenic 3km (2-mile) section of the wall has been heavily developed, and may even attract the odd traffic jam in summer. There is an irritating "shopping street" around the main ticket office (a peculiarly modern curse visited on many Chinese tourist attractions), two **cable cars,** and a fun-but-gimmicky **toboggan ride.** It's certainly well on its way to becoming Badaling, Mark II. However, with 23 watchtowers in total, Mutianyu is a

Day Trips from Beijing

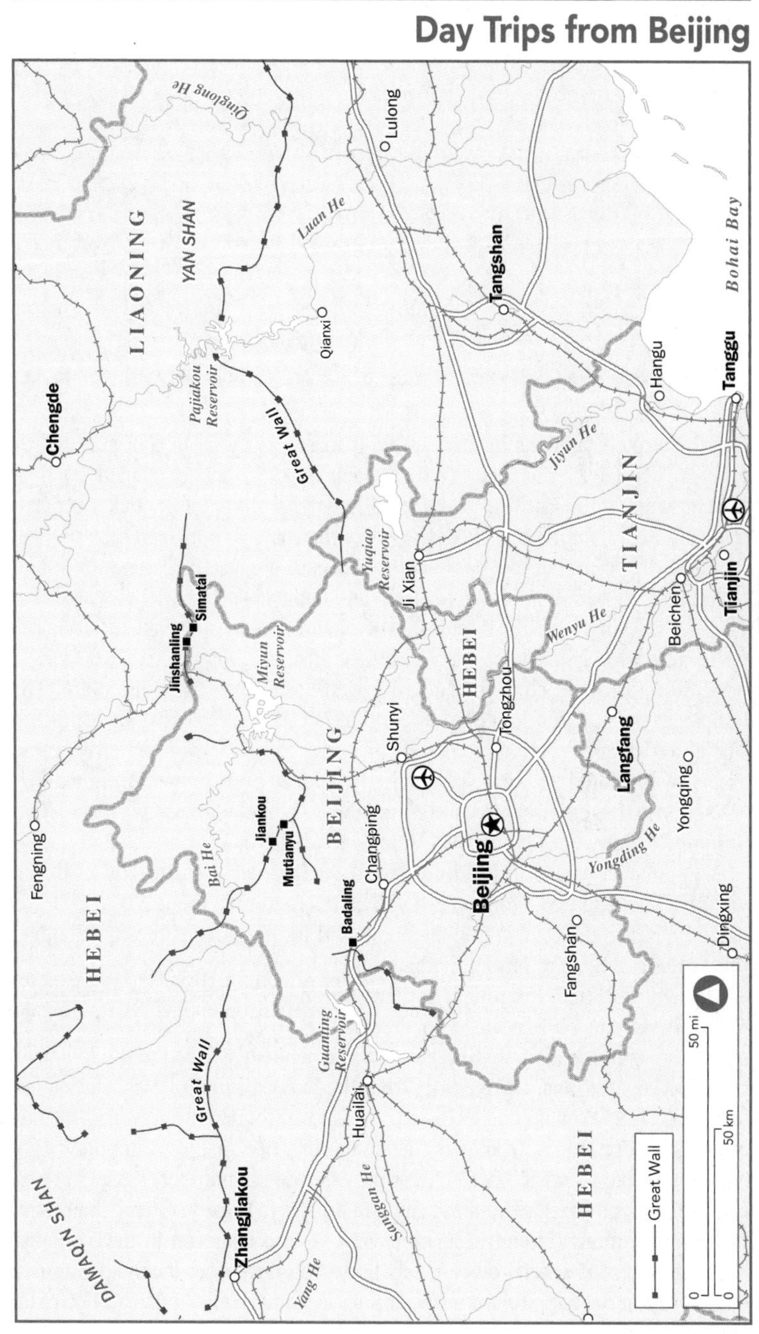

ON THE wild wall

Sections of the Great Wall listed below are easy to reach and suitably stunning, but they represent only a part of what the Wall has to offer. People with time and an inclination to explore beyond these sections are strongly encouraged to join one of the excellent, usually multiday "Wild Wall" trips to the crumbling **"unofficial" sections of the Wall** that snake through more remote areas north of Beijing. Most weekend trips cost RMB3,600 and are based at one of two **modernized farmhouses** (one better outfitted than the other). The fee includes guided hikes, two nights' accommodation, six meals, drinks and snacks, research and conservation contribution, and a souvenir book. Details and booking information about weekend trips, day hikes, and "extreme" treks can be found on the Wild Wall website at **www.wildwall.com**.

lengthy stretch, and it's not too difficult to get away from the worst of the crowds. Mutianyu was first restored back in 1986 and expanded by three watchtowers in the last few years. It's a lengthy walk from the ticket office to the wall, and a shuttle bus (RMB10) plies the route. It's a steep hike up from the drop-off point, but two cable-car routes ease the strain. The newer, longer one is an enclosed gondola-style affair, and connects ground level with Tower 14 (RMB50 single, RMB80 return). The older lift is an open, ski-lift-style ride up to Tower 6. It forms an easy circuit with the toboggan (RMB60 single, RMB80 return), which loops back down to earth from the same point. This looks tacky when you first clap eyes on it, but ultimately proves a lot of fun. The newly opened section of wall, from Tower 21 to 23, is particularly scenic, and crowds should be fairly sparse. Sadly, a fence prevents you from walking farther onto the tempting unrestored sections. The ticket office is open 6:30am to 6pm (7:30am–6pm Nov–Mar). Admission is RMB45.

A popular circuit is to head up with the larger cable car to Tower 14 and walk back to Tower 6, from where you can descend via the toboggan. Unfortunately, return tickets can only be purchased for the same cable car/toboggan link, so you'll need to buy individual tickets to make this work.

Mutianyu is 90km (56 miles) north of Beijing. Many hotels and hostels run tours. **Taxis** can be bargained for between RMB550 and RMB600 for the return day trip. It's also possible to visit independently. Head to the Dongzhimen Wai **bus** terminal (take exit H from the Dongzhimen subway station and turn left). Look for bus no. 916, which departs for Huairou every 10 to 15 minutes. There are two routes on the same line: one fast, one stopping (look out for the character for "fast"—快, *kuai*—beside the number). Once in Huairou (60 min. approx.), get out at Mingzhu Square (Mingzhu Guangchang) and pick up a minibus (*miandi*) (30 min.; RMB15) to take you to the Mutianyu roundabout, from which you can walk north uphill to reach the main entrance.

Tip: If you opt for public transportation, ignore all unsolicited advice at the Dongzhimen Wai bus terminal. A common scam is to claim the bus you want has been canceled and to invite you onto another apparently going in the same direction. Scammers often dress up in bus-driver garb to make a more convincing case. If someone approaches you and speaks to you in English, be suspicious. Follow their advice and you may well end up somewhere you really don't want to go.

SIMATAI ★★

The trek from Jinshanling (see box) to Simatai was one of *the* classic Great Wall walks until Simatai closed its series of watchtowers for renovation in 2010. Simatai reopened several years later with barriers to block the path of any hikers who hadn't paid their dues, and a vast new commercial development back down at ground level. The **Gubei Water Town (Gubei Shui Zhen)** has turned the old villages clustered around the entrance to the wall into an interconnected plaza of shops, restaurants, hotels, and exhibition halls, all finished in the style of a Jiangnan canal village (see p. 265). Development, however, no matter how ersatz, cannot spoil what is one of Beijing's remotest and wildest sections of wall. The steep, narrow passages are still here, though the gaps and gravel have been patched up in the recent work. Simatai was once so treacherous in places that multiple deaths had been reported here over the years, which partly explains why all visitors are now required to register their visit by reserving a place one day in advance (visit **www.wtown.com**). You'll also need to show your passport at the massive new ticket hall (daily 8am–5pm). Admission is RMB40. (It's an extra RMB40 to get into the Gubei Water Town. This can be safely skipped.) The cable car runs April to November from 8am to 4:30pm; a round-trip ride to the No. 8 Tower costs RMB50. At the time of writing, only 10 watchtowers had been reopened. The walk to the remotest watchtower, Tower 10, and back takes about 3 hours, and you'll need sturdy footwear.

Simatai is 110km (68 miles) northeast of Beijing. The best no-hassle option is to go there with a tour from your hotel or hostel (these often round up travelers from various points in the city). For a seat on a minibus or coach, expect to pay

A great hike ON THE GREAT WALL

Along with Jiankou, the **Jinshanling ★★** section of the Great Wall is the best for hiking away from the crowds. It's not as steep as Simatai and is more heavily restored, but attracts fewer visitors. The eastward hike toward Simatai is 6km (4 miles) and takes 2 to 3 hours. It was once possible to walk the full 10km (6 miles) to the gate of Simatai, but this option has been closed off by recent development. Nevertheless, as the crowds thin out and the wall begins to crumble in the latter part of the hike, the experience remains a sublime one. A number of hostels provide transportation for this hike, including the Beijing Downtown Backpacker's Hostel (85 Nan Luogo Xiang; ✆ **010/8400-2429;** RMB280, even-numbered days of the month only). You can also take an air-conditioned bus from the Xizhimen long-distance bus station to Miyun (every 30 min.; 6am–4pm; RMB15), then hire a minivan *(miandi)* to drop you off at Jinshanling and pick you up at Simatai for around RMB150—make sure you withhold payment until after you're picked up.

approximately RMB220 between May and October and RMB180 from November to April. Alternatively, book a driver through the excellent Bespoke Beijing **(www.bespokebeijing.com)**. Free spirits may opt to try bus no. 980 from the Donzhimen bus terminal (see instructions for getting to Mutianyu, above) to Miyun, and change for a minibus to Simatai (1 hr.; RMB15). Organized independently, a round-trip **taxi** from Beijing may cost anything up to RMB900.

JIANKOU ★★★

Few tourist buses make the journey to the stunning section of wall at Jiankou, and there is no cable car shuttling out-of-shape tourists to the top. Even more amazing, there are no touts selling knickknacks. This section is for serious hikers only. Soon after the ticket office, take the first left into Xizhazi Village, and where the road dead-ends into a parking lot, follow a forest trail up to the wall (1 hr.). Turn right (west) once you reach the wall, and prepare yourself for an intense hike up and down some steep sections of wall. The tallest watchtower in the distance is Jiankou. Just before you reach it, there is a turn-off point to the right that is marked by a flat, paved section of the wall that leads you, slowly, back down to the road. From the road, it's a 20-minute walk back to the parking lot. In total, the loop makes for about 5 hours of walking. The ticket office is open 8am to 5pm. Admission is RMB20.

Jiankou is 70km (44 miles) northeast of Beijing. There are no public transportation options here. However, if you can make your way to Mingzhu Square (Mingzhu Guangchang) in Huairou (see Mutianyu, above), it should be possible to negotiate a taxi ride to the ticket-office entrance for around RMB120. A round-trip **taxi** from Beijing will cost around RMB600, including the driver's waiting time.

THE MING TOMBS ★

Of the 16 emperors who ruled China during the Ming dynasty (1368–1644), 13 are buried in this valley north of Beijing (hence the Chinese name, Shisan Ling, which translates as "the 13 Tombs"). The Yongle emperor, who also oversaw construction of the Forbidden City, consulted geomancers before choosing this site, considered advantageous because it is bounded to the north by a range of protective mountains. The geography of the valley is mirrored in the tombs themselves, with each emperor buried beneath a tumulus, or "Spirit Tower," protected from the rear by a mountain. Only three of the Ming Tombs—**Ding Ling, Chang Ling,** and **Zhao Ling**—have been restored, and only one (Ding Ling) has been fully excavated. Many of the buildings mirror Ming palaces found in the city. Because of this, the sight can be boring to people who've already had their fill of imperial architecture. However, several attractions make the trip worthwhile for those who have the time.

The drive into the valley is along the **Spirit Way (Shen Dao) ★** (RMB35). It is essentially a 7km-long (4-mile) driveway, but things get interesting around the imposing Great Palace Gate (Da Hong Men). This leads to an attractive pavilion that houses China's largest memorial stele, and a walkway, slightly curved to fool evil ghosts, which is lined on either side with willows and carved stone animals and human figures. Several miles along the valley is the largest and best preserved of the tombs, **Chang Ling ★** (RMB45), which houses the remains of the Yongle emperor. It is essentially a Forbidden City in miniature, but probably underwhelming if you've seen the real thing. Most striking is the **Hall of Eminent Favors (Ling'en Dian),** an immense hall in which the interior columns and brackets have been left unpainted, creating an eye-catching contrast with the green ceiling panels. To the west of Chang Ling is the rather underwhelming **Ding Ling** (RMB65). The main feature here is the 4,000-sq.-m (13,000-sq.-ft.) **Underground Palace.** This was the burial place of the Wanli emperor, his wife, and his favorite concubine. It was discovered in 1956, just 10 years before the Red Guards swept through and ransacked the place. The corpse was dragged out and posthumously "denounced" and the coffins destroyed, now replaced with replicas. The burial objects that survived the looting have been moved to aboveground display rooms. Just over a ridge, slightly west of Ding Ling, is **Zhao Ling** (RMB35), the resting place of the Longqing emperor. It's quiet and peaceful but too much like the other tombs to be worth visiting if time is short.

The valley is 48km (30 miles) north of Beijing, on the same road that goes to the touristy Badaling section of the Great Wall. Many **tours** to Badaling also come here, but if you want time to explore some of the unrestored tombs (highly recommended), you'll have to make a separate trip and hire transportation to get you around what is a sprawling area. From Beijing, you can reach the Ming Tombs via **bus no. 872,** which departs from a stop on the north side of Deshengmen, around 500m (164 ft.) east of the Jishuitan subway station. It stops at all the attractions listed here, other than Zhao Ling, and can be used to get around once at the site. A **taxi** hired in Beijing should cost about RMB500, more if you want to be chauffeured around the various points within the valley.

CHENGDE ★★

Hebei Province, 233km (146 miles) NE of Beijing

Aside from the Great Wall, if you can do only one side trip from Beijing, make it Chengde—the summer camp of the Qing emperors. Here, in a walled enclosure containing numerous palaces, pavilions, and pagodas, the emperors escaped Beijing's blazing summer temperatures, entertained delegations from home and abroad, and practiced the mounted military skills that had originally gained them their empire. The design of the resort, built between 1703 and 1794, was shaped by its varied diplomatic functions: Some buildings were plain and undecorated to show visiting tribesmen that the emperors had not lost touch with their roots or been too softened by luxury; others were copies of some of China's most famous and elegant buildings; and some were giant edifices with hints of minority architecture, intended both to show the emperor's sympathy for the traditions of tributary- and border-dwelling peoples, and to overawe their emissaries.

In 1793, Britain's Lord Macartney arrived on a mission from George III, and not finding the Qianlong emperor at home in Beijing, followed him up to Chengde. It was here that Macartney famously failed to kowtow to the emperor, as tradition demanded, and set about a doomed attempt to impress the emperor with his gadgets of Western science. The meeting paved the way for four decades of mutual mistrust, which led to outright hostility in 1839 at the outset of the Opium War.

The Jiaqing emperor died here in 1820, as did the Xianfeng emperor in 1861, having signed the "unequal" treaties that marked the close of the Second Opium War (1856–60). The place came to be viewed as unlucky, and was already decaying by the fall of the Qing in 1911. But the **Imperial Mountain Retreat** and the **Eight Outer Temples** around its perimeter still form one of the greatest concentrations of ancient buildings in China. It's an 18th-century version of a "Splendid China" theme park (as seen in Shenzhen), but with oversize buildings rather than the miniatures offered there.

Chengde was the traditional summer retreat for Qing royalty and retains that seasonal emphasis. It can be packed at the height of summer, but, conversely, is quiet out of season. A visit during the winter months makes for more peaceful explorations, but the landscaping is less attractive, particularly within the Imperial Mountain Retreat. Bear in mind its size, too. It's just about possible to see most of the retreat in one day, thanks to the shuttle bus (RMB50), but you'll need to stay the night to have any hope of seeing the outer temples too.

Getting There

At the time of writing, construction on the new Jingshen high-speed railway linking Beijing and Shenyang was underway but incomplete. A new station at Chengde South is expected to be the first major stopping point along this route and will cut the train travel time from an average of more than 5 hours to less than 1. Once the route is open, Chengde will instantly become an easy day-trip. Work on the line was long delayed by protests, so predicting *exactly* when it will be complete has proved a risky business. Expect it sometime in the 2018–2020 bracket, but ask your concierge the latest news, and visit **www.travelchinaguide.com** for updated timetable information.

High-speed rail is the only realistic way to see Chengde in a day. Currently the fastest train to Chengde leaves Beijing Railway Station at 7:36am and takes 4 hours and 35 minutes. A returning train departs at 7:15pm and arrives back in Beijing just over 4 hours later. It's a slow and fairly uncomfortable ride. Thanks to a new highway, **bus** is a better option. The fastest and most frequent departures are from the Dongzhimen Long Distance Bus Station (45 Dongzhimen Wai Xijie; subway: Dongzhimen). The trip costs RMB73 for an air-conditioned coach, with departures about every 30 minutes from 5:40am to 6:40pm. The journey takes around 3 hours. Buses run to and from the forecourt of Chengde Railway Station.

Getting Around

Chengde **taxi** base fare is theoretically RMB5 in town, but the meter is often not used. If the meter is started, the base fare includes 1km; then it's RMB1.40 per km, jumping 50% after 8km (5 miles). A **shuttle bus** operates *within* the Imperial Mountain Resort (RMB50). **Bus** no. 118, from Yingzi Dajie next to the Imperial Mountain Resort main entrance, will take you to the northern group of temples (RMB1).

Exploring Chengde

If Beijing's Forbidden City was unambiguously the creation of the indigenous Ming dynasty, the summer palace at Chengde was entirely the brainchild of the Manchu Qing and was located between their ancient homeland, the frigid plains of Manchuria, and Han China. Here the emperor and the Manchu nobility would play at the equestrian and military talents that had won them China in the first place, both with formal contests in archery and with hunting in the well-stocked park. The lakes and many pavilions provided the emperor and his consorts with more refined diversions.

The summer palace was once a unified royal estate, but it's been splintered by the march of time, with various parks and temples each charging individual entrance fees. The central attraction is the walled **Imperial Mountain Retreat (Bishu Shanzhuang)** ★ (daily 6am–6pm; RMB120). It's not dissimilar from the Summer Palace back in Beijing, dotted with lakes, temples, and pavilions, and could easily consume half a day of exploration. Many of the buildings shown as lying within the park have long since vanished. The most important remaining is the **Palace of Righteousness (Zheng Gong).** The message here is one of simplicity and frugality (the beams and columns are very plain, although actually made of hardwoods brought long distances at great expense), with a pleasing elegance in great contrast to the usual Qing gaudiness. The palace now serves as a museum, displaying ancient military equipment in the front rooms, and period furnishings and antiquities at the rear.

Of greater architectural interest are the **Eight Outer Temples (Wai Ba Miao)**, a series of massive structures modeled on existing buildings elsewhere in the expanding Qing kingdom as a show of respect and admiration. Each charges individual entrance fees, though it's possible to buy a combination ticket (*tao piao*) for RMB80, which includes entry to the Temple of Happiness and Longevity, the Potala Temple, the Temple of Distant Peace, and the Temple of Joy.

The **Potala Temple (Putuozongcheng Zhi Miao)** ★★ is perhaps the most visually impressive of the lot (Shizi Gou Lu; admission May–Oct RMB40; Nov–Apr RMB30; May–Oct 7:30am–6pm, Nov–Apr 8:30am–5pm). Its tapering windows and slab-sided walls were designed in homage to the Dalai Lama's famous palace in Lhasa. Several of the outbuildings are solid, intended to add to the splendor in general rather than serve any particular purpose. Items on display in the surrounding galleries include two young girls' skulls fused with silver and once used as drinking vessels, and anatomically detailed esoteric statuary of sexual acts. Five minutes' walk away is the **Temple of Happiness and Longevity (Xumifushou Miao) ★**, inspired by the Tashilhunpo Monastery in Tibet and constructed specifically to make the Panchen Lama, number two in the Tibetan religious hierarchy, feel at home during a visit in 1780 (Shizi Gou Lu; RMB30; daily 7:30am–6pm).

The Temple of Universal Peace (Puning Si) ★ is among the most grand of the temples and also comes with the Tibetan theme, modeled on the Samye Monastery near Lhasa (Puning Si Lu; admission RMB50; RMB100 including ticket to climb the Buddha figure). The main Hall of Mahayana is impressive—story upon story of red walls and yellow roofs, topped with a gold knob surrounded by four mini-pagoda-like points. More impressive still are its contents, a giant copper-colored wooden Guanyin figure more than 22m (73 ft.) high, the largest of its kind in the world. It's possible to climb three stories to look the figure in the eye as she sits in dusty gloom (RMB50). While other sights in Chengde are managed by the sleepy local tourism bureau, this temple is run by an entrepreneurial group of monks. The temple now sports a hotel (see below) and a tacky but entertaining recreation of a Qing market, and offers an evening show promising blessings and exorcisms by "real Tibetan lamas."

Puyou Temple (Puyou Si) is beautiful but not an essential attraction, mainly interesting for its collection of statues of the 500 arhats (the first followers of the Sakyamuni Buddha). **Temple of Universal Joy (Pule Si)** was built to receive annual tributary visits from defeated Mongol tribes. The most striking element is the copy at the rear of the circular Hall of Prayer for Good Harvests from the Temple of Heaven in Beijing (p. 83). The **Temple of Distant Peace (Anyuan Miao)** is another example of architectural diplomacy, built in imitation of a temple (now long-vanished) in Yining on China's remote western borders to please Mongol tribes that were resettled around Chengde. It's one of the least popular temples, and all the more pleasant for it.

Tip: The Temple of Universal Peace and the other northern temples are on morning itineraries for tour groups, followed by the Temple of Universal Joy and the eastern temples in the afternoon. If you're traveling independently, try to do this circuit in reverse to avoid the worst of the crowds.

Where to Stay & Eat

From the first week of May to the first week of October, the town is busy, weekends particularly so, but only during the weeklong national holidays should it be difficult to find a room. There are a number of new hotels in the center of town, but one of the most interesting stays can be had at the **Puning Hotel (Puning Si Shangketang Da Jiudian) (✆ 0314/205-8889).** Run by the market-savvy monks of the Temple of Universal Peace, this guesthouse offers cozy accommodations within the west wing of the temple. The **Qi Wang Lou Hotel** (1 Bifengmen Dong Lu Bei; www.qiwanglou.com; ✆ **0314/218-2288**) butts up against the Imperial Mountain Retreat and is built in the same imitation style of Chengde's many temples. It's a comfortable four-star but not particularly cheap, so only stay if you can get a decent discount.

The **night market** on Yingzi Dajie runs through the heart of town. Stalls sell kebabs for RMB1 and other Chinese fast food, eaten at tables behind each stall. As befits a former hunting ground, Chengde's specialty is game. Deer, pheasant, and wild boar can be found on menus around town, each cooked in a quintessentially Chinese way. Stir-frying makes venison tough, but wild boar softens up nicely while retaining its gamy flavor. The best restaurants are in larger hotels. The **Xin Qianlong Da Jiudian,** just south of the Shenghua Hotel on Xinhua Lu (✆ **0314/207-2222**), has attentive service, good portions, and a picture menu. Plump dumplings stuffed with donkey meat and onions are called *lurou dacong shuijiao*; 200 grams or four *liang (si liang)* should be enough per person. *Cong shao yezhurou* (wild boar cooked with onions) and *zhenmo shanji ding* (nuggets of pheasant with local mushrooms) are both good. As long as you don't venture into scorpion or roe deer backbone marrow, a meal costs around RMB100 for two.

6 XI'AN

Spread across a basin between the rugged Wei and Yellow river valleys, Xi'an lies near modern China's geographic center. With miles of loam hills to the north and lush terraces of rice and tea to the south, this has long been a fertile land, and rulers from 11 dynasties established their court here, leaving behind archaeological treasures that only Ancient Egypt can rival. At its 8th-century peak, Xi'an was the largest and grandest city in the world, the terminus for the "Silk Road" traders who wended along the dusty corridor between the Gobi Desert and the Tibetan Plateau. The modern city may only be a humble provincial capital by comparison, but there's a palpable sense of history and plentiful reminders of the city's rich, cosmopolitan past.

Xi'an was first made capital of China under the Zhou dynasty in the 11th century B.C. The city rose and fell again and again until the Tang dynasty (A.D. 618–907), when Xi'an—known then as Chang'an—enjoyed almost three uninterrupted centuries as China's political and cultural center. Scholars and merchants flocked from all corners of the known world, and the city became a huge, cosmopolitan melting pot. From the north came Mongolian foods and weapons; along the network of canals to the east flowed silk; and, from the distant west, the spices, fashions, and metals of Central Asia were carted in by horse and camel. There was also a great flowering of the arts, sciences, and religion. Manicheans, Nestorian Christians, and Buddhists mingled freely in what was the first millennium's most tolerant and globalized capital. Buddhism in particular enjoyed imperial patronage and inspired painting, sculpture, and poetry, which survive to this day.

The scale of the metropolis is readily imagined. What are now referred to as the "city walls" were rebuilt during the Ming dynasty (1644–1911) on merely the inner sanctum of the Tang city. The real city walls created an enormous rectangle and stretched for 36km (22 miles), with the south gate opening onto a tree-lined avenue that was 150m (500 ft.) wide.

With the passing of the Tang, Xi'an lost its lead role to the cities of the east, though its slow fadeaway perhaps proved its modern saving-grace. While European colonial powers ransacked many of China's coastal cities during conflict and colonization, Xi'an was a distant backwater. It remained so when **Red Guards** marched through during the Cultural Revolution, vandalizing what symbols of the feudal past they could find. In 1974, just as things were settling down, an impoverished farmer accidentally bored a well into the awe-inspiring tomb of 3rd century B.C. emperor Qin Shihuang. The Terracotta Warriors found inside became the poster boys China needed, just as international tourism boomed—and Xi'an hasn't looked back since. The find prompted other digs that have turned up more archaeological treasure and cemented Xi'an's reputation as the cradle of Chinese civilization.

Locals beam with pride at belonging to such a grand historic narrative, but there's a sadness that their city ever fell so far behind. But herein lies Xi'an's more unexpected appeal: Where Beijing and Shanghai are highly internationalized, showcase cities, Xi'an is earthier, rawer, and more representative of the Chinese heartland. Yes, it's crowded, cluttered, and horribly polluted at times. But it's also genuine (Tang dinner shows aside, see p.173), and all the more charming for it.

The local government has sought to broaden the city's attractiveness to tourists in recent years. Xi'an's Tang heritage is at the heart of huge new developments such as the **Daming Palace, Tang Paradise,** and the **Tang Western Market,** all constructed on or around historic sights. There's the distinct feeling of history being forcibly foisted on Xi'an as opposed to bubbling up by itself, but there's a certain epic quality to these developments, and anything that can draw the masses away from the Terracotta Warriors is probably to be welcomed.

Xi'an is more compact than Beijing, with a grid layout that's easy to navigate. The main city-center sights can be seen in a day or two, though the famous tombs, the **Terracotta Warriors** foremost among them, are actually a long way outside the modern city, and you may need to arrange independent transportation. A new subway network is gradually making getting around easier and will one day stretch all the way to Qin's famous mausoleum, though not in time for readers of this book.

ESSENTIALS

Arriving

BY PLANE Daily flights connect **Xi'an Xianyang International Airport** with all major cities in China, including multiple daily flights to and from Beijing and Shanghai, as well as select international destinations within Asia. It's not currently possible to fly directly to Xi'an from North America, Australia, or Europe. The airport is 37km (23 miles) from the center of Xi'an. **Airport shuttle buses** run along eight different routes, though none travel to points within the city walls, meaning an additional taxi ride will be required. The fee is RMB26 regardless of destination. All buses depart from both Terminal 2 and Terminal 3. Buy tickets from the desks just after baggage claim in either terminal. The most useful routes are **Route 1,** which runs to the Aviation Hotel on Laodong Nan Lu, west of the city walls; **Route 2,** which goes to the old Railway Station, right on the north city wall (and from which certain parts of the old city are walkable); and **Route 6,** which goes to the Xi'an Hotel on Chang'an Bei Lu, south of the city walls, the nearest point for those staying in Qujiang. Buses run from around 7pm to 9pm, though Route 1 operates until the last flight has landed. If traveling in the opposite direction, aim to leave the city center at least 3 hours before your flight. A **taxi** from the airport into town costs about RMB150 to RMB180, depending on the time of day. Drivers are obliged to use their meter when collecting passengers from the airport but may still try to agree to a set fare. Drivers traveling from the city center *to* the airport will invariably refuse to use the meter. RMB150 is the going rate for a daytime fare, though hagglers may get a RMB10 discount.

BY TRAIN The most likely destination for rail passengers into and out of Xi'an is the huge new **North Railway Station.** Like all of China's new bullet-train stations, it's remote from the city center, 14km (8.7 miles) to the north of the Bell Tower. Line 2 of the subway connects to the city center. There's a huge new taxi stand, but Xi'an cars dry up completely between 3 and 4:30pm when drivers change shifts. If you arrive between these hours, the subway is your only option.

The fastest train from Beijing is the G87 which takes just 4 hours and 25 minutes but runs only once a day (RMB515.5 for a second-class seat). The other five bullet trains take between 5.5 and 6 hours. At the time of writing, there were no bullet trains to or from Shanghai. The fastest train is an overnight D-class train that has only "soft-sleeper" beds or hard seats and takes 10 hours and 36 minutes (RMB843 for a soft sleeper). The old **Xi'an Railway Station** is located just outside the northeast side of the city wall and has connections to local cities such as Luoyang and Lanzhou and some of the slower, overnight trains to and from Beijing and Shanghai. Bus no. 603 runs from the station square to Xi Dajie where some of the main hotels are located.

BY BUS **Xi'an Bus Station** is located on Jiefang Lu just south of Xi'an Railway Station, accessible by first passing beneath the city walls. Regular buses connect with Luoyang (425km/264 miles; 4 hr.; RMB108), Taiyuan (685km/425 miles; 8 hr.; RMB190) and Tianshui (380km/236 miles; 4 hr.; RMB120). For Huashan (2 hr.; RMB22), buses leave from east of the station square.

Visitor Information

As in Beijing and Shanghai, the "tourist information" booths you'll see dotted around the central sights are basically fronts for private tour operators and of little use for offering impartial information. The **Tourist Administration of Xi'an** runs an English-language website (http://en1.xian-tourism.com) that has some generic information on Xi'an culture and food, but information is badly in need of an update. Most five-star hotels provide guests with free maps of the city, as well as information about local attractions. You'll be able to pick one up by asking the concierge, even if you are not staying. Xi'an has a modest but growing number of Western expats living in or around the city (a huge, US$7 billion chip factory, opened by Samsung in 2014, boosted the numbers considerably). They are now served by an English-language expat magazine, **Xi'anese.** As well as reviews of restaurants and bars, the magazine has information about Xi'an's ever-changing transportation situation, as well as useful listings for services. The magazine is free and distributed around many foreigner-friendly bars and restaurants, and most city-center Starbucks cafes (there's one beside the Bell Tower). It can also be downloaded as a PDF from the magazine's website (www.xianease.com).

City Layout

Much like Beijing, Xi'an takes its layout cues from an imperial grid pattern of old. Central Xi'an is the area within the bounds of the city walls and surrounding moat. This is divided by a series of wide, straight boulevards, the most important of which radiate outward from the Ming-era **Bell Tower (Zhong Lou)** and lead to the four main city gates. Many hotels and restaurants lie on these arteries, which are named **Bei** (North), **Nan** (South), **Dong** (East), and **Xi** (West) **Dajie** (Avenue). Planning regulations have limited the height of buildings within the city walls (though the odd building obviously got through before rules were properly enforced), making this a relatively low-rise part of Xi'an. The lack of lucrative development opportunities means that, away from the main boulevards, central Xi'an can feel rather ramshackle. Outside the city walls, the apartment complexes, shiny malls and gleaming office blocks instantly spring up. Commercial development is particularly notable south of the old city, along **Chang'an Bei Lu.** As in Beijing, the **Second Ring Road** (Er Huan) performs a huge loop around the old city, roughly marking the scope of the city walls as they were during the Tang dynasty. Beyond this, to the southwest, is the **Xi'an High-Tech Development Zone,** of little interest to tourists but a hub for the city's growing expat community and home to some of the plusher hotels and restaurants. To the southeast of the Second Ring Road is **Qujiang District,** which has been specifically developed for tourism and is home to a clutch of brand new five-star hotels and major mall developments, as well as Xi'an's most luxurious villas. A third ring road makes an even larger loop around the city and comprises chunks of various interstate highways. To the northwest is Xi'an Airport, as well as Emperor Jingdi's Mausoleum. To the east is the Banpo Neolithic Village, while even farther out in this direction is **Lintong District,** the site of Qin Shihuang's Mausoleum and the Terracotta Warriors.

Neighborhoods in Brief

Though the city has several official administrative districts, these are not particularly meaningful for visitors and have not been used here. The walled city center is the main anchor for orientation, though it contains only a few of Xi'an's most important sights.

Lintong Lintong was once a desperately down-at-heel suburb but now boasts museums, schools, and spa resorts, all thanks to 30 years of mass tourism prompted by the discovery of **Qin Shihuang's Mausoleum** and the **Terracotta Warriors.** Staying here makes little sense for the average visitor, as it's so far from the other downtown sights, but there's a good chance that it'll be the first place you visit upon arrival in Xi'an.

City Center Xian's Ming dynasty wall marks the boundary of the modern city center. The eastern half has most of the plushest hotels, while the western and southern sections have the most tourist appeal. **The Bell Tower** lies in the middle, just south of center, and the **Drum Tower** is a short walk west. Nearby is the fascinating **Muslim District,** busy, chaotic, but fun to wander. The **South Gate** is the most spectacular of the old city entrances. Nearby **Defu Xiang** is Xi'an's official "bar street," though the indie bars along the inside of the south wall are more fun. Just to the west of the South Gate is **Shuyuanmen,** great for shoppers and pedestrian exploration. It leads the way to the **Forest of Steles Museum.**

Inner Ring Road The giant ring of urban Xi'an that lies outside the moat but within the Second Ring Road is a jumble of new commercial and residential developments and home to both of Xi'an's major universities. To the south of the walled city is the **Small Wild Goose Pagoda** and the **Tang Western Market,** while to the northeast is the **Daming Palace National Heritage Park,** the restored site of the oldest Tang-dynasty imperial palace.

Qujiang Taking top prize for the most transformed neighborhood in Xi'an is Qujiang. At the northern edge of this area is the **Shaanxi History Museum,** but the most obvious development has taken place around the **Great Wild Goose Pagoda,** with great bronze statues, landscaped gardens, a brand new elevated railway, the **Tang Dynasty** theme park, and a panoply of luxury hotels all having been built in the last decade.

GETTING AROUND

By Subway

Xi'an was fairly late to the subway-building business but is now on the map with two operating lines (perhaps three by the time you read this). Commercial development has taken precedence over tourism, and the lines are not hugely helpful in getting to and from the major sights, with only four stations within the city walls. One of these is the **Bell Tower (Zhong Lou),** and most of central Xi'an's most interesting spots are walkable here (making the station incredibly busy, especially on weekends). The station is on **Line 1,** which transfers passengers from the huge new Xi'an North Railway Station to the city center and beyond, cutting a perfectly straight path north-to-south. **Line 2** intersects at Bei Dajie, a station within the city walls, and runs east-to-west. The expected arrival of **Line 3** in 2016 should help connect Qujiang, currently stranded to the south, with the current network. In total, 17 subway lines are planned, including one that runs all the way to Lintong and the Terracotta Warriors, but the development timetable extends to 2030, and there's no confirmation on when further lines are expected to be finished.

Signs on platforms tell you which station is next in each direction, and English announcements are made on trains. Tickets cost RMB2 to RMB5, depending on the number of stops, though most city-center journeys will be RMB2. It's possible to buy a government transportation card, but these are not sold in subway stations themselves, and it's unlikely you'll hang around long enough for it to be worth the money. See the subway map on the inside back cover.

By Taxi

Xi'an's taxi system borders on the dysfunctional. If you are able to hail one, Xi'an taxis are cheap, starting at RMB6 for the first 3km (2 miles), then RMB1.5 per km thereafter (with an extra RMB1 "fuel surcharge" sometimes added). This isn't necessarily a good thing. Rates are so cheap that many local drivers struggle to make a living. It's more common here than elsewhere to find drivers parked up at the side of the road, waiting to negotiate a fare rather than relying on the meter and wasting petrol as they roam. If you do find a cab, it's not unusual for drivers to deliberately take a circuitous route to eke out a few extra RMB profit. There's also a city-mandated shift-swap between 3 and 4:30pm, making it very hard to find cabs midafternoon. The arrival of taxi-hailing apps on smartphones has only exacerbated the problem. Assuming you don't have a Chinese SIM card, a taxi-hailing app, and Mandarin skills, you'll probably need to rely on hotel concierges and restaurant staff to help book you a ride. If you do try to negotiate a ride, trips within the city walls should be around RMB10.

By Bus

As elsewhere in China, using the crowded but numerous local bus services is not recommended. Regular buses cost RMB1, while air-conditioned buses charge RMB2. However, signs are only in Chinese script, and there are no English-language announcements on the bus, making navigation stressful.

The one (important) exception is the dedicated "**tourist buses.**" There are 10 routes in total, the majority of which depart from the east side of the square next to Xi'an Railway Station. The most important route is **Line 5** (also known as the **no. 306**), which takes passengers out to the Terracotta Warriors at Lintong and runs every 15 minutes or so (RMB8). For those in a hurry, **free tourist shuttle buses** run between Xi'an North Railway Station and the Terracotta Warriors. They depart between 8am and 4pm and return between 10:30am and 7:30pm. You can ride for free by showing your train ticket (which must display that day's date) and an entrance ticket to the Terracotta Warriors attraction. This can be purchased in advance at the Tourist Service Center on the basement level of the station.

By Bike

Xi'an is flat and seems a likely city for widespread biking. However, the streets are congested, and traffic rules are often ignored by motorists. Aside from a ride along the top of the city walls (see p.154), cycling in Xi'an is only recommended for the experienced urban cyclist. The difficulty in registering to use one of the 8,000 hop-on, hop-off public bicycles is a further disincentive. You'll need to buy a public transportation card (*Chang'an Tong Ka)*, not easy in itself as they are not sold at all subway stations, and then register the card for bike rental by paying a RMB300 deposit. This can only be done in one of five application offices. It can be done, but you'll probably need help, so see if your concierge can offer assistance if you are determined to cycle Xi'an.

On Foot

The walled city of Xi'an is just about small enough to be walkable. If you are finding it difficult to get a taxi, and the crowded buses are off-putting, consider taking a stroll. Most roads follow a north-south-east-west trajectory, making

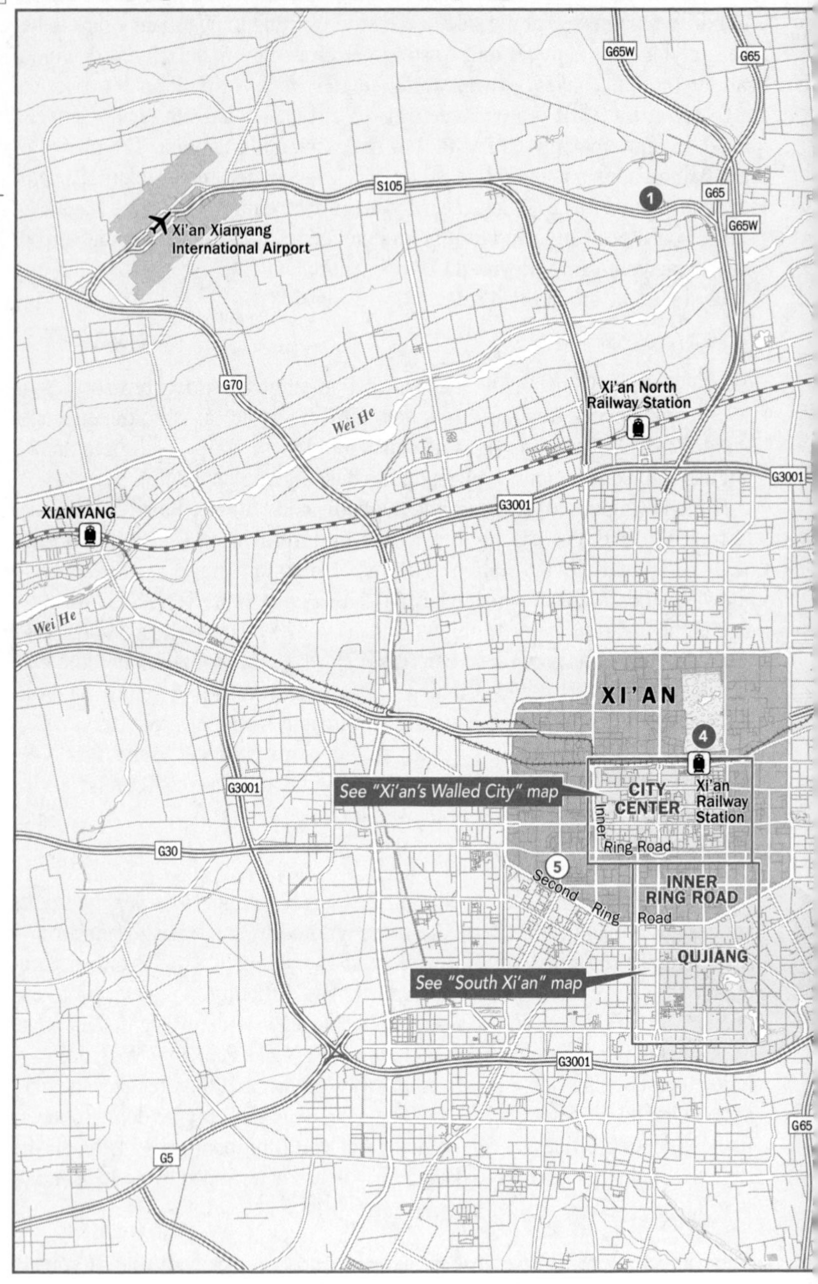

Xi'an Xianyang
International Airport
S105
G65W
G65
G65
G65W
1
G70
Wei He
Xi'an North
Railway Station
G3001
G3001
XIANYANG
Wei He
XI'AN
4
Xi'an
Railway
Station
CITY
CENTER
Inner
Ring Road
See "Xi'an's Walled City" map
G3001
G30
5
Second
Ring
Road
INNER
RING ROAD
QUJIANG
See "South Xi'an" map
G3001
G65
G5

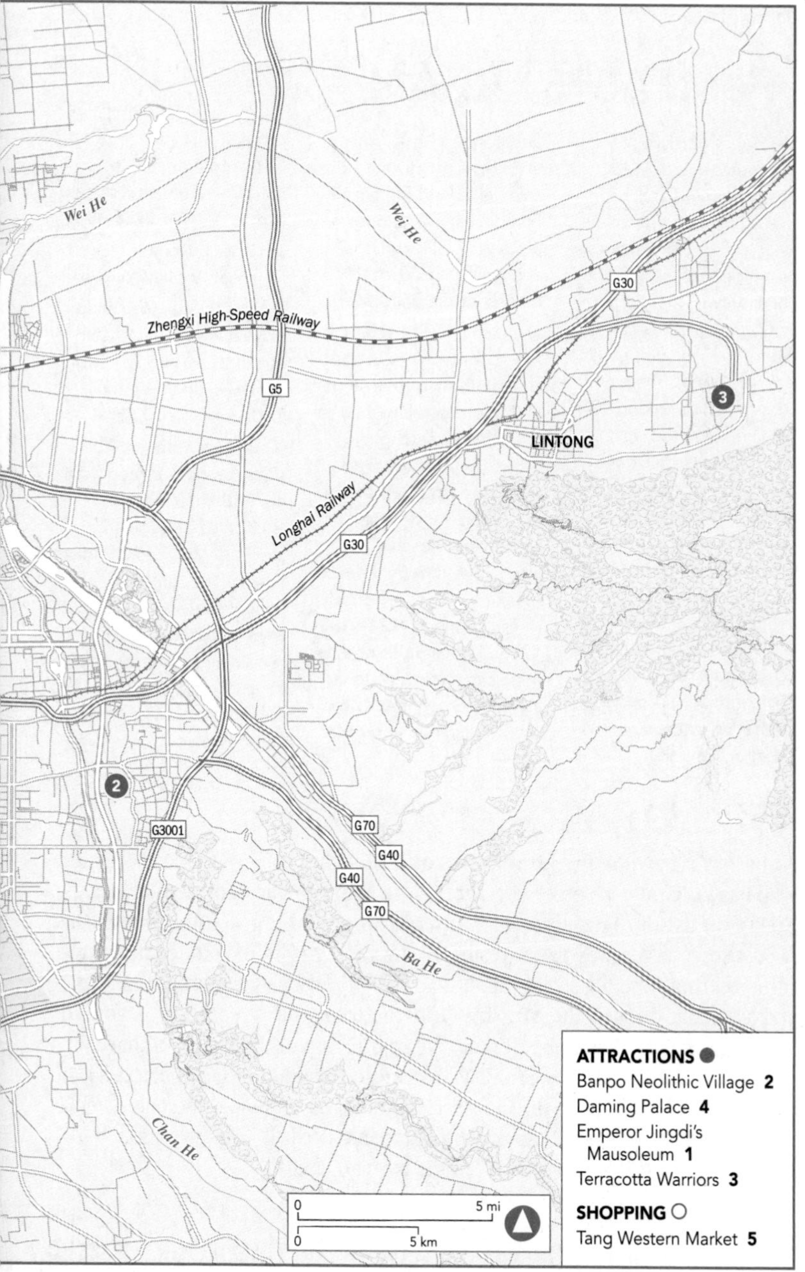

ATTRACTIONS ●
Banpo Neolithic Village **2**
Daming Palace **4**
Emperor Jingdi's Mausoleum **1**
Terracotta Warriors **3**

SHOPPING ○
Tang Western Market **5**

navigation easy. The downside is the sidewalks, which, as in many third-tier cities in China, are often crowded with the spillover of adjacent shops and parked cars.

[FastFACTS] XI'AN

Banks, Foreign Exchange & ATMs Plenty of banks around town offer cash and traveler's check exchange, credit-card advances, and ATMs. The city branch of the **Bank of China** is at 21 Jiefang Lu (Mon–Fri 9am–6pm, Sat and Sun 9am–4pm). There are other branches around 500m (1640 ft.) east and west of the Bell Tower on Dong Dajie and Xi Dajie, respectively. If staying in Qujiang District, there is a Bank of China ATM within the Xinlehui Mall, just opposite the entrance to the Great Wild Goose Pagoda. A cluster of banks and ATMs, Bank of China included, is on nearby Cuihua Lu, just south of Xiaozhai Dong Lu.

Books & Maps Maps and English-language books are available at the Shaanxi Foreign Language Book Store at 349 Dong Dajie, approximately 500m (1640 ft.) east of the Bell Tower.

Doctors & Dentists Xi'an's rise as an expat destination has led to a handful of English-speaking medical practitioners setting up shop. The **Xi'an International Medical Center** is a private operation that runs within Liren Hospital and offers care from English-speaking staff (30 Keji Lu, Hi-Tech Zone; ✆ **137-0188-4285**). **Welcome Dental** has three clinics dotted around the southern fringes of the city. The nearest to the city center is just south of the southeast entrance to Jiaotong University on Xingqing Nan Lu (✆ **186-2932-8883**).

Internet Access See "Internet Access," p. 295.

Post Office The **main branch** is at the northeast corner of the Bell Tower at 1 Bei Dajie, and is open 8:30am to 6pm.

Visa Extensions Extensions can be obtained from the **PSB** at 58 Xi Dajie (✆ **029/8727-5934**). They are open Monday to Friday 8:30am to noon and 3 to 6pm. Visas can take up to a week to process. You'll need a certificate from your hotel proving where you are staying and a passport-size photograph.

EXPLORING XI'AN

Xi'an has a bewildering array of historic sites that can confound the visitor who has little time to spare. The **Terracotta Warriors** are a must, likewise the **Shaanxi History Museum** and **Emperor Jingdi's Mausoleum** (though this is best seen on the way to, or from, the airport). Within the city center, make sure you find time for a bike ride along the city walls—an eternal favorite—and a wander through the **Muslim Quarter,** trying the street food as you go. These are the bare *essentials* for any Xi'an trip. Top of the list if you have any surplus time should be the **Small Wild Goose Pagoda** (and connected **Xi'an Museum**). The **Great Wild Goose Pagoda** is, as the name indicates, more famous, but it's not as accessible or photogenic. Visit if you have time, but if it comes down to a toss-up between the two, go small.

Lintong

Terracotta Warriors (Bingmayong) ★★★ ARCHAEOLOGICAL SITE/MUSEUM There's no use pretending. The tens of thousands of global travelers who flock to Xi'an each year are not here to taste Tang culture or marvel at Ming glories. There's really only one show in town, and it's warrior-shaped. Discovered by accident in 1974 by a farmer who bored a well and came up with a general's clay head, Qin Shihuang's funerary army represents one of the greatest sights on Earth. This was less a tomb and more an attempt by China's most fearsome leader to carry his newly won empire with him into the afterlife. The great man's mausoleum, beneath the burial mound just to the west, is supposedly booby-trapped, and excavation has barely begun, but legend says it includes a full reconstruction of the ancient capital, complete with rivers and lakes of mercury. According to Han historian Sima Qian, over 700,000 workers were drafted for the project, and those involved in the construction of the tomb were rewarded with graves beside their emperor.

The modern museum is made up of four main sections. It's hard not to get a shiver down your spine as you enter the great hangar of **Pit 1,** home to the largest congregation of warriors, arranged in battle formation stretching back 182m (600 ft.). Originally painted in bright colors, they were constructed from interchangeable parts sealed together by clay. Because the heads were hand-molded, no two appear the same. Qin Shihuang's army was drawn from all over his vast empire, and this ethnic diversity is reflected in the variety of hairstyles, headdresses, and facial expressions. Even on the mass-produced bodies, the level of detail is striking, down to the layering of armor, and the studs on archers' shoes that prevented them from slipping. The average height of the warriors is 1.8m (5 ft. 11 in.)—slightly taller than soldiers of the time—while senior officers are even taller. There are thought to be around 8,000 warriors in total, 6,000 of them in this pit alone (though only 1,000 or so are currently visible). Most of the soldiers in **Pit 2** are less intact than those in Pit 1, although the statues show greater diversity of posture. In total there are thought to be around 1,400 soldiers here, though again, only a fraction have been excavated. The very best finds have been encased in glass cabinets around the edge of the pit. Look out for the imposing 2m-tall (6½-ft.) general. **Pit 3** is much smaller and houses the command post for the underground army, with 68 senior officers.

The **Cultural Relics Exhibition Hall,** just to the right of Pit 1, contains a display of two magnificent bronze chariots, reconstructed from nearly 3,500 excavated fragments.

It is unthinkable to visit Xi'an without making the (lengthy) trip out to Lintong to view the spectacle in person, but it's worth being aware of a few minor annoyances. Most difficult to overcome is the baggage you'll likely be carrying in your head. After years of exposure to glossy magazine features and gorgeous slow-pan TV travel segments, it's possible you'll be underwhelmed by the reality, which can be a little cold and remote. Secondly, the crowds can be overwhelming. If you're able to arrange independent transportation, your best bet is to arrive at the crack of dawn and race straight into the most photogenic part of the exhibition, Pit 1. Thirdly, the RMB150 entrance cost is too steep, particularly given the local wage and comparable cost of Beijing's more storied sights. Finally, and most annoying of all, is the

ATTRACTIONS ●
Beiyuanmen ("Muslim Street") **12**
Bell Tower **18**
City Walls **34**
Drum Tower **14**
Forest of Steles Museum **39**
Great Mosque **11**
Temple of the Eight Immortals **7**

HOTELS ■
Citadines Central Xi'an **27**
Grand Noble **23**
Hilton Xi'an **6**
Jano's Backpackers **36**
Mecure **4**
Melody Hotel **15**
Sofitel on Renmin Square **5**
Xi'an Forest Green Hotel **1**
Xiangzimen International Youth Hostel **33**

RESTAURANTS & NIGHTLIFE ◆
Aperture Club **25**
Belgian Bar **37**
De Fa Chang **17**

Ding Ding Xiang **29**
Fanji Lazhi Roudian **26**
Isola Del Nord **3**
Jiasan Guantang Baozi **13**
Lao Sun Jia **22**
Lao Wan **31**
Near Wall Bar **32**
Noodle King **28**
On the Road **24**
Shanxi Thirteen **10**
Zoo **30**

SHOPPING ○
Century Ginwa **16**
Dong Da Jie **20**
Huajue Xiang **9**
Kaiyuan Square **19**
Luomashi Pedestrian Street **21**
Shuyuanmen **35**
Sanxue Jie **38**
Tang Western Market **40**
Temple of the Eight Immortals Antique Market **8**
Xicang Market **2**

seemingly endless bazaar strung between the bus drop-off and museum entrance. You can walk the 1km (half-mile) route yourself, but don't expect to make quick headway through the crowd. Definitely consider hiring one of the electric carts for RMB5. If you can overcome, or overlook, these problems, the Terracotta Warriors still have a chance of being *the* defining memory of a trip to China.

An English-speaking guide (RMB150) can be hired at the main entrance, though you'll also get offers on the walk into the museum (which are best ignored). An audio guide is also available (RMB40, with RMB200 deposit), but this is not particularly compelling. There are free shuttle buses running between the Terracotta Warriors exhibit and **Qin Shihuang's Mausoleum** itself. This is technically a separate attraction, though there's not a great deal to see here other than a vast grassy mound.

Off Qintang Da Dao. ✆ **029/8391-1961.** Admission: Main exhibits Mar–Nov RMB150, Dec–Feb RMB120. 8:30am–5:30pm. Bus: Tourist Bus 5 (no. 306) leaves from the east side of the square at the front of the railway station (RMB8; daily 7am–7pm; 40 min.). Round-trip taxi from the city costs RMB200–RMB300.

City Center

Bell & Drum Towers ★ LANDMARK Originally built in 1384 during the Ming dynasty, the **Bell Tower** lies at the heart of Xi'an's old city and is easily the most beautiful building still standing within the old city walls. It sits at the center of a giant roundabout and is a landmark for both travelers and drivers, with roads radiating out toward the four city-wall gates. The Bell Tower originally housed a giant Tang bell, rung at dawn to mark the beginning of the day's imperial activities, with the nearby **Drum Tower** signaling dusk, and the end of the bartering and politicking. The Bell Tower is a resplendent two-story pagoda, 36m (118 ft.) in height including the giant stone base, and beautifully lit up at night. However, though there are bell-ringing performances at 9:10am, 10am, 11am, 3pm, 4pm, and 5pm, it's hard to justify the RMB35 entrance cost (RMB50 if you also want to enter nearby Drum Tower). You can climb relatively high within the pagoda, but it's less interesting to look out *from* the pagoda than it is to look *at* the pagoda itself.

Jnc. of Bei Dajie, Nan Dajie, Xi Dajie, and Dong Dajie (entrance from the circular underpass). Admission RMB50 combined ticket, RMB35 to visit either Drum or Bell Towers. Apr–Oct 8:30am–9:30pm; Nov–Mar 8:30am–6pm. Subway: Bell Tower.

City Walls (Cheng Qiang) ★★★ MONUMENT The largest and best-preserved city wall in China is an essential stop. It's a 14km (8¾ mile) loop along a magnificently wide cobbled boulevard, which can be conducted on foot, bicycle, or by golf cart. The walls are monumental, wider than they are tall, making it one of the few places where you can pedal with total freedom without fear of being mown down by maniac drivers. Four watchtowers stand in each corner, while the four ancient city gates look like small palaces in miniature, with three separate and photogenic towers. The walls as they currently appear were built during the early Ming dynasty, on the remains of the

Tang-city's inner core. The city walls were much farther out, well past the Great Wild Goose Pagoda. There are great views over the surrounding moat and landscaped parkland to the high-rise development outside the city. Bike is by far the best means of transportation on the wall. The rental centers are sited beside each of the four historic gates. However, the **South Gate (Nan Men)** is the obvious place to begin and end your explorations, as its rental center is open the latest. Sturdy individual (RMB40) and tandem bicycles (RMB60) may be rented (per 2 hr.) from just west of the gate and returned any time up until final closing (8pm). The bike ranks elsewhere shut up shop at 6:30pm. The entire loop takes 3 to 4 hours by foot. Fast cyclists complete the circuit in 45 minutes, but allow 2 hours for a leisurely pedal and plenty of picture stops. Start out just before dusk and enjoy the night scenery. Finally, there is an interesting museum at the **Zhuque Gate** (along the south flank of the wall), which has packed-earth parts of the ancient wall exposed for close inspection.

Entrance to South Gate from Nan Dajie. Admission RMB54. Daily 8am–8pm.

Forest of Steles Museum (Beilin Bowuguan) ★ MUSEUM Formerly the Shaanxi Provincial Museum, the Forest of Steles Museum is situated in a charming Confucian temple (ca. 1087) beside the city walls. Steles are carved tablets, and these were originally created as standard set scholarly texts for the Tang literati. There's only limited English, and the steles can be a little hard to appreciate for non-Chinese-speakers, but the serene atmosphere of the courtyards and their gnarled old trees require no translation.

Located in the main courtyard, the first major stele was composed by the Xuanzong emperor in 745 and was an exposition on filial piety. This work predates the "Three Character Classic" *(San Zi Jing)*, the definitive classical text on the subject. Room 1 houses the Confucian classics, including "The Analects," "The Spring," and "Autumn Annals." Candidates for official examinations would pore over rubbings taken from these steles and would be expected to know the classics by heart—a form of rote learning that survives today, in modified form, in Chinese schools. Immediately to your left in room 2 is the Nestorian Stele. Nestorian Christians were drummed out of the Church for maintaining that Jesus was both human and divine and that Mary was the mother of "the man Jesus," and not the mother of God. The stele records the visit of a Nestorian priest to Chang'an and the founding of a Nestorian chapel, providing evidence of a Nestorian presence in China as early as A.D. 635. The influence of other faiths is clear—the Maltese cross is set amid Taoist clouds, supported by a Buddhist lotus flower. Rooms 2 and 3 also house the work of master calligraphers such as Wang Xizhi, whose writings are still used as models by calligraphy students. Room 4 has pictorial steles, including a famous image of Confucius. Here you will encounter a demonstration of "rubbing," whereby moistened paper is hammered onto the inked stones, color is tapped on using a wooden disk wrapped in a cloth, and the impression is dried before being gobbled up by Korean tour groups. It isn't a gentle process, and it's easy to see why many steles are almost unreadable.

Double back to your left to enter rooms 5 to 7, as well as a gallery of stone sculptures containing an exquisite statue of a bodhisattva that shows Indian influences.

The museum is nestled amid the charming shopping streets of **Sanyuanmen** and **Sanxue Jie,** which are well worth seeing on your way in, or way out (see "Shopping," p. 173).

18 Wenyi Bei Lu. ✆ **029/8725-8448.** Admission RMB75. Summer 8:30am–6pm; winter 8:30am–5:30pm. Subway: Yongningmen, then 15-min. walk east.

Great Mosque (Da Qingzhen Si) ★★ TEMPLE Founded during the height of the Tang dynasty in 742, this exquisite courtyard mosque is the largest and most important of the 38 city-center temples that serve Xi'an's large Muslim community. Half the adventure is getting there. The covered entrance alleyway, Huajue Xiang, is essentially a bazaar with good-humored vendors selling all manner of merchandise (see "Shopping," below), and it may take you a few attempts to find the mosque amongst the din. The courtyards are spacious and have a gardenlike feel, with a wonderful fusion of Arabian and Chinese architectural styles. To the right of the entrance is a hall filled with exquisite Ming furniture. The central courtyard has a triple-eaved octagonal "minaret" from which worshipers were traditionally called to prayer, although it is far more akin to a Chinese pagoda. The prayer hall is normally closed to non-Muslims. As this is an active mosque, be circumspect in taking photographs. Avoid visiting on Friday, when access to the mosque is restricted. The mosque is on the tourist radar, hence the RMB25 entrance fee. If you balk at either the crowds or the cost, venture a block or two north. Both **Da Yuan Pi** and **Xiao Yuan Pi** have mosques whose doors are open all day and where there is no admission gate. Though not quite as big, the architecture is nearly identical to the Great Mosque, and outside prayer time at least, there's a good chance you'll be able to enjoy almost complete serenity, a precious thing within the often-chaotic Muslim Quarter.

30 Huajue Xiang. ✆ **029/8727-2541.** Admission RMB25. Apr–Oct 8am–7pm; Nov–Mar 8am–6pm. Subway: Bell Tower, then 10-min. walk west.

The Muslim Quarter ★★★ NEIGHBORHOOD A wander through the timeless lanes of the Muslim Quarter is one of the highlights of a visit to Xi'an, and provides an alluring taste of what lies farther west for travelers setting out along the Silk Road. The Hui have been living here for centuries, and in the lanes, men wearing white skullcaps and women in headscarves tend small noodle and kebab houses, while carts laden with fruit and nuts bustle by. North of the Drum Tower, **Beiyuanmen** (also known as **"Huimin Jie"** or its translation, **"Muslim Street"**) is the natural entrance to the quarter, and is a fun place to wander for a while or grab a kebab meal. However, be warned: This is ground-zero for domestic tourists, and it can become swamped during busy evening hours when the neon splatter is almost as bright as it is back in Shanghai. To really experience the feel of the quarter, you need to head out into the side streets. Take a left off Beiyuanmen, pass the stalls along

Xiyangshi, and turn right onto Guangji Bei Jie before wandering north and west at your leisure. The crowds will thin out, and you may even stumble across a deserted mosque or two.

Beiyuanmen, Xiyangshi & Guangji Bei Jie are the busiest lanes in the Muslim Quarter. Subway: Bell Tower, then 5-min. walk.

Inner Ring Road Attractions

Daming Palace (Daming Gong) ★ MUSEUM/PARK This massive park, just to the north of the walled city, occupies the site of the royal Tang palace and is so large that you could fit four Forbidden Cities inside it. Two-thirds of the area is now public parkland, while one-third houses exhibits and displays from the archaeological work that has been undertaken here since the 1950s. The Danfeng Gate (Danfeng Men) in the south of the complex has been rebuilt anew beside a huge, sparse, public square. North is the **Hanyuan Palace (Hanyuan Gong),** which encloses several museums and exhibition sites and requires a ticket. There's a 3-D cinema with a looped movie explaining the glories of the Tang empire, as well as an impressive scale-model of the original palace. Beyond that is a sprawling network of lawns, paths, and water features that make for a pleasant ramble. Sadly, there isn't anything left of the original palace, and having only opened in 2010, the park is not yet mature. History buffs might get something out of a visit, but it shouldn't be a vital part of your itinerary.

Danfeng Gate entrance off Ziqiang Dong Lu. Admission: Free to park, RMB60 for cultural preservation exhibits, RMB90 for combo ticket including 3-D cinema and archaeological museum. Daily 8am–8pm; museums 9am–6pm. Subway: Anyuan Men, then exit C and a 10-min. walk west along Ziqiang Dong Lu.

Small Wild Goose Pagoda (Xiao Yan Ta) & Xi'an Museum (Xi'an Bowuguan) ★★ TEMPLE/MUSEUM Though normally regarded as the lesser cousin to the more famous Great Wild Goose Pagoda in the south, the Small Wild Goose Pagoda is well worth a couple of hours of your time in Xi'an. The area is huge, comprising parkland, a beautiful 7th-century temple complex, and the modern Xi'an Museum, and makes for a refuge from the relentless noise and traffic of the modern city. The temple is all courtyards and moon gates, with the elegant 13-story brick pagoda, built in 707, standing at its northern edge. The tower, 43m (142 ft.) high, was reduced from its original 15 stories by a succession of earthquakes, most devastatingly in the Shaanxi Earthquake of 1556, but the state of slight disrepair makes it more charming than most of Xi'an's newly polished "old" sights. In the western half of the park lies **Xi'an Museum,** which, like the pagoda, is sorely underrated. It's smaller in scope than the Shaanxi Provincial History Museum, comprising just three halls of jade, seals, and Buddhist sculpture. However, the exhibits are perhaps even more beautifully displayed here than at its sister museum, placed behind ropes rather than being glassed in. The series of stone Buddhist reliefs are simply stunning. Look out too for the fabulous marble map in the circular lobby, best viewed from the mezzanine. This depicts Xi'an's shifting center of gravity, with the Tang city cut in red marble, the smaller Ming city shown in beige, and the ancient Han city rendered in gray.

72 Youyi Xi Lu. ✆ **029/8523-8032.** Daily 8am–5pm for pagoda, 8am–6pm for museum, 8am–10pm for parkland. Admission: Free for park and museum (bring passport), RMB30 to climb pagoda. Subway: Nanshaomen, then 5-min. walk west.

Temple of the Eight Immortals (Ba Xian An) ★ TEMPLE Tucked away in a narrow alley the tour buses can't reach is the most charming temple in Xi'an. As with the Great Mosque, the walk into it is half the adventure, with a flea market out front in some of the temple's old buildings. This becomes a huge antiques market on Sunday mornings (see "Shopping," below). Inside the temple, monks play chess with their hair tied up in traditional Taoist fashion, and are often keen for a chat. The folk legend of the **Eight Immortals (Ba Xian)** is said to have originated here during the late Tang dynasty. The temple was expanded during the Qing dynasty and was a favorite haunt of Empress Dowager Cixi during the time she spent in Xi'an after her escape from Beijing following the Boxer Rebellion (see p. 35). As you look at the temple murals, note the influence of Confucianism on its supposed alter ego, Taoism (see p. 30). The Eight Immortals have a strict hierarchy, with Lu Dongbin in front on his tiger, the rotund Tieguai Li waddling along with his crook to his side, and the one woman, He Xiangu, near the back, carrying a lotus flower.

Wu Dao Shizi Dongjie (from An Ren Fang, continue east 135m/450 ft. before heading south down the first alley on your right. Turn right when the road meets a T-junction. Immediately take a left and continue south to the back of the temple, following the incense vendors). Admission RMB3. Daily 8:30am–6pm. Subway: Fukang Lu, then 10-min. walk southwest.

Qujiang

Great Wild Goose Pagoda (Da Yan Ta) ★ TEMPLE If you were one of the many Brits or Aussies entranced by the cult TV show "Monkey" as a child, the historic Great Wild Goose Pagoda is an essential stop. The Monkey King (*Sun Wukong*) was the fabled companion of the Buddhist monk Xuanzang in Wu Cheng'en's classic novel "Journey to the West" *(Xi You Ji)*. The monkey may not have been real but Xuanzang (596–664) certainly was. His travels to India and subsequent translations of sacred texts helped the spread of Buddhism within China and across East Asia. These texts are housed here in the huge pagoda specifically built for the purpose. The seven-story tower was built in a style similar to those seen by Xuanzang in India—hence the simple, tapering structure. Xuanzang is credited with translating 75 texts into over 1,000 volumes, an amazing feat since the originals contained a host of specialized terms with no Chinese equivalents.

The pagoda lies at the center of the Da Ci'en Temple. Halls at the back contain murals depicting Xuanzang's journey—in many pictures, he is shown holding a fly whisk, intended to send evil spirits into flight. To the left and right of the pagoda's south entrance are prefaces to the texts written by Taizong and Gaozong. Above the east and west doors are barely visible Tang carvings of the Buddha.

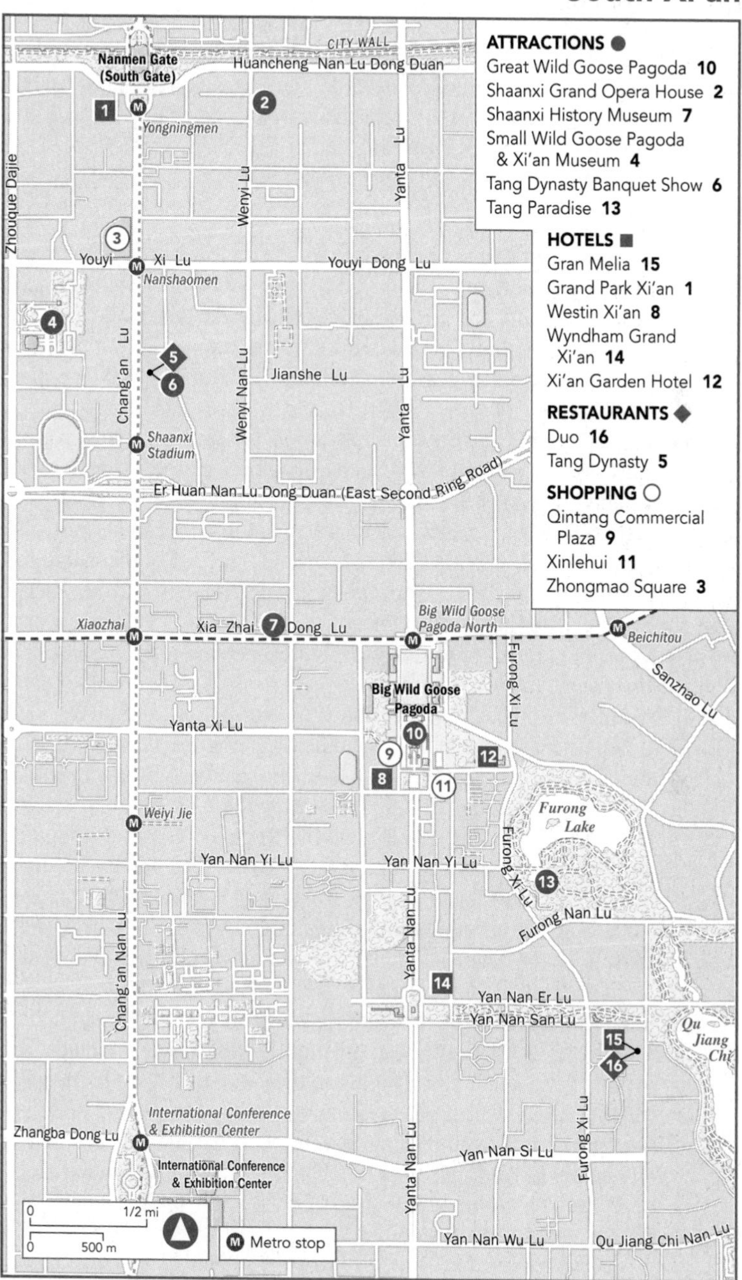
ATTRACTIONS ●
Great Wild Goose Pagoda 10
Shaanxi Grand Opera House 2
Shaanxi History Museum 7
Small Wild Goose Pagoda & Xi'an Museum 4
Tang Dynasty Banquet Show 6
Tang Paradise 13
HOTELS ■
Gran Melia 15
Grand Park Xi'an 1
Westin Xi'an 8
Wyndham Grand Xi'an 14
Xi'an Garden Hotel 12
RESTAURANTS ◆
Duo 16
Tang Dynasty 5
SHOPPING ○
Qintang Commercial Plaza 9
Xinlehui 11
Zhongmao Square 3
CITY WALL
Nanmen Gate (South Gate)
Huancheng Nan Lu Dong Duan
Yongningmen
Zhouque Dajie
Wenyi Lu
Yanta Lu
Youyi Xi Lu
Youyi Dong Lu
Nanshaomen
Chang'an Lu
Jianshe Lu
Wenyi Nan Lu
Shaanxi Stadium
Er Huan Nan Lu Dong Duan (East Second Ring Road)
Xiaozhai
Xia Zhai Dong Lu
Big Wild Goose Pagoda North
Beichitou
Furong Xi Lu
Sanzhao Lu
Big Wild Goose Pagoda
Yanta Xi Lu
Furong Lake
Weiyi Jie
Yan Nan Yi Lu
Furong Nan Lu
Chang'an Nan Lu
Yanta Nan Lu
Yan Nan Er Lu
Yan Nan San Lu
Qu Jiang Chi
International Conference & Exhibition Center
Zhangba Dong Lu
Yan Nan Si Lu
Yan Nan Wu Lu
Qu Jiang Chi Nan Lu
0 1/2 mi
0 500 m
Metro stop

The temple's perimeter has undergone massive and rather glitzy redevelopment, finished with parks, plazas, malls, and a new monorail. To the north is a giant square, which boasts a large pool of fountains, benches, and retail shops lining the mall. A water-fountain-and-light show kicks off nightly at 8pm. Stretching south is a grand boulevard known as the **Great Tang All Day Mall (Da Tang Bu Ye Cheng),** punctuated with a series of huge bronze statues of historical personalities, including one of Xuanzang himself.

Admission RMB50, plus an additional RMB40 to climb the tower. Daily 8am–5pm. Subway: Da Yan Ta.

Shaanxi History Museum (Shanxi Lishi Bowuguan) ★★★ MUSEUM Xi'an's best museum may have a provincial focus, but Shaanxi's astonishingly rich history and archaeological finds make this one of the country's top museums. Around 375,000 items ranging from the Neolithic period to the later years of dynastic rule are held in three chronologically organized exhibition halls, none of which are particularly large, making this one of China's more accessible and concise dips into its generally dizzying history.

Hall 1 gets underway a million years ago, ramps things up with Neolithic finds, before diving wholeheartedly into the stunning filigree bronze-work of the Zhou (1046–256 B.C.), which stands testament to an elaborate ritualized culture. Turn the corner into the Qin (221–206 B.C.) section of the hall to find a small battalion of Terracotta Warriors staring menacingly at you. Though their number are fewer here than at the archaeological site at Lintong, visitors are able to get right up close to the huge figures, making it *the* place to land your close-up photograph.

Hall 2 features exhibits from the Han (226 B.C.–A.D. 220) and Wei (A.D. 220–534), but China's gallop into its golden age becomes clear in hall 3, which features the increasingly elegant and extravagantly colored statuettes of the Sui (581–618) and Tang (618–907). Perhaps the most startling exhibits come in the last hall. From the Song (960–1279) period comes the stunning **Zhongshan Grotto,** complete with a giant seated Buddha and two walls of 10,000 miniature acolytes. Later exhibits from the globetrotting Ming (1368–1644) include stunning **ceramic tomb guardians** that point to a lively trade with the outside world. There's a trader from Africa and a fanciful depiction of a man on horseback battling a leopard.

English, French, and Korean audio guides can be rented from the front desk for RMB30 (RMB100 deposit), but ludicrously, this doesn't include earphones, so bring your own if you want to avoid another RMB10 hit. The guide frustrates with a heavy accent and a numbing focus on numbers, sizes, and dates. However, it's still worth having in your pocket. Though every item in the museum is *labeled* in English, only a handful give any additional detail, and the guide can help to bridge the gap. Allow 2 hours for your entire visit and don't forget to bring your passport.

91 Xiaozhai Dong Lu. http://e.sxhm.com. ✆ **029/8525-4727.** Free Admission. Visitor numbers are restricted to 2,500 in the morning and 1,500 in the afternoon, so get there

early and take your passport. Tues–Sun 8:30am–5pm (last admission 4pm). Closed Mondays. Subway: Xiao Zhai, then 10-min. walk east.

Tang Paradise (Da Tang Fu Rong Yuan) ★ THEME PARK Much of the modern-day Qujiang District lies on the site of the Tang-era imperial gardens, and the local government has tried to capitalize by lavishing money on a series of themed tourism developments in recent years. Tang Paradise is the most lavish of them. To all intents and purposes, it's a theme park (minus the fast rides), and you'll need to be in the mood for Tang kitsch to fully enjoy it. There are 12 zones around a huge central lake, with a number of indoor performances showcasing Tang fashion and music; the biggest and most flamboyant is the 70-minute "Dreams of the Great Tang" (*Meng Hui Da Tang*) pageant, staged at 5:15pm and 8:30pm, extra ticket required. The parkland is undeniably pleasant and the buildings (though new) are impressive in scale and highly photogenic, but the historical aura is not exactly authentic. The park is at its most charming lit up after dark. Come at this time, and you'll also get to enjoy the evening "water film," where lights and images are projected onto the mist generated by dozens of dancing water fountains. It starts at 7:45pm and lasts exactly 23 minutes.

Ticket gate at junction of Yan'nan Yi Lu and Furong Xi Lu. www.tangparadise.cn (Chinese only). Admission: RMB120. Daily 9am–10pm. Subway: Da Yan Ta, then 10-min. walk east.

Other Major Out-of-Town Attractions

Banpo Neolithic Village (Banpo Bowuguan) ★ ARCHAEOLOGICAL SITE/MUSEUM Based around an ongoing archaeological excavation site amid towering new high-rise developments, this extensive museum details life as it was lived in this spot six to seven thousand years ago. The museum is right on top of a Neolithic settlement, dated to around 5000 B.C., making it one of the oldest examples yet found of the "Yangshao" stone-age culture, which prefigured modern Chinese civilization. Given the amount of material unearthed here since its discovery in 1953 (including tools, pottery, and burial jars), it's amazing that only one-fifth of the site has been excavated (mostly due to the cost of preserving what has been discovered). The museum is in three parts, focusing on daily life, burial habits, and pottery-making. There are full-size reproductions of village scenes and Neolithic houses that can be explored. If you are interested in archaeology or ancient Chinese history, it's an essential trip, but can be skipped if time is short. It is, however, the only major Xi'an sight, outside of the city center, which had decent subway access at the time of writing.

155 Banpo Lu. Admission RMB60. 8:30am–5:30pm. ✆ **029/8246-7977.** Subway: Ban Po, then Exit A and walk 5 min. east along Changle Dong Lu. Turn left into Banpo Lu and the museum is 5 min. farther, on your left.

Emperor Jingdi's Mausoleum (Han Yangling) ★★★ ARCHAEOLOGICAL SITE/MUSEUM Discovered by a works crew building the new airport road in 1990, Han Yangling, the mausoleum of Han dynasty emperor Jingdi (157–141 B.C.), deserves far more attention than it has received to date. Few tourists make it here, and though it doesn't quite have the instant wow-factor of the Terracotta Warriors, the beautifully presented underground museum and lack of crowds allow for better appreciation of the amazing archaeological finds.

As across town, the chief highlight is the thousands of clay figurines, displayed in their originally discovered state. In total there are 10,000, located in 81 pits that radiate out from the emperor's protruding burial mound. Only the 21 pits to the northeast of the emperor's tomb have been excavated to date. Visitors can get views unavailable at Lintong, thanks to a beautifully low-lit glass walkway that runs directly over the top of the pits and then down alongside them. In some of the pits, the figures are toppled like bowling pins; in others, they remain caked in loess, with only columns of protruding heads to indicate what lies beneath. There are also examples of the molds used to cast the figures, which help to illustrate their production, said to have taken some 17,000 workers nearly three decades. The figures were cast without arms, which were fashioned from wood and added later. More important figurines were also clothed in miniature silk garments, but both wood and silk have long since perished. Some of the figures are clearly identifiable as eunuchs, and as such, this is the earliest evidence of this practice in the Chinese court.

A comparison with the "original" warriors offers insight into the changes in the seven short decades between Qin Shihuang's death and that of Jingdi. The Terracotta Army was built during a turbulent time when Qin was trying to establish absolute supremacy and unify the country for the first time. Emperor Jingdi ruled over a less militarized empire and was a devoted Taoist. Thus, alongside soldiers, nobles, and servants, there are herds of pigs, sheep, and cows. Jingdi obviously felt less need for grand gestures; while the Terracotta Warriors were significantly *taller* than real soldiers of the time, Jingdi's figures come in at a third of human height.

Toward the end of the museum is a holographic film screening (RMB10), worth seeing for the technology more than the content. Past the emperor's burial mound, to the south, a Tang palace has been built around the remains of the south gate to the mausoleum site. There's not much to see here, just two giant platypus-shaped mounds of loess, but it gives an idea of the scale of the original complex. There's no English language audio guide, but an English-speaking guide can be hired at the underground museum for RMB120 (40 min.). The site is close to the airport and is a perfect way to begin, or end, your trip. Allow 90 minutes.

Han Yangling (15-min. drive from the airport). Admission Mar–Nov RMB80; Dec–Feb RMB55. 8:30am–5pm. RMB250–RMB300 taxi return from Xi'an (having the driver take you to the museum en route to the airport and waiting while you explore should cost about the same).

WHERE TO STAY

Xi'an's hotel scene has come a long way in recent years. The shiniest new hotels are being built down in Qujiang District, where a huge amount of development cash has gentrified what was once a fairly downmarket suburb. Staying here puts you within easy reach of the Great Wild Goose Pagoda, the Shaanxi History Museum, and Tang Paradise, as well as surrounding restaurants and shops. There's a slightly exclusive, resort feel to the area, and it's less crowded than staying in town, but the location is inconvenient for central sights. The opening of Line 3 of the subway (expected to be in 2016) will make it easier to jump on the subway into the city center. Staying within the walled city remains the best option for most short-stay visitors. The big-brand foreign hotels are mainly located toward the fringes, while the most central hotels, around the Bell Tower, are Chinese-managed three- and four-stars. There are some decent options but there's a price to be paid for proximity to central sights. Xi Dajie and Dong Dajie (where the majority of the hotels are located) are both busy commuter thoroughfares, and traffic noise is high. Generally speaking, the main sights are toward the southern end of the walled city, with far less to do and see in the north. In the south, there are a few quieter, simpler options, including boutique backpacker lodges and apartment hotels. Staying close to the Terracotta Warriors out in Lintong has limited appeal. Apart from Qin's famous tomb, there is really not much to do, and the ride into town is both expensive and time-consuming.

Most hotels listed below will offer some discount, and reductions of as much as 50% off the rack rates can be achieved with bargaining out of peak season.

City Center

EXPENSIVE

Hilton Xi'an ★★ A few years younger than its nearby rival, Sofitel, the Hilton Xi'an has been well maintained and is probably the most luxurious of the major hotels within the city walls. The downstairs lobby sparkles in marble and is festooned with bombastic art pieces inspired by local history. Upstairs, rooms have large windows, 42-inch TVs, and carpets that have retained their bounce, while bathrooms have generous tubs and separate showers. It's worth paying a little extra to stay in one of the deluxe rooms above the sixth floor. Those facing the interior courtyard have a pleasant outlook but are quieter than city-view rooms. Amenities are excellent, including a beautiful pool and gym complex, and an outdoor garden on the sixth floor. Stay for five-star comfort and top service, though know that the city-center attractions are just out of easy reach on foot (the walk is 30 min.). The difficulties in getting a taxi make this matter more than it probably should.

199 Dongxin Jie. www3.hilton.com/en/hotels/china/hilton-xian-XIYHIHI/index.html. ✆ **029/8738-8888.** 309 units. RMB780 standard rooms, RMB930 deluxe, RMB2,980 suite. Subway: Wulukou. **Amenities:** 3 restaurants; bar; gym; roof garden; swimming pool; spa; babysitting service; Wi-Fi: RMB20 per hour; RMB60 per day (included in some room rates).

Sofitel Renmin Square ★ The Sofitel has enjoyed nearly a decade at the top of Xi'an's five-star market but is showing a bit of strain now that the competition has been ramped up in recent years. The pros remain: the attractive twin-winged building and the excellent location, occupying center stage in a quiet, off-street development close to the central city sights (Muslim Street is about a 20-min. walk). The restaurants and bars are among the city's best fine-dining options, albeit expensive. However, service levels have dropped off as staff have apparently been poached by the other big hotels coming through, and the rooms, though still perfectly pleasant, are looking a touch dated. All this is reflected in the prices, which are, if anything, cheaper now than a few years ago, making this a good value five-star stay. Sofitel's sister hotels, the Grand Mercure, and Mercure, are in the same compound and provide cheaper alternatives, if needed.

319 Dongxin Jie. www.sofitel.com. ✆ **029/8792-8888.** 414 units. RMB800–RMB1,000 standard rooms. Subway: Wulukou, then 15-min. walk. **Amenities:** 4 restaurants; 2 bars; gym; swimming pool; free Wi-Fi.

MODERATE

Citadines Central Xi'an ★★★ Ascott has three Citadines-branded apartment hotels scattered around Xi'an. They're primarily aimed at the increasing numbers of Korean and Western expats who stay in Xi'an for long periods, often with family in tow. This city-center location offers rich rewards for short-stay visitors, mainly on account of its fabulous location. It's close to the Drum Tower and Muslim Quarter but occupies a peaceful niche just off the main drag. Studio rooms are spacious, though slightly dated, with a lounge and bedroom area divided by a screen and a wall-mounted TV that slides between the two. There's great wardrobe space and a kitchenette in each room. Deluxe rooms on the top floor have one- or two-bedroom options and have been recently renovated, with new furniture and beige wood floors. All rooms open onto balconies that overlook a lovely garden atrium that runs from the 6th to the 12th floor. Below are meeting rooms and a self-service laundry, while on the top floor is a fabulous gym—with a view, a large pool table, and access to the roof of the building where guests can hang out during the summer and look across the Xi'an rooftops.

36 Zhubashi (south of the Drum Tower). ✆ **029/8576-1188.** 6 units. RMB450–RMB500 studios, RMB640 1-bedroom deluxe rooms, online advance discounts available. Subway: Zhong Lou. **Amenities:** Restaurant; self-service laundry; roof terrace; games room; gym; free Wi-Fi.

Grand Noble ★ Rising above the hectic thoroughfare of Dong Dajie, the huge Grand Noble is one of the few locally managed hotels clustered around the Drum Tower that will appeal to budget-conscious travelers looking for a comfy central stay. The rooms have three-star quality fittings and furniture, though the glass desks and wall-mounted flatscreens lend a touch of class. Bathrooms are a touch cramped but liberally decked with glass and mirrors. Public areas are surprisingly polished. The breakfast spread is foreigner-friendly, with American, European, and Korean options, while Gordon's bar is always busy at night and good for socializing with the many overseas tour groups that breeze through. Though the immediate surrounds are nothing to write home about, the Bell and Drum Towers are an easy 10-minute walk away.

334 Dong Dajie. www.gnhotel.com. ✆ **029/8769-0000.** 428 units. RMB698 standard rooms. Subway: Zhong Lou. **Amenities:** Restaurant; bar; massage rooms; gym; free Wi-Fi.

INEXPENSIVE

Jano's Backpackers ★★★ Don't be put off by the name, which sneakily hides the fact that this is one of Xi'an's funkiest boutique hotels. Downstairs it's traditional backpacker stuff, with foosball, a reading room, and the doodles of past guests scrawled over the walls. Upstairs the mood is completely different: The five private rooms are each decked out in beautiful antique furniture and have hardwood floors, artwork hanging from the walls, and tidy bathrooms with fetching Ming-style blue-and-white porcelain washbowls. The finishes are classy rather than luxurious. However, mattresses and bedding are three-star standard, and rooms are a touch gloomy, owing to the fact that the hostel is in the shadow of the south city wall. On the plus side, this also makes it a fantastic location for exploring the most interesting part of old Xi'an, especially given the very reasonable cost. Family travelers will appreciate the dedicated family room, where parents can sleep on a high mezzanine.

69 Shuncheng Nan Lu (75m east of the South Gate). http://xian-backpackers.com. ✆ **029/8725-6656.** 5 private units, plus dorms. RMB320 superior rooms, RMB390 family rooms. Subway: Yongningmen. **Amenities:** Cafe; attached bar; games room; free Wi-Fi.

Mercure ★ The smallest and cheapest of the three Accor hotels that make up the Renmin Square complex, Mercure offers a cheap, functional stay amid the quiet of this leafy, former-government compound, a 15-minute stroll from the center of the old city. Rooms are a bit cramped, with bulky, old-style TVs, but beds are comfy and bathrooms positively plush (no baths). Breakfast is served on-site, though guests are welcome to use the excellent facilities in the two neighboring hotels.

319 Dongxin Jie. www.mercure.com/gb/hotel-5975-mercure-on-renmin-square-xian/index.shtml. ✆ **029/8792-8888.** 103 units. RMB450 standard rooms. Subway: Zhong Lou, then 15-min. walk. **Amenities:** Restaurant; free Wi-Fi; free use of sister hotels' facilities, including gym and swimming pool.

Melody Hotel ★ An old-timer on the Xi'an hotel circuit, Melody got the renovation it had been crying out for in late 2014. It's a hotel in the Home Inn style, with zero amenities and simple rooms fitted with air-conditioning, a kettle, a TV, and a small bathroom (no baths). However, everything is new, from the TVs and carpets in the room to the newly marbled and surprisingly stylish lobby. Best of all, you are right on top of the Muslim Quarter and the Bell and Drum Towers, with the city walls only a short walk south. The more expensive rooms face the Drum Tower directly, but these can be noisy, so ask for a room facing south or west, as high up as possible. Melody is a simple hotel, and staff speak only halting English, but it will please those looking for presentable rooms at a low price in a central spot.

86 Xi Dajie (opposite the Drum Tower). www.melodyhotelxian.cn. ✆ **029/8728-8888.** 138 units. RMB398–RMB498 standard room. Subway: Zhong Lou. **Amenities:** Free Wi-Fi.

Xiangzimen International Youth Hostel ★ Conjuring the feel of a Beijing courtyard residence, Xiangzimen is an attractive hostel boasting a fantastic location beside the south wall. Basement rooms are windowless and dreary, but ensuite rooms on the second floor are large and airy and have TVs and windows overlooking the quiet street outside. Avoid third-floor rooms, which allow smoking and are particularly stale. The public areas have the feel of an old-time inn, with wooden fittings and charming museum pieces, like the full-size rickshaw on the second floor. Desk staff are young and friendly and speak excellent English. Downstairs, there's a long, conservatory-style dining room with simple Western dishes, as well as a small, convivial bar at the front.

16 Xiangzimiao Jie (close to Defu Xiang). www.yhaxian.com. ✆ **029/6286-7999.** RMB200 standard ensuite room. Subway: Yongningmen. **Amenities:** Restaurant; bar; laundry; games room; free Wi-Fi.

Inner Ring Road

MODERATE

Grand Park Xi'an ★ One of the grand old dames of the Xi'an hospitality scene, this Hong Kong–managed hotel was built in 1992 in a brilliant location, overlooking the South Gate of the old city walls. It's showing its age a little in the guestrooms, which are clean and spacious but uninspired. Amenities are similarly simple, with a modern gym and attached sauna the highlight, though the cavernous lobby lounge is unexpectedly swanky, overlooked by the room balconies and glass elevators. When booking, ask for one of the east-facing rooms looking out over the wall. The South Gate and surrounding watchtowers sparkle in neon after dark, and this is probably the best hotel view in all of Xi'an. Despite being outside the walls, it's only a 10-minute walk to get to the Shuyuanmen pedestrian street and south wall bars, and 15 minutes to the Bell Tower.

12 Xi Duan, Huancheng Nan Lu. www.parkhotelgroup.com/xian/default-en.html. ✆ **029/8760-8888.** 325 units. RMB600 standard room. Subway: Yongningmen. **Amenities:** Restaurant; bar; fitness center; free Wi-Fi.

INEXPENSIVE

Xi'an Green Forest Hotel ★ Brushing shoulders with a number of dreary-looking motels and guesthouses just north of the city walls, Green Forest is a budget hostel with boutique aspirations that attracts a young, friendly crowd. It's not particularly easy to find, tucked away inside a building that has other budget hotels. The fourth-floor lobby has a pleasant, loungy ambience, with bookshelves and a number of comfy booths for beer and chatting. Guest floors go up to a hip little roof bar overlooking the main drag and a view back to the North Gate of the city walls. "Queen" ensuite rooms have attractive pine beds and exposed brickwork, though they're small, and the soundproofing is quite poor. Try to bag a room on the sixth or seventh floors, far enough away from both lobby and roof bar to minimize noise. It's not inside the city walls, but with the North Gate subway station only 100m away, this is a decent low-budget base from which to explore the city.

4/F, 9 Beiguan Zhengjie. www.greenforesthostel.com. ✆ **010/6445-7463.** 48 units. RMB178 standard room. Subway: Anyuanmen. **Amenities:** Restaurant; bar; free Wi-Fi.

Qujiang District

EXPENSIVE

Gran Melia ★★ The Spanish chain is a latecomer to the hotel business in China and has focused on inland cities where competition is less intense. Beijing's loss is Xi'an's gain, as on design, service, and facilities, the Gran Melia is probably the best five-star in town. Rooms are exceptionally large and have advanced electronics for controlling curtains and lights, luxuriant new carpets, high ceilings, and a fabulous glassed-in bathroom with freestanding bath tub. The showcase restaurant, Duo, continues the Spanish theme, with tapas and sangria, and has patio tables beside landscaped gardens and a lake. The breakfast buffet in Café Gran Mercado compares with Shanghai's finest, while the pool and spa are spotless. The hotel is part of a mammoth commercial complex, and at the time of writing, it was still struggling to pull in the patrons. It means that the hotel is likely to be quiet, at least in the short-term. The location is the biggest drawback by far. Though the adjacent lake and gardens create a resort feel, the hotel is far from the sights of the city center and—with the exception of Tang Paradise—even sights within Qujiang are not easily walkable.

1666 Qujiangchi Xi Lu. www.melia.com/en/hotels/china/xian/gran-melia-xian/index.html. ✆ **029/6821-6666.** 389 units. RMB1,200 standard rooms including breakfast. Subway: None. **Amenities:** 3 restaurants; piano lounge; cigar lounge; spa; Turkish baths; swimming pool; free Wi-Fi.

Westin Xi'an ★★ The first luxury hotel to join the gentrification game down in Qujiang is by far the most popular, attracting a nice mixture of local tourists, expat families, business types, and young Korean and Japanese travelers. This is not your average five-star high-rise. The Westin has been built in the mold of a Tang-dynasty palace, with *guzheng* (a classical Chinese zither) music serenading guests as they step into the stylish lobby, and a private museum in the basement. Rooms take shape around a series of quiet atriums, and it can be a long tramp along vast corridors to get to the front-of-house facilities. Rooms are comfortable, with beds as wide as they are long, though the porthole windows don't allow much of a view and the bathrooms are, if anything, *too* big for their own good. The Japanese restaurant is superb and has a great all-you-can-eat a la carte lunchtime deal. It's an all-Asian staff at the breakfast buffet, and Eastern tastes, particularly Korean, take precedence over Western staples. The Westin's big draw is its location, immediately next to the Great Wild Goose Pagoda and the adjacent landscaped gardens.

66 Ci'en Lu. www.starwoodhotels.com/westin/property/overview/index.html. ✆ **029/6568-6568.** 320 units. From RMB850 standard rooms. Subway: Da Yan Ta. **Amenities:** 3 restaurants; cocktail bar; kids' play area; private museum; free Wi-Fi.

Wyndham Grand ★ The Wyndham Grand is a blockbuster celebration of the tastes of newly rich locals. Everything is supersized, from the floor-to-ceiling windows and giant desks in the rooms, to the long corridors—50% wider than anything else in the city—to the imposing white marble lobby.

Rooms are also huge and warmly decorated, with the bathrooms particularly resplendent in Mediterranean mosaics, dark wood, and rich marble. The front-desk service is as warm and welcoming as you'll get in Xi'an. For interior comforts, it's nigh-on-faultless, and anyone seeking space will enjoy the vibe. However, it will probably please business travelers and conference organizers more than your average tourist, not least because of the rather awkward location, 1.5km (1 mile) south of the Great Wild Goose Pagoda.

208 Ci'en Dong Lu. www.wyndhamgrandxian.com/index.php. ✆ **029/6821-9999.** 565 units. RMB1,000 standard rooms, RMB3,400 suites. Subway: None. **Amenities:** Restaurant; bar; spa; swimming pool; gym; free Wi-Fi.

MODERATE

Xi'an Garden Hotel ★ At the time of writing, the Xi'an Garden Hotel was about to undergo a yearlong period of renovation. It's an old, state-run guesthouse dating from the mid-'90s, and rooms were extremely tired. However, the location is good, blending into the landscaped gardens around the Great Wild Goose Pagoda, and the hotel grounds are among the most charming in Xi'an. Based in three wings around a beautiful central lake, the Tang Garden is dotted with wildlife and pretty cherry trees that blossom spectacularly in the spring, made to please the Tang-obsessed Japanese who used to dominate tourism here. The hotel is due to reopen in summer 2016, with refreshed rooms and amenities. Assuming no changes to the landscaping or staffing, expect rudimentary local service standards and a charming garden setting, with brand new rooms.

40 Yanyin Lu. www.gardenhotelxian.cn. ✆ **029/8760-1111.** 280 units. RMB650 standard rooms, approx. Subway: Da Yan Ta. **Amenities:** Restaurant; massage rooms; teahouse; free Wi-Fi.

WHERE TO EAT

Xi'an's city-center dining scene is a peculiar hybrid. There are broadly four kinds of local restaurants: First up are the clutch of officially sanctioned **"famous" restaurants** (a few are okay, but they tend to live off their "time-honored-brand" status, awarded by the city's tourism authorities, without needing to put in much effort); secondly, there are a number of small **Shaanxi chain diners** (these are normally safe, cheap, and tasty and have simple English language menus, but there's little wow-factor); there's far more glitz at the coterie of all-dancing **Tang banquets** aimed at tour groups (these are highly packaged and the food is mass-produced, but they can be fun, at least the first time you try one); finally, there's **street food.** Xi'an has some of the most celebrated snacks in China, but finding a reliable restaurant to bag yourself a *Rou Jia Mo* or a bowl of *Yangrou Paomo* (see "Xi'an Specialties" box) is not easy. The Muslim Quarter is the place to head, packed as it is with stalls and family-run hole-in-the-wall joints. Here there's little English on the menus, and none spoken, so travelers will likely need to use the point-and-gesture method. I recommend heading into one of the busier restaurants along **Da Pi Yuan,** which runs west from the top end of Beiyuanmen (Huimin Jie).

Restaurants here are packed night after night with plastic tables and chairs spilling out onto the street. This is where local Xi'an residents come to sample the halal delights of the Hui kitchens. Beiyuanmen (aka "Muslim Street") itself is a riot of garish neon and sizzling platters. Though a handful of stalls have English-language signs, this is not actually the best place to eat, with prices high and quality often slapdash. It's convenient for a quick snack, but don't plan on having a proper meal here.

The best examples of the local restaurants listed above are given below. If you're staying in Xi'an long, it's more than possible you'll tire of the various bread, broth, and mutton combos. Xi'an has no shortage of the big American fast-food chains (McDonalds, KFC, and Subway are all well represented). There are a growing number of Chinese-run "Western" restaurants that appeal to Xi'an's new wealthy with a distinctly sinicized take on French or Italian food. The very best Western dining is—unsurprisingly—in the top hotels, which have some fantastic restaurants, but the high prices are not always reflected in presentation and service standards.

With one exception, the restaurants reviewed below are all in the city center—by far the best place to eat. If you are feeling hungry while touring

Xi'an Specialties

Xi'an has some of the best street food in the country. Though the most famous have come to define Shaanxi cuisine, it's not hard to see the cosmopolitan blend that has gone into their invention. The most famous dish, ***Yangrou Paomo*** (羊肉泡馍), torn bread soaked in a mutton broth, combines Mongolia's mutton habit, the doughy breads beloved of Central Asia, and the kind of steaming soup drunk across China's freezing north. Start out with two flattened and condensed slabs of bread, tear these into tiny pieces, and pop them into the empty bowl. When you've finished, your bowl will be taken away and refilled with broth and noodles. Stir in the coriander and chili, and when your palate gets greasy, nibble a clove of garlic. Xi'an's most famous snack is ***Rou Jia Mo*** (肉夹馍). If you're struggling with the pronunciation, trying saying the name of James Bond actor "Roger Moore," and you'll be nine-tenths of the way there. This is Xi'an's answer to the hamburger, with finely chopped pork pressed between two halves of a lightly toasted bun with a slightly sweet gravy dripped in. Served cold and soggy, they can be most unpleasant, but made properly and eaten fresh, there's almost nothing better. Noodles are a particular specialty and come in a variety of guises. ***Biang Biang Mian*** are wide noodle slabs that resemble lasagna pasta sheets, dunked in meat gravy and chili oil and served with shredded pork and pickled condiments. ***Ma Jiang Liang Pi*** (麻将凉皮), or *Niang Pi* in the local vernacular, is thick, udon-like noodles served cold and slopped with a rich, fragrant sesame paste. Though more commonly associated with the nearby city of Lanzhou, ***La Mian*** (拉面)—pulled noodles—shops are rife in Xi'an. Noodles are made in front of customers through a noisy process of rolling, pounding, and pulling, and served in a mutton broth. The listings here will point you in the direction of some of the more famous restaurants specializing in these dishes, but the Muslim Quarter has dozens of small, family-run restaurants that may well serve them all.

elsewhere, head to the nearest major hotel or mall (see the "Where to Stay" section for hotel locations, and the introduction to the "Shopping" section for information about malls).

De Fa Chang (德发长) ★★ DUMPLINGS A great example of one of Xi'an's "time-honored brands," De Fa Chang is a loud and lively restaurant, strung with socialist banners and staffed by elderly waitresses who look like they haven't had a day off in 50 years. The entrance is on the first story in the middle of the crumbling old block that runs between the Bell and Drum Towers. The canteen downstairs is always bustling and serves a variety of multicolored dumplings and side dishes, ordered from a garish McDonalds-style counter and dished up from wheeled carts in the style of Cantonese dim sum. Upstairs it's a little more refined, with an 18-course dumpling banquet (RMB118) on offer. Tasty *xiaochi* (snacks) will come in a steady stream to your table. All in all, De Fa Chang is rough and ready, but for delicious dumplings and lovely cut-price views over the Bell Tower Square, it's well worth a visit.

1/F, 3 Xi Dajie, Zhonglou Guangchang. ✆ **029/8721-4060.** Meal for two RMB60–RMB200. No credit cards. Daily 10:30am–9:30pm. Subway: Bell Tower.

Ding Ding Xiang (顶顶香) ★★ SHAANXI A conveniently located branch of one of Xi'an's best local chains, Ding Ding Xiang's specialty is *Suan Dou Jiao Rou Mo*, oily piles of pickled peppers and ground meat that can be gathered up in thin, Peking Duck–style pancakes. These come in traditional wheat (*jian bing*) or lurid green vegetable (*shucai jian bing*) varieties. The sour and spicy *tu dou si* (shredded potato) is also a marvel. The dining space is surprisingly trendy, with birdcages, mirrors festooning the downstairs space, and retro posters of major American and European cities lining the walls upstairs. Waitstaff speak no English, but the menus have excellent English explanations, as well as large pictures of the food.

130 Nanyuanmen, Fen Xiang (on south side of Fen Xiang, just west of Zhubashi). www.ddxcy.com (Chinese only). ✆ **029/8728-8022.** Meal for two RMB60–RMB100. No credit cards. Daily 10:30am–midnight. Subway: Bell Tower, then 10-min. walk.

Duo ★★ SPANISH Authentic Spanish food is hard to come by in China, but this new restaurant in the basement of the Gran Melia is about as good as it gets away from the motherland. Both the head chef and restaurant manager are from Spain, and in the best Iberian traditions, the menu is seafood-heavy, with dishes like Barcelona Black Rice with Aioli Sauce (RMB336 for two) and Lobster Rice (RMB676) emerging in skillets. Staff carry iPads to offer a visual aid to menu selections, and there's a superb selection of imported wines. The indoor space is sleek, but Xian's warm summer weather can be enjoyed out on the lakeside terrace. It's well worth visiting on Thursday, when all-you-can-eat mini tapas and sangria are served from the bar, reminiscent of a Barcelona *pinxtos* bar. The downside to all this authentic goodness? It's expensive.

1666 Qujiangchi Xi Lu, Qujiang. ✆ **029/6821-6666.** Meal for two RMB600–RMB1,000. Daily 11am–2pm, 5:30–10pm. Subway: Bei Chi Tou, then 15-min. walk.

Fanji Lazhi Roudian (樊记腊汁肉店) ★★ MUSLIM An open secret among in-the-know locals, Fanji Lazhi Roudian is perhaps the best vendor of Shaanxi's most widely consumed snack, *Rou Jia Mo* (see Xi'an Specialties box). One is unlikely to fill you up, but it's perfect for a snack on the run, or a couple can be combined with the tasty wonton soup to make a simple but hearty meal. There's no English on the frontage; just look out for the turquoise wipe-clean tables and chairs. However, a single, tatty English-language menu is lodged behind the front desk. Smile and look interested, and it will be magically produced. Ask for the good-quality *(youzhi)* bun (RMB8).

53 Zhubashi (50m south of Xi Dajie on the road's east side). ✆ **029/8727-3917.** Meal for two RMB40. No credit cards. Daily 8am–9pm. Subway: Bell Tower, then 10-min. walk.

Isola del Nord ★ ITALIAN You'll be forgiven for thinking you've been magically transported to Hong Kong on arrival at Isola del Nord, not for the cracking Cantonese fare but rather for the fact that only in Hong Kong will you find a restaurant so bizarrely located. Head past the security guards of an anonymous high-rise block, into the commuter lifts used by office workers, tiptoe down nondescript white-tiled corridors, and just when you think you've taken a wrong turn, open a door onto a Chinese approximation of Mediterranean paradise: walls painted in sun-kissed yellow, laid-back jazz riffs over the PA, and the aroma of tomatoes and olives pervading the air. The menu is simple, offering pizzas (RMB75–RMB90) and pastas with tomato and cream bases (RMB60–RMB80), while there's draft Belgian blonde beer (RMB40) on the drinks list, as well as sangria. This is a Chinese-run Western restaurant, make no mistake, and it attracts well-to-do Chinese families more than it does expats. Nevertheless, it makes a pleasant break from the street clamor at prices well below what you'll find in five-star Western restaurants. It's odd, but kind of charming.

11/F, B Tower, Kai'ai Dasha, 1 Xi Huamen Dajie. (It's the compound on the north side of the street, right at the junction with Bei Dajie. Walk along a driveway beneath the first building and into the block behind.) ✆ **029/8720-1501.** Meal for two RMB150–RMB250. Daily 11:30am–9:30pm. Subway: Bell Tower, then 5-min. walk.

Jia San Guantang Baozi (贾三灌汤包子) ★ MUSLIM This old stalwart of Muslim Street has been expanded in recent years, with locals tending to rub shoulders on the busy first-floor dining space, and the slightly quiet upstairs rooms favored by foreigners and tour groups. There's no English on the exterior—you'll know you're there when you see the monstrous golden signs over the entrance and a wall festooned with photographs of Xi'an notables—but it's one of the few Muslim Quarter restaurants to have English on menus. The specialty dish is *Guantang Baozi,* bready dumplings that come in a choice of beef, lamb, or "three flavors"—lamb, mushroom, and shrimp. The dumplings have piping-hot soup inside, so let them cool before testing your chopstick skills. This dish is best washed down with *Ba Bao Tian Xifan,* a sweet rice porridge filled with peanuts, raisins, and hawthorn and medlar berries.

93 Beiyuanmen (135m north of Drum Tower on the east side of the street). ✆ **029/8725-7507.** Meal for two RMB50. No credit cards. Daily 8:30am–11pm. Subway: Bell Tower, then 5-min. walk.

Lao Sun Jia (老孙家) ★ SHAANXI Lao Sun Jia first opened its doors in 1898, and it remains a top spot for sampling Xi'an's most celebrated dish, *Yangrou Paomo* (see Xi'an Specialties box). One of three modern branches, this outlet is hidden away on the fifth floor of a mall complex. Upon leaving the glass elevator from street level, guests are led into a cavernous inner dining hall, with the restaurant's historic credentials paraded in various wall displays. Waitstaff are clearly on low-wage, iron-rice-bowl contracts and can be surly, but an English menu helps with ordering. Customers *must* break their own bread here—Chinese diners would not have it any other way. Simply take two or three slabs and get tearing, though be prepared for a condescending snort from the waitress when she sees how poorly you've done your job. Expert diners grind their bread into virtual crumbs for maximum flavor, and it's unlikely a first-timer will make the grade. If the headline dish doesn't fill you up, try the lamb dumplings *(Suan Tang Shuijiao)* and a local favorite, *Fenzheng Yangrou,* lamb "breaded" with pieces of broken rice.

334 Dong Dajie, just west of Nan Xinjie (look for the 1898 sign and take the lift to the 5th floor). ✆ **029/8742-1858.** Reservations recommended. Meal for two RMB150. No credit cards. Daily 9am–9pm. Subway: Bell Tower, then 10-min. walk.

Lao Wan (老碗) ★★ SHAANXI Tucked away on the north side of Xiangzimiao Jie, Lao Wan (literally "Old Bowl") opens up from an easy-to-miss frontage (where there's no English) into a labyrinthine interior, charmingly clad in wood finishings and latticework. It's noisy and bustling, with flush-cheeked waitresses bellowing into the cacophony as they dash between the various semi-private rooms. There's page after page of local specialties on the menu, the highlight being the *hulu* whole chicken (RMB58), soaked in soy sauce, steamed, and then flattened before being deep-fried to a crisp. If that sounds a little too adventurous, Lao Wan also does a mean sweet-and-sour pork, not so different from the takeout back home. If that doesn't sound foreigner-friendly enough, there's even imported German wheat beer on the menu.

55 Xiangzimiao Jie (nr. jnc. with Dachejia Xiang). ✆ **029/6889-3666.** Meal for two RMB60–RMB150. 11:30am–9:30pm. Subway: Yongningmen, then 10-min. walk.

Noodle King (Biang Biang Mian) ★ SHAANXI A bona fide hole-in-the-wall joint but one of the most famous places to sample the restaurant's eponymous specialty. It's old-fashioned bumpkin service, with the giant "belt" noodles chucked in front of you in quick-time. However, the incongruous wall-hung pictures of Chinese film and TV stars who have visited is testament to the restaurant's peculiar popularity. There's no English-language menu; order at the front desk as you go in. *Biang biang* noodles are the only item on the menu, but choose between different toppings. The best of the (few) options is the *san he yi* (three-in-one), where the meat, gravy, and chili are slopped on in liberal quantities. The restaurant's English name is writ small on the red sign, beneath the Noodle King logo, a bespectacled, goateed face. It's on the south side of Fen Xiang, just opposite Nanyuanmen alley.

South side of Fen Xiang, close to Nanyuanmen. ✆ **029/8725-6611.** Meal for two RMB32. No credit cards. 9am–9:30pm. Subway: Bell Tower, then 15-min. walk.

Catching Chinese Shadows

Before karaoke, *Piying* was the staple entertainment of rural Shaanxi folk. The puppet performers are carved from leather and dyed dazzling colors. There are over 600 different plays, ranging from legends to love stories to kung-fu epics. Unlike opera, this is loud, irreverent entertainment for the masses. *Piying* is a dying art form; it takes 10 years to learn the craft, and for most, driving a taxi is a more appealing option. However, tourism may just save the day, and short performances can now be seen on request at **Gaojia Dayuan** (8:30am–11pm; entrance RMB30) on the western side of Muslim Street (144 Beiyuanmen) in the Muslim Quarter. This traditional courtyard residence, once home to Qing official Gao Yuesong, has been attractively restored and also contains an art gallery and a teahouse.

Shanxi 13 (Shan Shi San) ★★ DESSERTS A wonderful dessert shop, dressed up like a sophisticated teahouse of old, which puts the lie to the notion that Xi'an snacks are all about bread and mutton. There are a variety of sweet snacks, but most of the customers who stream through are here for the ice cream, which comes in a dizzying variety of flavors, from traditional Chinese fruits (dragon fruit, mandarin, and mango) to spectacular savory options such as glutinous rice, taro, and tofu. There's a takeout counter at the far end, but better to find a seat amid the bookshelves and beneath the hanging lamps and soak up the atmosphere.

270 Beiyuanmen (near Da Pi Yuan, northern end of Muslim Street). ✆ **029/8726-5413.** Dessert for two RMB60. Daily 9:30am–10pm. Subway: Bell Tower, then 15-min. walk.

Tang Dynasty (Tang Yue Gong) ★ BANQUET The oldest of the two big Tang extravaganza shows is still just about the best. Managed by a Hong Kong company with a clear eye for the foreign market, the impressively grand space opens as a buffet at lunchtime but gets packed in the evening when a six-course "Tang Dynasty" banquet (rice wine included) is punctuated by performances on the huge main stage. The dance is all about mass choreography and lavish costumes, while the musical interludes are played on traditional instruments, such as the *pai xiao* bamboo flute. A slightly cheaper dumpling banquet is an alternative to the main offering. If you can get past the slickness and the feeling that it's just for foreigners (the voice-overs are all in English), the show makes a spectacular night out. Dinner starts serving at 6:30pm; the show (70 min.) begins at 8:30pm. Ask your concierge to book a table.

75 Chang'an Bei Lu. www.xiantangdynasty.com. ✆ **029/8782-2222.** Reservations required. Tang Dynasty banquet and show RMB500; Dumpling Banquet and show RMB400. Daily 11am–2:30pm, 6–10pm. Subway: Between Nanshaomen and Tiyu Chang stations.

SHOPPING

The rise of affluent middle-class shoppers in Xi'an has led to an explosion of shops and malls in recent years. The crowds heave at weekends along **Dong**

Dajie (just east of the Bell Tower) and **Luomashi Pedestrian Street** (which runs south of Dong Dajie). It's mainly local fashions here, though there's no shortage of knockoff and luxury-brand imitations, along with Western coffee shops and fast-food joints. The Bell Tower Square (Zhonglou Guangchang) itself is also a riot of commerce. Souvenir stalls line the first-floor verandah between the Drum and Bell Towers, and Hong Kong's **Century Ginwa** (Shiji Jinhua) runs a popular mall. To the southeast of Bell Tower Square is **Kaiyuan Square (Kaiyuan Guangchang),** home to a handful of (genuine) branded stores and an outlet of the British department store Debenhams. Luxury brands such as Prada and YSL feature at the goliath **Zhongmao Square (Zhongmao Guangchang)** development, off Nanguan Zheng Jie, which stretches from just south of the city walls all the way to the Small Wild Goose Pagoda. Just southeast of the Great Wild Goose Pagoda is the **Xinlehui** mall, which has a bunch of upmarket Chinese chain restaurants and bars, while just to the west of the main temple entrance is the **Qintang Commercial Plaza,** notable for an extraordinary giant screen covering the entire ceiling.

With their expensive imported goods, Xi'an's new malls mainly serve local tastes. Travelers should look to one of the souvenir shopping streets listed below. Xi'an is a great place to pick up knick-knacks, but it's worth being very suspicious of anyone offering you genuine antiques. Though there *are* tales of peasants digging up treasure from their farm plots, you're far more likely to be offered one of the meticulously fashioned "antiques" that have been made within the last few months at the increasingly sophisticated knockoff factories. Don't buy **replica Terracotta Warriors** *at* the site unless you are able to bargain low prices (numbers should be in the low 10s, not the 100s). You'll be assured of the superior quality of these "authentic" replica statuettes, but it's almost certain to be the same stuff you can buy downtown for a fraction of the cost.

The Best Shopping Streets

Shuyuanmen ★★★ Souvenir-hunters should make this restored Tang-themed pedestrian street, close to the south city walls, their first port of call. The street begins off Nan Dajie, beside the South Gate roundabout, and runs east for 300m (984 ft.). There are a number of street stalls that sell everything from replica Terracotta Warriors, painted face masks, framed paper-cuttings, beads, hairpins, and ceramic flutes to fans, necklaces, inkstones, and Communist kitsch (such as plates and holograms of Chairman Mao). Everything is cheap, and prices are, amazingly, labeled. Feel free to bargain, but the marked prices are not unreasonable, so don't expect big discounts. Behind the stalls are shops selling more expensive items such as jade and tricolor ceramics. On the south side of the street, shortly before the junction with Anju Xiang, is the **Shuyuanmen Antique and Art City (Xi'an Shuyuanmen Guwan Yishu Cheng),** a quiet courtyard where a number of calligraphers-for-hire have set up shop. Even if you're not in the market for originally produced scrolls, it can be fascinating to watch these artists at work. Do a right at **Anju Xiang** to meet the calligraphy and painting stalls along **Sanxue Jie** (see below).

Shuyuanmen. Daily 9am–9pm approx. Subway: Yongningmen, then 5-min. walk north

Huajue Xiang ★★ There's no shortage of souvenirs for sale along the Muslim Quarter's main two thoroughfares, **Beiyuanmen** ("Muslim Street") and **Xiyangshi** ("Western Market"). Most of these are of the edible variety, including a rich assortment of preserved fruit and nuts that can be bagged up and carried home. For even more lasting gifts, head to Huajue Xiang, a covered alley that leads south from Xiyangshi down to the Great Mosque. Shopping here is a blood sport, and you are the game, but the vendors are friendly. Most of the stuff is generic—T-shirts, sunglasses, and headphones—but there are a number of interesting finds for those willing to hunt around. Look out for glamorous *qipao* dresses, *feng shui* compasses, Tibetan prayer wheels, and copies of the "Little Red Book" in French. Shops open here until the mayhem on nearby Beiyuanmen dies down around 11pm.

Huajue Xiang (between Beiyuanmen and Xiyangshi). Shuyuanmen. Daily 9am–10pm approx. Subway: Bell Tower, then 5-min. walk west.

The Best Markets

Tang Western Market ★ Less a market than a megamall, this huge new development, sited on the historic Silk Road–era "Western Market," is worth visiting for those with an interest in jade or jewelry. The "Antique City" (Da Tang Guwan Cheng) is a maze of beautifully lit stores selling sparkling jade pieces from the size of a thimble to giant wall installations. Other shops sell antique bank notes, refined teapots, and historic coins. Shops can provide antique certification, though caution is still required. Below the development's main central hotel is "Jewelry Street" (Zhubao Jie), where there are cheaper pearls, necklaces, and jade. Elsewhere there is a huge *Da Run Fa*, a local supermarket, which will be fun to wander if you've not witnessed local groceries. Elsewhere, Western-branded coffee shops and fast-food joints are in no short supply.

Jinshi Guangchang, off Laodong Nan Jie. Daily 10am–9pm. Bus 201 from Bell Tower. (Bus stop is just east of the Bell Tower on Dong Dajie. Take stop on north side of road, heading *toward* the Bell Tower).

Temple of the Eight Immortals Antiques Market ★ Held every Sunday within the Eight Immortals Temple (Ba Xian Gong) compound, west of the city walls, this is one of Xi'an's best surviving antique markets. Despite a sign warning that antiques must be declared with Customs before you leave China, there's no guarantee that what you buy is genuine. But there is a buzz to the place, and you can find some wonderful Cultural Revolution kitsch, ceramics, bronze Buddhas, and Qing coins.

Wu Dao Shizi Dong Jie. (From An Ren Fang, continue east 135m/450 ft. before heading south down the 1st alley on your right; turn right when the road meets a T-junction. Immediately take a left and continue south to the back of the temple, following the incense vendors.) Admission RMB3. Sun 8:30am–6pm. Subway: Fukang Lu, then 10-min. walk southwest.

Xi Cang Market ★★ By far the least touristy market in Xi'an is held every Thursday and Sunday morning around the rectangular loop of Xi Cang alley in the north of the Muslim District. The main products are exotic plants, birds, and insects, making it unlikely you'll ferret out that perfect souvenir. There are some ceramics, jewelry, and trinkets sold in the old-fashioned way from mats spread out across the pavement. However, the most interesting and attractive sections are those crowded with hanging cages and alive with birdsong and chirruping.

Xi Cang Dong Lu, Xi Cang Nan Lu, Xi Cang Xi Lu and Xi Cang Bei Lu. Sun & Thu 6:30am–noon. Subway: Sanjinqiao, then 5-min. walk south.

Arts & Crafts

Sanxue Jie ★★ One block south of Shuyuanmen is this narrow paved lane dedicated entirely to painting and calligraphy. The eastern section features a number of shops that hawk original and imitation paintings. Many are of superb quality and very reasonably priced. You'll find everything from reproductions of famous Western paintings to eye-catching calligraphic swirls. The curiously named **Mediocre Art Salon** at the far western end of the street is particularly impressive in its variety of oils, selling everything from impressionist European cityscapes to peasant portraits, to dreamy abstract work. On the eastern end of the street, close to the **Forest of Steles Museum (Beilin Bowuguan),** there are stalls that sell brushes and simpler calligraphic scrolls.

Sanxue Jie. (From the South Gate, walk east along Shuncheng Nan Lu beside the city wall. Take the first left beside the Belgian Bar, then the first right.) Daily 9am–9pm. Subway: Yongningmen, then 5-min. walk north.

NIGHTLIFE

Xi'an's nightlife scene offers a taste of middle China. Bars are now awash with sophisticated beers—some imported from Europe, some home-brewed—but old drinking habits die hard, particularly the fondness for liar's dice, karaoke, and heavy smoking. It's a quirky blend, but in the unlikely event you've traveled to Xi'an looking to party, don't expect to be bowled over.

Those looking to paint the town red should head to Xi Dajie, where there's a buzz every night of the week. In the section between the Bell Tower and Qiaoxinkou, you'll find palatial karaoke parlors and giant nightclubs. These tend to come and go, but at the time of writing, the biggest were **Shasha** (within the same complex as the clearly signed Parkson mall on the junction of Xi Dajie and Guangji Bei Lu) and **Le Nest** (300m/984 ft. farther west, on the south side of Xi Dajie within the Rongmin Hotel). For more laid-back drinking options, head to the south of the city center. **Defu Xiang** is officially "Bar Street," but it's not particularly appealing. The drinking holes here are utterly generic, dark, and smoky, and live local bands play Mandopop (Mandarin pop) covers. The best of a bad bunch is probably the oldest, **De Fu Lou** (at the north end of the main strip, just as the road bends). Xi'an's top bars are to be found along the wall, on either side of the South Gate. The best have been listed below. For those staying in **Qujiang,** there is (another) "Bar Street" along Ci'en Dong Lu, on the east side of the **Xinlehui** mall, just south of Ci'en Lu.

Bars

Belgian Bar ★★ Run by an Australian-Chinese couple, the Belgian Bar is the most Westernized of Xi'an's many watering holes. There's a superb selection of imported beers, with well-known brands such as Hoegaarden and Leffe sitting alongside more adventurous Trappist and monastery beers such as Chimay and Rochefort. It's a top choice for a summertime drink, with the tables spilling out onto the street right beside the Ming-era wall.

Shuncheng Xiang Zhong Duan (150m/492 ft. east of the South Gate). www.belgian-bar-xian.com. ✆ **029/8725-6656.** Subway: Yongningmen, then 5-min. walk.

Near Wall Bar ★★★ The craft beer at this popular bar is brewed in-house, as two-stories' worth of shiny vats and pressure gauges testify. The hoppy-as-hell Porter beer is unique in Xi'an (RMB60 for a large glass) and can be enjoyed alongside a hookah pipe, which is occasionally passed around. The nightly live music features heaps of sing-along English-language hits, while there's a smoky games room out back with a foosball table.

Shuncheng Xiang Xi Duan (200m/656 ft. west of South Gate on the inside of the wall). www.xianbrewery.tumblr.com. ✆ **185/9177-7896.** Subway: Yongningmen, then 5-min. walk.

On The Road (Zai Lu Shang Jiu Ba) ★ An old-timer on the Xi'an circuit, this slightly grungy and pleasingly cheap Tibetan-themed bar attracts travelers and underpaid English teachers in equal measure. There's a large pool table and a stage, decorated with prayer flags, where nightly bands play a mixture of modern pop alongside the odd folk set.

Yinmachi (off Juhuayuan, south of Dong Dajie). ✆ **029/8751-0265.** Subway: Bell Tower, then 10-min. walk east.

Zoo Bar ★ Hidden on the first floor of a particularly ramshackle building on the south wall, this trendy cocktail bar pulls in the rich kids too cool to play dice. It's the kind of place you'll bump into returnees from foreign universities who speak decent English and dress to impress. A couple of extravagant day-beds on the far wall make for a loungy atmosphere.

Shuncheng Xiang Xi Duan (20m east of Zhuque Gate). ✆ **029/8761-8950.** Subway: Yongningmen, then 15-min. walk.

Live Music

Aperture Club (Guang Juan Julebu) ★★ Most Xi'an bars regard cover bands as an essential part of the furniture, but for those looking beyond bland Mandopop, there's only one show in town. This is a small club and has been at the heart of Xi'an's nascent live-music scene for several years. The stage is cramped, the walls are sticky, and the lighting rig looks like it breaks all known health-and-safety regs, but this is a wonderfully atmospheric place, especially when Xi'an's young punks come out to see one of the traveling Chinese and international bands that routinely pass through. A small bar at the back serves local beers.

Yinmachi (off Juhuayuan, south of Dong Dajie). No phone. Subway: Bell Tower, then 10-min. walk east.

Performing Arts

Two companies stage Tang-themed banquets and musicals to entertain visitors. They're kitschy and entirely ahistorical, but if you can get over the fact they are aimed almost exclusively at tour groups (voice-overs are in English and Chinese), they can be fun.

Shanxi Grand Opera House (Shanxi Gewu Da Xiyuan) ★ While it can't compete with Tang Dynasty (see below) as a spectacle, this opera company has a more authentic feel, with revolutionary credentials tracing its origins to the Northwest Culture Work Group in Yan'an. If you opt for the dinner, you'll gorge on dumplings with 20 different fillings. Be sure to book in advance. Dinner starts at 7pm, and the show starts at 8pm.

161 Wenyi Bei Lu. www.tang-dynastyshow.com. ✆ **029/8785-3295.** Reservations required. Dinner and show RMB298, show only RMB238. Subway: Yongningmen, then 10-min. walk east.

Tang Dynasty (Tang Yue Gong) ★ Run by a Hong Kong entrepreneur, this show lives up to all your Orientalist dreams: lavish costumes modeled on the Mogao cave paintings, a six-course banquet (watch out for the rice wine), hammy acting, and some amazing music and dance. Gao Ming's performance of the Spring Oriole's Song on a vertical bamboo flute, the *pai xiao*, is almost worth the money in itself. If you can get past the kitsch, the show makes for a spectacular night out. Dinner starts at 6:30pm; the show begins at 8:30pm.

75 Chang'an Bei Lu. www.xiantangdynasty.com. ✆ **029/8782-2222.** Reservations required. Tang Dynasty banquet and show RMB500; Dumpling Banquet and show RMB400. Daily 11am–2:30pm, 6–10pm. Subway: Between Nanshaomen and Tiyu Chang stations.

DAY TRIPS FROM XI'AN

7

You'll probably already feel like you've done a day trip from Xi'an if you've visited one or other of the city's most famous tombs. The Terracotta Warriors and Emperor Jingdi's Mausoleum are both a ways outside the city, and many local tours combine them with other outlying (but nonessential) sights such as the Huaqing Hot Springs and Famen Temple. High-speed rail has brought two slightly more distant, and very different, attractions within easy reach—the mountain scenery of Huashan and the historic grottoes of Luoyang. Both are east of the city and can be visited on a day trip or seen on the way back to Beijing or Shanghai. Xi'an marks the current terminus of high-speed rail, so trips to the spectacular dry landscapes of western China will require more than a day's outing.

HUASHAN ★★

Shaanxi Province, 120km (74 miles) E of Xi'an

China is a nation that *loves* lists, categories, and classifications. It comes as no surprise then that there are five officially sanctioned "great mountains," so called because of their associations with past emperors. Huashan is the westernmost of these, declared holy by long-reining Han emperor Wudi (reigned 141–87 B.C.), who claimed that sacrifices had been made on the mountain by the very first Shang kings 1,500 years earlier. The mountain's present popularity with Chinese tourists has a couple of modern fillips: Jin Yong's martial-arts novel, "Hua Shan Lun Jian," has heroic swordsmen, mythical beasts, and beautiful maidens carrying on in melodramatic fashion on the granite bluffs, hanging off the precariously perched pine trees, and dangling from precipitous peaks; more prosaically, a brand-new station has been built for Huashan along the high-speed rail route from Beijing to Xi'an, making it easy to build into an itinerary. Huashan sees comparatively few foreign visitors, but the scenery is spectacular, the Taoist monks are friendly, and the air is (often) clear enough to make the sunrise worth seeing. The best times to visit are mid-autumn, when the trees are a magical, colorful jumble, or spring, when the wildflowers bloom. Winter is picturesque but bitterly cold.

Day Trips from Xi'an

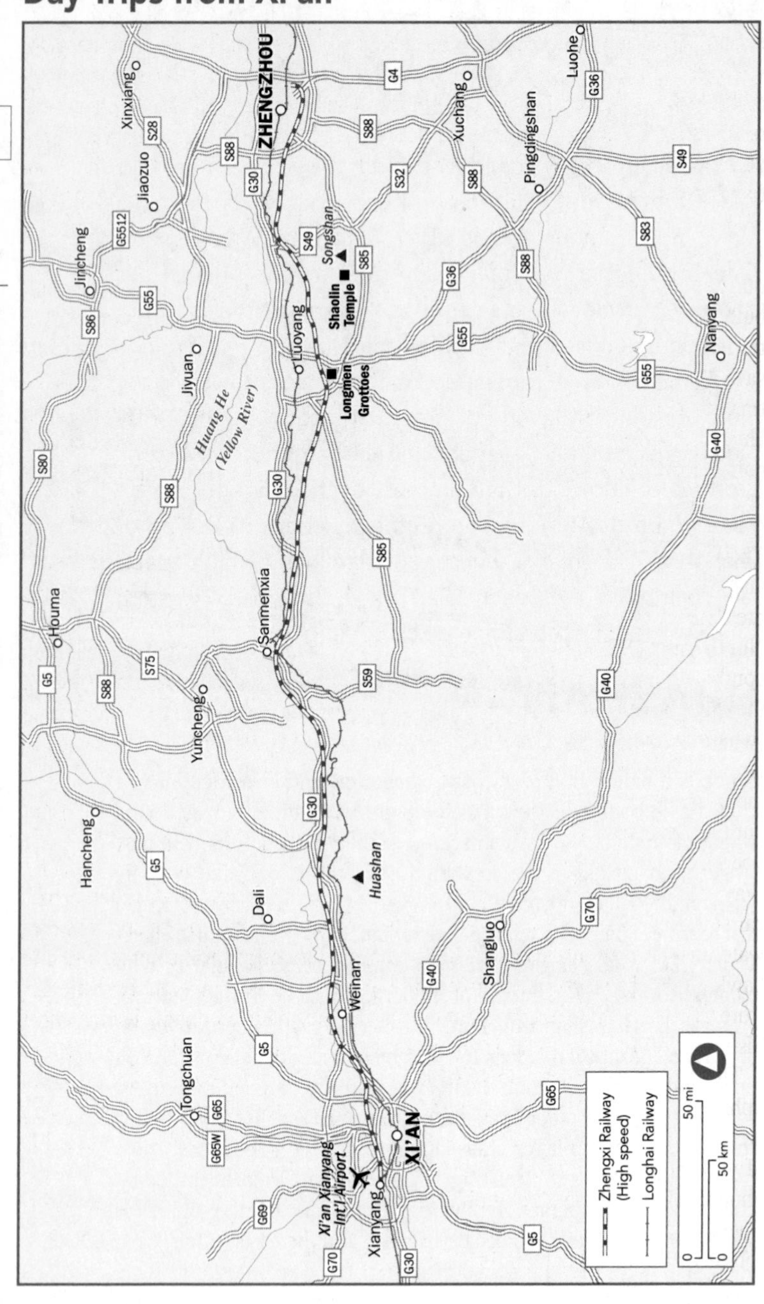

Getting There

Huashan can be visited within a day from Xi'an. An air-conditioned **coach** (Tourist Line 1) departs from the east side of Xi'an Railway Station's southern square at 7am (2 hr.; RMB22) and takes passengers all the way to the main ticket hall at the park's east gate. Entrance to the scenic reserve costs RMB180 (Apr–Oct) or RMB100 (Nov–Mar). Cable cars lead to the North Peak and West Peak, but you'll need to take a further shuttle bus (RMB20/40 respectively). The coach back to Xi'an departs from the Eastern Gate at 5pm. Smaller minibuses run until 7pm.

High-speed G-class **trains** to and from Xi'an take just 35 minutes and run 11 times throughout the day. Tickets cost RMB54.5. Though the trip is much quicker, rail is not necessarily the most convenient option: The new, purpose-built stations in Xi'an and Huayin (Huashan's nearest city) are both north of their respective cities. If you take the subway in Xi'an, and a taxi in Huayin, you may save 15 minutes or so of travel time. However, it is a three-leg journey (subway–train–taxi/bus). The first train leaves Xi'an at 7:53am, and the last train back from Huashan North is at 8:49pm. From the station, there is a free green minibus every half-hour to the Eastern Gate (35 min.), or you can hail a taxi for RMB25.

Exploring Huashan

The Huashan scenic reserve is a cluster of five peaks—north, south, east, west, and central—which are joined by narrow walkways that pass between some breathtakingly sheer cliff faces. The most popular angle of attack is to first scale **North Peak (Bei Feng),** at 1,613m (5,295 ft.), the lowest of the five, and then continue, via some spectacular narrow walkways, to the loop that runs between the other peaks. This route begins at the main ticket office at the Eastern Gate (where the tourist bus drops passengers). Inside is a shuttle bus (RMB20) to the North Park cable car terminus (RMB150 round-trip; RMB80 one-way). The incredibly steep cable-car ride gets you onto the mountain in 10 short minutes, but there can be long lines, especially during holiday season and weekends. If you fancy a challenge, or don't fancy waiting in line, there's also the "Soldiers' Way" mountain path, built from 3,999 steps, which begins close to the cable-car station. Expect to spend 2 hours sweating and toiling, and be sure to bring water, as there are no shops en route (though you might come across the odd hawker). A less-steep, alternative walking route (8km; 5 miles in length) runs from Huashan Village and eventually joins the main mountain loop a short distance after the cable-car terminus. It takes around 4 hours to reach the top.

The North Peak can be busy with crowds. From the cable-car station, head uphill and across **Green Dragon Ridge (Cang Long Feng),** where the steps are carved from the granite and the mountain falls away sharply on either side of you. This path can be crowded, and the crossing will test those with acrophobia. This leads to a large circular loop that connects the four other peaks. There are only short, sharp climbs from here on, as each of the other peaks is roughly the same height, a little over 2,000m (6,562 ft.).

A good alternative to the often crowded North Peak route is the new **West Peak (Xi Feng)** cable car (RMB140 one-way). After buying your ticket at the

Eastern Gate, head *back out* into the parking lot to take one of the shuttle buses (RMB40) to the West Peak cable-car station. It's a slightly longer upward ride, but because of the extra distance and cost, it's normally a bit quieter. It also allows for more time on the mountain itself. The best option is to head up via the West Peak cable car, spend a day on the mountain, and then return to ground level from the North Peak cable car.

If you have more time, consider staying at one of the simple guesthouses on the mountain. The main attraction in this is being able to enjoy the mountain paths after the crowds have left, and (pollution permitting), a sunrise or sunset vista. Some Chinese guidebooks recommend climbing up at night with a flashlight to see the sunrise (presumably skipping the entrance fee). The locals say, "You don't fear what you can't see" ("*Bu jian bu pa*"). This is not sensible.

Huashan is a proper mountain (not always a given at Chinese "mountain" attractions), so be prepared for some serious hiking and/or climbing, especially if you're not intending to use the cable cars. Water should be readily available on the mountain, but not necessarily on the climb up, so bring provisions. Most importantly, pack plenty of cash. If you follow the suggested route above, you'll probably be hit for tickets on five separate occasions (entrance, shuttle bus × 2, cable car × 2), so be prepared.

Huashan does not seem to attract that many foreign visitors, and you'll likely be gawked at by the many Chinese group-tourists bedecked in yellow hats and white gloves as you pass. Souvenirs, bottles of water, and cucumbers will no doubt be waved in your face, but there is an enjoyable spirit of camaraderie among the hikers. As at many of China's holy mountains, Chinese visitors have their names engraved on a brass padlock wishing good health for the family (or a long and happy relationship for young couples) and attach it to one of the many chain railings.

Where to Stay & Eat

Before early May and after mid-October, there is a surplus of accommodations on Huashan, so discounts of 30% to 50% are easily obtained. Dining on the mountain is basic and overpriced; take as much food as you can carry.

If you arrive at Huashan late at night, there are a couple of passable hotels in **Huashan Kou,** and unlike the lodgings on Huashan itself, they have ensuite showers. The best places to stay in the village are the **Huashan Kezhan** (✆ **0913/465-8111;** RMB580 twin; look for a discount of up to 45%) and the newer **Bijiayi Kuaijie Jiudian** (✆ **0913/465-8000;** RMB238 standard twin).

On the mountain, facilities are basic, there are no private bathrooms or showers, and pit toilets are common. The **North Peak Hotel (Bei Feng Fandian),** RMB240 twin without bathroom, is a 5-minute walk from North Peak cable car and is convenient for the lazy, or the late. Both the sunset and the sunrise can be enjoyed from the North Peak. The hotel offers a competent staff, clean rooms, a restaurant, and magnificent views, and as a result, it is often fully booked. Other decent mountaintop options include the **East Peak Hotel (Dong Feng Binguan),** RMB320 double, which is great for easy sunrise viewing.

YAODONG cave dwellings

North of Xi'an is a vast plateau of loess, a distinct yellowy earth made up of packed sand and silt. Since at least the 2nd millennium B.C., this fertile soil has been terraced by Chinese peasants for both farming and dwelling, and the culture continues to this day. Even within Xi'an's suburban sprawl, it's quite common to find entire villages of *yaodong*, or "house caves," which have been excavated horizontally from the thick loess walls. This earth acts as an insulator, maintaining heat during the cold seasons and keeping the caves icy cool in the sweltering summer months. Scientists and scholars have begun to take an interest in the miraculous properties of these dwellings, and they've also crept onto the radar of tour companies. **Xi'an Insiders** (www.xianinsiders.com; ✆ **138-1761-6975**) runs several tours that take visitors out to such a *yaodong*. One of these, the "Grand Escapade," whisks you out to Xi'an's eastern suburbs in either a jeep or sidecar and passes vineyards, temples, and the Terracotta Warriors on the way to a suburban cave dwelling. A rustic dinner is cooked by the cave owner and served under the stars in the quiet courtyard, and guests then spend a night in one of three cave bedrooms (RMB2,450 per person). Pretty much the only difference between now and 4,000 years ago is the delightful electric blanket.

LUOYANG ★★

Henan Province, 322km (200 miles) E of Xi'an

Situated in western Henan Province at the junction of the Grand Canal and the ancient Silk Road, Luoyang (literally "north of the river Luo") was the capital of nine dynasties from the Eastern Zhou (770–221 B.C.) to the Late Tang (A.D. 923–36). Today, this industrial town with a population of 1.3 million is better known as home to the magnificent UNESCO World Heritage Site **Longmen Grottoes (Longmen Shiku).** Alongside the Mogao Caves in Dunhuang and the Yungang Grottoes in Datong, they're among the most important repositories of Buddhist sculpture in China and an awe-inspiring sight, especially if you have the remotest interest in Buddhist history or art. The grottoes' after-dark opening hours mean that it's technically possible to squeeze in a visit to **Shaolin Temple** in what would be a very busy day (though a taxi would need to be hired on arrival at the station). Avoid visiting in April when Luoyang's famous **Peony Festival** attracts hundreds of thousands of visitors. The benefits of the beautiful flowers are outweighed by the extra crowds at the various tourist sights.

Getting There

Luoyang was previously too remote to consider as a day trip from Xi'an, but the new **high-speed train** network has put it within reach. Beginning at 7:41am, trains run throughout the day between Xi'an North and the new Luoyang Longmen Station, conveniently located close to the grottoes. Tickets cost RMB174.5 each way (1 hr. 40 min.). The last train back to Xi'an departs Longmen at 8:21pm.

Luoyang's small airport is located about 11km (7 miles) north of the city center. Daily **flights** connect Luoyang with Beijing (1½ hr.) and Shanghai (1½ hr.).

Getting Around

Taxis charge RMB5 for 3km (2 miles), then RMB1.50 per kilometer until 10km (6 miles), after which the price rises to RMB2.25 per kilometer. From 10pm to 5am, prices rise to RMB5.80 for 2km (1¼ miles), then RMB1.75 per kilometer thereafter. **Bus** rides cost RMB1. From the Longmen Railway Station, bus **nos. 67** and **71** run to the Longmen Grottoes.

Longmen Grottoes ★★

Located 13km (8 miles) south of the city center, on the banks of the Yi River (Yi He), the Longmen Grottoes (Longmen Shiku) are considered one of three great sculptural treasure-troves in China. The first caves were carved in the Northern Wei dynasty in A.D. 493, when the emperor moved his capital from Pingcheng (today's Datong) to Luoyang. Over the next 400 years, cave art and sculpture flourished, reaching their zenith during the Tang dynasty (618–907) and even continuing into the Northern Song. Benefactors of the Longmen caves included imperial families, high-ranking officers, Buddhist leaders, and merchants, as well as more "common" folk, many of whom could only afford the smaller honeycomb niches. Today, there are 2,300 caves and niches with more than 2,800 inscriptions and over 100,000 Buddhist statues on both East Hill and West Hill. Some have been disfigured (and sometimes entirely removed) over the centuries. The last century wasn't particularly kind. If statuettes weren't stolen by colonial schemers, they stood a good chance of being vandalized during the Cultural Revolution. A sign points out in which foreign museums some of the more prominent statues are known to reside. About 30% of the caves are from the Northern Wei dynasty (A.D. 386–584); their statues are more elongated, static, and lacking in complexity and detail than the later Tang-dynasty sculptures with their fuller figures, gentle features, and characteristic liveliness. The highlight is the 1km-long (½-mile) stretch on the **West Hill** side of the Yi River, which includes the caves listed below. A walkway takes visitors up close to the cave entrances cut from the rock, though it's generally not possible to actually enter the grottoes. Two bridges cross the river, creating a long circular loop of the site, though you can't reenter the popular West Hill once you have left. The grottoes on the **East Hill** are not quite as spectacular, but the pleasant **Xiangshan Temple** and **Bai Juyi's Tomb** are located on this side of the water.

Listed here are the most magnificent of the many caves, starting at the entrance and running south. Displays have rudimentary English captions, but even for the most independent traveler, this is one of those times when a guided tour is highly recommended. English-speaking guides are available for hire just inside the main entrance for RMB100.

As at the Terracotta Warriors back in Xi'an, a frustratingly long 2km (1¼-mile) "pedestrian street" (translation: shopping precinct) has been built between the parking lot and the main gate to the grottoes. Golf carts are on hand to ease the strain. A round trip costs RMB15 and is well worth it during hot summer months.

Finally, the grottoes are now open until 10:30pm, with some of the caves lit up after dark. It makes for an entrancing spectacle, though enjoying the night scene will be tough outside winter months if you are hoping to make it on the last train back to Xi'an (which departs at 8:21pm).

Three Binyang Caves (Binyang San Dong) ★ Work here began in the Northern Wei dynasty in A.D. 500, but the carver died in 523 after completing only the middle cave. The other two were finished later. All three were commissioned by the Xuan Wu emperor, who dedicated the middle cave to his father, the Xiao Wen emperor, the southern cave to his mother, and the northern cave to himself. The figures in the middle cave are comparatively longer and thinner than their fleshier, curvier, Sui- and Tang-dynasty counterparts in the other two caves. Missing reliefs are now in the Metropolitan Museum of Art in New York and the Nelson-Atkins Museum of Art in Kansas City.

Ten Thousand Buddha Cave (Wan Fo Dong) ★★ Finished in A.D. 680, this exquisite cave actually contains carvings of 15,000 Buddhas, mostly in small niches in the north and south walls, with the smallest Buddha measuring only 4cm (1½ in.) high. Even more remarkable is the fact that this cave was commissioned by two women, an indication perhaps of the comparatively elevated status of females during Empress Wu Zetian's reign. The centerpiece is the Amitabha Buddha, whose delicate rounded features are said to be modeled on those of one of the cave's patrons.

Lotus Flower Cave (Lianhua Dong) ★ Carved during the Northern Wei dynasty around A.D. 527, this cave's highlight is a lotus flower, measuring 3m (10 ft.) in diameter, carved in high relief on the ceiling. Representing serenity and purity, lotus flowers are common motifs in Buddhist art. Surrounding the lotus are some faded but still fine *apsaras* (Buddhist flying nymphs).

Ancestor Worshiping Temple (Fengxian Si) ★★★ Carved in the Tang dynasty between A.D. 672 and 675, this majestic cave is the largest and most beautiful at Longmen. Originally started by the Tang Gaozong emperor, it was expedited by Empress Wu Zetian, an ardent Buddhist, who poured money (from her cosmetics budget, it is said) into its completion, no doubt because the central Buddha's face is thought to be modeled on hers. This main Buddha, Vairocana, seated on a lotus flower, is a stunning 17m (56 ft.) tall, with a 4m-high (13-ft.) head, 1.9m-long (6-ft.) earlobes, a wide forehead, a full nose, and serene eyes, which were painted black at one time.

Flanking the Buddha is the disciple Kasyapa (the elder) to the left, and Sakyamuni's cousin, the clever disciple Ananda (the younger), to the right. Beside the disciples are two attending bodhisattvas (Buddhas who delay entry into nirvana in order to help others), Manjusri and Samantabhadra, who are decorated with exquisitely fine beads and ornamental drapes. It is said that this tableau of statues is a distilled replica of the Tang imperial court, with the dignified main Buddha representing the emperor (or empress), the obedient disciples representing the ministers, the heavenly kings standing in for the warriors and soldiers, the richly dressed bodhisattvas evoking the imperial concubines, and the flying *devas* (spirits) recalling palace maids.

Medical Prescription Cave (Yaofang Dong) ★ This small cave was first carved in the Northern Wei dynasty but appended in subsequent dynasties. The main Buddha here is a Northern Qi (A.D. 550–577) creation, its rounder figure emblematic of the transition from the thin Wei figures to the fuller Tang sculptures. At the entrance are steles, carved with Chinese medicine prescriptions for 120 diseases, including diabetes and madness.

Old Sun Cave (Guyang Dong) ★ First carved during the Northern Wei sometime between A.D. 488 and 528, this is the oldest cave at Longmen, though additions were being made well into the Tang dynasty by different benefactors. Nineteen of the famous "Longmen Twenty" (20 pieces of calligraphy deemed especially fine and representative of their time) are found here. The central Buddha's head was restored during the Qing dynasty, and is said to resemble Taoist master Laozi.

Stone Room Cave (Shiku Dong) ★ This last of the major caves was carved in the Northern Wei between 516 and 528 and has the best worshiping scenes in Longmen. On both sides of the wall are niches with low-relief carvings of officials in high hats, court ladies in flowing robes carrying single lotus flowers, and servants carrying sheltering canopies, all in a procession to honor Buddha.

Luolong Lu (5km/3 miles) south of Luoyang Longmen Train Station. Admission RMB120. Daily 7am–10:30pm. Public buses 67 & 71 from Luoyang Longmen Station to Longmen Grottoes (RMB1) or free shuttle bus during busy periods (entrance tickets can be bought at the station itself and entitle you to a free shuttle). A taxi ride costs around RMB20.

OTHER ATTRACTIONS

White Horse Temple (Baima Si) ★ It is more than likely that earlier Buddhist temples were built along the Silk Routes in what is today's Xinjiang (the path by which Buddhism entered China), but this is widely held to be the first officially sanctioned Buddhist temple built in China proper. Located 13km (7 miles) to the east of Luoyang, the temple was built by the Eastern Han Mingdi emperor (reigned A.D. 58–76) to honor and house two Indian monks who, the story goes, came from India bearing Buddhist scriptures on two white horses. Two stone horses (likely from the Song dynasty) stand guard outside the gate to today's temple, mostly a Ming construction. Just inside the main entrance in the southeastern and southwestern corners of the complex are the tombs of the two Indian monks. In the impressive Yuan dynasty Great Hall (Daxiong Dian), there are 18 *arhats* (disciples) of ramie cloth.

Baima Si Lu. ✆ **0379/6378-9053.** Admission RMB50. 7am–6pm. Bus: 56 (from the Xigua stop on Zhongzhou Zhong Lu).

Ancient Han Tombs (Gumu Bowuguan) ★★ This fascinating exhibition features 25 reconstructed underground ancient tombs dating from the Western Han dynasty (206 B.C.–A.D. 9) to the Northern Song dynasty (960–1127). By the Eastern Han dynasty (A.D. 25–220), the use of hollow bricks with painted designs gave way to larger stone vaults made of solid carved brick. Eleven of the tombs also have elaborate wall murals, the most famous of which is the Western Han "Expelling the Ghost Mural Tomb," which features a faded but still gorgeous fresco of celebrants holding a feast before the exorcism. The tombs are about 10km (6 miles) north of town on the road to the airport.

Jichang Lu. ✆ **0379/6226-5737.** Admission RMB20. 8:30am–5pm. Bus: 83 (Gumu Bowuguan stop).

Luoyang Museum (Luoyang Bowuguan) ★★ This excellent museum only opened in 2007 and presents its treasure in well-lit vaults with newly installed English language explanations. Standouts include a section dedicated to the Xia (B.C. 2200–1700) and Shang dynasties (B.C. 1700–1100), with an emphasis on items excavated at Erlitou (an important Shang site 30km/18 miles east of Luoyang), including jade, bronzes, and pottery artifacts, plus Han dynasty exhibits of painted pottery and tomb frescoes, and some fine Tang-dynasty glazed pottery.

298 Zhongzhou Zhong Lu. ✆ **0379/6990-1020.** Admission RMB20. 8am–5pm. Bus: no. 4, 11, or 50.

Wangcheng Park (Wangcheng Gongyuan) ★ Every April during the Luoyang Peony Festival (Apr 15–25), this park, built on the former site of a Zhou dynasty city, Wangcheng, is awash in a riot of colors: red, white, black, yellow, purple, pink, blue, green, and every shade in between. Luoyang produces the best peonies China has to offer, so don't miss paying a visit if you're in town then. For an extra RMB15, you can visit the zoo. The zoo and gardens, which open at the crack of dawn, are perfect for early risers.

Zhongzhou Zhong Lu. ✆ **0379/6393-8545.** Free admission to park, zoo entrance RMB15, 6am–6pm. Park is open 24 hr. Bus: 2, 4, 101, 102, or 103.

Beyond Luoyang

Located south of the Yellow River in northwest Henan Province, **Songshan** is the most central of the five holy Taoist mountains. It's made up of two mountain ranges, the greater range **Taishishan** and the lesser range **Shaoshishan.** Both have numerous peaks and are dotted throughout with temples and pagodas, making them a fantastic destination for serious trekkers. However, most visitors to Songshan today come for the **Shaolin Temple (Shaolin Si),** birthplace of the eponymous brand of kung-fu martial art (*Shaolin Gongfu*) that has long been popular in Asia but has become increasingly well-known in the Western world. The main town serving Songshan is **Dengfeng** (meaning "Ascending to Bestow Honor"), named by the Tang-dynasty empress Wu Zetian, who preferred Songshan to Taishan (Mount Tai) in Shandong Province, traditionally the favorite mountain of most emperors.

Though it's a further 76km (47 miles) east of the Longmen Grottoes, Songshan *can* be visited on a trip to Luoyang, though to see both the grottoes and Shaolin Temple, you'll probably need to be on the first train out (arriving at 9:18am), getting the last train back (departing Luoyang at 8:21pm) and expecting to rush at both attractions. Should you go for this ambitious trip, I recommend negotiating a taxi ride from Luoyang Longmen Railway Station (expect to pay around RMB500 return, including time spent waiting at Shaolin Temple, but don't expect the driver to wait around for you at the Longmen Grottoes), visiting the temple first and the grottoes on the return leg. The grottoes are only 5km from the train station and open until 10:30pm, meaning you'll be able to better plan the journey home when you know how much time remains of your day. Alternatively, stay overnight in either Luoyang or the small town of Dengfeng.

Shaolin Temple (Shaolin Si) ★ Most visitors come to Songshan not for the mountain-climbing but for this famous monastery, better known for its martial arts than for its religious affiliations. Today's Shaolin, more loud marketplace than quiet monastery, is overrun with vendors, tourists, and martial-arts students.

Located at the northern base of Shaoshishan, the monastery was built in A.D. 495 during the Northern Wei dynasty. Legend has it that the Indian monk Bodhidharma (Damo in Chinese), founder of the Chan (Zen) school of Mahayana Buddhism, retreated here in 527 after failing to convince the emperor of Liang in Nanjing of the "nothingness" of everything. With the

TREKKING ON songshan

To get the best out of a visit to Songshan, stay overnight in Dengfeng and aim to spend an entire day on the mountain. Ascending **Taishishan,** to the northwest of Dengfeng, is the greater challenge, as there are no cable cars to bail out the weary. The trail typically starts behind the Songyang Academy (Songyang Shuyuan). Stone steps lead all the way up to the 1,470m-high (4,900-ft.) **Junji Peak (Junji Feng),** where, unlike at China's other sacred mountains, there is no temple or building at the summit, just patches of grass and all of Songshan below you. Allow 4 hours to reach the top. A RMB100 entrance fee gets you into the Taishishan Scenic Area, which contains the **Songyue Temple Pagoda.** You can use the same ticket to get into Shaolin Monastery. Climbing **Shaoshishan,** the lesser range to the west, is made easier by three cable cars. Just west of the Forest of Stupas (Ta Lin) is the **Shaolin Suodao** (RMB30), which runs up the northern side of the mountain and has back views of the monastery and the forest. A better option, the **Songyang Suodao,** is up the road another 150m (492 ft.). This pleasant RMB30, 20-minute ride on a chairlift runs less than halfway up the mountain. The ride (or hike) back down affords some marvelous views of the Shaolin Monastery and the Forest of Stupas nestled in the foothills. The **Song Shan Shaolin Suodao** is another 300m (984 ft.) from the lower terminus of the first gondola, and is a RMB50 one-way (RMB60 round-trip), 40-minute cable-car ride that goes past Ladder (Tizi) Gully to just below the summit. From here, trails lead to the **Song Shan Diaoqiao,** a suspension bridge stretched over a deep ravine of tall bald rocks. You can climb back down either the northern side of Shaoshishan underneath the cable cars, or the sheer southern face lined with steep narrow trails. At the parking lot below **Sanhuang Palace (Sanhuang Xinggong),** you can hire a taxi back to Dengfeng. For the relatively fit, climbing Shaoshishan takes 5 to 6 hours round-trip.

Chan emphasis on meditation, Damo is said to have sat praying in a cave for 9 years. As an aid to, or perhaps relief from, meditation, Damo's disciples apparently developed a set of exercises based on the movements of certain animals like the praying mantis, monkey, and eagle, which eventually developed into a form of physical and spiritual combat known as Shaolin kung-fu *(gongfu)*. In the Tang dynasty, Prince Li Shimin (later to be the Tang Taizong emperor) was rescued from a battle by 13 Shaolin monks. Thereafter the emperor decreed that the monastery always keep a troop of fighting monks, a practice that reached its apogee during the Ming dynasty (1368–1644), when 3,000 Shaolin monks were engaged in fighting Japanese pirates off the coast of China. The Shaolin monks' exploits, depicted in countless Hong Kong and mainland-Chinese films, have in recent years caught on with Western audiences. Indeed, it's not uncommon to see Western faces leaping and stomping at the more than 60 martial-arts schools around the monastery.

Pugilism aside, the temple itself has a number of religious relics and frescoes worth viewing. In the **Wenshu Hall (Wenshu Dian),** visitors can squint through the protective glass casing at a piece of rock supposedly imprinted with Damo's shadow from all those months of meditation. On the base before you get to the final three halls, stop to take a look at the bas-reliefs. Instead of the same old dragon carvings seen at other temples, there are peaceful-looking monks in kung-fu and meditation poses. In the last hall, the **Thousand Buddha Hall (Qian Fo Dian),** there is a gorgeous Ming dynasty fresco of 500 *arhats* (Buddhist disciples) worshiping Pilu, a celestial Buddha embodying wisdom and purity. About 400m (1,312 ft.) west of the temple is the impressive **Forest of Stupas (Ta Lin)** ★, the monastery's graveyard, where 243 brick stupas built between the Tang (618–907) and Qing (1644–1911) dynasties contain the remains of notable monks. The oldest stupa, honoring Tang-dynasty monk Fawan Chanshi, was built in 791 and features a simple stupa on a two-tiered brick pedestal. High on the mountain behind the forest is the **Damo's Cave (Damo Dong)**, where the main man was said to have meditated for those 9 long years.

Finish your visit with one of the free kung-fu shows that take place near the entrance at the **Shaolin Martial Arts Training Center (Shaolin Wushu Guan).** Shows take place every half-hour between 9:30am and noon, and 2 and 6pm. Come at least 20 minutes in advance if you want a seat.

Shaolin Si. ✆ **0371/6274-8276.** RMB100 includes admission to the Forest of Stupas. Daily 6:30am–6pm.

Where to Stay & Eat

Luoyang's hotels are mainly Chinese-run three- and four-stars that can be a little grubby. Most hotels regularly give 20%–30% discounts unless otherwise noted. There is usually a 5% city tax but no additional service charge. If you're going to be in town for the Peony Festival, book a room in advance.

There are a few exceptions to the otherwise downbeat hotel scene in Luoyang. The **Holiday Inn Express Luoyang City Center** (28 Jinchenzhai Jie,

© **020/3349-9520;** RMB350 for a standard double) is a clean, spacious, and modern hotel just north of the Longmen Train Station. It's no-frills but very comfortable for the price and convenient for both the station and the grottoes. More in the heart of the city, north of the river, is **Christian's Hotel** (56 Jiefang Lu, © **0379/6326-6666;** RMB750 for a standard room), another new-build that has many of the trappings of a five-star, albeit with local service standards.

For Western food, hotel dining offers the most reliable fare. The **Luoyang Peony Hotel (Luoyang Mudan Da Jiudian),** at 15 Zhongzhou Xi Lu (© **0379/6468-0000**), has a Western dining room that serves fish and chips, pizzas, and lamb chops for dinner at RMB30 to RMB90. Otherwise try the unpretentious **Old Luoyang Noodle House (Lao Luoyang Mianguan)** at Changchun Xi Lu, close to the junction with Jinghua Lu (© **0379/6861-1658**), which serves Henanese cuisine and is nearly always packed with locals. The *zhajiangmian* (noodles with bean sauce) and the *tangcu liji* (sweet-and-sour fish) are both delicious.

SHANGHAI

8

It's been 175 short years since Shanghai started her journey from the boonies to the big time. Hers is a Hollywood tale of soaring highs and crashing lows, shot through with glamour and greed. Bankers and gangsters, socialites and shysters, colonials and "coolies," aristocrats and revolutionaries, all have been lured into Shanghai's seductive embrace and shaped the city's sometimes sordid history. Today Shanghai is China's economic engine-room, and it's the huddled masses who march toward the bright lights at the mouth of the Yangtze, seeking a slice of the pie amid China's relentless boom.

It was undoubtedly colonialism that gave Shanghai her first, bittersweet break. Before the Opium War (1839–1842), Shanghai was a semi-prosperous market town that few people outside the Yangtze Delta would have heard of. The Treaty of Nanjing, which ended hostilities, carved open the area for colonial occupation. The enclaves that were established—first by Britain, then the United States and France—became a magnet to both foreign adventurers and domestic migrants. Shanghai was seen as a safe haven during the bloody Taiping Rebellion, and later, during the chaotic Warlord Era, when the Communist Party secretly set up shop under unsuspecting French noses. By the early 1900s, Shanghai was entering its "golden age," fattened on overseas investment, cheap labor, opium, and extortion. If you were on the right side of the racket, life couldn't be sweeter. Away from the champagne parties and dance halls, the bodies of half-starved unskilled local laborers (known as "coolies"), prostitutes, and criminals were regularly fished from the portside.

The population of Shanghai's well-defended foreign concessions swelled again when Japan overran China in 1937 but then suffered as the Japanese took complete charge 4 years later, making servants of those who had once been masters. Most of the population assumed it would be business-as-usual after 1945, and some even carried on dreaming after the Communists' civil war victory in 1949, but they were spectacularly mistaken. Mao didn't care for Shanghai's infamous "anything goes" culture, and his ascent to power led to the private clubs, swanky hotels, and gambling dens shutting their doors for good.

The Mao era was unkind to Shanghai. The Cultural Revolution, which ravaged China during the Great Helmsman's last years, began in Shanghai and was directed from the city by the so-called "Gang of Four." Thousands were sent from their urban homes to the countryside for reeducation. Four decades of radicalism and repression ended in 1991 when Shanghai's mayor, Zhu Rongji, got a promotion to the head table in Beijing. The city was opened to the world once more, but rather than merely "reform," as instructed, Shanghai flung herself into the largest urban transformation in human history. There's hardly been any let-up since. If the American Dream was distilled from the dusty plains of the West, China's current dash for wealth and power has risen from the boggy flats east of the Huangpu.

The city's new architecture symbolizes this spirit, with glass and chrome totems being summoned from the swamps like something out of an alien invasion. The mightiest of them, the 128-story Shanghai Tower, now looms over the 101-story World Financial Trade Center, and its paltry 88-floor neighbor, the Jinmao Tower. They haughtily look down at the colonial buildings of the Bund just opposite—past and present, divided by a muddy river.

The faint echoes of "swinging" Shanghai's decadent heyday have lately become unmistakable boom-box thuds. The nightclubs are as exclusive as they ever were back in the 1920s, with added diamonds and designer suits. The gap between rich and poor has again become a chasm, with hapless Dickensian slop boys coexisting with dot.com.cn billionaires. And the new wealth has produced hedonism. Prostitution and drugs have both returned, though neither is legal, as they once were. History doesn't repeat, but it does rhyme.

Like many of those who live in life's fast lane, Shanghai gets depressed; she is sinking by roughly a centimeter each year. Indeed, if that master of killjoys— global warming—has his way, she will be one of the first to find herself underwater. However, there's little sense of impending doom. This is a city that revels in danger.

The Shanghainese are famed for their frankness, efficiency, business acumen, and general contempt for anyone unfortunate enough not to have been born in this blessed city. There's no doubt they have created China's most outward-looking, modern, and brash metropolis. In a city once dubbed the "Whore of the Orient," you may not always find yourself in "good" company. But there's no denying the folks 'round here are a lot of fun.

ESSENTIALS

Arriving

BY PLANE Shanghai has an older airport to the west, **Hongqiao International Airport,** and a newer airport to the east, **Pudong International Airport,** which began operations late in 1999. Virtually all of the international carriers use Pudong, which serves all major international destinations from Amsterdam to Vancouver. Every major city in China is also served with multiple daily flights. Most use Hongqiao, but flights to and from Beijing and Xi'an also use Pudong.

The **Pudong International Airport** (www.shairport.com; ✆ **021/96990**), your likely point of arrival, is located about 45km (28 miles) east of downtown Shanghai. Transfers into the city take 45 minutes to 1 hour. The airport has two terminals serving both international and domestic flights that are connected by a central walkway as well as free shuttle buses. Hotel counters, money exchange, and ATMs are in both terminals.

Hongqiao Airport (www.shairport.com; ✆ **021/62990**), now largely reserved for flights within China, is located 19km (12 miles) west of the city center. There are also two terminals, both with hotel counters here, ATMs, and money exchange. Domestic flights, including regular shuttles to and from Beijing, are run by a number of airlines including China Eastern Airlines (www.ceair.com), its subsidiary Shanghai Airlines (www.shanghai-air.com), Air China (www.airchina.com.cn), and Hainan Airways (www.hainanairlines.com).

Hotel Shuttles: Many of Shanghai's hotels maintain service counters along the walls in the main arrivals halls in both airports, though in most cases, the hotel's airport staff is primarily there to help you find a taxi or arrange for an expensive private car to take you to your hotel in the city.

Airport Taxis: The legitimate taxis are lined up just outside the arrivals halls of both airports at Pudong, and outside arrival at Terminal 2 at Hongqiao Airport. Taxis into town from Hongqiao Airport take anywhere from 20 to 40 minutes depending on traffic and should cost between RMB40 and RMB70 for most central hotels. Taxi transfers from Pudong run between 45 minutes and 1.5 hours for RMB150 and up. Insist on seeing the meter started.

Subway: The world's first commercially operating maglev (magnetic levitation) line uses German technology to whisk you the 30km (19 miles) between Pudong Airport and the Longyang Road subway station in Pudong. It's a thrilling 8-minute ride (RMB50 one-way; RMB80 round-trip within 7 days). Maglev trains depart Pudong every 20 minutes between 7:02am and 9:42pm daily. Travelers can connect to the Shanghai subway at Longyang Road, though it's an awkward transfer if you're hauling heavy luggage. The maglev and subway are in different buildings, and passengers need to navigate several escalators, narrow barriers, and security checks.

Airport Buses: There are eight bus routes making transfers from **Pudong** airport into town. They run between 7am and 11pm and pick up from both terminals (there's a late-night bus that runs up until 45 minutes after the final arrival and stops at multiple city-center points). The most useful regular routes are: Airport Bus Line 1, which goes to Hongqiao Airport and Hongqiao Railway Station; Line 2, which goes to Jing'an Temple; and Line 5, which goes to the Shanghai Railway Station. Fares range from RMB16 to RMB30. Shuttle buses no longer run between Pudong Airport and select hotels.

Only public buses run from **Hongqiao** Terminal 1. Terminal 2 does have several bus routes, but they mainly serve local destinations and make regular stops. Airport Bus Line 1 does whisk passengers across to Pudong airport, but for city-center customers, taxi is by far the easiest option.

BY TRAIN **Shanghai Railway Station** is massive. You will have to walk a block to the subway station (follow the signs for lines 1, 3, and 4) or wait in line

Shanghai Neighborhoods & Outlying Attractions

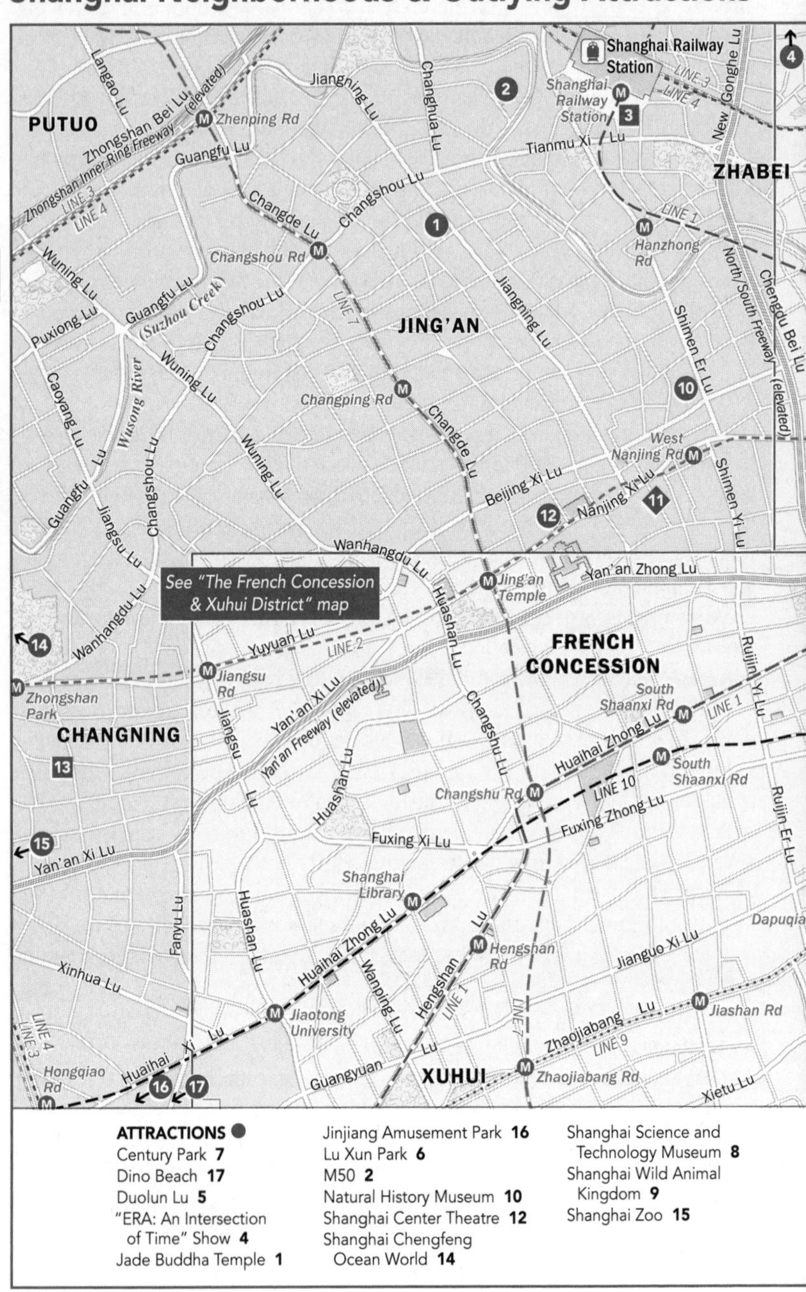

ATTRACTIONS ●

Century Park **7**
Dino Beach **17**
Duolun Lu **5**
"ERA: An Intersection of Time" Show **4**
Jade Buddha Temple **1**
Jinjiang Amusement Park **16**
Lu Xun Park **6**
M50 **2**
Natural History Museum **10**
Shanghai Center Theatre **12**
Shanghai Chengfeng Ocean World **14**
Shanghai Science and Technology Museum **8**
Shanghai Wild Animal Kingdom **9**
Shanghai Zoo **15**

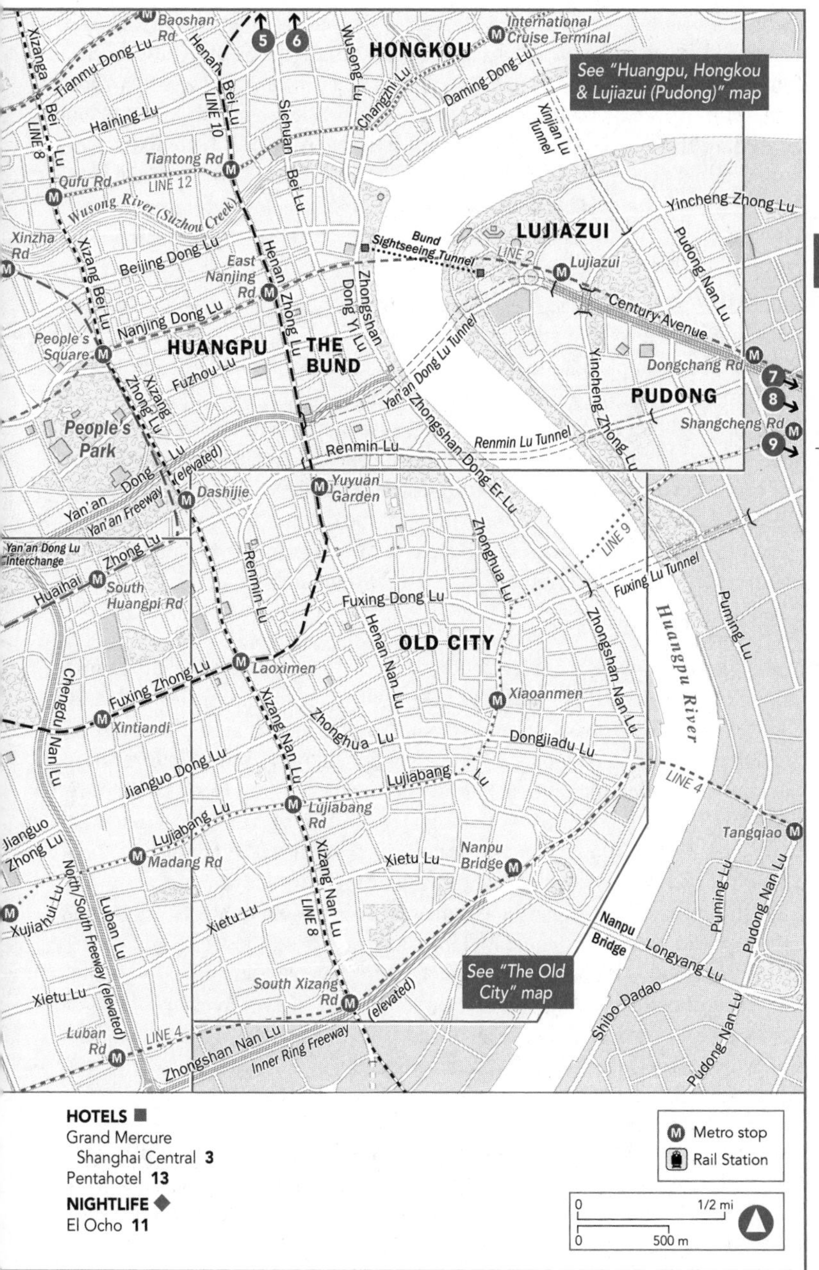
HONGKOU
International Cruise Terminal
See "Huangpu, Hongkou & Lujiazui (Pudong)" map
Baoshan Rd
Tianmu Dong Lu
Xizang Bei Lu
LINE 8
Henan Bei Lu
LINE 10
Sichuan Bei Lu
Wusong Lu
Changzhi Lu
Daming Dong Lu
Xinjian Lu Tunnel
Haining Lu
Tiantong Rd
Qufu Rd
LINE 12
Wusong River (Suzhou Creek)
Xinzha Rd
Beijing Dong Lu
East Nanjing Rd
Henan Zhong Lu
Zhongshan Dong Yi Lu
Bund Sightseeing Tunnel
LUJIAZUI
LINE 2
Lujiazui
Yincheng Zhong Lu
Pudong Nan Lu
Century Avenue
Nanjing Dong Lu
People's Square
HUANGPU
THE BUND
Yan'an Dong Lu Tunnel
Dongchang Rd
Fuzhou Lu
Xizang Zhong Lu
PUDONG
People's Park
Renmin Lu
Renmin Lu Tunnel
Zhongshan Dong Er Lu
Shangcheng Rd
Yan'an Dong Lu
Yan'an Freeway (elevated)
Dashijie
Yuyuan Garden
Yan'an Dong Lu Interchange
Huaihai Zhong Lu
South Huangpi Rd
Renmin Lu
Zhonghua Lu
LINE 9
Fuxing Lu Tunnel
Fuxing Dong Lu
Henan Nan Lu
OLD CITY
Zhongshan Nan Lu
Huangpu River
Puming Lu
Chengdu Nan Lu
Fuxing Zhong Lu
Laoximen
Xintiandi
Xizang Nan Lu
Zhonghua Lu
Xiaoanmen
Dongjiadu Lu
Jianguo Dong Lu
Lujiabang Lu
LINE 4
Lujiabang Rd
Tangqiao
Jianguo Zhong Lu
Madang Rd
Xietu Lu
Nanpu Bridge
Xujiahui Lu
North/South Freeway (elevated)
Luban Lu
Nanpu Bridge
Longyang Lu
Pudong Nan Lu
Puming Lu
Shibo Dadao
See "The Old City" map
South Xizang Rd
Xietu Lu
Luban Rd
Zhongshan Nan Lu
Inner Ring Freeway (elevated)
Pudong Nan Lu
HOTELS
Grand Mercure Shanghai Central 3
Pentahotel 13
NIGHTLIFE
El Ocho 11
Metro stop
Rail Station
0
1/2 mi
0
500 m

for a taxi at the large, underground stand. Express T trains run to destinations such as Beijing, Nanjing, and Xi'an, though faster bullet trains serve each of these destinations from Hongqiao Station (see below). Most trains arriving from Hangzhou and select destinations arrive at the **Shanghai South Railway Station** in the southwestern part of town. This station is reachable by subway lines 1 and 3. However, by far the most useful station for travelers is the ultramodern **Hongqiao Railway Station.** Spread over four levels, it feels more like an airport terminal than a station and serves several high-speed bullet trains, including trains to Nanjing, Hangzhou, and the Beijing-Shanghai high-speed railway. Located west of the city center, the station connects to Hongqiao International Airport (see above) and lies on lines 2 and 10 of the Shanghai subway.

BY SHIP Shanghai receives many cruise passengers, the majority from Japan and Korea. Where you disembark will depend on the size of the vessel. Smaller cruise ships that are able to navigate the Huangpu River will stop at the **Shanghai International Cruise Terminal** at 500 Dongdaming Lu, not far north of the Bund. From here, it's easier to take an onward taxi or jump on the subway line 12 at the new Cruise Terminal Station. Large ships will stop at the **Wusong Kou Passenger Terminal,** at the confluence of the Huangpu and the Yangtze rivers, 24km (15 miles) north of the city proper. If you arrive here as an independent traveler, you will have to hail a taxi at the passenger terminal to reach your hotel, which is around a 30-minute drive away.

Visitor Information

The best source of visitor information is the 24-hour **Shanghai Call Center** (http://en.shio.gov.cn; ✆ **021/962288**), with very helpful English-and-Chinese-speaking university graduates providing information on almost all Shanghai-travel-related topics. There are about a dozen **Tourist Information Service Centers** in the city, including one at 561 Nanjing Dong Lu (✆ **021/5353-1117**), but they mainly work as agents for domestic tour companies and are of little help to foreigners. The best sources of **current information** about Shanghai events, shopping, restaurants, and nightlife are the generally free English-language newspapers and magazines distributed to hotels, shops, and cafes around town. They are: **"Time Out"** (www.timeoutshanghai.com), **"City Weekend"** (www.cityweekend.com.cn/shanghai), and **"That's Shanghai"** (http://online.thatsmags.com/city/shanghai). "City Weekend" has an Android or iOS app that can be downloaded for free, while "That's Shanghai" can be downloaded as a PDF from the website.

City Layout

Shanghai is divided by the Huangpu River into Pudong (east of the river) and Puxi (west of the river). The majority of Shanghai's sights are still concentrated **downtown** in Puxi, whose layout bears a distinct Western imprint. After the First Opium War in 1842 opened Shanghai up to foreign powers, the British, French and Americans moved in, carving for themselves their own "concessions" where they were subject not to the laws of the Chinese government but to those established by their own governing councils. Colonial Shanghai is especially visible in the neo-classical buildings along the western shore of the Huangpu River at the **Bund** and in the busy streets behind. From here, stretching west for around 1.6km (1 mile) is **Nanjing Dong Lu,** the main thoroughfare of the U.S.-British administered "International Settlement," and in its day, the most famous shopping street in Asia. The road connects the Bund and **People's Square,** the center of downtown Shanghai. Three of Shanghai's main subway lines meet here, and it's home to the Shanghai Museum, Shanghai Art Museum, and Shanghai Grand Theatre, as well as government offices.

South of the Bund is Shanghai's **Old City,** full of tangles of *shikumen* neighborhoods and some of the most famous tourist sights, including Yuyuan Garden and the surrounding temples and bazaar. This area, sometimes known as Nanshi (literally "South City"), predates colonialism by several centuries. The ancient wall was knocked down early in the 20th century, but the circular shape is visible in the form of Renmin Lu and Zhonghua Lu.

Fanning out west from the Old City is Shanghai's most famous colonial settlement, the former **French Concession.** Just as it was during the interwar years, this is one of Shanghai's trendiest neighborhoods, crammed with fashionable clubs, bars, and boutiques. It's also home to the mega-development of **Xintiandi** and its earthier alternative, **Tianzifang.** Farther west still is **Xujiahui,** a former hub of Jesuit missionary activity and the site of Shanghai's most magnificent colonial cathedral, St. Ignatius.

North of Xujiahui are the districts of **Jing'an** and **Changning.** In colonial days, this was mostly countryside, but they're now home to some of Shanghai's most upmarket residential and commercial developments. Jing'an, in particular, has some of Shanghai's top hotels.

North Shanghai comprises the Hongkou and Zhabei districts, which have a scattering of interesting sights, including the Jade Buddha Temple, the Lu Xun Museum, and the Shanghai Jewish Refugees Museum. **South Shanghai** has the Longhua Pagoda.

East of the Huangpu River, **Pudong** is a vast, sprawling residential area. Facing the Huangpu, across from the Bund, is **Lujiazui.** With its now-iconic coterie of skyscrapers, this is the most recognizable chunk of Pudong, but the district stretches beyond, as far as the sea, and includes lots of luxury low-rise villa developments and new apartment complexes. There's not a huge amount for tourists to see here, but it is where modern Shanghai has taken shape.

Neighborhoods in Brief

The Shanghai municipality consists of 16 districts and the outlying island of Chongming. It's one of four "municipalities" in China—cities so big or important that they function as entire provinces in their own right. The three districts of most interest to visitors are the huge, sprawling areas of Huangpu and Pudong, but this rundown uses more historical (and more useful) definitions of neighborhood boundaries.

Huangpu After recent mergers, Huangpu District now comprises nearly all of Shanghai city-center west of the river (Puxi) but can be more usefully subdivided into three areas. The old definition of "Huangpu," used here, refers to the original heart of the former colonial concession run by Britain and the United States—the International Settlement.

It lies in a rectangle, bounded by the elevated highways of Yan'an Lu and Chengdu Lu, and the waterways of the Huangpu River and Suzhou Creek. Contained within are the key central tourist sights of the Bund, Nanjing Dong Lu, and People's Square.

The Old City Now part of Huangpu District, Shanghai's Old City is marked by the loop formed by Renmin Lu and Zhonghua Lu that marks the old city wall (demolished in 1912). It has a distinct atmosphere in its narrow lanes and *shikumen* dwellings. This has historically been one of Shanghai's poorest areas, but demolition and creeping gentrification are changing this day by day. Of interest for tourists are Yuyuan Garden, the surrounding Yuyuan bazaar, and the serene Shanghai Confucius Temple.

The French Concession Shanghai government has worked hard to remove the term "French Concession" from day-to-day conversation. However, the label is still widely used, not least because this charming swath of central Shanghai maintains a distinct atmosphere. It runs from the circular Old City in the east to snaking Huashan Lu in the west, and takes in everything south of Yan'an Lu and north of Zhaojiabang Lu. Standout sights include Fuxing Park, the shopping avenue of Huaihai Lu, Xintiandi, and the lanes of Tianzifang, but the area is as much about villa architecture and ambience as it is attractions. At the far-west fringe of the original concession is **Xujiahui.** This area is famed for modern malls and historic buildings such as St. Ignatius Cathedral and Jiaotong University. South of here, in Xuhui District, are Longhua Pagoda and the Shanghai Botanical Gardens.

Jing'an District North of the French Concession and part of the former International Settlement, this district has its share of colonial architecture, as well as the modern Shanghai Center. Two of the city's top Buddhist shrines, Jing'an Temple and the Jade Buddha Temple, are located here, as well as the arts district of M50 and a number of Shanghai's top hotels and restaurants.

Hongkou and Zhabei North of the bend in the Huangpu is Hongkou. This was the original American Concession but it was later absorbed into the British-controlled area to form the International Settlement. After 1931, it became a de facto Japanese "concession" and one of the only refuges for Jews escaping persecution in Europe. The Ohel Moshe Synagogue now survives as a museum to this heritage. West of Hongkou is Zhabei, a fairly anonymous district north of Suzhou Creek, but home to the Lu Xun Museum and the Duolun Commercial Street.

Pudong Located across the Huangpu River from the Bund, Pudong (literally "east of the Huangpu") was formerly boggy farmland before 1991 when it was selected by Vice-Premier (and former Shanghai mayor) Zhu Rongji as the place to reboot China's free-market miracle. Today, it is home to the Lujiazui financial district with its modern totems of "progress" (Shanghai Tower, Shanghai World Financial Center, Jinmao Tower), as well as the Shanghai Stock Exchange, huge department stores, and a riverside promenade. Farther out are Pudong International Airport and the 2010 World Expo grounds.

GETTING AROUND

By Subway

The Shanghai subway only came into being in the 1990s and retains the feel of a new, modern network. At the time of writing, there were 14 lines and 341 miles of track, making it the largest network in the world. There are even plans to expand farther, with another four lines scheduled to open by 2020. It's by far the fastest way to cover longer distances and is exceptionally cheap. The most useful routes for visitors are lines 1 and 2. **Line 1,** the red line, winds in a roughly north-south direction, connecting the Shanghai Railway Station in the north, through the French Concession, to the Shanghai South Railway Station and points southwest. Its central downtown stop is People's Square, where it connects with **Line 2,** the green line, which runs east-west across downtown Shanghai. The line stretches the whole way between Shanghai's two very distant airports, and is also the way to the bullet trains departing Hongqiao Railway Station. In its packed middle section, it connects the financial district of Lujiazui with the hotels and apartment complexes around Jing'an and is the quickest way for visitors to cross the Huangpu River. Other useful lines include **Line 3,** the yellow line, which is an elevated light-rail for much of its route. Encircling the western outskirts of the city, it provides a fun way to breeze through suburban Shanghai above ground level, though it's not hugely helpful for getting to tourist sights. **Line 4,** the purple line, forms a complete loop, connecting Pudong and Puxi. Its eastern hub, Century Avenue, is the biggest and busiest on the network, joining four major lines. **Line 8** runs north-to-south and bypasses the World Expo site, the Old City, and People's Square. **Line 9** runs from Pudong in the east to the far southwest, passing Xujiahui and the river town of Qibao en route. See the map on the inside back cover for all stops.

NAVIGATING THE SUBWAY Most rides will cost RMB3 to RMB4, but costs can go up to RMB9 for very long distances. To determine your fare, consult the fare map posted near the ticket counters or use the ticket vending kiosks. These all have excellent English language functionality and are the easiest way to buy tickets on a fare-by-fare basis. If you're staying for a few days, get a "Shanghai Public Transportation Card" (*Jiaotong Ka*). These can be purchased at most service centers within subway stations and require a refundable RMB20 deposit. They can also be used to pay for taxis. One- and three-day subway cards are also available (RMB18 and RMB45, respectively), but you'll need to take at least five or six rides within a day for it to be worth buying. Subway platform signs in Chinese and English indicate the station name, including the English language translation (hence why we have used the English names for subway stations throughout this book), as well as the name of the next station in each direction. Maps of the subway system are posted in each station and inside the subway cars. English announcements of upcoming stops are also made on trains. **Note:** Hang on to your electronic ticket, which you have to insert into the exit barrier when you leave.

DRAWBACKS Airport-style scanners have been installed in all stations, and you'll need to submit your bag for inspection before entering the ticket area. Trains run between approximately 5:30am and 11pm, so it's not to be relied on if you plan to stay out late (the ease of finding a taxi in Shanghai makes this less of a problem than in Beijing). Finally, though many new stations have quick and easy interchanges, the walk between lines at People's Square can be both long and very, very, (very) crowded.

By Taxi

With over 45,000 cabs roaming the streets, it's easier to get a taxi in Shanghai than in any other city in China, and this remains the best way to make short, city-center journeys. Various companies operate, but though colors may be different, the cars, prices, and quality of service are indistinguishable. All drivers should display a license number and photograph in the front of the taxi, along with a telephone number for complaints. Regardless of the company, the fare is RMB15 for the first 3km (1¾ miles) and RMB2.2 for each additional kilometer. There's a 30% surcharge for trips after 11pm. Expect to pay RMB15 to RMB35 for most excursions in the city and up to RMB60 for longer crosstown jaunts. Drivers are obliged to use the meter at all times and invariably will without being prompted. No tip is expected.

On the downside, the arrival of taxi-hailing apps such as **Uber** and **Didi Da Che** have made it a little less easy to find a cab from any given street corner. Moreover, it can be next to impossible to find a taxi in poor weather. If you are stranded, grab a map and head for the nearest subway (it's unlikely to be too far away). Language can also be a problem. The English name of your destination may be quite different from the Chinese name, so pointing at written text will not always work. Drivers may not recognize written Pinyin (the Romanized form of Chinese). If possible, have someone write your destination *in Chinese.* Try dialing the Shanghai Call Center, at ✆ **962288,** if confusion persists. An English-language operator will be able to mediate. If there is any argument or confusion at the end of a taxi ride, ask the driver for a *fa piao*, which they are legally obliged to give. These printed receipts give details of your journey and will discourage drivers who might be tempted to squeeze you for extra cash.

Most cabs in Shanghai are sedans, colored in metallic blue, green, or red. There are a few larger white Volkswagen Tourans that operate. These were introduced for the 2010 Expo but now serve regular customers. Prices are the same, and drivers are more likely to speak some basic English.

By Bus

Public buses mostly charge RMB2, but they are more difficult to use and less comfortable than taxis or the subway. Tickets are sold on board by a roving conductor, though some buses have no conductors and require exact change. Be prepared to stand and be cramped during your expedition, and take care with backpacks and purses.

By Bridge, Boat & Tunnel

Shanghai is divided by the wide Huangpu River. To shift the thousands of daily visitors between east (Pudong) and west (Puxi) Shanghai, there are a multitude of routes. Most cars and taxis in the city center will cross via one of three **tunnels** where Yan'an Lu, Renmin Lu, and Fuxing Lu burrow beneath the water, though taxis are prohibited from using the tunnel during rush hour. There are also three bridges—the **Nanpu Bridge,** the **Lupu Bridge,** and the **Yangpu Bridge**—but these are a ways from the action in the middle of town. For those on foot, there are several **passenger ferry** routes. The two most useful routes for visitors are: the line from the terminal at the southern end of the Bund, which connects with the southern end of Binjiang Da Dao (near Dongchang Lu) in Lujiazui; and the route between Gongping Lu, in Hongkou, and Taidong Lu, just north of the main towers in Lujiazui. The fare is RMB2. Subway lines 2, 4,

7, 8, and 9 also make the crossing (though only **Line 2** goes to Lujiazui, the most important Pudong station). Finally, for pedestrians moving between Lujiazui and the Bund, there is the **Bund Sightseeing Tunnel** (RMB40 one-way, RMB50 round-trip). It's a glass tram car that chugs through a tacky subterranean light show with music and narrative. It's not supposed to be a commuter link, but travel at rush hour, and it may be your best bet for crossing.

[FastFACTS] SHANGHAI

If you don't find what you're looking for in these listings, try the **Shanghai Call Center** (✆ **021/962-288**) or inquire at your hotel desk.

Banks, Currency Exchange & ATMs The most convenient place to exchange currency is your hotel, where the rates are the same as at the Bank of China, and exchange desks are often open 24 hours. Convenient **Bank of China** locations for currency exchange and credit-card cash withdrawals are located on the Bund at the Bank of China building, 23 Zhongshan Dong Yi Lu, beside the north-south flyover at 580 Nanjing Xi Lu, and beside the Changshu Lu subway station at 1285 Huaihai Zhong Lu. Bank hours are Monday to Friday from 9am to noon and 1:30 to 4:30pm, and Saturday from 9am to noon.

There are also branches of the **Hong Kong and Shanghai Bank (HSBC)** at the Shanghai Centre (1376 Nanjing Xi Lu) and at G/F, HSBC Tower, Lujiazui Huan Lu, Pudong, that can change U.S. traveler's checks and cash. All have 24-hour **ATMs.** Although there are thousands of ATMs around town with international logos for Plus or Cirrus, not all of them take international cards. It's best to stick to Bank of China, ICBC, HSBC, or Citibank ATMs.

Doctors & Dentists Shanghai has the most advanced medical treatment and facilities in China. The higher-end hotels usually have in-house or on-call doctors, but almost all hotels can refer foreign guests to dentists and doctors versed in Western medicine. The following medical clinics and hospitals specialize in treating foreigners and provide international-standard services: **Parkway Health,** Suite 203, Shanghai Center, 1376 Nanjing Xi Lu (24-hr. hotline; www.parkwayhealth.cn; ✆ **021/6445-5999**) has several clinics around town, 24-hour emergency services, offers Western dental care, and OB-GYN services; walk-in hours at the Nanjing Lu branch are from 9am to 7pm Monday through Friday, 9am to 5pm on weekends. Call for times at other clinics. **Huashan Worldwide Medical Center,** 12 Wulumuqi Zhong Lu, Jing'an District (www.sh-hwmc.com.cn; ✆ **021/6249-9295**), has a special Foreigner's Clinic on the eighth floor of building 1. A representative office of **International SOS,** Unit 1801–1806, Tower B, Baoland Plaza, 588 Dalian Lu, Yangpu District (✆ **021/5298-9538**) provides medical evacuation and repatriation throughout China on a 24-hour basis.

Dental care for foreign visitors and expatriates is provided by **Parkway Health** dental centers Monday to Saturday (see above) and by the **Shanghai United Family Hospital Dental Clinic,** 1139 Xianxia Lu (www.ufh.com.cn; ✆ **021/2216-3900**), with multilingual Western-trained dentists and their own lab.

Embassies & Consulates The consulates of many countries are located in the French Concession and Jing'an District. The consulates are open Monday through Friday only, and often close for lunch from noon to 1pm. The Consulate General of **Australia** is in CITIC Square on the 22nd floor, 1168 Nanjing Xi Lu (www.shanghai.china.embassy.gov.au; ✆ **021/2215-5200**). The **British** Consulate General is at the British Centre, Garden Square, 968 Beijing Xi Lu (www.gov.uk; ✆ **021/3279-2000**). The **Canadian** Consulate General is at ECO City Building, 8th floor,

1788 Nanjing Xi Lu (www.canadainternational.gc.ca; ✆ **021/3279-2800**). The **New Zealand** Consulate General is at Rooms 2801-2802A, 5 Corporate Avenue, 150 Hubin Lu (www.nzembassy.com; ✆ **021/5407-5858**). The Consulate General of the **United States** is at 1469 Huaihai Zhong Lu (http://shanghai.usembassy-china.org.cn; ✆ **021/6433-6880**), although U.S. citizen services are available at the Westgate Mall, 8th floor, 1038 Nanjing Xi Lu (✆ **021/3217-4650**).

Hospitals See "Doctors & Dentists," above.

Internet Access Wi-Fi Internet access is standard in all Shanghai's hotels. Most offer free Internet, though a handful of the upper-end hotels may still charge a daily fee. The majority of Shanghai restaurants and cafes also offer free Wi-Fi access to their patrons, and there's even government-provided public Wi-Fi, though you'll need to use a China SIM to register.

Maps & Books The biggest and best selection of English-language books in Shanghai, as well as the bilingual Shanghai Tourist Map, can be found at the **Shanghai Foreign Language Bookstore,** 390 Fuzhou Lu (✆ **021/6322-3200;** 9am–6pm). **Garden Books,** 325 Changle Lu (✆ **021/5404-8728**), also has an extensive English-language book selection. The **Shanghai Museum,** 201 Renmin Da Dao (✆ **021/6372-3500**), has selections of books on Shanghai and Chinese art and culture, as do the gift shops and kiosks in major hotels. Most hotel concierges should also be able to provide bilingual maps of the city.

Pharmacies The best outlet for Westerners is **Watson's,** which has branches throughout town, including at 787 Huaihai Zhong Lu (✆ **021/6431-8650;** daily 10am–10pm). Watson's is also a reliable vendor of anti-pollution face masks. Prescriptions can be filled at the **Parkway Health Medical Center,** Suite 203, 1376 Nanjing Xi Lu, Shanghai Centre (✆ **021/6279-7688**).

Post Office Most hotels sell postage stamps and will mail your letters and parcels, the latter for a hefty fee. The main post office is located at 276 Bei Suzhou Lu (✆ **021/6325-2070;** daily 7am–10pm), just north of Suzhou Creek; international parcels are sent from a desk in the same building, but its entrance is actually around the corner at 395 Tiantong Lu 395. Another post office where employees can speak some English is in the East Tower of the Shanghai Center, 1376 Nanjing Xi Lu (✆ **021/6279-8044**).

Taxes Most four- and five-star hotels levy a 10% to 15% tax on rooms, while a few restaurants and bars have taken to placing a similar service charge on bills. There is no sales tax.

Taxis See "Getting Around," above.

Visa Extensions The **PSB** office for visa extensions is at 1500 Minsheng Lu (✆ **021/2895-1900**; subway: Shanghai Science and Technology Museum) in Pudong. Hours are Monday to Saturday 9am to 5pm.

Weather Both the Google Play Store and the Apple App Store offer a selection of free China weather apps. It's also a good idea to be able to predict the pollution. If the AQI is 150 or above, you should be wearing a face mask if you plan to spend any serious time outside (see "Pharmacies" above for advice on where to buy masks). The **Shanghai Air Quality** takes its data from the U.S. Consulate in Shanghai. More traditional weather information can be found in the "Shanghai Daily" newspaper or on CCTV 9, China Central Television's English channel (broadcast in most hotels).

EXPLORING SHANGHAI

Shanghai has few sights on the scale of the Forbidden City or the Great Wall, but the treasures it does have—its colonial neighborhoods, historic homes, museums, parks, and shopping avenues—reveal a unique inheritance. Shanghai is by far the most compact and easily navigable of the three featured cities in this book, and 2 days (the average time overseas visitors spend here) are sufficient to tick off the central landmark attractions. But Shanghai is about more than just its guidebook-listed sights. If all you do is run between the attractions, Shanghai is likely to disappoint. Indeed, it's one of those places where first-time visitors often come away underwhelmed, or even appalled, at the brashness and commercialism. It's only by lingering a while that a visitor can begin to appreciate its cultural and architectural complexity, and soak up its industrious, dynamic, and entrepreneurial spirit.

The best way to see Shanghai is on your own, armed with a good map and this guide, and using a combination of taxis, subways, and your own two feet. Transportation facilities and many of the sights described here are very user-friendly, even for the non-Chinese-speaking, first-time visitor. Taxis are easy to hail (certainly compared to those in Beijing and Xi'an), and the subway is the world's most extensive, meaning you'll rarely have to walk far from a subway station.

Huangpu District

THE BUND (WAITAN) ★★★

The Bund is the name given to the waterfront running along the west shore of the Huangpu River, forming the eastern boundary of old downtown Shanghai. This was the focal point for colonial business: The junks and sailboats that once docked outside the walled city, to the south, swiftly found a more lucrative port of call here, and banks and trading houses were built to both manage and glorify this bustling trade. They became grander and grander as the years went on. All but four of the neoclassical structures that stand today date from between 1901 and 1929, colonial Shanghai's boom years. Pedestrians can walk along the shadow of these buildings on the pavement that lines Zhongshan Dong Yi Lu, or, across the street, on a riverside promenade with its elevated view of the sci-fi towers of Pudong. There can be few places in the world where past and present meet so spectacularly. The description below details a walk from south to north along the pavement, and looping back north to south along the riverside.

ZHONGSHAN DONG YI LU WALK

Most Bund buildings operate as banks or converted commercial spaces and are open to the public in one way or another. Start at the former **Shanghai Club** (no. 2), reopened as the Waldorf Astoria Hotel in 2010. Its famous "Long Bar" survives, while the lobby has caged elevators. The former **Union Insurance Company Building** (no. 3, or "Three on the Bund") contains some of Shanghai's chichiest drinking-and-dining venues, and has a free art gallery on the third floor. The beautiful domed roof of the former **Hong Kong and Shanghai Bank** (no. 12) is now the Pudong Development Bank. Head in for a view of the dazzling mosaic ceiling mural. The **Customs House** (no. 13) next door is one of the few buildings with no public access, but the clock-tower bell, shipped from London to Shanghai in the 1920s, still marks time for all. The grand old **Cathay Hotel** (no. 20) is the newly renovated Fairmont Peace Hotel and a treasure trove of Art Deco styling. Nonguests can stroll through the wings of the finely restored lobby, where the small Peace Gallery, up on the mezzanine, has some intimate portraits

Huangpu, Hongkou & Lujiazui (Pudong)

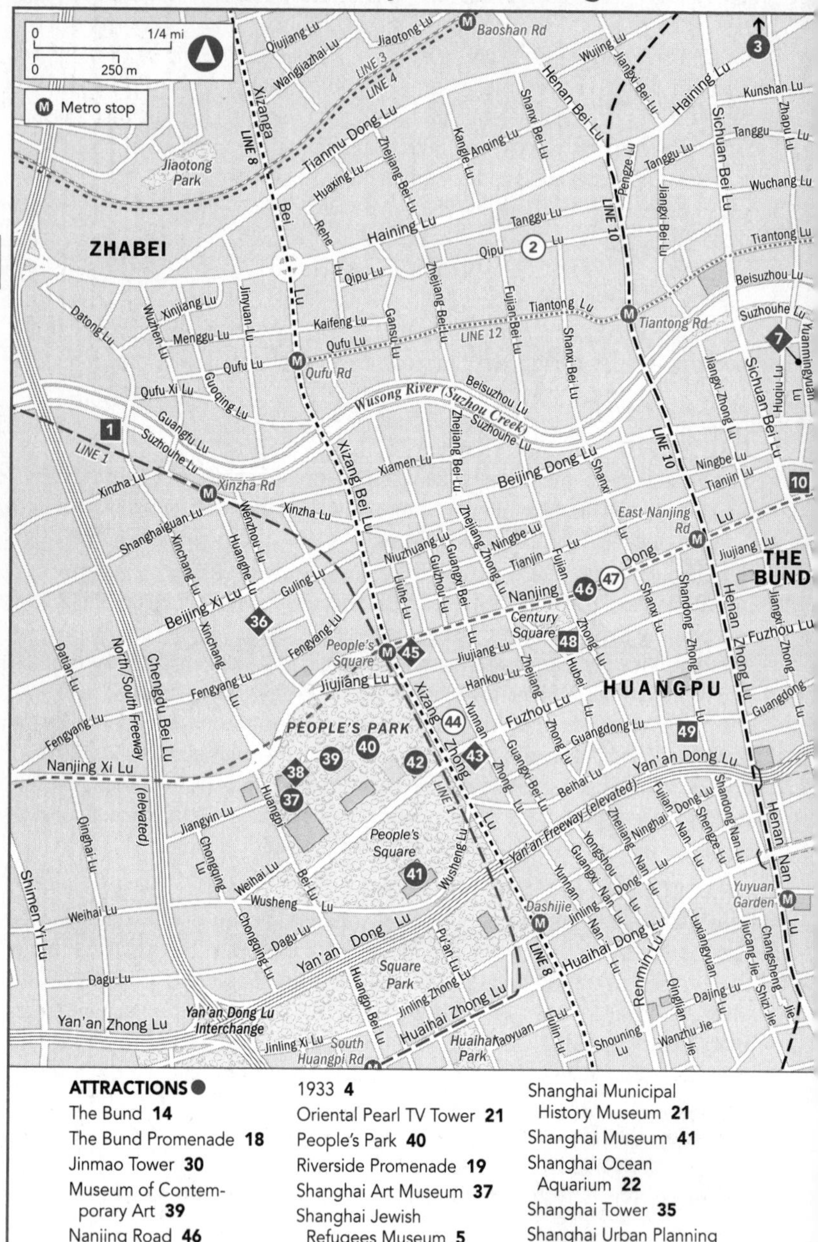

ATTRACTIONS ●

The Bund **14**
The Bund Promenade **18**
Jinmao Tower **30**
Museum of Contemporary Art **39**
Nanjing Road **46**
1933 **4**
Oriental Pearl TV Tower **21**
People's Park **40**
Riverside Promenade **19**
Shanghai Art Museum **37**
Shanghai Jewish Refugees Museum **5**
Shanghai Municipal History Museum **21**
Shanghai Museum **41**
Shanghai Ocean Aquarium **22**
Shanghai Tower **35**
Shanghai Urban Planning Exhibition **42**

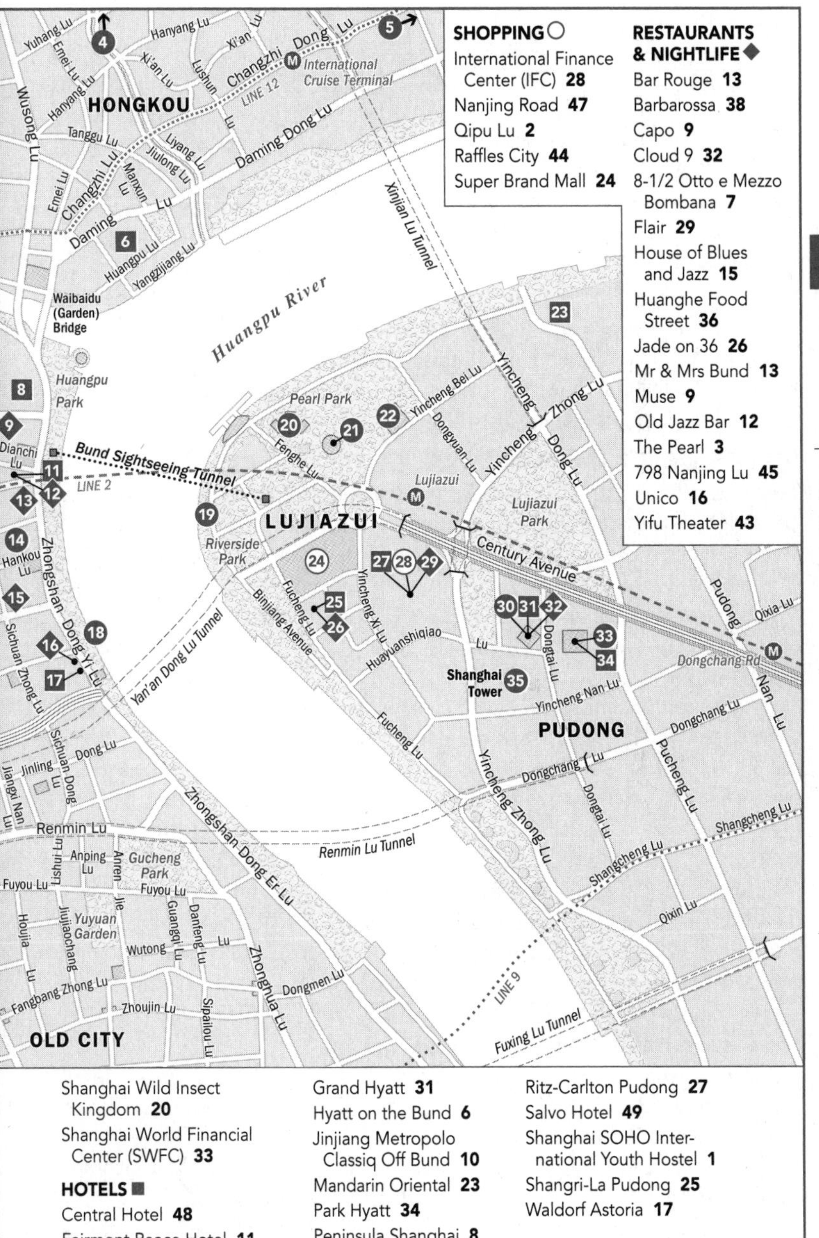
SHOPPING
International Finance Center (IFC) 28
Nanjing Road 47
Qipu Lu 2
Raffles City 44
Super Brand Mall 24
RESTAURANTS & NIGHTLIFE
Bar Rouge 13
Barbarossa 38
Capo 9
Cloud 9 32
8-1/2 Otto e Mezzo Bombana 7
Flair 29
House of Blues and Jazz 15
Huanghe Food Street 36
Jade on 36 26
Mr & Mrs Bund 13
Muse 9
Old Jazz Bar 12
The Pearl 3
798 Nanjing Lu 45
Unico 16
Yifu Theater 43
Shanghai Wild Insect Kingdom 20
Shanghai World Financial Center (SWFC) 33
HOTELS
Central Hotel 48
Fairmont Peace Hotel 11
Grand Hyatt 31
Hyatt on the Bund 6
Jinjiang Metropolo Classiq Off Bund 10
Mandarin Oriental 23
Park Hyatt 34
Peninsula Shanghai 8
Ritz-Carlton Pudong 27
Salvo Hotel 49
Shanghai SOHO International Youth Hostel 1
Shangri-La Pudong 25
Waldorf Astoria 17
HONGKOU
LUJIAZUI
PUDONG
OLD CITY
Huangpu River
International Cruise Terminal
Waibaidu (Garden) Bridge
Huangpu Park
Pearl Park
Riverside Park
Lujiazui Park
Bund Sightseeing Tunnel
Century Avenue
Shanghai Tower
Yuyuan Garden
Gucheng Park
Xinjian Lu Tunnel
Yan'an Dong Lu Tunnel
Renmin Lu Tunnel
Fuxing Lu Tunnel
LINE 2
LINE 9
LINE 12
Zhongshan Dong Yi Lu
Zhongshan Dong Er Lu
Yincheng Zhong Lu
Daming Dong Lu
Changzhi Dong Lu
Wusong Lu
Sichuan Zhong Lu
Renmin Lu
Zhonghua Lu
Dongchang Lu
Pucheng Lu
Pudong Nan Lu
Lujiazui

of the hotel's famous guests, such as Charlie Chaplin and Noël Coward. Alternatively, head to the eighth-floor terrace (cover charge) for a superb view down the length of the Bund and across the Huangpu to the towers of Pudong.

Turn away from the river at Beijing Dong Lu and turn right into cobbled Yuanmingyuan Lu. This offers access to the old **British Consulate** compound, which once occupied the most precious slice of real estate at the northern end of the Bund. The consulate buildings have been renovated and converted into private exhibition space, though those opposite contain luxury shops and restaurants. The distinctive **China Baptist Publishing Building** (no. 209) was where Shanghai's most-celebrated Art Deco architect, Ladislaus Hudec, had his offices. Turn right at the late 19th-century **Union Church** to see the former **Shanghai Rowing Club** building, opened by the Brits and Americans in 1863. Walk along Nan Suzhou Lu, to where Suzhou Creek enters the Huangpu River. Here stands the 18m-wide (59-ft.) iron **Waibaidu Bridge,** built in 1906 to replace the original 1856 wooden bridge, where a toll was charged to anyone entering or leaving British territory.

RIVERSIDE PROMENADE WALK

There are a few other attractions for those walking along the riverside promenade. On the shore stands a granite obelisk, **Monument to the People's Heroes,** erected in 1993 and dedicated to Chinese patriots (as defined by the Communist Party) beginning in the 1840s. The **Bund History Museum** (Mon–Fri 9am–4:15pm; free admission), which contains some interesting photographs of the Bund, stands at its base. Just south of the monument is **Huangpu Park,** originally the British Public Gardens built in 1868. In the early days, only Chinese servants accompanying their foreign masters were allowed to enter the park. Dogs were also prohibited, leading in later years to the apocryphal NO CHINESE OR DOGS ALLOWED sign being attributed to the park. The park was eventually opened to Chinese in 1926, but today, has simply become part of the Bund promenade with the recent renovations.

South of here, across from the Fairmont Peace Hotel, is the entrance to the pedestrian **Bund Sightseeing Tunnel (Waitan Guanguang Suidao),** open daily 8am–10:30pm (admission RMB55 round-trip, RMB45 one-way), which runs under the Huangpu. Complete with tram cars and a light show, the tunnel connects downtown Shanghai to the Pudong New Area and the Oriental Pearl TV Tower. Also here is a **statue of Chen Yi,** Shanghai's first mayor after 1949 and a dead ringer for Mao Zedong, at least in bronze.

Farther south, opposite the former Hong Kong and Shanghai Bank, is the **Bund Bull,** Arturo Di Modica's reprisal of his "Charging Bull" on Wall Street, though younger, stronger, and "redder" for the Chinese setting.

Close to the intersection with Yan'an Dong Lu is the elegant **Meteorological Signal Tower,** a slender, round brick structure that served as a control tower for river traffic during colonial days. Built in 1907, the tower was moved 20m (66 ft.) during the widening of Zhongshan Lu in 1993. About a 20-minute walk farther down the promenade are the docks for the Huangpu River cruises (p. 223).

SHANGHAI art deco

Emerging in the late 1910s and first labeled a "movement" in 1925, Art Deco enjoyed a short-lived reign as the dominant architectural motif. The style was singled out by sleek, geometric designs that took inspiration from the dawning era of mass production and consumerism. Owing to historical coincidence, colonial Shanghai found itself being built anew just as the Art Deco era got into its swing. The city's "anything goes" reputation only encouraged the experimental (and young) foreign architects who imbued the spirit of the era in their designs. Where many of Europe's best Art Deco buildings were destroyed by war, Shanghai's survived the years of conflict, and the city is up there with Napier, in New Zealand, as one of the world's great repositories of this unique form. Many of the most striking examples are either on or around the Bund.

No Art Deco enthusiast should miss the **Fairmont Peace Hotel** (see p. 227), with its signature green-copper pyramid roof. Just up the way on the Bund, the **Bank of Communications Building** (no. 14) was the last colonial-era Bund building to go up, opening a year before revolution struck in 1949. Just north of the Waibaidu Bridge is the **Broadway Mansions,** a onetime luxury apartment block modeled on the Chinese character for the "lucky" number eight. The **Metropole Hotel,** part of a dazzling intersection two blocks west of the Bund (at Jiangxi Lu and Fuzhou Lu), was the birthplace of Shanghai jazz. Elsewhere in Shanghai, the **Cathay Theatre** (Maoming Nan Lu and Huaihai Lu), the **Park Hotel** (north of People's Square), and **1933** (see p. 221) are also must-see sights for Deco aficionados.

Nanjing Road (Nanjing Dong Lu) ★★ NEIGHBORHOOD The main thoroughfare of the former International Settlement, Nanking Road (as it was then known) was once the most famous street in Asia, renowned for its towering architecture and modern department stores. It's still a hub for hawking and commerce, though these days you're more likely to come across cheap souvenir knickknacks than you are elegant evening wear. It's a sea of tourists throughout the day, while there's a distinctly noirish feel at night when the neon burns bright. At the junction with Zhejiang Lu, China's first two department stores face each other across the frenetic plaza. The Sincere and the Wing On, built in 1917 and 1918 respectively, are easy to spot thanks to their copycat cathedral-like spires.

Nanjing Dong Lu (between Xizang Zhong Lu and the Bund). Free. Shops 8am–11pm. Subway: East Nanjing Rd.

PEOPLE'S SQUARE (RENMIN GUANGCHANG) ★★

Shanghai's central hub was fashioned from the International Settlement's horse-racing track, where colonial high society amused itself as long ago as 1863. Two years after the Communist takeover of Shanghai, it was repurposed as a grimly utilitarian concrete plaza, later used as a public reckoning ground during the Cultural Revolution. In 1994 the square came in for wholesale rejuvenation, and it's now the city's foremost cultural center and busiest subway interchange. The original 12 hectares (30 acres) of the racecourse have been parceled out. In the north is People's Park (Renmin Gongyuan), a thickly forested space filled with lotus ponds, rock gardens, and a small amusement ground. Clusters of old folks come to play mah-jongg or chess, and the **Museum of Contemporary Art** (below) and the Moroccan-themed restaurant **Barbarossa** (p. 251) are both hidden within. To the west is the **Shanghai Art Museum** (below), which once acted as the race club where the most well-to-do of racegoers would watch the action. Along Renmin Da Dao, the road that dissects the square, are the **Grand Theatre,** the **Shanghai Urban Planning Exhibition Hall** (p. 209), and the Shanghai government's 20-story administrative headquarters. To the south are the landscaped gardens that surround the **Shanghai Museum** (below).

Museum of Contemporary Art (Shanghai Dangdai Yishuguan) ★★ GALLERY This fabulous art space is essentially a giant greenhouse in the middle of People's Park. A sweeping glass ramp guides visitors onto a mezzanine, overlooking a frequently changing (but invariably puzzling) ground-floor installation. It's fun, youthful, and exuberant—art by young people for young people. At the front of the second floor is a thickly carpeted area with multicolored kids' chairs where visitors are encouraged to get out the crayons and take inspiration from what they've just seen. For those immune to the charms of modern art, the building itself is quite interesting and can be appreciated gratis by heading up to the third-floor restaurant. The terrace here has great views across the green canopy and out to the buildings that surround the park.

People's Park (Gate 7), 231 Nanjing Xi Lu. www.mocashanghai.org. ✆ **021/6327-9900.** Admission RMB20. Daily 10am–6pm. Subway: People's Square (exit 11).

Shanghai Art Museum (Shanghai Meishuguan) ★ GALLERY The artwork in this gallery's 12 exhibit halls is certainly noteworthy, ranging from modern traditional oils to recent pop canvases, but it's overwhelmed by the fastidiously restored, wood-and-marble interiors of this five-story, neoclassical landmark building. The clock tower, erected in 1933, marks the location of the original grandstand of 1863.

325 Nanjing Xi Lu, (nr. Huangpi Lu). www.sh-artmuseum.org.cn. ✆ **021/6327-2829.** Admission RMB20. Tue–Sun 10am–6pm (last tickets sold 4pm). Subway: People's Square (exit 11).

Shanghai Museum (Shanghai Bowuguan) ★★★ MUSEUM Frequently cited as the best museum in China, the Shanghai Museum has 11 state-of-the-art galleries arranged across four floors, all encircling a spacious cylindrical atrium. Designed by Shanghai native Xing Tonghe to mimic the shape of a *ding* (a bronze cauldron used in ritual feasting and sacrifice), the museum looks beyond Shanghai's relatively short history and plunders the almost limitless reserves of cultural treasures. Around 120,000 items are beautifully displayed in spotlit and soundproofed galleries and arranged into logical themes. There are separate displays on bronzes, sculpture, ceramics, paintings, calligraphy, seals, jade, coins, furniture, and ethnic minority art—and it's easy to skip any that don't take your fancy. In a city where Han

Chinese dominate, the Minority Nationalities Art Gallery is especially interesting for its colorful face masks and folk costumes.

201 Renmin Da Dao (south side of People's Square). www.shanghaimuseum.net/en. ✆ **021/6372-3500.** Free admission (passport required), though tickets limited to 8,000 per day. Audio guide RMB40. Daily 9am–5pm. Subway: People's Square (exit 1) or Da Shijie (exit 4).

Shanghai Urban Planning Exhibition Center (Shanghai Chengshi Guihua Zhanshiguan) ★★ EXHIBITION HALL If you want to see what a city of the future is really going to look like, wander over to the eastern edge of People's Square. Housed in a striking, modern, five-story building made of Microlite glass, this is one of the world's largest showcases of urban development and is much more interesting than its dry name suggests. The highlight is on the third floor: an awesome, vast, scale model of urban Shanghai. The clear plastic models indicate structures yet to be built, and there are many of them. Beleaguered Shanghai residents wondering if their current cramped downtown houses will survive the bulldozer (chances are not good) need only look here for the answer. The fourth floor also has displays on proposed forms of future transportation, including magnetic levitation (maglev), subway, and light-rail trains that are going to change even the face of the Bund. It's well worth an hour of your time.

100 Renmin Da Dao (entrance off Xizang Zhong Lu). www.supec.org. ✆ **021/6372-2077.** Admission RMB30. Daily 9am–5pm. Subway: People's Square (exit 2).

The Old City

YU GARDEN & SURROUNDINGS

Yu Garden (Yu Yuan) ★ GARDEN Bearing the burden of being the most complete classical garden in urban Shanghai and therefore a must-see for every tourist, this overexposed Ming-dynasty estate overflows daily with hordes of visitors, and is no longer the pastoral haven it once was. Built between 1559 and 1577 by local official Pan Yunduan as a private retreat for his father, *Yu Yuan* (meaning Garden of Peace and Comfort) is a maze of pavilions, elaborate rock gardens, arched bridges, and goldfish ponds. Each of the six areas is separated from the others by gray-tile "dragon walls," each undulating toward a sculpted dragon's head. The most famous of the historic buildings within is the **Hall of Heralding Spring (Dian Chun Tang)**, where, in 1853, the secret Small Sword Society (*Xiaodao Hui*) plotted to join the peasant-led Taiping Rebellion and help overthrow the Qing. The eventual Taiping defeat led to the gardens being trashed. Stick to a general clockwise path from the main entrance and you'll get around most of the estate and arrive eventually at the Inner Garden (*Nei Yuan*) and the exit.

18 Anren Jie (north entrance off Fuyou Lu, south entrance southeast of Huxinting Pavilion, within Yuyuan Bazaar). ✆ **021/6326-0830.** Admission RMB45. Daily 8:30am–5pm. Subway: Yuyuan Garden.

Yuyuan Bazaar (Yuyuan Shangcheng) ★ LANDMARK Never one to let historical authenticity interfere with money-making opportunities, the

The Old City

ATTRACTIONS ●
Baiyun Temple 4
Confucius Temple 13
Dajing Pavilion & Ancient City Wall 3
Huxinting Teahouse 9
Peach Garden Mosque 12
Power Station of Art 20
St. Francis Xavier's Church 18
Shiliupu Marina (Ferries) 14
Yu Garden 10
Yuyuan Bazaar 7
HOTELS ■
Fraser Residences Shanghai 1
Hotel Indigo 15
Waterhouse at South Bund 17
RESTAURANTS & NIGHTLIFE ◆
Char 16
Shouning Lu 2
Sipailou Lu 11
SHOPPING ○
Bird, Flower, Fish, and Insect Market 5
Fuyou Antiques Market 6
South Bund Soft Material Spinning Market 19
Yuyuan Bazaar 8
Metro stop
OLD CITY
Huangpu River
Yan'an Dong Lu
Yan'an Freeway (elevated)
Renmin Lu
Renmin Lu Tunnel
Gucheng Park
Yuyuan Garden
Henan Nan Lu
Zhongshan Dong Er Lu
Zhonghua Lu
Fuxing Dong Lu
Zhongshan Nan Lu
Laoximen
Xiaoanmen
Lujiabang Rd
Lujiabang Lu
Nanpu Bridge
LINE 4
LINE 8
LINE 9
LINE 10
0 1/4 mi
0 250 m

Shanghai government surrounded the western boundary of Yu Garden with a cacophonous commercial plaza in the 1990s. As malls go, this is one of the most impressive, with its upturned eaves and lattice windows evoking palatial Ming architecture. Amid the many souvenir shops are Western brand stores, including (but not limited to) McDonalds and Starbucks. For nonshoppers, the main reason to visit is to get to Yu Garden itself, but it's well worth pausing at the Huxinting Teahouse en route. It was built in 1784 by cotton-cloth merchants as a brokerage hall and is thought to be the model for the wildly popular Blue Willow tableware of the same period. The photogenic, five-sided, two-story pavilion is reached via the traditional Bridge of Nine Turnings, so designed to deflect evil spirits who are said to travel only in straight lines. In the south of the complex is the Temple of the Town God (Chenghuang Miao). This shrine of Taoist worship dates from 1403 but was completely destroyed during the Cultural Revolution (1966–76), being resurrected amid the bazaar's restoration. The temple's main courtyard is usually jammed with worshipers praying before the statues of Huo Guang (a local military hero) in the front hall, and the town god in the back. The smell of incense is overpowered only by the smell of money wafting from the nearby shops.

Teahouse: 257 Yuyuan Lu (inside the Yuyuan Bazaar). ✆ **021/6373-6950.** Free admission. Daily 8:30am–9pm. Subway: Yu Garden. **Temple:** 249 Fangbang Zhong Lu (north side of street, near Anren Lu). www.shchm.org. ✆ **021/6386-5700.** Admission RMB10. Daily 8:30am–4:30pm. Subway: Yu Garden.

AROUND THE OLD CITY

Baiyun Taoist Temple (Baiyun Guan) ★ TEMPLE Originally built in 1863 and moved here in 2004, this temple is one of only two Taoist temples in China to possess the precious Ming Dynasty Taoist Scripture (*Dao Zang*). The two-story temple is housed in a courtyard building with red walls, lattice windows and doors, and a beautiful ornamented roof. Incense-bearing supplicants pray before a dizzying array of gilded Taoist deities, each entrusted with a specific cause. If your timing is right, you may be able to catch a Taoist service, which is highly ritualized, often resembling pageants complete with music, chanting, and processions of monks in colorful robes.

239 Dajing Lu (east of Renmin Lu, next to Ancient City Wall). ✆ **021/6328-7236.** Admission RMB5. Daily 8am–4:30pm. Subway: Dashijie or Yu Garden.

Confucius Temple (Wen Miao) ★ TEMPLE Built in 1855 on the site of an earlier temple, and restored in 1999 to celebrate the 2,550th birthday of Confucius, this temple honoring China's great sage offers quiet refuge from the crowded streets of the old Chinese city. As at all Chinese Confucian temples, there's a *lingxin men* (gate) leading to the main hall. Inside are statues of Confucius flanked by his two disciples, Mengzi (Mencius) and Yanhui, and his two favorite musical instruments, a drum and a set of bells. To the northeast, the Zunjing Ge, formerly the library, now houses a display of unusually shaped rocks. Back near the entrance, Kuixing Ge is a three-story, 20m-high (66-ft.) pagoda dedicated to the god of liberal arts, and the only original structure left on these tranquil grounds. A lively bookfair is held here on Sunday mornings.

215 Wenmiao Lu (one block east of Zhonghua Lu). ✆ **021/6377-1815.** Admission RMB10. Daily 9am–4:30pm. Subway: Laoximen.

Dajing Pavilion & Ancient City Wall (Dajing Ge) ★ HISTORIC SITE In 1553 during the Ming Dynasty, Shanghai built a city wall to defend itself against Japanese pirates. Following the course of today's Renmin Lu and Zhonghua Lu, the wall measured 8.1m (27 ft.) high and 4.8km (3 miles) around, and had 10 gates. All that remains today is 50m (164 ft.) of wall at this intersection of Dajing Lu and Renmin Lu (the rest was pulled down in 1912). The visible section of the remaining wall dates to the Qing Dynasty, as is evident by brick markings bearing the names of Qing emperors Xianfeng (1851–61) and Tongzhi (1862–74). The newly rebuilt Dajing Ge Pavilion atop the wall was one of the 30 towers along the structure. There's a small exhibit here on life in the old Chinese city.

269 Dajing Lu (jnc. with Renmin Lu). ✆ **021/6326-6171.** Admission RMB5. Daily 9am–4pm. Subway: Dashijie.

Peach Garden Mosque (Xiao Taoyuan Qingzhensi) ★ TEMPLE Shanghai's largest and most active mosque dates from 1917, though the current reconstruction is from 1925. Its main prayer hall can hold several hundred worshipers (restricted to Muslim males only). There is a separate worship hall for women. The courtyard contains a minaret (for calls to prayer). Shanghai's oldest mosque (1870) is in the north of the Old City at 378 Fuyou Lu.

52 Xiao Taoyuan Jie (nr. jnc. of Fuxing Dong Lu and Henan Nan Lu). ✆ **021/6377-5442.** No subway. Sunrise–sunset.

St. Francis Xavier's Church (Sheng Fangjige Shawulüe Tang) ★ CHURCH Located in the southern part of the old Chinese city, this was the first large cathedral in Shanghai, built in 1853 in the early Spanish baroque style. It's a fine-looking building with arched roofs, thick pillars, and lotus-designed bas-reliefs inside. Chinese couplets are inscribed on both inside and outside walls, and four of the church bells are said to be original. A huge new altarpiece was unveiled in 2010 featuring depictions of key events in Jesus' life. The 14 fresco paintings were made by Spanish artist Kiko Argüello and blend traditional and modernist styles. Services (in English and Chinese) attract large congregations, and nonlocals are made welcome with no vetting of your Catholic credentials.

185 Dongjiadu Lu (west of Zhongshan Nan Lu). ✆ **021/6378-7058.** Services Mon–Fri 7am (in Chinese), Sat 5pm (English), Sun 8am (Chinese), 10:30am and 12:30pm (both English).

BEYOND THE OLD CITY

Power Station of Art ★ MUSEUM Open since 2012, this art museum is located inside a stunningly renovated, glass-and-red-steel-encased power station overlooking the Huangpu River, a short distance south of the Old City. The permanent exhibition comprises a number of pavilions, many dedicated to educating Chinese about the diversity of world societies. Currently there's not enough on display to fill up the cavernous museum, so parts of the space feel cold and empty. However, the building is beautiful, admission is free, and views of the Huangpu River from the upper floors are stunning, so it's worth an hour or two if you have time to kill. The museum is about 20 minutes from the nearest subway station, so taxi is the best bet.

200 Huayuangang Lu (nr. Miaojiang Lu). www.powerstationofart.org/en. ✆ **021/3127-8535.** Free admission. Closed Mon; Tue–Sun 9am–5pm. Subway: Xizang Rd., 20-min. walk.

The French Concession

The French Concession comprises a large swath of central Shanghai. There are several interesting sights, listed below, but the real charm is in walking (or, better still, cycling) along its tree-lined boulevards, past gated villas, and through its *lilong* neighborhoods. The central thoroughfare in French times was Avenue Joffre, modern-day **Huaihai Zhong Lu.** The eastern section is one of Shanghai's premier shopping strips, lined with luxury malls. However, the western section provides a useful guide for those conducting independent explorations. A great way to get a feel for the area is to head east from Changshu Road subway station. Stay within two or three blocks, north or south, of Huaihai Zhong Lu, until you reach Fuxing Park.

Included in these listings are the sights of Xuhui district, which extends out from the French Concession's southwest boundary. **Xujiahui** is the site of the oldest Jesuit settlement in mainland China, established by a local Mandarin who was baptized by Italian missionary Matteo Ricci (see p. 34) in the early 17th century. French Jesuits were active here from the earliest colonial times, and it was absorbed into the French Concession as it gradually expanded through the 19th and early 20th centuries. In a typically Shanghainese reversal, it's now a relic-studded shopping district.

THE HEART OF THE FRENCH CONCESSION

Fuxing Park (Fuxing Gongyuan) ★ PARK Formerly a private estate, Fuxing Park was purchased by foreign residents and opened to the French public on July 14, 1909. It was popularly known as French Park, styled after your typical Parisian city park with wide, tree-lined walks and flowerbeds. Today, this is one of the city's most popular parks, home to a number of restaurants and nightclubs, as well as to pleasant fountains, a children's playground with a carousel and bumper cars, a rose garden to the east, 120 species of trees, and near the north entrance, a statue of Karl Marx and Friedrich Engels in front of which Chinese couples often practice ballroom dancing.

2 Gaolan Lu (entrances off Gaolan Lu, Yandang Lu, and Fuxing Zhong Lu). ✆ **021/6372-6083.** Free admission. Daily 6am–6pm. Subway: Xintiandi.

Hengshan Road Community Church ★ CHURCH Established in 1925 and also called the International Church (Guoji Libai Tang), this is the best known of Shanghai's Protestant churches among foreign residents and visitors, and is the largest in use. The ivy-covered English-style building and grounds are beautiful, fully in keeping with this upscale, colonial-style

The French Concession & Xuhui District

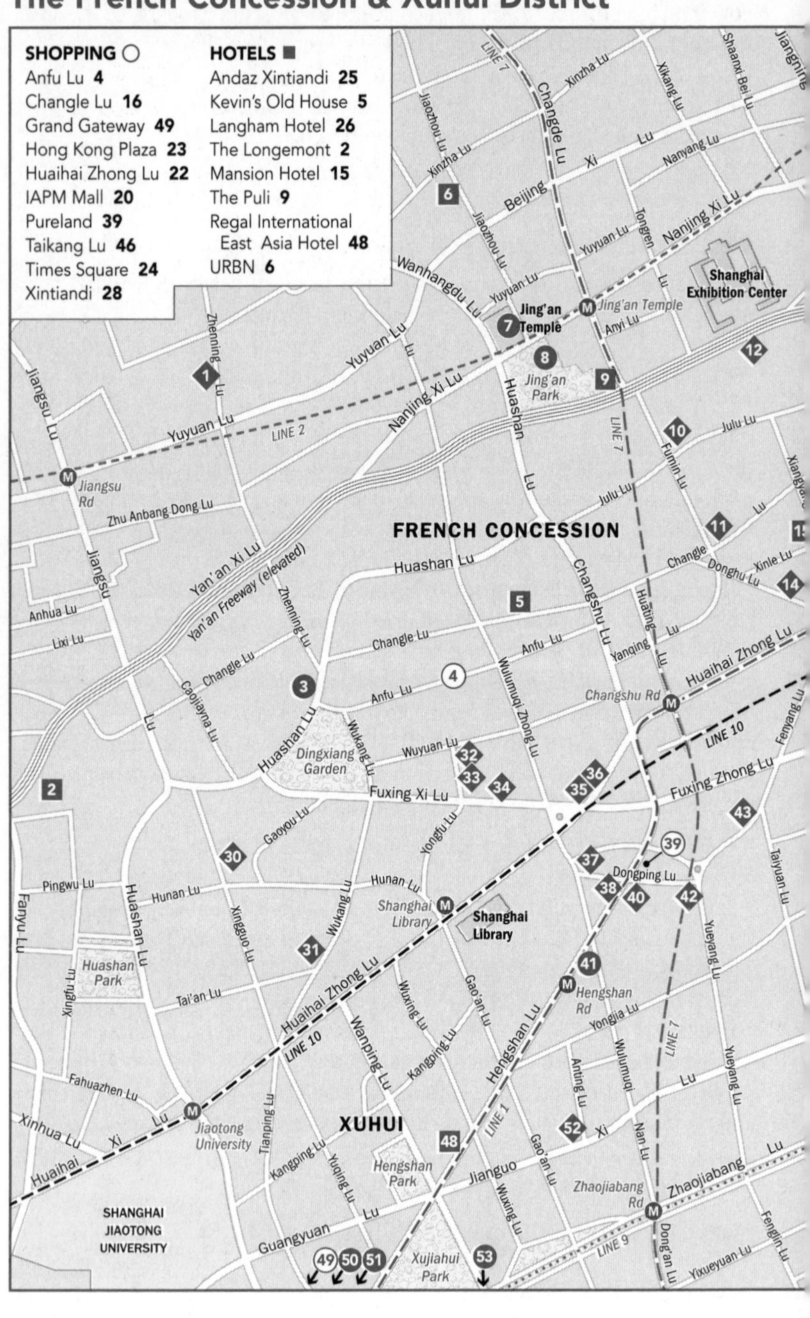

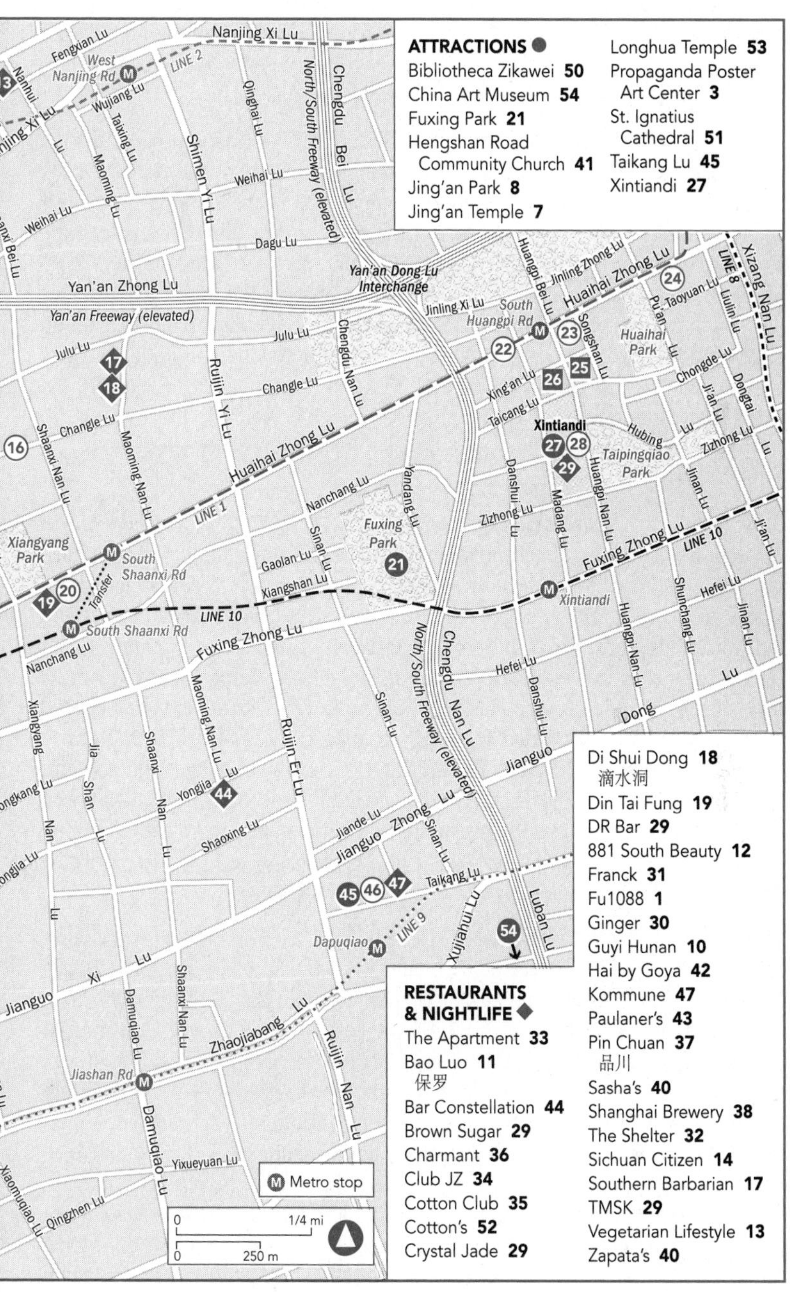

ATTRACTIONS
Bibliotheca Zikawei 50
China Art Museum 54
Fuxing Park 21
Hengshan Road Community Church 41
Jing'an Park 8
Jing'an Temple 7
Longhua Temple 53
Propaganda Poster Art Center 3
St. Ignatius Cathedral 51
Taikang Lu 45
Xintiandi 27
RESTAURANTS & NIGHTLIFE
The Apartment 33
Bao Luo 11 保罗
Bar Constellation 44
Brown Sugar 29
Charmant 36
Club JZ 34
Cotton Club 35
Cotton's 52
Crystal Jade 29
Di Shui Dong 18 滴水洞
Din Tai Fung 19
DR Bar 29
881 South Beauty 12
Franck 31
Fu1088 1
Ginger 30
Guyi Hunan 10
Hai by Goya 42
Kommune 47
Paulaner's 43
Pin Chuan 37 品川
Sasha's 40
Shanghai Brewery 38
The Shelter 32
Sichuan Citizen 14
Southern Barbarian 17
TMSK 29
Vegetarian Lifestyle 13
Zapata's 40
Metro stop
0 1/4 mi
0 250 m
Nanjing Xi Lu
Fengxian Lu
West Nanjing Rd
LINE 2
Wujiang Lu
Nanhui Lu
Qinghai Lu
Taixing Lu
Maoming Lu
Shimen Yi Lu
Weihai Lu
North/South Freeway (elevated)
Chengdu Bei Lu
Dagu Lu
Shaanxi Bei Lu
Yan'an Zhong Lu
Yan'an Freeway (elevated)
Yan'an Dong Lu Interchange
Jinling Xi Lu
Jinling Zhong Lu
Huangpi Bei Lu
South Huangpi Rd
Huaihai Zhong Lu
Taoyuan Lu
Pu'an Lu
Liulin Lu
LINE 8
Xizang Nan Lu
Huaihai Park
Songshan Lu
Chongde Lu
Julu Lu
Chengdu Nan Lu
Changle Lu
Ruijin Yi Lu
Xing'an Lu
Taicang Lu
Ji'an Lu
Dongtai Lu
Xintiandi
Hubing Lu
Taipingqiao Park
Zizhong Lu
Shaanxi Nan Lu
Maoming Nan Lu
LINE 1
Nanchang Lu
Yandang Lu
Danshui Lu
Madang Lu
Huangpi Nan Lu
Jinan Lu
Xiangyang Park
South Shaanxi Rd
Transfer
Gaolan Lu
Sinan Lu
Fuxing Park
Xiangshan Lu
Fuxing Zhong Lu
LINE 10
Hefei Lu
Shunchang Lu
Jiangguo Dong Lu
Xiangyang Nan Lu
Jia Shan Lu
Shaanxi Nan Lu
Ruijin Er Lu
Yongkang Lu
Yongjia Lu
Shaoxing Lu
Jiande Lu
Jianguo Zhong Lu
Taikang Lu
Xujiahui Lu
Luban Lu
Dapuqiao
LINE 9
Jianguo Xi Lu
Damuqiao Lu
Zhaojiabang Lu
Ruijin Nan Lu
Jiashan Rd
Taiyuan Lu
Yixueyuan Lu
Xiaomuqiao Lu
Qingzhen Lu

shopping district within the French Concession. Special services for foreign passport holders are currently held here on Sundays at 2 and 4pm. The surrounding lanes off Hengshan Lu are great for pedestrian exploration.

53 Hengshan Lu (west of Wulumuqi Nan Lu). ✆ **021/6437-6576.** Services Sun 7:30am & 10am (Chinese), 2pm & 4pm (English). Subway: Hengshan Rd.

Propaganda Poster Art Center ★ GALLERY If you have just the wall space for some revolutionary art, this place has just the right "leftist" poster for you. Tucked away in the basement of a French Concession apartment building is the personal collection of a private individual, Mr. Yang Peiming. It comprises more than 5,000 Communist propaganda posters from 1949 to 1979. The presentation is a bit haphazard, but the posters themselves are quite interesting. Chairman Mao figures prominently, of course, as do eager, ruddy-cheeked young workers and fervent Red Guards. Vintage posters are for sale as well (from around RMB700 and up), but not necessarily the most interesting ones. The center is worth a peek if you're in the area.

B/F, Building B, 868 Huashan Lu (nr. Wukang Lu). ✆ **021/6211-1845.** Admission RMB20. Daily 10am–5pm. No subway.

Taikang Lu (Tianzifang) ★★★ NEIGHBORHOOD What began as a collection of small galleries and studios fashioned from a single factory building is now a labyrinthine leisure district, geared as much to coffee and shopping as it is to art. "Tianzifang" is the collective name given to the three parallel lanes, running north to south between Taikang Lu and Jianguo Zhong Lu. It feels like an earthier version of Xintiandi, and despite being "found" by mass tourism, they exude an unmistakably bohemian vibe. Art-lovers should head to the place that kick-started the area's transformation—Lane 210, Taikang Lu. The **International Artists Factory** at no. 3 is now populated mainly with cool indie stores. **The Original Works Artists' Studio,** at no. 5, is a more dedicated artistic venue, with 15 studios and small galleries over three floors.

Lanes 210, 248, and 274, Taikang Lu (between Taikang Lu and Jianguo Zhong Lu). Free admission. Shops and cafes from 9am–late. Subway: Dapuqiao.

Xintiandi ★★★ NEIGHBORHOOD/MUSEUM Part old, part new, part tourist sight, part dining mecca, Xintiandi stylishly sums up modern China's many contradictions. In one besieged corner of this gorgeous slice of urban redevelopment is the **Site of the 1st Congress of the Chinese Communist Party** ★ (76 Xingye Lu; ✆ **021/5383-2171;** free admission; daily 9am–5pm). It serves up socialist slogans with a straight face to hordes of schoolchildren while, outside, Armani-wearing businessmen do million-dollar lunch deals. As the anchor of the urban renewal project, the museum has been expanded to include several new galleries. There is the expected hagiographic treatment, given the history of the Communist Party, but also more interesting displays of a Qing Dynasty bronze cannon, swords, and daggers used by rebels during the Taiping and Small Swords rebellions in 19th-century Shanghai. The *shikumen* (see "Shikumen Lilong" box) houses of this formerly working-class neighborhood have kept their original 1920s facades, though the bars and lifestyle

THE BEST french concession villas

The French Concession's colonial villas were home to magnates, revolutionaries, and gangsters in equal measure in the 1920s and '30s. They were islands of exclusivity where the elite could cavort, or conspire, away from prying eyes. Most remain sealed off today, but the crowbar of commerce has prized open one or two. Hoteliers have done much of the breaking and entering: The **Moller Mansion** (jnc. of Yan'an Zhong Lu and Shanxi Nan Lu) is a gigantic gingerbread mansion of brown-tiled steeples, gables, and spires. Built by Swedish shipping magnate Eric Moller in 1936, it mixes architectural styles with childlike abandon and is now a boutique hotel. The lobby of the **Mansion Hotel** (jnc. of Xinle Lu and Xiangyang Lu) is a veritable museum of period pieces. The building was one of many owned by gangster Du Yuesheng. "Big Ears Du" was a bank director, a member of the concession's governing council, and a man fond of sending coffins to those who suggested he was anything other than a pillar of the community. The **InterContinental Ruijin** (off Ruijin Er Lu, south of Fuxing Zhong Lu) is housed within the former walled estate of colonial media magnate Henry Morris, proprietor of the "North China Daily News." It is set around a number of converted 1920s villas looking out over a French Concession lawn where racehorses were once trained. If you're shopping on Huaihai Lu, be sure to check out the gorgeous **Twin Villas** colonial mansion at no. 796 (Huaihai Lu, nr. Ruijin Er Lu). It's a three-story neoclassical complex, set back from the street, where the wooden staircases and Art Deco stained glass epitomize aristocratic wealth and excess. Alfred Dunhill and Vacheron Constantin share the space and have masters of their respective disciplines working in open laboratories. Aside from commercial enterprises, there are a number of museums crafted from concession villas. The **Shanghai Arts and Crafts Museum** (jnc. of Fenyang Lu and Taiyuan Lu; ✆ **021/6431-4074;** RMB8; daily 9am–4pm; subway: Changshu Road) is worth visiting as much for its well-clipped lawn, teak-paneled library, marble fireplace, and creaking floorboards as it is for its displays of jade and lacquerware. Finally there are three "former residences" of China's political aristocracy. The **Former Residence of Sun Yat-sen** (7 Xiangshan Lu; ✆ **021/6437-2954;** RMB20; daily 9am–4:30pm; subway: Xintiandi) has interior living quarters preserved from the 1920s, when China's first president was resident. **Soong Ching-ling's Former Residence** (1843 Huaihai Zhong Lu; ✆ **021/6437-6268;** RMB20; daily 9am-4:30pm; subway: Jiaotong University) is a beautiful villa, owned by Sun Yat-sen's widow, with two black sedans in the driveway, one presented by Stalin in 1952. The emphasis at **Zhou Enlai's Former Residence** (73 Sinan Lu; ✆ **021/6473-0420;** free admission; 9am-4:30pm; subway: Xintiandi) is on austerity rather than extravagance. This was the Communist Party's Shanghai office prior to the 1949 revolution, and Zhou, Mao's much-loved right-hand man, kept a spartan room on the first floor.

boutiques that have taken up within the brand-new interiors are as modern as they come. Those more interested in seeing how life was really lived can visit the **Shikumen Open House Museum** (181 Taicang Lu; ✆ **021/3307-0337;** admission RMB20; daily 11am–11pm), which presents several rooms furnished with furniture from the 1920s and 1930s. Look for the hanging clothes, wicker baskets, ladies' makeup on the powder tables, and old photos in frames that give the house an authentic, lived-in feel. It's a short 30-minute stop, but worthwhile.

Xintiandi fills the two city blocks south of Taicang Lu, between Madang Lu and Huangpi Nan Lu. Free admission. 24-hr. Subway: South Huangpi Rd. or Xintiandi.

XUJIAHUI

Bibliotheca Zikawei ★LIBRARY The first of the two buildings of this 1847 library has a second-floor public reading room presided over by two boxwood friezes, one of St. Ignatius of Loyola on his deathbed, and the other of St. Francis. But the real treasure is in the adjacent two-story Bibliotheca built in 1897, with a first floor designed in a Chinese style with separate alcoves for the keeping of local records, and the second floor given over to the collection of Western books. Here, stacked neatly on wall-to-wall, floor-to-ceiling shelves are some 560,000 musty, fragile volumes in about 20 languages including Latin, English, French, German, Chinese, and Russian, and covering everything from literature and philosophy to politics, history, and religion. The oldest book, a Latin tome by John Duns Scotus, dates to 1515. Remarkably, the library, which had become a part of the Shanghai City Library in 1956, did not lose a single volume during the Cultural Revolution (1966–76), as librarians defended the collection zealously from Red Guards. The Bibliotheca is only open for touring on Saturday afternoons, but the reading room is open to the public during regular business hours.

80 Caoxi Bei Lu. ✆ **021/6487-4095.** Free 15-min. library tours Sat 2–4pm. Reading room: Mon-Sat 9:30am-7pm. Subway: Xujiahui.

Longhua Temple (Longhua Si) ★ TEMPLE Shanghai's largest and most active temple is one of its most fascinating, featuring the city's premier pagoda. Local lore has it that the Longhua Pagoda (Longhua Ta) was originally built around A.D. 247 by Sun Quan, the king of the Wu Kingdom during the Three Kingdoms period, but today's seven-story, eight-sided, wood-and-brick pagoda, like the temple, dates to the Song Dynasty (A.D. 960–1279). For a long time the tallest structure in Shanghai, today it can only be admired from a distance. The extensive temple grounds are often crowded with incense-bearing supplicants. There are four main halls (only a century old), the most impressive being the "Grand Hall" (Daxiong Bao Dian), where a gilded statue of Sakyamuni sits under a beautifully carved dome. Behind the third and fourth halls is a basic, but popular, vegetarian restaurant (daily 11am–2pm). Longhua is also famous for its midnight bell-ringing every New Year's Eve. The Bell Tower's 3,000kg (3.3-ton) bronze bell, cast in 1894, is struck 108 times to dispel all the worries said to be afflicting mankind. For a small fee, you, too, can strike the bell, but three times only.

2853 Longhua Lu. ✆ **021/6456-6085.** Admission RMB10. Daily 7am–5pm. Subway: Longcao Rd.

St. Ignatius Cathedral (Xujiahui Tianzhutang) ★CHURCH Shanghai's great colonial-era cathedral was opened by the Jesuits who had a church

shikumen LILONG

Li means "neighborhood," and *long* means "alley." Combined, the word normally refers to one of Shanghai's many gated neighborhoods, comprising a matrix of adjoining lanes, each lined with identically designed homes. Chinese refugees poured into Shanghai in waves throughout the early colonial era, and these *lilong* (also known as "*longtang*") catered to the new arrivals, offering cheap(ish) housing in identical two-to-three-story buildings. There are various styles, but the most interesting are the *Shikumen Lilong*. A home-grown design unique to Shanghai, *shikumen* translates as "stone frame door," the name deriving from the gray stone that surrounds the black wooden front doors. If the facades look more European, the interiors were very Chinese, with the sparse amenities offset by a private courtyard—a design feature used in nearly all traditional Chinese architecture—where residents could cook and wash. There are miles of cramped *lilong* in the southern part of the Old City, but it's easy to get lost. Some of the tidiest and most attractive *shikumen lilong* are in Jing'an District. Ride the subway to West Nanjing Lu in Jing'an, and walk south along **Taixing Lu** until you reach Weihai Lu. The alleys that run east and west off this rather grand *lilong* exhibit beautiful *shikumen* features. There's another impressive alley a little way west along Nanjing Xi Lu. Enter the Jing'an Bieshu (1023 Nanjing Xi Lu) from a gate just west of Maoming Nan Lu and walk south past 10 rows of well-kept *lilong*. For a more polished and commercial take on *shikumen* architecture, visit **Xintiandi** (p. 216). Alternatively, try one of the 1-, 2-, or 4-hour tours offered by **Shanghai Insiders** (www.shanghaiinsiders.com), a company that specializes in taking visitors to some of Shanghai's most atmospheric back lanes, using a distinctly colonial form of transportation—motorbike and sidecar.

here as early as 1608 (today's structure dates to 1910). As a missionary center, the cathedral grounds once included a library, an orphanage, a college, a publishing house, and its own weather station. Today, only the church, part of the school, and the reopened Bibliotheca Zikawei (see above) remain. This largest of Shanghai's cathedrals, with space for more than 2,500 inside, sports a gargoyled roof and twin red-brick spires that were destroyed in the Cultural Revolution (1966–76) and rebuilt in 1980. Its vast interior of altars, stone columns, Gothic ceilings, stained-glass windows, and paintings of the Last Supper and Stations of the Cross is yet another chapter in Shanghai's living history of European architecture.

158 Puxi Lu (west side of Caoxi Bei Lu). ✆ **021/6438-2595.** Services Mon–Sat 6:15am and 7am, w/an additional 6pm Mass on Sat; Sun 6am, 7:30am, and 10am; open to visitors Sat–Sun 1–4pm. Subway: Xujiahui.

Jing'an District

Jade Buddha Temple (Yufo Si) ★ TEMPLE Though an active Buddhist monastery today, the real emphasis at Shanghai's most popular temple is squarely on tourism. What the busloads come for are the two gorgeous white jade Buddhas, each carved from an individual slab of Burmese jade and brought to Shanghai in 1881 by the monk Huigeng, who was on his way back from Burma to his hometown on nearby Putuo Island. The first of the two treasures is a lustrous, beatific, seated Buddha weighing 205kg (452 lb.), measuring 1.9m (6¼ ft.) and adorned with jewels and stones. The other Buddha is reclined, his peaceful expression signaling his impending entry into nirvana. Opposite is a larger, coarser replica donated by the Singapore Buddhist Friendship Association in 1988.

170 Anyuan Lu (west of Jiangning Lu). ✆ **021/6266-3668.** Admission RMB20. Daily 8am–4:30pm. Subway: Changshou Rd.

Jing'an Park (Jing'an Gongyuan) ★ PARK This pleasant little park was completely remodeled in 1999 when the new Jing An subway station was created. Its north side consists of a sunken cement courtyard flanked by a few shops, cafes, and the subway entrance; the south side, dominated by a pond that is an artful recreation of a classic southern Chinese garden, is a pretty spot to stroll, people-watch, or enjoy an evening drink at the bar in the adjacent Indonesian restaurant (Bali Laguna). Mornings are a perfect time to watch (or join) tai chi classes, while Sunday morning (8:30–11am) brings out the polyglots (mostly Chinese who want to practice their English) to the multilanguage corner (*wai yu jiao*) at the eastern end of the park.

189 Huashan Lu (nr. Yan'an Zhong Lu). ✆ **021/6248-3238.** Free admission. Daily dawn–late. Subway: Jing'an Temple.

Jing'an Temple (Jing'an Si) ★ TEMPLE Always lively and crowded, this garishly decorated temple has the longest history of any shrine in Shanghai (about 17 centuries, though the shopping annex is considerably more recent, as is the 63m-tall/207-ft. gold pagoda at the back, completed in 2010). The temple's chief antiquities are a Ming-dynasty copper bell (the Hongwu Bell) that weighs in at 3,175kg (3½ tons), and stone Buddhas from the Northern and Southern States period (A.D. 420–589). Although its name means "Temple of Tranquility," it is hardly the place for quiet meditation these days, nor was it in the past. Before 1949, this was Shanghai's richest Buddhist monastery, presided over by the Abbott of Bubbling Well Road (Nanjing Xi Lu, as it was known in colonial times because of a well that was located in front of the temple), an imposing figure who kept seven mistresses and a White Russian bodyguard. Today's southern-style main halls all have renovations using Burmese teakwood (*youmu*).

1686 Nanjing Xi Lu (nr. Changde Lu). ✆ **021/6256-6366.** Admission RMB50. Daily 7:30am–5pm. Subway: Jing'an Temple.

M50 ★ GALLERY Shanghai's answer to Beijing's trendy 798 art district, M50 (50 Moganshan Lu) is a former factory district on the banks of Suzhou Creek that has been turned into a showcase for the best of modern Chinese art. The district is wonderfully raw and grimy, all exposed brickwork, wheezing air-conditioning units, wrought-iron window frames, and unswept cobwebs. **ShanghART** (Buildings 16 and 18; www.shanghartgallery.com; ✆ **021/6359-3923**) is one of the few spaces big enough to host major installations, while

M97 (97 Moganshan Lu; www.m97gallery.com; ✆ **021/6266-1597**) is a great fine-art photography gallery a few doors down. As in 798, there has been creeping expansion of the original space, and a nearby alleyway at **M20** (20 Moganshan Lu) also has a cluster of raw art spaces. The setting is fairly bleak, so it's not one for a cold winter's day, but artsy types will love it, and it's less crassly commercial than Beijing's 798.

50 Moganshan Lu. Tue–Sun 10:30am–6pm. Subway: Shanghai Railway Station, plus short cab ride.

Natural History Museum ★★ MUSEUM Appearing as a natural outgrowth of the pleasant-but-otherwise-unremarkable Jing'an Sculpture Park, Shanghai's relocated Natural History Museum is a marvel of environmental engineering. The curling shape of the building was inspired by the nautilus shell, "one of the purest geometric forms found in nature," according to the architects, and there's more "biomimicry" in its core structures, the central "cell" column, the green "living" wall, and the "stone" wall suggesting shifting tectonic plates. Six floors have artifacts from seven continents, including deep-sea monsters, Ming-dynasty mummies, and an enormous dinosaur skeleton. There's also an IMAX cinema. As so often in China, the standards of the English-language captions reduce the engagement among older kids, but youngsters will enjoy the sheer spectacle.

Jing'an Park, 128 Shimen Er Lu. www.snhm.org.cn. ✆ **021/6862-2000.** RMB30 for adults. Tue–Sun 9am–5pm. Subway: West Nanjing Rd.

Hongkou & Zhabei

1933 ★★ LANDMARK Opened in 2008 as a Hongkou alternative to Xintiandi, 1933 has never quite taken off as the imagined "fashion and lifestyle hub" as intended, but the building is still well worth seeing if you are in the neighborhood. Inside the International Settlement's grimly efficient ex-slaughterhouse is a dizzying network of concrete ramps and bridges used to herd 300 cows, 500 sheep, and 300 pigs toward their doom daily. The shops and restaurants that have sprung up in the gaps are likely to be unerringly quiet, but anyone with the remotest interest in Art Deco (see p. 207) can get their kicks from the building alone.

10 Shajing Lu (nr. Haining Lu). www.1933shanghai.com. ✆ **021/6514-7439.** Daily 10am–9pm. Subway: Hailun Rd.

Duolun Lu Culture Street ★ NEIGHBORHOOD A 20-minute walk south from the Lu Xun Park and Memorial Hall (see below) is Duolun Lu, Shanghai's "culture street." A number of leftist artists and writers— Lu Xun, Mao Dun, and Guo Moruo, among others—lived here during the 1930s under Japanese occupation, making this one of Shanghai's foremost cultural and literary hubs. The stately brick homes and shops on this 1km (½-mile) stretch of the street have been preserved and refurbished, and cars are now banned, making it a fine pedestrian mall of bookshops, teahouses, antiques shops, and historic homes. As you enter from Sichuan Bei Lu, the Duolun **Museum of**

Modern Art (no. 27; www.duolunmoma.org; ✆ **021/6587-2530;** Tues–Sun 10am–6pm; admission RMB10) on your left showcases the works of international modern artists. A few doors down at no. 59, the Great Virtue Christian Church (Hong De Tang) was built in 1928 with upturned Chinese eaves. The street curves to the right, passing the stately bell tower Xishi Zhong Lou (no. 119), the wonderful Old Film Cafe (no. 123), where you can sip coffee while watching old Chinese movies from the 1920s and 1930s, and antiques and curio shops selling everything from art to Mao memorabilia. At Lane 201, no. 2 is the **League of Leftist Writers Museum** (9:30am–4pm; admission RMB5). The last architectural treasure on the curving lane is the Kong Residence, a splendid 1924 creation sadly not open for public viewing. The street is not really worth a special trip out here, but if you're interested in Shanghai's colonial architecture, or radical history, then Duolun Lu is a must.

Duolun Lu (jnc. with Sichuan Bei Lu, three blocks north of Dong Baoxing Lu Light Rail Station). Free admission. Sunrise–late. Subway: Dongbaoxing Rd.

Lu Xun Park and Memorial Hall (Lu Xun Gongyuan/Lu Xun Jinianguan) ★ PARK/HISTORIC SITE What was originally Hongkou Park (1905), once a foreigners' park opened to the Chinese only in 1928, has been renamed for China's best-known 20th-century writer, Lu Xun (1881–1936), who lived in this neighborhood from 1927 until his death. Known as the "father of modern Chinese literature," Lu Xun was a prolific writer who translated science-fiction novels into Chinese just as easily as he penned scathing critiques of Confucianism and the alternately submissive and arrogant Chinese character. Extolled as a political revolutionary (Mao Zedong penned an inscription on Lu Xun's tomb, which lies at the north end of the park), Lu Xun was himself never a member of the Communist Party. At the eastern end of the park is a memorial hall devoted to his life. The main exhibit room on the second floor displays his many books and old photographs, as well as his hat, goatskin gown, and death mask. Signs are in English. A 10-minute walk east of the park, **Lu Xun's Former Residence** (Building 9, Lane 132, Shanyin Lu, nr. Sichuan Bei Lu; RMB8; daily 9am–4pm) is a three-story brick house where he lived from 1933 to his death, and is still largely decorated as it was then.

146 Dong Jiangwan Lu (Memorial Hall inside park on east side). ✆ **021/6540-2288.** Admission free. Daily 6am–6pm. Memorial hall and residence daily 9am–4pm. Subway: Hongkou Football Stadium.

Shanghai Jewish Refugees Museum ★ MUSEUM One of the most fascinating of Shanghai's many little-known histories is its role as a safe haven for European Jews. Between 1933 and 1941, around 30,000 headed to Shanghai to flee the Nazi menace, though most were re-ghettoized under Japanese occupation in 1941. This onetime synagogue lies in the heart of the former ghetto. There's some interesting documentary video in the main building, while the yard behind contains two outhouses exhibiting salvaged memorabilia, and a new 37m-long (121-ft.) copper wall whose surface is etched with the names of all the Jewish people known to have taken shelter in Shanghai.

The lanes of the former ghetto, surrounding the museum, are also well worth wandering.

62 Changyang Lu (nr. Zhoushan Lu). ✆ **021/6512-6669.** Admission RMB50. Daily 9am–5pm. Subway: Tilanqiao.

Pudong

Century Park (Shiji Gongyuan) ★ PARK Built to herald the new millennium, this sprawling 140-hectare (346-acre) park lies at the southern terminus of Shiji Da Dao, which runs from the Oriental Pearl TV Tower. Designed by a British firm, the park is divided into seven scenic areas and includes a minigolf course, a man-made cobblestone beach, a bird-protection area, and an international garden area. The center of the park contains a lake where fishing poles and paddleboats can be rented. There's plenty here to distract the kids, but it's an even better place to watch local families enjoy themselves.

1001 Jinxiu Lu. ✆ **021/3876-0588.** Admission RMB10. Daily 7am–6pm (to 5pm Nov 16–Mar 15). Subway: Century Park.

China Art Museum ★★ MUSEUM Those who missed the opportunity to attend the 2010 Shanghai World Expo will appreciate the reincarnation of the spectacular China Pavilion as an art museum. Like most Chinese fine-art museums, it is divided into nearly a dozen sections that include bronzes, jade, sculptures, paintings, and the furniture of various dynasties. It features contemporary art from China as well as from international exhibitions in one of 27 halls encompassing more than 650,000 square feet. One of the most popular exhibits is in Hall 5—an electronic recreation of one of China's most famous historic murals, the "Riverside Scene at Qingming Festival." Admission to this

HUANGPU river cruises

The Huangpu River (Huangpu Jiang) is the city's shipping artery to the mouth of the Yangzi River, which the Huangpu joins 29km (18 miles) north of downtown Shanghai. It has also become a demarcation line between two Shanghais, east and west, past and future. Cruises offer fabulous views of both the Bund and the glittering towers of Pudong and are particularly scenic around dusk. A number of companies run tourist ships that depart from the **Shiliupu Marina (Shiliupu Matou),** at 531 Zhongshan Dong Er Lu, accessible via a 20-minute walk south from the Bund. Tickets can be purchased through your hotel desk or at the marina. During the day, the choice is either a long 3-hour cruise to the mouth of the Yangzi (Wusong Kou) and back (RMB150 approx.), or an hour-long cruise from the Bund to the Yangpu Bridge (RMB100 approx.). Nighttime cruises are more scenic but shorter (RMB100; 45-min. approx.), often doing no more than running up and down the length of the Bund. There's little you see from the boat that you can't see from land, but the ride is fun nonetheless. Specific prices vary depending on the company, the boat, and the season, so check ahead. Cruises are particularly popular with Chinese tour groups, and English-language commentary is rarely offered.

THE SHANGHAI tower

After a 7-year construction project, cranes were being dismantled at the latest tallest-building-in-China as this book was going to press, and it should be open to the public by the time you read this. With China facing an economic slowdown and falling real-estate prices, it looks like the 632m-tall (2,073-ft.) hulk was completed in the nick of time. The gracefully twisting, three-sided building has 121 floors and employs a transparent double-glass facade. The building's core consists of nine cylindrical stacks encased within a giant glass tube. Between this and the angular outer facade are nine "public" atriums, each due to be fitted out with gardens, cafes, and retail space, and providing stunning 360-degree city views. The Shanghai Tower has been designed to "harmonize" with its near neighbors, the Jinmao and the SWFC (see p. 226), and as with those buildings, a hotel will occupy the upper reaches, this one operated by Shanghai's own Jinjiang Group. A museum is also slated. This said, the building's owners, a consortium of Chinese companies, were reported to be using an international leasing agent to find tenants, suggesting that it may still be some time before the Shanghai Tower is fully operational. When that day comes, it may have lost its tallest-in-China crown to the Ping An Finance Center in Shenzhen (financial shocks notwithstanding).

hall is RMB20, though otherwise the museum is free. You need not be an art-lover to enjoy a visit. The iconic building, an inverted red pyramid structure, graced dozens of magazine covers back in 2010 and alone makes the trip worthwhile. You cannot enter without reserving on the website or at various ticket booths around the city 2 days in advance. See the website for more details.

Former World Expo Site, 161 Shangnan Lu (nr. Guozhan Lu). http://china.artmuseumonline.org. ✆ **021/6327-2425.** Free admission. Tue–Sun 9am–5pm (closed Monday). Subway: China Art Museum.

Jinmao Tower ★★★ LANDMARK Rising to 421m (1,381 ft.), the Jinmao was by far the tallest building in China when it was built in 1998 as a Sino-American joint venture. These days, it's struggling to hold onto its top-10 spot, but it remains the nation's most beautiful skyscraper by far. Blending traditional Chinese and modern Western tower designs, the building, which boasts 88 floors (eight being an auspicious Chinese number), consists of 13 distinct tapering segments, with high-tech steel bands binding the glass like an exoskeleton. The result is a building that appears to be bending outward, like windswept bamboo, at the same time as being sucked to a fine point, like a calligraphy quill. Offices occupy the first 50 floors, the Grand Hyatt hotel the 51st to the 87th floors, while a public observation deck on the 88th floor ("the Skywalk") offers views that beat those of the nearby Oriental Pearl TV Tower (its admission charge is also lower). High-speed elevators (9m/30 ft. per sec.) whisk visitors from Level B1 to the top in less than 45 seconds. The views are spellbinding, and you can also look down at the 152m-high (499-ft.) atrium of the Grand Hyatt. A less touristy alternative is to see the Grand Hyatt's impressive atrium from below before heading up to the 87th floor Cloud Nine bar. There's a steep minimum charge (RMB120), but you at least get to enjoy the view in exclusive conditions, accompanied by tapas and cocktails.

2 Shiji Da Dao. ✆ **021/5047-5101.** Admission RMB88. Observation Deck daily 8:30am–10:30pm (last ticket sold 10pm). Subway: Lujiazui.

Oriental Pearl TV Tower ★ LANDMARK The earliest symbol of the new China, this hideous gray tower with three tapering levels of pink spheres (meant to resemble pearls) still holds a special place in many a local heart and is still one of the first stops in town for Chinese visitors. Built in 1994 at a height of 468m (1,535 ft.), it is hailed as the tallest TV tower in Asia and the third-tallest in the world. It's hard to recommend for views, given there are less touristy and loftier platforms available at Lujiazui's adjacent three skyscrapers. However, if you don't mind crowds, the observation deck in the middle sphere (263m/863 ft. elevation), reached by high-speed elevators staffed by statistics-reciting attendants, is at a perfect height to take in Shanghai old and new, neither too high nor too low. Far more worthwhile is the excellent Shanghai Municipal History Museum, located in the basement.

1 Shiji Da Dao. ✆ **021/5879-1888.** Admission RMB100–RMB150, depending on sections visited. Daily 8am–9:30pm. Subway: Lujiazui.

Riverside Promenade (Binjiang Da Dao) ★ NEIGHBORHOOD Pudong's answer to the Bund, this green strip along the east bank of the Huangpu River offers a fine view of the Bund at a distance. After dark, when the Bund's buildings are lit up and beacon lights sweep the river lanes, the view is one of the best in Shanghai. The Riverside Promenade also affords marvelous views of Pudong's skyscrapers and the Shanghai International Conference Center and its twin globes. Extending from Dongchang Lu and the river ferry terminal in the south to Taidong Lu in the north, the 2.5km-long (1½-mile) promenade consists of manicured lawns, flower beds, and a broad walkway dotted with kiosks. Starbucks and Häagen-Dazs have staked out the best spots in the middle section around the Pudong Shangri-La hotel, so you can now have your view and your latte and ice cream too.

East shoreline Huangpu River (entrances on either side of Lujiazui Lu). Free admission. Daily 6:30am–11pm (midnight in summer). Subway: Lujiazui.

Shanghai Municipal History Museum (Shanghai Shi Lishi Chenlieguan) ★★★ From the replica rickshaw by the entrance to the scale models of famous French Concession buildings by the exit, this superb museum paints Shanghai history in vivid tones. In contrast to the slightly academic feel of the Shanghai Museum, the story unfolds through superbly rendered dioramas and waxworks, working in tandem with some surprisingly tasteful sound effects and textured surfaces. The galleries are divided into three sections, post-revolution, colonial, and precolonial, the latter contesting the often peddled myth that foreigners were responsible for creating this city. What makes the museum all the more remarkable is the fact that it's lodged in the basement of the city's most awful tourist trap, the Oriental Pearl TV Tower. Ignore the line for the elevators and instead head straight for the basement. Other intriguing bits include boulders marking the concessions' boundaries and visiting chits used in brothels. The museum takes about an hour to tour. Tickets are purchased at the Oriental Pearl TV Tower gate. Audio headsets (RMB30) are not crucial, as displays are well annotated in English and Chinese.

B/F, Oriental Pearl TV Tower, 1 Shiji Da Dao. www.historymuseum.sh.cn. ✆ **021/5879-1888.** Admission RMB35. Daily 9am–11pm. Subway: Lujiazui.

Shanghai World Financial Center (Shanghai Huanqiu Jinrong Zhongxin) ★ LANDMARK The tapering, 101-story, 492m-high (1,614-ft.) SWFC enjoyed a 7-year spell as China's tallest building before the big beast beside it came along to make it look more like a dinky little bottle-opener (see "The Shanghai Tower" box). There is a stunning all-glass 100th-floor observatory at a height of 474m (1,555 ft.). The rarefied air and views from up top are unparalleled, but can be stomach-churning for those prone to acrophobia. The 94th-floor exhibition space, and the 97th-floor skybridge are nothing special, but the Park Hyatt Hotel, on the 79th to 93rd floors, is certainly good for a meal or drink after your visit, as are the restaurants in the basement.

100 Shiji Da Dao. www.swfc-observatory.com. ✆ **021/5878-0101.** 94th fl. only RMB100; 94th–97th fl. RMB110; 94th–100th fl. RMB150. Daily 8am–11pm (10pm last entry). Subway: Lujiazui.

WHERE TO STAY

Shanghai's hotel scene reflects its often stark wealth divide. Since the turn of the millennium, a *lot* of money has poured into the top-end of the hospitality market. With practically every international hotel chain and brand-name now in town, the visitor is spoiled for choice when it comes to high-end accommodations. There are some areas where you can barely move for the next "luxury" five-star trying to tempt big-spending locals with lavishly priced cocktails, spa treatments, or staycations. At the other end of the spectrum, there are a huge number of hostels, budget motels, and guesthouses, though conditions can be quite dismal. In between, things look a little thin, with the market dominated by the two biggest Chinese hotel-management groups, Jinjiang and Hengshan. Between them they run nearly all of the city's heritage hotels. These storied buildings once catered to Shanghainese high society, and they retain their handsome colonial frontages. However, interiors are often shabby, service levels can be atrocious, and management is geared almost exclusively toward the hordes of domestic tour groups that charge through each day.

In the last few years, there have been signs that both overseas and domestic brands are recognizing the long-suffering middle-class traveler unwilling to blow entire pension pots for the privilege of a few downtown creature comforts. Apartment hotels, glam midmarkets, and even bed-and-breakfasts have started appearing, a welcome alternative to the cookie-cutter chain hotels. However, the wait goes on for hotels to emerge from Shanghai's charming old *shikumen* neighborhoods in the way that has happened in Beijing's *hutong*.

Shanghai has some definite advantages when it comes to hotels. One is the levels of service, which are generally higher here than anywhere in China. English is certainly not *widely* spoken, but you've got a better chance of being understood by receptionists, porters, and bellboys here than in Beijing or Xi'an.

Also handy for travelers is the geography. Shanghai is the most compact of the three major cities in this book. Where Beijing and Xian both have only two or three workable hotel hubs, Shanghai's hotels are liberally spaced, and there's no need to plant yourself in Huangpu, the most "downtown" area, given the ease of moving between neighborhoods. However, if you are staying in Lujiazui, east of the river, you'll need a taxi to cross after 11pm when the subway stops running. There are no bridges to this area—pedestrian or road—and ferries also stop early. This is a minor inconvenience rather than a deal-breaker, as taxis are numerous and cheap.

Prices are generally high in Shanghai, but the fierce competition from the glut of hotels has led to significant discounts during parts of the year. However, these discounts disappear almost entirely during big conventions, meetings, and special citywide events, such as the annual Formula One Grand Prix race in the spring. Because Shanghai is more of a financial, commercial, and industrial city than a tourism-driven one, hoteliers like to claim that they have no low season. In reality, you can get the biggest discounts between December and February, while rates are highest from May through October. With so many international chains and new luxury hotels, Shanghai offers excellent accommodations but few bargains. The room rates listed are rack rates, but you'll be able to negotiate much better rates in person. All rooms have TVs with foreign channels unless otherwise noted, and free Wi-Fi is very much the norm.

In general, payment for your room is made up front. If asked how long you're staying, always say one day (or you'll be asked to pay for however many days you plan on staying). You can then pay as you go. Keep all receipts, from proof of your room payment to any room-key deposit you might have to make. The top hotels usually levy a service charge of 10% to 15%, though this may be waived or included in the final negotiated price at smaller hotels. Children under age 12 usually stay free in their parent's room.

Huangpu & the Old City

Fairmont Peace Hotel ★ Known in its heyday as the Cathay Hotel, the Fairmont Peace Hotel completed a highly awaited renovation in 2010, with rooms updated, and lobby and common areas restored to glittering condition. The hotel's vintage Art Deco style is a welcome change from the modern, sleek luxury hotel that has dominated the Shanghai scene in recent years. When you walk the hallways of the Peace Hotel, you can almost feel the weight of China's history since this building was erected back in 1929. It's long been a draw for high-profile foreigners, including Charlie Chaplin and Noël Coward (in 1930, the latter wrote "Private Lives" in Room 314). Service is professional and friendly, but there are still a few kinks to be worked out as the Peace Hotel's iconic name merges with the Fairmont Hotel brand. Even if you don't stay here, it's well worth your time to saunter into the masterful Art Deco lobby, stare at the majestic artwork—don't forget to look up at the glass rotunda—and head over for a drink at the world-famous Jazz Bar, which has live music every night and is usually packed full of tourists. The outdoor balcony beside the top-floor Cathay Room restaurant is fantastic for pictures down the length of the Bund and across the water to Lujiazui. Guests can saunter up for free, though nonguests can get access by paying a cover.

20 Nanjing Dong Lu, near the Bund. www.fairmont.com/peacehotel. ✆ **021/6321-6888.** 270 units. RMB2,900 standard; 3,500 executive level. Subway: East Nanjing Rd. **Amenities:** 3 restaurants; deli; lounge, bar; health club; indoor pool; spa; free Wi-Fi.

Hotel Indigo ★★ This swanky high-rise hotel has a location right beside the Shiliupu tourist ferry terminal on the waterside walkway, a 15-minute walk from both the Bund and Yu Gardens. Rooms are well worth boutique status, festooned with one-of-a-kind design pieces and decorated whimsically in splashes of vivid color. Views across the river, over to the twinkling towers of Lujiazui, are outstanding, and it's worth paying the premium to upgrade. Upstairs the Char Grill boasts fancy cuts of imported meat. Prices are hefty for food that is good but not outstanding, so you might find the best value in grabbing a drink at the Char bar and enjoying the views up the length of the Bund from the outdoor patio. Though the river views are fantastic, you are about as far as it's possible to get in Shanghai from a subway station (the nearest is a 20-minute walk away), making it a little inconvenient for hopping around town.

585 Zhongshan Dong Er Lu. www.ihg.com/hotelindigo/hotels/us/en/shanghai/shgnb/hoteldetail. ✆ **021/3302-9999.** RMB1,700 standard rooms. Subway: Yu Garden. **Amenities:** Restaurant; bar; swimming pool; fitness center; library; free Wi-Fi.

The Peninsula Hotel ★★★ The luxurious Peninsula Hotel sets a new standard for luxury hotels in Shanghai. Located at the top of the city's most famous street next to the former British Consulate, the 14-story Peninsula is the only property allowed to be built on the Bund in the last 60 years. Tops at the hotel are the guest rooms—large, elegant, and fully appointed with walk-in closets, a nail dryer, a Nespresso coffee machine, a 46-inch plasma TV, a multimedia reader, free Wi-Fi, and a VoIP system that allows guests to call home anywhere in the world for free. What's especially impressive is that the hotel gets the smallest details right to ensure maximum guest comfort: Afraid you might wake up in the dark confused as to where you are? Wave your hand, and the bedside lighting panel will slowly illuminate. Deluxe rooms with Bund and river views are well worth splurging on. Fully expect the refined and attentive service for which the Peninsula is well known. Those not staying here can still drop in for the famous high tea (daily 2–6pm), with a traditional 1930s tea dance held the first Saturday of every month.

32 Zhongshan Dongyi Lu, near Beijing Dong Lu. www.peninsula.com. ✆ **021/2327-2888.** RMB3,200 standard room. Subway: East Nanjing Rd. **Amenities:** 3 restaurants; basement bar; children's programs; health club; indoor pool; spa; free Wi-Fi.

The Waterhouse at South Bund ★ An achingly cool offering by a Singaporean boutique hotelier, The Waterhouse is a picture of industrial chic, from the exposed brickwork and sleek furniture in the lobby to the spacious rooms, where glassy textures jar against factory-gray walls. Those who prefer traditional digs will probably feel like they're staying in a bomb shelter, but there's something undeniably hip about the decor. The riverside location means there are some stunning river views, while the upstairs terrace is a top spot for gazing upon the towers of Lujiazui across the water. One of the city's best restaurants, Table No. 1, is on-site. No two rooms are alike. Some have balconies; some have showers rather than baths, so the advice is to book by phone. Nonalcoholic drinks are free from the minibar.

1–3 Maojiayuan Lu, near Zhongshan Nan Lu. www.waterhouseshanghai.com. ✆ **021/6080-2988.** RMB1,500 standard. Subway: Xiaonanmen, 15-min. walk. **Amenities:** Restaurant; bar; health club; free Wi-Fi.

Waldorf Astoria ★★ Along with the Peace Hotel, the Waldorf Astoria is one of the few luxury properties in Shanghai with history in the building. The hotel's Long Bar has its origins back in 1911, when the first British Consul General in Shanghai established an exclusive gentleman's club for the city's movers and shakers. The bar's leather and dark-wood paneled interiors hark back to an earlier era, and it boasts one of the finer selections of scotch available in Shanghai; the best seat in the house is still at the end of the bar closest to the windows with the Bund view. The Waldorf Astoria consists of two buildings: the restored Heritage Building—which has 100-year-old marble floors and contains the hotel's restaurants, bar, and 20 carefully restored suites—and the recently constructed 24-story Waldorf Astoria Building, where the majority of rooms are located. Rooms are wonderfully luxuriant, with lovely Art Deco touches, high ceilings with chandeliers, and modern conveniences such as televisions embedded in some bathroom mirrors. This is a good choice for guests who want to experience the Bund and Shanghai history, yet want some distance from the tourist crowds that flock to the Fairmont Peace Hotel.

2 Zhongshan Dongyi Lu. http://waldorfastoria3.hilton.com/en/hotels/china/waldorf-astoria-shanghai-on-the-bund-SHAWAWA. ✆ **021/6322-9988.** Subway: East Nanjing Rd., 10-min. walk. **Amenities:** 2 restaurants; 2 bars; spa; gym; swimming pool; free Wi-Fi.

MODERATE

Jinjiang Metropolo Hotel Classiq Off Bund ★★★ More famous for managing crumbling heritage hotels beloved of tour groups, the state-backed Jinjiang Hotel Group has been winning admiring glances for its Metropolo brand hotels in recent years. Opened in late 2014, the Metropolo Classiq Off Bund is its finest offering, located immediately next to the far more expensive Fairmont Peace Hotel and just yards from the Bund. The style takes hints from the colonial heritage of its sister properties but injects much needed glam. Units are like hip living rooms, with woolly carpets, leather armchairs, and oversized mirrors. Of the nine suites upstairs, three have their own private balcony, a rare treat in this storied part of old Shanghai. Guestrooms are spread across 11 floors, so this shouldn't be thought of as a boutique hotel, but it has got a definite attitude and is the perfect choice for those who have a budget to look after but want to stay centrally without slumming it.

98 Nanjing Dong Lu, near Sichuan Zhong Lu. http://jjhotels.jinjiang.com. ✆ **021/6321-1666.** RMB1,200 standard rooms. Subway: East Nanjing Rd. **Amenities:** Restaurant; bar; fitness center; free Wi-Fi.

INEXPENSIVE

Central Hotel ★ You can't beat this hotel for an affordable, well-located place to stay near all the city's attractions. One street away from the shopping and restaurants on and around Nanjing Dong Lu and a hop from two major subway stations, Central Hotel's clean and spacious rooms are a great place to come back to after a day of sightseeing. Amenities are a touch above basic (for example, there's no pool, staff are not accustomed to servicing Wi-Fi issues so sometimes there's no online access, and the Chinese-style lobby looks a bit dated), but at these prices for Shanghai, you won't care.

555 Jiujiang Lu. www.centralhotelshanghai.com. ✆ **021/5396-5000.** RMB500 standard rooms. Subway: People's Square, East Nanjing Rd. **Amenities:** Gym; games room; sauna; spa; indoor minigolf, free Wi-Fi.

Salvo Hotel ★ The Salvo Hotel is just a few minutes from Nanjing Dong Lu, Shanghai's central thoroughfare, and its namesake subway station from which you can reach almost anywhere conveniently and quickly. The hotel is equidistant between People's Square and the Bund. Rooms have Chinese-style decor and could use renovation, and the dark woods, patterned wallpaper, gilded armchairs, and low ceilings can make accommodations feel dated and small. Also, don't expect the English-speaking staff and service you might find in a five-star hotel (for example, there's no published telephone number; instead, book online via the hotel's website or various travel engines).

FADING stars

There are two types of hotels in China: Sino-foreign joint-venture hotels, which are Chinese-owned properties with foreign management, and wholly Chinese-owned-and-managed hotels. The former tend to be four-and-five-star hotels with familiar brand names, while the latter can range from five-star outfits to unrated hovels. The Chinese government ranks hotels on an almost meaningless star system whereby five-star accreditation is handed out by a central authority, while ranks of four stars and below are determined by local authorities, none of whom are beyond being wined, dined, and having their palms greased. Even five-stars must suffer political meddling. Five annual inspections seem somewhat excessive, especially when you consider the beautifully ambiguous assessment criteria: demanding that 70% of rooms be bigger than 20sq.m (215 sq. ft.) is one thing; saying that style should be "outstanding," management systems "appropriate," and that the PA systems should supply "good-quality background music" is something else entirely. In short, it's more sensible to trust the brand than an official star rating.

Stay here if you want a basic room you don't expect to spend much time in. For the location, the price can't be bettered, but don't expect stardust in either service or room quality.

339 Guangdong Lu. www.salvohotelshanghai.com. No phone. Email: reservation@salvohotelshanghai.com. RMB350 standard rooms. Subway: East Nanjing Rd. **Amenities:** Gym; games room; bar; free Wi-Fi.

French Concession

EXPENSIVE

Andaz Xintiandi Shanghai ★★ This "contemporary boutique" arm of the Hyatt opened up in Shanghai's tourist and business district Xintiandi in 2013 and has drawn a young, trendy crowd ever since. It's not a boutique hotel in the traditional sense; rising to 28 stories, this is a busy, bustling, and large hotel. However, there is a definite with-it, urban ambience, with informal check-ins conducted by roaming concierges; in-room, rock-slab bathrooms; and artworks by artists with Shanghai connections. All room controls—blinds, TV, air-conditioning included—are made from an iPad. The LED lighting can be customized according to a series of presets to suit various moods, while the guests can help themselves to free nonalcoholic drinks and snacks from the minibar. The pool and fitness center are privately run businesses, housed within the same building, but are available for guests to use for free. The location is great for exploring Xintiandi, right on your doorstep, and only a 5-minute walk from the subway station.

88 Songshan Lu. www.andazshanghai.com. ✆ **021/2310-1234.** 307 units. RMB1,500 standard rooms. Subway: South Huangpi Rd. **Amenities:** 4 restaurants; free welcome cocktail 6–8pm on day of arrival; free use of private gym and fitness center.

Langham Hotel ★★ Resplendent with a 35-seat martini bar, a great outdoor terrace, and three top restaurants, the five-star Langham is an oasis of calm at the crossroads of two of Shanghai's most interesting places for visitors. The tree-lined streets of the historic former French Concession and the bars, boutiques, and restaurants of Xintiandi are both on your doorstep, with other central locations not far away. The award-winning T'ang Court restaurant serves up fine Cantonese dishes alongside an international buffet-style restaurant and an outdoor lounge and bar. The layout of the restaurant is unusual, as most tables are tucked into nooks and crannies to maximize privacy. Just a few minutes after 7pm every day, guests can head to the atrium to watch the Langham's multitiered chandelier change colors during a brief light-show. The guestrooms have an old-world feel, with dark woods, patterned carpet, and some leather furniture. A big plus is the VPN built into the free Wi-Fi, giving guests easy access to familiar Western websites that are otherwise blocked.

99 Madang Lu. xintiandi.langhamhotels.com. ✆ **021/2330-2288.** RMB2,000 and up. Subway: South Huangpi Rd or Xintiandi. **Amenities:** 4 restaurants; 2 bars; spa, swimming pool; gym; free Wi-Fi.

Mansion Hotel ★ Fashioned from a French villa once belonging to infamous gangster "Big Ears Du," the Mansion feels like a smaller, more exclusive version of one of the state-run heritage hotels but suffers a few of the same service issues. The lobby is a marvel, festooned with traditional Chinese furnishings and colonial-era museum pieces, such as the grandfather clocks and the gramophone. Rooms are each uniquely laid out, though consistent in their high ceilings, bathroom Jacuzzis, thick carpet, and hardwood furniture. The Bose iPod docks add a modern touch. There's a great outdoor terrace in the upstairs restaurant and champagne bar. For all its opulence, management is of a Chinese rather than international standard, and service can be poor. Though there are no major sights on the doorstep, the location is absolutely superb for pedestrian exploration of the French Concession.

82 Xinle Lu. www.mansionhotelchina.com. ✆ **021/5403-9888.** RMB2,050 standard rooms. Subway: Shaanxi South Rd. **Amenities:** 2 restaurants; bar; free Wi-Fi.

MODERATE

Fraser Residence Shanghai ★★ Fraser Residence provides serviced apartments particularly well suited for business travelers, tourists, and families wanting a kitchen and laundry facilities. This property got an overhaul in 2013, when meeting facilities and rooms were upgraded and air-and-water filtration systems were installed throughout. Choose from studios all the way up to three-bedroom apartments. It's great value, and also well located for sightseeing to Yu Gardens, People's Square, and the Bund. Most rooms come with a balcony, and all are decorated with light and modern flourishes, such as minimalist Scandinavian-style furniture and light wood floorings in the rooms. If you want to stay on the Pudong side of Shanghai, check out Fraser Residence in Lujiazui.

98 Shouning Lu. http://shanghai.frasershospitality.com. ✆ **021/2308-0000.** RMB600 standard rooms. Subway: Dashijie or South Huangpi Rd. **Amenities:** Restaurant; gym; pool; free Wi-Fi.

Regal International East Asia Hotel ★★ Located right in the heart of the former French Concession, with its plane trees that arch over the roadways, the Regal International East Asia provides excellent value for its accommodations and location. Folks who want to spend time exploring the surrounding historic French Concession neighborhoods will especially appreciate the location, although those who want to spend most of their time near the bustling Nanjing Road, Bund, or People's Square might find it a bit too far away. Rooms are spacious, clean, and decorated with an Asian flair, and the Western and Asian breakfast hits all the mainstays (including cereal, coffee, and yogurt for the foreigners, and congee for Chinese visitors). Skip lunches and dinners and instead head out the door to any of Shanghai's great restaurants. At the Regal, you'll find some of the best fitness facilities available anywhere in the city, with squash, seven indoor and outdoor tennis courts, bowling alleys, and a pool.

516 Hengshan Lu. www.regalhotel.com/regal-international-east-asia-hotel. ✆ **021/6415-5588.** 320 units. RMB700 standard rooms. Subway: Hengshan Rd. **Amenities:** Restaurant; bar; gym; swimming pool; squash courts; tennis court; bowling alley; spa; free Wi-Fi.

Jing'an

EXPENSIVE

The Puli Hotel & Spa ★★★ Located right beside leafy Jing'an Park, the Puli deploys moody design notes to create a hotel that has the feel of a giant spa. Rooms are stylishly dressed in dark woods and gray slate. Tibetan-themed Bayankala bathroom products add extra fragrance, and there are twinkling skyline views from the windowside bathtubs. The downstairs pool complex feels like something out of a Bond lair, with sliding doors and an infinity pool within a high-ceilinged cavelike space. The innovative Jing'an Restaurant and pampering Anantara Spa complete the amenities, but this is not a hotel that has a long shopping list of services and features. Rather, the Puli wins for its great rooms, great vibe, and convenient location, separate from, but well linked to, the tourist sights slightly farther east. The crowd is hip, and fashionistas will feel especially at home.

1 Changde Lu, near Yan'an Zhong Lu. www.thepuli.com. ✆ **021/2216-6973.** RMB3,380 standard rooms. Subway: Jing'an Temple. **Amenities:** 2 restaurants; bar; health club; indoor pool; spa; free Wi-Fi.

MODERATE

Longemont Hotel ★★ This formerly foreign-managed five-star can't compare to the newer luxury properties in Shanghai but retains an air of quality despite the pleasing price cut. For around US$130, you'll get clean, spacious rooms, a fantastic fitness club and pool, and several top-draw restaurants. The Longemont Hotel attracts more of a business- than a tourist-crowd, and it is favored more by Japanese and other Asian travelers. This is a great place to stay if you want a hotel with international-level standards at reasonable prices. A well-priced Cantonese restaurant on the third floor, Royal China, is good enough to bring in non-hotel guests; try the dim sum. Kids will love the huge fish, lobster, and crab tanks on display. Though you are right on the elevated Yan'an Lu highway, there are no subway stops within easy reach, making transportation a little bit awkward, though taxis are cheap and easily hailed.

1116 Yan'an Xi Lu. www.thelongemonthotels.com. ✆ **021-6115-9988.** RMB800 standard rooms. Subway: Jiangsu Rd or Jiaotong University. **Amenities:** Two restaurants; bar; swimming pool; spa; free Wi-Fi.

Kevin's Old House ★★ One of the few hotels to make a home in the city's *lilong* neighborhoods, Kevin's Old House is a charming bed-and-breakfast-style guesthouse. Those nostalgic for old Shanghai style will love the six suites, simply but tastefully refurbished with antique furniture, four-poster beds, and hardwood floors. Bathrooms, however, are thoroughly modern, with cozy hot tubs. Breakfast is included, served in a lovely outdoor terrace, though those expecting to sleep-in should request a room away from the restaurant, which can get noisy. The inn is located in the western reaches of the French Concession, largely low-rise, and filled with tree-lined avenues and small boutiques.

No. 4, Lane 946, Changle Lu. www.kevinsoldhouse.com. ✆ **021/6248-6800.** RMB950 Subway: Changshu Rd. **Amenities:** Restaurant; bar; free Wi-Fi.

Pentahotel ★ This casual hotel overlooking Zhongshan Park is in a busy residential area of Shanghai, away from the city center. By staying slightly away from Shanghai's touristy areas, you'll get a more authentic feel for Chinese city life, and also get more bang for your buck than you would at one of the ritzier hotels closer to the city center. You can still subway into People's Square in about 15 minutes; just avoid traveling during morning or afternoon rush hour, if possible. Rooms have been redone with new carpet and combinations of bright and neutral tan colors. Furniture is modern, and rooms are bright.

1525 Dingxi Lu. www.pentahotels.com. ✆ **021-6252-1111.** RMB600 standard rooms. Subway: Zhongshan Park. **Amenities:** Gym; bar; pool table; free bike rental; free Wi-Fi.

URBN Hotel ★ A former postal-warehouse-turned-hotel, URBN claims environmental kudos for being decorated with locally sourced or recycled materials. Its carbon-neutral claims have been toned down in recent years, but there's still a certain designer chic to the place. Rooms have a quirky design, with beds on elevated platforms, and sunken wraparound lounges designed with parties in mind. Whether you find this funky or impractical will depend on whether you are likely to get up in the night. Those who do should light the way to risk injury. Such design and functional quirks are allied with occasionally spotty service, but this is a popular and often-busy boutique hotel. Guests may use the nearby One Wellness gym, and there's a nice downstairs restaurant that spills out into the bamboo courtyard during summer months.

183 Jiazhou Lu, near Xinzha Lu. www.urbnhotels.com. ✆ **021/5153-4600.** 26 units. RMB1,500 standard rooms. Subway: Jing'an Temple. **Amenities:** Restaurant; bar; access to nearby gym; free Wi-Fi.

Hongkou & Zhabei

EXPENSIVE

Hyatt on the Bund ★ This well-established five-star has great river views and a superb top-floor bar/restaurant, though it has gone from being ultrahip to a touch tired in just 10 short years. The name is a bit of a misnomer, as it's a 10-minute walk to the northern end of the Bund, but it's still easily accessible by taxi and subway on the better side of the river for the main action. Rooms are comfortable but fairly bland in beiges and browns and are already starting to feel old-fashioned. Upper-story River View rooms have a spectacular vantage point, looking down the length of the Huangpu from the crook of the river. It pays to be in the West Tower for both the Bund views and the proximity of the restaurants. Staff are well drilled and helpful, and the hotel's restaurants are both excellent: Xindalu for exquisite Peking Duck, and VUE for contemporary Western with a view. The attached VUE bar *is* true to its name in offering a brilliant lookout, as well as a top-floor outdoor whirlpool and surrounding daybeds. The ride up in the external glass elevator is an extra thrill.

199 Huangpu Lu. www.shanghai.bund.hyatt.com. ✆ **021/6393-1234.** RMB1,800 standard rooms. Subway: International Passenger Transport Center. **Amenities:** 3 restaurants; bar; health club; indoor pool; spa; free Wi-Fi.

MODERATE

Grand Mercure Shanghai Central ★★ You'll like the higher-end feel of this Mercure chain location along with its lower-end prices, which are increasingly hard to find in Shanghai. Nearby are the Jade Buddha Temple and the Shanghai Railway Museum, but otherwise you'll need to hop on the subway or catch a taxi to visit other popular Shanghai attractions. This is a spacious and modern hotel, with rooms dressed classily with crisp linens, dark-wood screens, and local art on the walls. However, it's lacking in many international touches such as a pool, Western-standard service with English-speaking staff, or a full American breakfast. But the relatively low prices leave you plenty of room in your budget for food and entertainment. Beware of the fact that it's located right next to a busy thoroughfare, so those who are sensitive to noise might want to look elsewhere or ask for a room situated away from the main road.

330 Meiyuan Lu. www.mercure.com. ✆ **021/6353-5555.** RMB500 standard rooms. Subway: Shanghai Railway Station. Amenities: Restaurant; gym; bar; free Wi-Fi.

INEXPENSIVE

Shanghai SOHO International Youth Hostel ★ This excellent YHA hostel has a peaceful location beside Suzhou Creek and is a 5-minute walk to Line 1 of the subway. The friendly staff speak English, there's free Wi-Fi in reception, cheap food, a bike-rental service, and a roof terrace. It's particularly popular with Chinese backpackers and students, who tend to opt for the dorm rooms, but there are also spacious ensuite double rooms (the cheapest of which have no windows). Book one of the slightly more expensive

CHINESE BUSINESS motels

For many Chinese business travelers to Shanghai, the no-frills business chain motels (such as the Jinjiang Inn, Super Motel, and Green Tree Inn) that have sprouted up around town have become a popular lodging option. Usually housed in dull, unremarkable buildings, these motels have basic, but relatively new and clean rooms (some even with very modern decor) with air-conditioning, hot water, television, telephone, and free Wi-Fi for the business or professional traveler who would prefer to stay away from the backpacking hostel scene. There is usually a restaurant on the premises that serves *"jiachang cai"* (home-style Chinese cooking), as well as a business center that can handle airplane and train bookings. Not much English is spoken at these places, so it may be more suitable for foreigners who already have some grasp of Chinese. Still, if you're bemoaning the lack of decent but affordable lodgings in town, here are three of the better-located choices. **Jinjiang Star,** located downtown in Huangpu District at 33 Fujian Nan Lu (www.jj-inn.com; ✆ **021/6326-0505**), has basic en-suite standard rooms for RMB349; **Green Tree Inn** (at 111 Yan'an Zhong Lu, just west of Fumin Lu (www.998.com; ✆ **021/3617-4888**), has standard rooms starting at RMB399; while **Super Motel 168,** located in western Shanghai at 1119 Yan'an Xi Lu (www.motel168.com; ✆ **021/5117-7777**), across from the Longemont Shanghai, has standard rooms starting at RMB298.

upstairs options, which do have natural light, and specify nonsmoking. Aside from the price, the main draw here is the location. It's on a riverside pedestrian walkway and feels far from Shanghai's madding, and sometimes maddening, crowd, though People's Park is just over 10 minutes' walk away.

1307 Nan Suzhou Lu (nr. Chengdu Lu). www.yhachina.com. ✆ **021/5888-8817.** RMB200 for basic ensuite rooms, RMB280 for rooms with a window. **Amenities:** Bar; laundry; games room; free Wi-Fi.

Pudong

EXPENSIVE

Grand Hyatt Shanghai ★ Back in the late 1990s when the Jinmao skyscraper opened, the Grand Hyatt was among the highest hotels in the world, taking the top floors of the building and catering to diplomats and business executives. Since then, the competition in luxury high-rise hotels has multiplied, and this spot is working to catch up, although rooms overlooking the city are still breathtaking. All rooms have been renovated since 2013, bringing a little extra color and comfort. The hotel still has luxury and style, but is value-priced relative to some of the newer five-star hotels in Pudong. Try the Cucina Italian restaurant, which is among the better Italian restaurants on the Pudong side of the city. Of all the restaurants in the hotel, it also hogs the best views as it overlooks the Pearl Tower. The three nightlife venues have live music every night, and the Cloud 9 Sky Bar circles the top floor with 360-degree views of the city.

Jinmao Tower, 88 Shiji Da Dao. http://shanghai.grand.hyatt.com/en/hotel/home.html. 555 units. ✆ **21/5049-1234.** RMB1,700 and up, standard rooms. Subway: Lujiazui. **Amenities:** 4 restaurants; bar; swimming pool; fitness center; free Wi-Fi.

Mandarin Oriental Pudong ★★★ This luxury Hong Kong chain is a latecomer to the Shanghai market, but the owners have used the time to size up the competition. Enjoy unusual benefits such as check-out times a full 24 hours from the time you check in, hotel gardens, and 24-hour pool access. If you've got cash to burn, this hotel boasts the largest luxury suites available in Shanghai, which have already attracted the likes of Justin Bieber, Jackie Chan, Vivienne Tam, and Italian opera superstar Cecilia Bartoli. Mere mortals can enjoy the still-expensive regular rooms, which are spacious and combine touches of Asian and Western design, or get a rubdown in one of the spa's cavernous treatment rooms. For service, design, and restaurant options, this is one of the best hotels in town, though the riverside location isn't ideal. It's a bit of a stroll into the financial district of Lujiazui, and crossing the river requires a further subway ride. On the plus side, taxis are easy to hail, and the lovely Binjiang Lu riverside promenade is on your doorstep. River-view rooms look out across the river to the Hongkou District, while views the other way let you peer into the thicket of skyscrapers. Ask to stay as high as you can.

111 Pudong Nan Lu. www.mandarinoriental.com/shanghai. ✆ **021/2082-9888.** RMB3,600 standard rooms. Subway: Lujiazui Station. **Amenities:** 3 restaurants; 2 bars; gym; swimming pool; spa; free Wi-Fi.

Park Hyatt Shanghai ★★ Occupying floors 79 to 93 of the World Financial Center, the Shanghai outlet of Hyatt's most exclusive brand was once the world's tallest hotel but now can't even claim top spot in the city. It is, however, undiminished in terms of its luxury and levels of service. The Japanese design theme creates a calming, Zen-like cool throughout, from the downstairs entrance (where you'll need to scan your bags for security) to the low-lit hallways linking the guestrooms. The view from the 87th-floor lobby is better than that from the building's official public viewing platform, above. Rooms are among the largest in the city, with high ceilings, windowside day-beds, and iPod docking stations. Bathrooms are beautiful, with large rain showers and deep hot tubs, while the infinity pool and spa upstairs enjoy a quite spectacular lookout. Room views are breathtaking—and very much part of what you pay for here— though the hotel is so high that both cloud and smog often obscure the view. To minimize potential disappointment, opt for a room facing the beautiful Jinmao Tower and the Oriental Pearl TV Tower, both of which shine through the gloom at night.

Shanghai World Financial Center, 100 Shiji Da Dao. www.shanghai.park.hyatt.com. ✆ **021/6888-1234.** 174 units. RMB3,000 standard rooms. Subway: Lujiazui. **Amenities:** 2 restaurants; lounge; 3 bars; health club and spa; indoor pool; free Wi-Fi.

Pudong Shangri-La ★★ As one of the earliest skyscrapers to go up in 1990s Lujiazui, this fantastic five-star looks like a relic from the outside but wins on comfort and impeccable service. The Shangri-La's largest global hotel has 952 guest rooms, divided between the River View Tower and the taller Grand Tower. River Tower rooms have views in all four directions—expect a premium of around RMB250 for the (recommended) Bund view, inclusive of binoculars and a great booklet introducing the neoclassical architecture across the water. Rooms here are airy and dressed in a hybrid East-West style, with chandeliers and willow patterns, while the Grand Tower has a darker, classier, business feel. The signature Chi spa offers indulgent extended treatments in a heavily scented interior cocoon. There's also a large, covered pool and health spa, while the arcade connecting the two towers houses the superb 24-hour E-Cafe where the world comes to you in 10 major global cuisines, served as a buffet at breakfast, lunch, and dinner. A staffed play area, just across the lobby, keeps the little ones occupied so you can better enjoy the food. A number of world-class restaurants are on-site, including Nadaman and Jade on 36 (p. 246).

33 Fucheng Lu, near Binjiang Da Dao. www.shangri-la.com. ✆ **021/6882-8888.** RMB1,850 standard rooms; RMB2,250 and up for executive level. Subway: Lujiazui. **Amenities:** 6 restaurants; 2 bars; health club; indoor pool; spa; tennis court; free Wi-Fi.

Ritz-Carlton Pudong ★ Located within the upscale IFC mall, the Ritz-Carlton Pudong is among the most luxurious of all five-stars in Lujiazui. The Bund-view rooms have wonderful vistas back toward Puxi, and the breakfast spread on the 52nd floor is among the best in town. The infinity pool is also nice, with a view of the Huangpu River and a large hot tub that will fit at least a dozen guests. The Flair bar is a destination for out-of-towners on account of its 58th-floor open-air patio (see "Bars with a View" box, p. 252). Rooms,

airport HOTELS

There are several hotels serving **Pudong Airport,** the major international hub. The best of the lot, **Ramada Plaza Pudong Airport** (1100 Qihang Lu; www.ramadaairportpd.com; ✆ **021/3849-4949**), is a 2-to-3-minute free shuttle ride or a 10-minute walk from the airport. The hotel has 370 rooms (RMB880–RMB1,080 standard), which are clean and comfortable with the usual amenities, including safes and in-room movies. Both Western and Chinese dining are available. If you want to be really close to the terminal and don't mind basic accommodations, the gigantic **Dazhong Airport Hotel** (6001 Yinbin Da Dao; www.motel168.com; ✆ **021/3879-9999**) is located right on top of the maglev station, just a few minutes' walk from both airport Terminals 1 and 2. The hotel has clean rooms with all the basic amenities, including free Wi-Fi, and prices starting around RMB398.

The **Shanghai International Airport Hotel** (368 Yingbinyi Lu; ✆ **021/96990**) is the closest to the terminal at **Shanghai Hongqiao Airport,** host of most domestic flights. Rooms are fairly uninspiring and go for around RMB500. The closest Western-brand hotel is the **Howard Johnson Hongqiao Airport Hotel** (1989 Huaxiang Lu; http://shanghai.hotel.hqa.hojochina.com; ✆ **021/5227-8888**), which is 5 minutes to the west and has a shuttle bus to and from Terminal 2. Rooms here are around RMB600.

however, are not the best in town. Though the Ritz is only a few years old, the furniture in the rooms already seems a little worn and dated, with faux-wood vinyl paneling and golden carpets and drapes.

Shanghai IFC Mall, 8 Shiji Da Dao. www.ritzcarlton.com/en/Properties/Shanghai-Pudong. ✆ **021/2020-1888.** RMB5,000 standard rooms. Subway: Lujiazui. **Amenities:** 3 restaurants; bar; swimming pool; fitness suite; spa, free Wi-Fi.

WHERE TO EAT

Gastronomes never had it so good in Shanghai. With restaurants serving a mind-boggling variety of Chinese cuisine, as well as a wide range of top-notch international fare, Shanghai is hands down the best city for upmarket dining. The prosperous 1990s that saw Shanghai take again to the world stage have reawakened the demand for *la bella vita,* as seen in the explosion of dining establishments in the last few years. For Shanghai residents, ever-attuned to the latest trends and tastes, eating out and trying new restaurants is now a pastime that rivals shopping.

While some of Shanghai's top restaurants can be found in hotels, there are scores of well-run private establishments that rival, if not surpass, the quality of hotel food, and usually at lower prices. Significantly improved hygiene standards should also allay any concerns you may have about eating out. Shanghai provides the unusual opportunity of dining one moment in a traditional teahouse and another in a restored colonial mansion.

Don't expect the Chinese food here to taste the same as that at home; expect it to be light years better. While you can eat your way through China by sampling all the regional Chinese restaurants in Shanghai, the emphasis is on Shanghai's own renowned cuisine, commonly referred to as *benbang cai.* Usually considered a branch of Huaiyang cuisine, Shanghai cooking has traditionally relied on soy sauce, sugar, and oil. The most celebrated Shanghai dish is hairy crab, a freshwater delicacy that reaches its prime every fall. Also popular are any number of "drunken" dishes (crab, chicken) marinated in local Shaoxing wine, and braised meat dishes such as lion's head meatballs and braised pork knuckle. Shanghai dim sum and snacks include a variety of dumplings, headlined by the local favorite *xiaolong bao*, as well as onion pancakes and leek pies, all of which deserve to be tried.

Huangpu

EXPENSIVE

8-1/2 Otto e Mezzo Bombana ★★ ITALIAN Known as "Bombana" for short, this is Italian chef Umberto Bombana's Shanghai version of his three-Michelin-star restaurant in Hong Kong of the same name. You will pay for the privilege of sitting in this ultraformal dining room overlooking the Bund, with its scrumptious seasonal prix-fixe and a la carte menus. There's no question that the contemporary Italian fare is creative and fresh, with seasonal seafood and meat tasting-menus. The braised short rib alongside pan-seared tenderloin offers some of the tenderest meats you'll find in Shanghai, although portions are small. Their Sicilian-style lobster fettuccine is also a crowd favorite. Bombana is popular with wealthy Chinese, who come to impress clients and paramours. Foreigners on expense accounts might do the same, but those who are wallet-conscious will find better value elsewhere.

6/F, 169 Yuanmingyuan Lu. www.ottoemezzobombana.com/shanghai. ✆ **021/6087-2890.** RMB500–RMB800 per person. Lunch noon–2:30pm, Dinner 6pm–11pm. Subway: East Nanjing Rd., then 15-min walk.

Capo ★ ITALIAN Designed to evoke the aura of a Roman basilica, with pillars and corridors flanking a main hallway, Capo is the well-executed venture of Enzo Carbone, the chef behind Shanghai's Italian restaurants Issimo and Matto. The centerpiece of this space is a pair of ovens—one for the meat and the other for pizzas. The *crudo* bar serves oysters and other shellfish, but the main reason to come to Capo is for the steak. The restaurant sources from a ranch in Australia, and the menu lets you know whether your cow was grain- or grass-fed, alongside a marbling score. The steaks leave the apple-fired oven with the right amount of char, and are rolled out on wooden chopping blocks and carved table-side. Capo is a great addition to the fine-dining options in Shanghai, although one door empties out into the adjoining nightclub, Muse. So don't sit near that exit if you don't want techno-music crashing your meal.

Yifeng Galleria, 5/F, 99 Beijing Dong Lu. www.caposhanghai.com. ✆ **021/5308-8332.** RMB800-plus per person. Subway: East Nanjing Rd., 10-min walk.

Mr and Mrs Bund ★★★ FRENCH Still one of Shanghai's most popular restaurants to celebrate anniversaries and birthdays, Mr and Mrs Bund serves up fine-but-casual French fare alongside stunning Huangpu river views. Even

PAUL PAIRET'S ultraviolet

Less restaurant and more all-senses-on-deck gustatory experience, Ultraviolet is the brainchild of the inimitable French chef Paul Pairet, Shanghai's very own Heston Blumenthal. Guests are whisked, blindfolded, from the chef's Bund restaurant (see "Mr and Mrs Bund") to a secret location where they are treated to an unblindfolded, hours-long smorgasbord within an intimate 10-seat multimedia room. Ultraviolet employs a production team, with video, sound, and "scent diffusers" used to establish a specific mood for each dish. Lobster, for example, may be served alongside images and sounds of crashing waves and a whiff of a sea breeze. There are two menus to choose from—the original UVA menu or the expanded, decadent UVB menu—with only one sitting per evening. A seat costs at least RMB3,000, depending on the menu, but don't think of the price tag as the cost of a meal but rather as a ticket for a private show. The "restaurant" is open Tuesday to Saturday, and it's a 6:30pm start. Needless to say, booking well in advance is necessary (visit www.uvbypp.cc). Simply put, Ultraviolet is seriously fun, or as Alain Ducasse put it, "*C'est magnifique et delicieux*!"

as Shanghai's restaurant scene has exploded with competition, bringing in chefs from every corner of the world, Mr and Mrs Bund still regularly tops best-restaurant lists. Try customer favorites such as the short rib and the lemon-and-lemon tart, and don't forget Chef Paul Pairet's longtime signature "meuniere with truffle bread," which was one of his favorite side dishes for years at home before it occurred to him to put it on his restaurant menu. Finer touches include a sourcing list that tells you where your food came from. Be sure to book in advance and ask for a Bund-view window table.

6/F, Bund 18, 18 Zhongshan Dong Yi Lu (nr. Nanjing Dong Lu). www.mmbund.com. ✆ **021/6323-9898.** RMB300–RMB500 per person. Weekday lunch 11:30am–2pm, 6pm–2am. Subway: East Nanjing Rd., 10-min walk.

French Concession

EXPENSIVE

Franck ★★ FRENCH, INTERNATIONAL Franck was one of the first French bistros to show up on the Shanghai scene back in 2007, and it's still competing well with the dozens of new fine international restaurants to appear on the scene (also with big-name chefs and investors). Franck's salmon appetizer—smoked in-house—is a divine combination of smoky and salty. Menus change daily and are displayed with flair on a series of portable marker boards; the service is attentive, and anything on the menu will be explained in French, English, or Chinese. Franck is packed most nights—the restaurant does not serve lunch and is open seven nights a week for dinner—so reserve well in advance. This restaurant was one of the original anchor tenants of Ferguson Lane before the alley became the swanky cafe-and-restaurant destination that it is today.

Ferguson Lane, 376 Wukang Lu. www.franck.com.cn. ✆ **021/6437-6465.** RMB600 per person. Daily 6pm–1am. Subway: Shanghai Library, then 10-min. walk.

MODERATE

Bao Luo (保罗) ★★ SHANGHAINESE Bao Luo used to be *the* go-to restaurant for late-night revelry, opening until 6am daily. It's now reverted to a slightly more humane closing time of midnight, but other than that, it's one of the few constants in Shanghai's dining merry-go-round. An apparently tiny diner, as seen from the outside, it actually stretches four houses deep, every square inch buzzing with barely controlled chaos. The story goes that Bao Luo's owner—a bicycle repairman who lived in this very lane—started the restaurant in his own home, but gradually bought up his neighbors' houses as business boomed. The extensive menu features many local favorites given a slight twist, including *huiguo rou jiabing* (twice-cooked lamb wrapped in pancakes), *songshu luyu* (sweet-and-sour fried fish), *xiefen hui zhenjun* (braised mushroom with crabmeat), and the sinfully fatty, but absolutely delicious, *hong shaorou* (braised pork belly).

271 Fumin Lu (north of Changle Lu). ✆ **021/6279-2827.** Meal for two RMB100–RMB150. No credit cards. Daily 11am–midnight. Subway: Changshu Rd.

Crystal Jade Restaurant ★★★ CHINESE A classy Singaporean chain, Crystal Jade promiscuously borrows from regional cuisines across the nation. The dining room of their Xintiandi branch somehow blends glam decor with a relaxed food-court feel and serves up some of the best *xiaolong bao* (steamed dumplings with broth) in town. Other perennial favorites include spicy Sichuanese *la mian* (hand-pulled noodles), and the sweet *char-siu bao* buns beloved of the Cantonese. The place becomes packed on Sundays for its legendary dim sum brunch. Reserve in advance or risk a long wait. There are two other branches in Shanghai, one in the nearby Hong Kong New World Plaza (North Block) at 300 Huaihai Zhong Lu.

2/F, 12A, Xintiandi South Block (enter from the main mall entrance in the southwest corner of the south block). www.crystaljade.com. ✆ **021/6311-2288.** Daily 11am–11pm (10:30am opening on Sun). Subway: Xintiandi or South Huangpi Rd.

Ginger ★★★ INTERNATIONAL, ASIAN FUSION This Asian fusion bar and bistro gets excellent marks for ambience, with a multistory venue with large picture windows overlooking greenery and a park, and an unhurried atmosphere that is unusual for Shanghai restaurants. The food is fantastic too, with the flavors coming from the globe-trotting ways of Singaporean owner Betty Ng. The *laksa* is rich and layered, the crab cakes are fresh, a wine-infused rosemary chicken is juicy but crisp on the outside, and the hand rolls and spring rolls are delicately wrapped. There's also a Wagyu beef burger and a lamb chop. Even though the menu is eclectic, you'll have trouble deciding, as dishes are consistently good, desserts included.

91 Xingguó Lu. www.gingerfoods.com/about.html. ✆ **021/3406-0599.** RMB250 per person. Mon–Sat 10:30am–11pm, Sun 10:30am–10pm. Subway: Shanghai Library, then 15-min. walk.

Hai by Goga ★★ FUSION Want skyline views alongside some of the tastiest Cal-Asian fusion cuisine the city has to offer? In 2011, San Francisco chef Brad Turley launched this companion to his signature Goga restaurant on the street level of the building entrance, adding a fully stocked bar and a versatile menu that's equally welcoming for post-work snacks, dinner, or late-night bites. While the original Goga serves up crowd favorites year-round (such as a lobster roll), Hai by Goga's menu changes more seasonally and allows Chef Brad room to experiment. In winter, enjoy a West Coast cioppino or a hearty foie gras bread pudding, while in summer you'll see lighter fare, such as chilled citrus-spiked ceviches and grilled seafood with crisp salads. You'll also see a rotation of imported oysters year-round. You'll find this seventh-floor terrace and lounge a great place to watch the sun set over cocktails and appetizers, and you'll likely see Brad himself checking in on tables on occasion.

7/F, 1 Yueyang Lu (nr. Dongping Lu). gogarestaurants.com. ✆ **021/3461-7893.** RMB300–RMB400 per person. Mon–Sat 5pm–midnight, closed Sunday. Subway: Changshu Rd.

INEXPENSIVE

Charmant ★★ TAIWANESE/CHINESE A family-owned restaurant that's been providing Taiwanese fare in Shanghai since 2003, Charmant religiously employs authentic old-school Taiwanese cooking methods, such as tossing both a young and old chicken together to boil for broth, to maximize both flavor and tenderness. They fly their crustaceans in from Taiwan for the Sakura shrimp fried rice, and desserts are heavenly. Try the almond jello, a sweet, white gelatin that is handmade every day from roasted almonds and coupled with diced fruits. Charmant's a favorite among local Chinese and expats alike, not to mention the Taiwanese who swear by their three-cup (*sanbeiji*) chicken recipe, which is a flavorful dish cooked in rice wine, soy sauce, and a sesame oil marinade.

1414 Huaihai Zhong Lu (nr. Fuxing Zhong Lu). ✆ **021/6431-8107.** RMB60–RMB90 per person. Daily 11am–2am. Subway: Changshu Lu.

Di Shui Dong (滴水洞) ★★★ HUNANESE Rivaling Sichuan cuisine for spiciness but relying on chilies over numbing *huajiao* peppercorns, the lesser-known cooking of Hunan province can be sampled at this delightful restaurant. Enter from a small French Concession storefront, up a flight of rickety wooden stairs, and into a bustling dining room dressed in peasant chic. Highly recommended are the *ziran paigu* (cumin ribs), *gan guo ji* (chicken in chili pot), *suan doujiao rouni* (mashed pork with sour beans), and the spiced bullfrog legs. The heat is complemented beautifully by the black Tsingtao stout (*heipi*) that's recently been added to the menu. It's seriously unpretentious, with the flush-cheeked staff observing few airs and graces. However, it's busy night after night with a pleasingly mixed, foreign-Chinese crowd, something that's a rarity outside superexpensive restaurants.

56 Maoming Nan Lu (nr. Changle Lu). ✆ **021/6253-2689.** Meal for two RMB80–RMB140. No foreign credit cards. 10am–1am. Subway: South Shanxi Rd.

Din Tai Fung (iAPM Mall) ★★ CHINESE, TAIWANESE Those who love Din Tai Fung's *xiaolong bao* (see "Xintiandi," above) will be thrilled to know there's another location tucked away on the third floor of the new high-end iAPM mall. This Taiwanese-owned restaurant chain seems to be growing at warp speed, with new locations popping up all over Shanghai. The classic pork soup dumplings at RMB68 for a basket of 10 are a must. Other favorites include the sesame noodles (*dan dan mian*), any of the stir-fried fresh green vegetables, the hot-and-sour soup, the shrimp-fried rice, the spicy wontons in a bowl, and any of the sago-and-fruit desserts. You can spend an afternoon shopping, stop in at the Apple Store, and finish up here for soup dumplings. Expect to have to line up for a table (no reservations).

3/F, iAPM Mall, 999 Huaihai Zhong Lu. www.dintaifung-china.com.cn. ✆ **021/5466-8191.** RMB150 per person. Daily 10am–11pm. Subway: South Shanxi Rd.

Pin Chuan (品川) ★★ SICHUAN Those who have lived in Sichuan will swear that this is some of the best, freshest Sichuan food you'll find in Shanghai. The quality of fish, meats, and vegetables here is top-notch, which is one reason it's favored by expats and fastidious Chinese. The food is not so spicy that you're reaching for water after every bite (and a good thing, because they only serve bottled water for a charge), and food is served to share. There's not much ambience—tables are pushed close together and the lights are bright—but really, you're here for the food. Try the *lazi* chicken (ask for bones removed if you prefer diced chicken) or the perch with fresh green Sichuan peppercorns. The kitchen standards are high, so the chicken is perfectly fried every time, and the fish is tender and cooked just right.

47 Taojiang Lu (nr. Wulumuqi Nan Lu). www.pinchuan-china.com. ✆ **021-6437-9361.** RMB100–RMB200 per person. Lunch 11am–2pm, Dinner 5–10pm. Subway: Hengshan Lu.

Sichuan Citizen ★★ SICHUAN Sichuan Citizen is a favorite with locals and expats alike, with great cocktails, stone-pot dishes, pepper beef, twice-fried eggplant, and other mouthwatering classics served in a casual, red-lantern-and-wood setting. The two-story restaurant is also good for hosting groups, as you'll get away with paying about RMB100 to RMB150 a head. It often tops best-Sichuan lists in Shanghai, but beware that flagging down a waiter is sometimes difficult, and you may leave with a feeling of being over-oiled and over-spiced, as this is by no means a "light" cuisine.

30 Donghu Lu (nr. Huaihai Zhong Lu). www.citizenshanghai.com. ✆ **021/5404-1235.** RMB100–RMB150 per person. Daily 11am–10:30pm. Subway: South Shanxi Rd.

Southern Barbarian ★★★ YUNNAN CHINESE This restaurant's been a favorite with locals since it opened in the late 1990s, especially among the expats who flock here for its authentic and flavorful Yunnan cuisine cooked by the owner, a native of China's interior Yunnan province. In 2013, the restaurant launched a new menu, but don't skip the old standbys of grilled goat cheese (a Yunnan specialty), Crossing Bridge Noodles, and beer chicken. It can be tough to find—you'll have to go to the back of the building and up a staircase—but you won't be disappointed. The imported beer selection is outstanding, and often wins awards from the foodie publications in town.

2/F, 169 Jinxian Lu (nr. Maoming Nan Lu, inside small Juroshine Life Art Space). www.southernbarbarian.com. ✆ **021/5157-5510.** RMB100–RMB200 per person. Mon–Fri 10am–10pm, Fri–Sun 10am–midnight. Subway: South Shanxi Rd.

FOOD streets

Shanghai can't compete with Beijing or Xi'an for street food, but there are a few decent neighborhoods for those looking to sample a more lo-fi take on Eastern cuisine. However, few have English menus or English-speaking staff. Among the best are: **Huanghe Lu,** (stretching north from People's Square), mainly populated by family-run sit-down restaurants doing great *mantou* (steamed bread) and dumplings; **Shouning Lu,** just west of the Old City, which specializes in the spicy crawfish *(xiaolong xia)* beloved of the Shanghainese and also sells Hairy Crab (*dazha xie*) during the season. **Sipailou Lu,** south of Fangbang Zhong Lu, just east of the Yuyuan Bazaar (see p. 210) in the Old City, is chock-full of temporary stalls selling every kind of local delicacy. **Wujiang Lu,** beside the Nanjing Xi Lu subway station in Jing'an, was once *the* place to go for street food, but is now more like a mall food court. Still, it's a compromise option for those worried about hygiene standards at the grungier joints on this list.

Jing'an District

EXPENSIVE

881 South Beauty (Qiao Jiang Nan) ★ SICHUAN The South Beauty restaurant chain has won huge popularity thanks to a fusion of top-draw Sichuanese dishes and elegant dining settings. This is its top spot in Shanghai, housed in an old financier's mansion off the old Avenue Edward VII (today's Yan'an Lu), which has been fitted out to resemble a romantic lounge bar. There's a more refined ambience out back where well-dressed diners enjoy floor-to-ceiling views of the garden, and a terrace that is popular during warmer months. The food is not excessively hot, perhaps to accommodate local and expatriate tastes, but you can always request them to *jia la* (add spice). Start with the Four Seasons Cold Dish Platter, where you can select four appetizers from a wide range of choices; for a main, try the "Australian Beef Tender in Hot Oil with Stones," which is cooked from raw at the table, in oil that's kept scalding by the presence of rounded pebbles; and save room for the *dan-dan* noodles in spicy peanut sauce. The only downside to the whole experience is the service. Anyone who looks like they'd rather not lose face by complaining should expect to be overcharged. Check your bill carefully.

881 Yan'an Zhong Lu (east of Tongren Lu). ✆ **021/6247-5878.** Reservations recommended. Meal for two RMB250–RMB400. Daily 11am–11:30pm. Subway: West Nanjing Rd.

Fu 1088 ★★★ SHANGHAI Tucked away behind an iron gate on a busy one-way street, this gem of a restaurant is in an unmarked three-story villa with glossy wallpaper and chipped mosaic floors. Dining is in one of 17 private rooms, each laden with early-20th-century furniture, cherrywood chairs, and chandeliers. Start with the chilled drunken chicken with rice-wine shaved ice, and go on to the glorious braised pork with soy and rock sugar, the deep-fried shrimp with wasabi mayonnaise, and the steamed egg with crabmeat. Two local dishes you're unlikely to find back home that are also worth trying include *huaiyang dazhu gansi* (bean curd sheet with garden greens and shrimp in thick soup) and the sautéed water bamboo in soy sauce. Though waiters only speak a small amount of English, kitchen staff are working to an international spec, evinced by the immaculate fine-dining presentation. There is a RMB300 minimum charge per person in the evening, but the RMB158 lunchtime tasting menu doesn't skimp an inch on quality.

375 Zhenning Lu (north of Yuyuan Lu). ✆ **021/5239-7878.** Reservations recommended. Meal for two RMB600–RMB900. Daily 11am–2pm and 5:30pm–midnight. Subway: Jiangsu Rd.

MODERATE

Guyi Hunan ★★★ HUNAN Diners flock to Guyi for reliably satisfying Hunan cuisine at reasonable prices—this is a great place to take guests who might want to try good Chinese food but are scared of anything too spicy or strange. There's nothing remarkable about the ambience—cloth-covered round and square tables are crammed into a single room— but it's the food you're coming for. The cumin-crusted ribs, spicy *lazi* chicken, and the eggplant and long beans are specialties for good reason; they're fresh and perfectly seasoned. (If you're a meat-lover, definitely order the ribs, which can be ordered by the piece.) The restaurant's official stance is that it doesn't take reservations, and you'll find a scrum of people crowding the doorways at dinnertime waiting for a table (although staff will usually take your name if you call ahead for a reservation before 6 pm). What you *can* reserve is one of the restaurant's two private dining rooms, which have a RMB1,500 minimum on food and beverage. That's very easily met if you have a table of at least 10.

87 Fumin Lu (nr. Yan'an Zhong Lu). ✆ **021/6249-5628.** RMB100–RMB200. Lunch 11am–2pm, Dinner 5:30pm–10:30pm. Subway: Changshu Rd.

Vegetarian Lifestyle ★★★ CHINESE VEGETARIAN This is the Chinese restaurant with the power to transform carnivores into vegetarians for life with little sacrifice. The all-veggie menu changes every few months, but the standbys, such as fake meat Kung Pao "Chicken," "pork" dumplings, and Wuxi-style "spareribs," will bring you back again and again. They do amazing, creative things with mushrooms, lotus roots, soybean-based products, and all kinds of other things you'd never thought would taste so good, including putting them into dumplings and deep-frying for satay with dipping sauces. As the Chinese get more and more health-conscious, they are starting to flock to organic, vegetarian options—but Vegetarian Lifestyle was the original, opening up in Shanghai in 2001. Prices are reasonable, and the menu comes with mouth-watering pictures for those who can't read Chinese. Lunch sets are a steal at less than RMB50, and include a soup, main, and rice. Those who enjoy upscale dining can try WUJIE The Bund, known for creative vegetarian fusion cuisine and started by the founder of Vegetarian Lifestyle after he donated his shares in that restaurant to charity.

258 Fengxian Lu (nr. Nanhui Lu). www.jujubetree.com. ✆ **021/6215-7566.** RMB100 per person. Daily 11am–9pm. Subway: West Nanjing Rd.

EASY bites

Shanghai has a number of Western-run chains that have an impeccable record of appealing to expat tastes, and will be of interest to anyone who's feeling jaded with Chinese cuisine after a long tour. Going since 1999, **Wagas** (www.wagas.com.cn) is now a national chain, specializing in sandwiches, wraps, pastas, and smoothies, all served up sans preservatives, additives, or MSG. Of the seven Shanghai restaurants, the most useful are in the Shanghai Center in Jing'an (1376 Nanjing Xi Lu) and Lujiazui's IFC Mall. **Element Fresh** (www.elementfresh.com) is one of the oldest expat "bankers" in Shanghai. It's American-managed, and does salads and sandwiches that are fresh, light, healthy, and an instant cure for any homesickness. There are outlets in Lujiazui's Super Brand Mall, the K.Wah Centre at 1028 Huaihai Zhong Lu, and Xintiandi. **Blue Frog** (www.bluefrog.com.cn) is a popular chain of American diners with outlets all over town. Portions are generous, the service is efficient, and there are discounted happy-hour drinks every day. There's a branch in the SWFC (see p. 226). Finally, **Kabb** (www.kabbsh.com) is an enduringly popular bistro bar. There are three branches, one in Xintiandi, another in the nearby iAPM mall (999 Huaihai Zhong Lu), and a final branch in the Kerry Center in Jing'an District (1238 Yan'an Zhong Lu).

Pudong

EXPENSIVE

Jade on 36 ★★ FRENCH Located on the top floor of the riverside wing in Lujiazui's oldest five-star hotel, Jade on 36 is as suave as ever, but far more accessible than in days gone by. This is a deliberate move on the part of chef Jeremy Biasiol, who looks to sell his homeland's famous fare not with flamboyant *haute cuisine* but on hearty, rustic portions made to share. Be sure to try the "Jade on 36 Garden," where you can pluck marinated mini-veggies from the onion mousse and edible "soil" like you're a community gardener. Prices are much reduced from the days when Paul Pairet (see "Ultraviolet" box, p. 240) ruled the roost, but the Adam Tihany-designed space remains gorgeous, and the views are simply divine. Be sure to request a window seat on reservation.

1/F, River Wing, Pudong Shangri-La Hotel, 33 Fucheng Lu. www.shangri-la.com/shanghai/pudongshangrila/dining/restaurants/jade-on-36. ✆ **021/6882-8888,** ext. 6888. Reservations recommended. Meal for two RMB250–RMB500. Mon–Fri 11:30am–1:30pm, Mon–Sun 5pm–10pm, Sun 11am–3pm. Subway: Lujiazui.

SHOPPING

Shanghai was raised on commerce, so it comes as no surprise to find a particularly virulent strain of the shopping bug coursing through the veins of most residents. During colonial days, Chinese from across the land dreamed of visiting the great port, not to sightsee, but to shop. Anything made or sold in Shanghai had the imprimatur of reliability and quality, a colonial equivalent of modern-day Germany. Many of the bourgeois merchants who made Shanghai (and themselves) wealthy before World War II fled to Hong Kong after the Communist revolution of 1949, transferring Asia's shopping crown in the process. However, Shanghai never lost her thirst for fine fashions and luxury goods. These days, the Shanghainese are able, and clearly willing, to snap up the best that both China and the wider world have to offer. The shopping experience has undoubtedly followed Hong Kong's lead in moving away from bustling street markets to increasingly large and luxurious malls. As part of the process, Shanghai's once notorious trade in fakes and knockoffs has come under serious strain, with crackdowns and street-beautification campaigns common. This said, Shanghai was never one to let rules and regulations get in the way of a good trade, and there are a few hidden spots. Even if you have no interest in doing your part for the Chinese economic miracle, it's still worth entering the fray (preferably with all your wits, commercial and otherwise, sharpened) to witness, if not join in, Shanghai's favorite pastime.

What to Buy

Furniture, old or new, in traditional Chinese styles can be purchased or custom-ordered at several antiques stores. Prices are high, but still lower than you'd pay at home; shipping, however, can add considerably to the bill.

Shanghai is also known for its selection and low prices in **silk** (both off the bolt and in finished garments). The Shanghainese people are connoisseurs of fashion and style, so shops selling **fashionable clothing** in cotton, wool, silk, and just about any imaginable material are a dime a dozen, and prices are low. **Traditional clothing** such as *qipao* (mandarin-collar dresses) and *mian ao* (padded jackets sometimes referred to as Mao jackets or Zhongshan jackets) are once again fashionable purchases.

Jewelry can be a bargain, particularly **jade, gold, silver,** and **freshwater pearls,** but bargaining and a critical eye are required. **Electronics, cameras,** and other high-tech goods are not particularly good buys, but if you need anything replaced, you'll find a wide selection from which to choose.

Among **arts and crafts,** there are also especially good buys in **ceramics,** hand-stitched **embroideries, teapots, painted fans,** and **chopsticks.** These are often sold in markets and on the sidewalks by itinerant vendors. Collectibles include **Mao buttons, posters of Old Shanghai** (covering everything from cigarette advertisements to talcum powder), old Chinese **coins, wood carvings,** and **screens**—all priced lowest at markets and stands. Other popular crafts made in Shanghai are **handbags, carpets, lacquerware, painted snuff bottles,** and **peasant paintings.** Prices vary considerably. The best rule is to find something you truly like, then consider how much it is worth to you.

Top Shopping Areas

Home to the first department stores in Asia, **Nanjing Dong Lu** (formerly Nanking Road) in the **Huangpu** district has long been Shanghai's most popular shopping street. Modern and traditional modes of retailing commingle at the **Nanjing Lu Pedestrian Mall,** though you're more likely to find souvenir novelties—cheap cheongsams or chopstick sets—than you are high-class goods. You'll be in the company of literally tens of thousands of people, mainly tourists, so don't expect to peruse at your leisure.

More refined shoppers should head to colonial Shanghai's "other" great shopping thoroughfare, **Huaihai Zhong Lu** (formerly Avenue Joffre), where you'll find a number of sleek Chinese-brand stores interspersed with names familiar from back home. Elsewhere in the rambling **French Concession** are a number of one-of-a-kind shops and outdoor mini-malls. There's a great cluster of stores on **Anfu Lu,** just west of Wulumuqi Bei Lu. Likewise, at the semi-circle formed by **Taojiang Lu** and **Dongping Lu,** on either side of Hengshan Lu. At 1 Hengshan Lu is perhaps the finest ceramics store in town, **Pureland** (www.pureland.cn; ✆ **021/6445-6806;** daily 10:30am–10:30pm), which sells trippy hand-painted porcelain busts and portraits. Some of the most interesting clothes and shoes in the French Concession are concentrated in the **Maoming Lu/Changle Lu** area. Meanwhile, in the south of the concession are the developments of **Xintiandi** (p. 216) and **Tianzifang** (p. 216). The former is the place to head for refined gifts for those more discerning friends back home, while the latter has a panoply of family-run craft stores and postmodern T-shirt shops.

In **Jing'an,** the area around **Jing'an Temple** is now a shopping mecca. The ever-popular Jiuguang Mall (Jiuguang Baihuo) rises from the Jing'an Temple subway station, while the streets immediately to the east and north of the temple itself are a riot of commerce. Suffice it to say the money-changers will not be thrown out anytime soon.

Down in the **Old City,** the **Yuyuan Bazaar** (see p. 209) is second only to Nanjing Dong Lu in the race for heaviest concentration of tourist stuff, though there are shops selling interesting local products along **Fangbang Zhong Lu.** The stretch between Yuyuan Bazaar and Henan Nan Lu is "Old Street," the place to head for local arts, crafts, and antiques, while east of the bazaar, it's packed with stalls selling cheap clothing.

The shopping in **Pudong** is mostly of the mall variety. See the section below for the best of these.

Malls

New malls go up in Shanghai with almost metronomic regularity, and keeping on top of the biggest, best, or brashest is next-to-impossible. Malls are often

bomb shelter SHOPPING

Purpose-built megamalls are crowded in Shanghai, and increasingly stuffed with identical big-brand names. For a refreshingly different, and quintessentially Chinese, shopping experience, check out the conjoined **D-Mall** and **Hong Kong Shopping Center** (daily 10am–10pm), one of several rambling arcades that encircle Shanghai's busiest subway stops. Formed from an old bomb shelter under People's Park, this rabbit warren of knock-off stores specializes in mid-to-low-end fashions, cosmetics, and jewelry. Underground shopping is a feature of many Chinese cities, and though the vibe tends to be down-market, the goods on sale are invariably cheap. Head to People's Park subway station on Line 2, and walk upstairs. You can't miss it.

of most interest to overseas visitors for people-watching or the usually excellent food courts within. **Nanjing Xi Lu** in the Jing'an District has three of Shanghai's oldest malls. **Plaza 66** (no. 1266) is at the base of a distinctive glass tower and carries wall-to-wall luxury brands. **CITIC Square** (no. 1168) is less chichi and has outlets by local designers, while the **Westgate Mall** (no. 1038) is the most charming of the three, resembling a Victorian-era railway waiting room. Farther west in Jing'an is the newer **Jing'an Kerry Center** (1563 Nanjing Xi Lu), which has clothes and electronics, as well as a cinema.

There are two other major concentrations of malls. The first is along **Huaihai Zhong Lu,** which has the new **iAPM** (no. 999), Shanghai's first "late-night" luxury mall. It goes until midnight every day and is generally packed. **One subway stop east are Times Square** (no. 99) and the **Hong Kong New World Plaza** (no. 300), two similarly mighty commercial plazas.

Another mini-mall cluster can be found in Lujiazui, Pudong. As in its original incarnation in Hong Kong, the **International Finance Center** has a luxury mall strung between two high-rise towers. The original and most spectacular of Lujiazui's malls is the **Super Brand Mall,** a mini-universe of electronics, fashions, accessories, and shoes with a South Beauty restaurant (see p. 244) taking up the top floor.

There are many other malls elsewhere in Shanghai, though the most likely destinations for readers of this book will be **Raffles City,** just to the east of People's Park (268 Xizang Zhong Lu), and the **Grand Gateway Mall** in Xujiahui (2118 Huashan Lu).

Markets & Bazaars

The once-renowned **Dongtai Lu Antiques Market** (Dongtai Lu, south of Chongde Lu) was hanging on to a handful of stalls as this book was going to press, but there were reports of imminent demolition, so it may not be around at all by the time you read this. It was once *the* place to buy crafts and curios, but it's an area that has come under pressure in recent gentrification. Nearby Xintiandi (p. 216) clearly has much to answer for.

The **Bird, Flower, Fish, and Insect Market** (Xizang Nan Lu, nr. Fuxing Dong Lu; subway: Laoximen) is not a million miles away but remains one of the few old-time markets that hasn't either been closed down or homogenized to death. There are a few jade stalls, but the main products are listed in the title and so may yield up obvious take-home gifts. Nevertheless, it's a wonderful place to wander for an hour or two, listening to (alternately) insect chirruping, birdsong, and crackly old-time radios of the mostly elderly vendors.

Bearing in mind that you're not going to find anything genuinely *antique*, the place to shop for old furniture, pendants, and porcelain is the **Fuyou Antiques Market** (457 Fangbang Zhong Lu, west of Henan Nan Lu; subway: Yuyuan Garden) on "Old Street." Three floors of the market building are open daily from 9am to 5pm, while the busier weekend market (on the third and fourth floors) runs from 5am to 6pm but tapers off by noon. There's more junk

faking IT

The disappearance of traditional markets over the last decade has partly been the result of beautification efforts, and partly a response to the huge quantity of counterfeit goods—luxury watches, designer bags, and choice Apple products included—which were freely changing hands. There are still a huge number of fakes, but they are now more dispersed across town. **Qipu Lu** is a favorite destination for "bargain hunters." The fakes are barely hidden within two huge, slightly dilapidated department stores around the road's junction with Henan Lu (subway: Tiantong Rd.). More central is **Han City Fashion and Accessories Market** (aka "The Fake Market," at 580 Nanjing Xi Lu, just west of the Chengdu Bei Lu flyover). It's between the People's Square and West Nanjing Road subway stations on the north side of the street.

than there are gems, but it can be a fun place to rummage for souvenirs. Expect to find "old" coins, Chairman Mao buttons, Buddhist statues, snuff bottles, and carved wooden screens. And be prepared to bargain hard.

Want a cashmere coat with tailor-made touches? The place for bespoke clothing remains the awkwardly named **South Bund Soft Material Spinning Market** (399 Lujiabang Lu, nr. Nancang Jie; subway: Nanpu Bridge). Textiles and made-to-measure outfits are sold from stalls along a series of claustrophobic corridors. Be ready to haggle and don't be surprised if prices end up being *higher* than what you might pay for retail ready-made garments in the West; vendors are well aware that tourists will pay for the privilege of custom-designing clothing. Expect to pay around RMB800 for a bespoke suit. There are plenty of ready-made shirts, scarves, ties, blankets, and other fabric knickknacks on offer also.

NIGHTLIFE

In the first half of the 20th century, Shanghai was the most notorious city in Asia, with a nightlife that rivaled that of Paris. Dubbed the "Whore of the Orient," old Shanghai presented countless opportunities for debauchery in its gambling dens, opium joints, nightclubs, and glamorous theaters. After the Communist Party came to power in 1949, Shanghai was cleaned up overnight; drugs and prostitution were ended by decree, and entertainment was reduced to a few politically acceptable plays and dances. Well into the 1990s, visitors retired to their hotels after dark unless they were part of a group tour going to see the Shanghai acrobats. In the last 20 years, however, the possibilities for an evening on the town have multiplied exponentially, and while Shanghai is not in the same league as Hong Kong or Paris quite yet, it is fast becoming once again a city that never sleeps.

Away from the major concert halls and theaters (of which Shanghai now has a surfeit, see below), the nightlife scene is a merry-go-round, with bars, clubs, and cocktail lounges opening and closing faster than night can turn to day. This is true of all major cities, perhaps, but in Shanghai the phenomenon is acute. Listed here are those venues that have stood the test of time, but there's still no guarantee they'll still be around when you visit. The best advice is to grab one of the expat magazines listed in the "Visitor Information" section (p. 196) and check out the latest news.

Bars, Pubs & Lounges

The big hotels often have elegant lounges on their top floors (see "Bars with a View" box, p. 252) and some of Shanghai's best bars around their lobbies. Independent spots outside the hotels run the gamut from upscale to down-and-dirty, but those listed here are frequented by plenty of English-speaking foreigners (residents and tourists alike) in addition to hip, well-to-do Shanghainese. In recent years, Shanghai's lively nightlife seems to have cleaved along the lines of the moneyed Bund crowd (favoring the many bars that have sprouted there) and those who wouldn't be caught dead anywhere near the place. Expect drink prices, especially for imports, to be fractionally higher than what you'd pay in the bars of a large city in the West. Tipping is not necessary, although bartenders are unlikely to complain.

For a decade, the **Bund** drinking scene was dominated by two bars, **Bar Rouge** ★ (7/F, Bund 18, 18 Zhongshan Dong Yi Lu) and Glamour. The latter fell victim to an overnight rent hike (the reason most Shanghai bars don't hang around long) in 2015, which put a question mark over how long the Bund's grand old lady can hang on. At the time of writing, she was still there, pulling in the jet set—alongside a sizable proportion of the high-class hooker community—with gorgeous views and creative drinks. The Bund's hottest property at the time of writing was **Unico** (2/F, Three on the Bund, 3 Zhongshan Dong Yi Li), a Latin-soul lounge in a grand space toward the south of the Bund strip.

Tucked away within the greenery of People's Park, **Barbarossa** ★★ (231 Nanjing Xi Lu, inside People's Park) has shown astonishing longevity through the years. It's both restaurant and lounge, comprising three floors of romantically lit interiors and maharajah chic. There's a fabulous rooftop terrace and half-price cocktails before 8pm.

The **French Concession** is where the best of the bars and lounges are hidden. **Constellation** ★★★ has expanded to three distinct venues over the years, though the wooden fixtures and leather furniture of the second iteration (33 Yongjia Lu, near Maoming Nan Lu) has the feel of a Victorian gentleman's club. Appropriately, whisky and cigars are among the most popular menu items. Set in a heritage villa in a sleepy corner of the French Concession, **Cotton's** ★★★ (132 Anting Lu, nr. Jianguo Xi Lu) exudes elegance and offers a warm welcome, helped by four open hearths. It's hugely popular with young expats. **Paulaner's** ★★ (150 Fenyang Lu, nr. Dongping Lu) is a German bar with a dozen outlets around the city. Its Shanghai HQ is by far the best for honest, Bavarian, beer-swilling fun. It's a gorgeous three-story mansion in the heart of the French Concession. **Shanghai Brewery** ★

(15 Dongping Lu, nr. Hengshan Lu) is an excellent microbrewery in the pleasant Dongping Lu area. Just across the way is the demure **Sasha's** lounge and restaurant ★★ (11 Dongping Lu, nr. Hengshan Lu), an old favorite set in a gorgeous 1920s French Concession villa with a patio out back. In the same compound is **Zapata's,** a cheap (in every sense of the word) and raucous disco where students (and the odd sleazy old dude) come to dance on the tables and prowl for mates come the weekend.

Xintiandi (see p. 216) is famous for its upscale restaurants and international shops. But this impressive development only truly comes alive after dark when Shanghai's hip and wealthy spill out of its pretty bars and lounges. The best-known are **DR Bar** (quiet and loungy), **TMSK** (bright and glam), and **Brown Sugar** (more clubby, with live music), though they're only worth visiting if you are already in the area. The same applies to the quieter bars and cafes of **Tianzifang** (see p. 216), including its oldest centerpiece bar, **Kommune.**

El Ocho ★★ (3/F, Bldg 3, 99 Taixing Lu, nr. Wujiang Lu) is a fabulous "craft" cocktail bar in a gorgeous new *shikumen* mini-mall on Taixing Lu. It's owned by Shanghai's most famous Spanish resident, chef Willy Trullas Moreno. The creative cocktails are served in a cool space with exposed-beam ceilings and long purple sofas.

BARS with a view

Shanghai's forest of high-rises, though spectacular to the newcomer, can tend to grind the long-term resident down. The remedy is to get out of the shadows, up onto the rooftops, and make like you *own* this town. It's virtually impossible *not* to feel like Donald Trump when looking out from **Flair** ★★★ (58/F, Ritz-Carlton Pudong, International Finance Center, 8 Shiji Da Dao). Despite the 58th-floor perch, there's a two-tier *outdoor* deck that overlooks a truly magisterial panorama. Equally amazing, the angle on the nearby Oriental Pearl TV Tower (see p. 225) is almost enough to make that monstrosity look *good.* Nearby **Jade on 36** ★★ (36/F, River Wing, Pudong Shangri-La, 33 Fucheng Lu) has no outdoor deck, and is certainly not the loftiest bar in town. However, the location, right on the Huangpu River, is peerless, and offers a spectacular lookout back toward the thicket of skyscrapers in Huangpu. The eccentric Adam Tihany design, complete with giant upturned lipstick case, is very much part of the appeal. Also in Lujiazui is **Cloud 9** ★ (87/F, Grand Hyatt, 88 Shiji Da Dao), worth visiting just to say you've been inside the gorgeous Jinmao Tower (p. 224). In its raw, metallic tones, Cloud 9 is supertrendy and remains begrudgingly tolerant of camera-toting tourists. **CHAR** ★ (31/F, Hotel Indigo, 585 Zhongshan Dong Er Lu) has some of the best bar views on the Puxi side of Shanghai. It's got an outdoor terrace that looks straight up the length of the Bund, while across the water are the glittering tower blocks of Pudong. **789 Nanjing Lu** ★ (66/F, Le Royal Meridien Shanghai, 789 Nanjing Dong Lu) is like a posh penthouse apartment smack-dab at Shanghai's geographic midpoint, with views to all corners of the city. Many of these bars only open at dusk, when happy-hour deals are common. There are few better places to watch the lights come on across one of the world's densest metropolises.

Dance Clubs

Shanghai has some of the most sophisticated and elaborate dance clubs and discos in China. Sadly, the minute they get popular, up go the rents and revelers are forced to look elsewhere for their late-night kicks. The dance-club scene relies heavily on DJs, whether foreign superstars brought in on a short engagement, or increasingly nimble locals. Though it's changed location a fair number of times, **Muse** ★ (5/F, 99 Beijing Dong Lu) has hung around long enough to become the daddy of Shanghai clubs. This is the most luxe version yet, with VIP lounges, KTV (karaoke) rooms, and a wading pool on a rooftop deck. It's a see-and-be-seen club, and attracts large groups of wealthy friends who think nothing of splashing several hundred bucks on a bottle of Dom Pérignon. Popular in the alternative scene is **The Shelter** ★★ (5 Yongfu Lu, nr. Wuyuan Lu), so named because it was built to protect the locals from World War II bombs. It resembles a London Underground station (with a bar where the trains should be) and serves drinks at student prices as well as heavy drum-and-bass beats. If Muse is too luxe and The Shelter too grungy, **The Apartment** ★ (44 Yongfu Lu, north of Fuxing Xi Lu) is the synthesis. It's more a lounge early on but has late-night DJs playing until 4am. The place expands over two floors and several rooms, and gets a decent mix of expats and locals.

The Performing Arts

Shanghai now has half a dozen world-class concert venues, several of which opened their doors in the last 5 years and boast the latest acoustic technology. Major international artists in fields as varied as opera, rock, and riverdance regularly tour here. Check the entertainment listings in the free English-language papers for tourists and expatriates for specific shows that may be on while you are in town (see "Visitor Information," p. 196).

ACROBATICS

Shanghai acrobatics are world renowned. The juggling, contortionism, unicycling, chair-stacking, and plate-spinning have firmly entered the age of high-tech staging. The near-nightly show at the Shanghai Circus World (*Shanghai Maxicheng*) is a Las Vegas–style variety act and a must-see when you're in town. **ERA: Intersection of Time** ★★★ (2266 Gonghe Xin Lu; www.era-shanghai.com; ✆ **021/5665-6622;** RMB80–RMB580; subway: Shanghai Circus World) is a stunning multimedia extravaganza and breathless display of organization, skill, and lionheart courage. Old Chinese acrobatic classics are blended with quite terrifying new stunts in a seamless performance that benefits from Cirque du Soleil-learned choreography. The Shanghai Acrobatic Troupe, one of the world's best, often tours the world but sometimes can be found performing at the **Shanghai Centre Theater (Shanghai Shangcheng Juyuan)** ★, at 1376 Nanjing Xi Lu (✆ **021/6279-8663**). Whether the big ticket troupe is in town or not, a 90-minute variety show begins nightly at 7:30pm, with tickets costing RMB100–RMB280. It's a far more traditional affair, but still worthwhile if you haven't got time to see ERA.

LIVE MUSIC

Shanghai was China's jazz city in the days before 1949 and is once again becoming the home of some of the most exciting jazz heard on the mainland. Many of the top-end hotel lounges and bars offer jazz performances, albeit of the easy-listening variety. Six musicians, including several octogenarians, perform easy-listening jazz at the **Old Jazz Bar** in the historic and recently renovated Fairmont Peace Hotel (20 Nanjing Dong Lu; nightly at 7pm), and a female vocalist joins at 9:45pm to add that old-time seductive edge. For more modern and improvisational sounds, check out the following spots: the smoky and long-running **Cotton Club** ★, at 8 Fuxing Xi Lu (www.thecottonclub.cn; ✆ **021/6437-7110**); the rather grander **House of Blues and Jazz** ★★, at 60 Fuzhou Lu (www.houseofbluesandjazz.com; ✆ **021/6323-2779**); and the jamming, jam-packed, and frankly brilliant **Club JZ** ★★★, at 46 Fuxing Xi Lu (www.jzclub.cn; ✆ **021/6431-0269**). Xintiandi's **Brown Sugar** (House 15, North Block; www.brownsugarlive.com; ✆ **021/5382-8998**) hosts international artists but is the most commercial of the venues here, with minimum-spends slapped on each table. Performances start around 9pm.

OPERA

Shanghai has its own Chinese opera troupe that regularly performs Beijing opera (*Jing Ju*) at the **Yifu Theatre** (701 Fuzhou Lu, east of Xizang Zhong Lu; ✆ **021/6351-4668**). Most opera performances consist of abridgements lasting 2 hours or less (as opposed to the "unabridged" 5-hour versions), and with their martial-arts choreography, spirited acrobatics, and fine costumes, these performances can be delightful. Regional operas, including the *Kun Ju* form, are also performed in Shanghai. Check with your hotel desk for schedules.

VAUDEVILLE & BURLESQUE

Various venues have tried to reinvigorate the burlesque traditions of raunchy old Shanghai over the years. The current star performer is **The Pearl** (71 Zhapu Lu, nr. Haining Lu; www.thepearl.com.cn; ✆ **137-6488-9962;** subway: Sichuan Bei Lu Hongkou district). Housed in a onetime Buddhist temple, The Pearl first became a burlesque club in colonial times when this part of town was known as "Chinatown" among expatriate residents. It's a glam, three-story space with a finely honed 1930s feel. Interspersed with cabaret performances are local theatre productions and music events.

SHANGHAI FOR KIDS

Shanghai is the most child-friendly city in China and will become all the more so when Disneyland opens in 2016 (see "Shanghai Disneyland" box). For a start, most of its parks actually allow kids to *play* on the grass, something that may shock Chinese and Westerners in equal measure—Chinese for the sheer audacity of the notion, Westerners for the (accurate) implication that there are parks in China where this is *not* the case. **Jing'an Sculpture Park** and **Century Park** (see p. 223) are perhaps the most interesting for kids. The former

SHANGHAI'S disneyland

Shanghai Disney Resort was still taking shape as this book went to press. Originally slated for a 2015 entrance, it should (*should*) be open by the spring of 2016. China had previously been wary of inviting in Disney, that great Trojan horse of American culture, and it's no surprise that the "joint venture" (majority-owned by a Chinese company) is described as a "Magic Kingdom–style Disney theme park" rather than a straight copy of what can be found in California and Florida. It's to be located on a 400-hectare (1,000-acre) site close to Pudong Airport, making it the third-biggest Disney theme park after the ones in Orlando and Paris. The centerpiece will be the largest and tallest Disney Castle in the world, featuring an underground boat ride. However, in addition to the usual rollercoasters, meet-and-greet opportunities, and themed "worlds," there is expected to be a number of Chinese stylings, including areas dedicated to indigenous mythical characters. Few specifics were confirmed as the book went to press, but suffice it to say that Shanghai, already the most child-friendly of Chinese cities, will likely become a veritable opium den for 21st-century kids in the very near future. Visit www.shanghaidisneyresort.com.cn to keep up with the latest news.

contains the excellent new **Natural History Museum** (see p. 221), while the latter has a minigolf course and an artificial beach, among other wily inducements. **Fuxing Park** (p. 213) and **Tianshan** and **Zhongshan Parks** in Changning District are also great for throwing a frisbee or flying a kite.

Lujiazui has a couple of obvious child-friendly attractions. The **Shanghai Ocean Aquarium ★★** is the largest in Asia (158 Yincheng Bei Lu; www.aquarium.sh.cn; ✆ **021/5877-9988;** admission RMB135 adults, RMB90 children under 1.4m/4½ ft., children under 80cm/2½ ft. free; daily 9am–6pm, open to 9pm July–Aug; subway: Lujiazui). Its state-of-the-art facilities boast 28 exhibit areas for more than 10,000 sea creatures from all continents: sharks, jellyfish, turtles, lionfish, sea otters, Yangzi sturgeon, and more. The centerpiece is the massive, sparkling, glass-surround observation tunnel. Nearby is the **Shanghai Wild Insect Kingdom** (1 Fenghe Lu; www.shinsect.com; ✆ **021/5840-5921;** RMB40 adults, RMB25 children; daily 9am–5pm; subway: Lujiazui), by no-means a "must-see," but with displays of live insects, reptiles, and amphibians, as well as a few hands-on exhibits, that will please little ones. The **Bund Sightseeing Tunnel** (see p. 201), which runs between Lujiazui and the Bund, may prove a mild diversion, but only take it if you're heading that way anyway as it's not exactly thrilling.

Elsewhere in Pudong is the **Shanghai Science and Technology Museum ★** (2000 Shiji Da Dao; www.sstm.org.cn; ✆ **021/6862-2000;** adults RMB60, children RMB20; Tue–Sun 9am–5:15pm; subway: Shanghai Science and Technology Museum), which is suitably modern but suffers a bit from dry English-language captions, steeped in the didactic style of Chinese education. Farther out again is the **Shanghai Wild Animal Park ★** (178 Nanba Gong Lu; www.shwzoo.com; ✆ **021/6118-0000;** adults RMB120, half-price children under 1.2m/4 ft.; daily 8am–5pm; subway: Safari Park), Shanghai's only drive-through safari, home to some 5,000 animals (200 species). Buses transport visitors through the grounds, and there's also a walk-through area with birds, monkeys, seals, and sea lions.

On the opposite side of Shanghai are a number of major child-oriented developments. The oldest is the **Shanghai Zoo ★** (2831 Hongqiao Lu, nr. Hongqiao Airport; ✆ **021/6268-7775;** RMB40, free for children under 1.2m/4 ft.; daily 7am–5pm, times vary slightly depending on season; subway: Shanghai Zoo). It's one of China's best, but still has a long way to go to equal the better preserves in the West. Spaces for animals are quite confined and depressing, but there is a panda center, playground equipment, and a Ferris wheel. **Dino Beach ★** (78 Xinzhen Lu; www.dinobeach.com.cn; ✆ **021/6478-3333;** RMB100 before 11am, otherwise RMB120, free for toddlers under 0.8m/31 in.; open Jul–Aug only, 9am–midnight; subway: Qibao, then taxi) is the best water park in Shanghai, boasting Asia's largest wave pool, a lazy river and rapids, eight water slides, and three pools for kids. **Jinjiang Amusement Park** (201 Hongmei Lu, nr. Huming Lu; ✆ **021/5420-4956;** RMB80 including six rides; daily 8:45am–5pm; subway: Jinjiang Park) is Shanghai's most complete modern amusement park (prior to Disneyland opening) and has a loop-the-loop rollercoaster. Finally, **Shanghai Changfeng Ocean World** (Gate 4 Changfeng Park, 451 Dadu He Lu; www.oceanworld.com.cn; ✆ **021/6223-8888;** adults RMB130, RMB90 for children between 1m and 1.4m/3¼ and 4½ ft., free for children under 1m/3¼ ft.; daily 8:30am–5pm; subway: Jinshajiang Rd.) is not as extensive as the Pudong aquarium but has a touch pool for kids to experience crabs, starfish, and urchins, as well as a penguin area and large tanks with underwater life from the Amazon to Antarctica.

DAY TRIPS FROM SHANGHAI

Of all the cities in this book, Shanghai is best positioned for out-of-town trips. The railways that radiate out in all directions have brought three of eastern China's prettiest and most historic cities within easy reach. They lie in a region informally known as Jiangnan—"south of the Yangtze." This is delta country, and even the biggest of cities are shot through with rivers and canals. Out in the countryside, beautiful water towns have been built around these waterways. They may not quite deserve the "Venice of the East" moniker some claim, but they make for a charming escape nonetheless.

9

SUZHOU ★

81km (50 miles) W of Shanghai

Suzhou is an ancient city lying at the heart of a modern sprawl. Its silk factories are the chief surviving elements of a cultural center that dominated China's artistic scene for long periods during the Ming and Qing dynasties. Now famed for its cobbled streets, genteel gardens, and interlocking canals, it is one of the many places that lay claim to the dubious "Venice of the East" label. Go with that in mind, and you'll most likely come back disappointed. Rapid development has robbed the city of much of its mystique. This said, the very heart of the city is a protected UNESCO-listed World Heritage site and retains a certain low-rise repose. If nothing else, it's completely different from Shanghai, and the rail link makes it a very straightforward day trip.

Getting There

All **trains** heading from Shanghai in westerly or northerly directions go through Suzhou, meaning there are more than 10 trains an hour between the two cities, running from very early until past 10pm. However, Shanghai to Suzhou is the one route in this book where it's *not* recommended to jump on the very fastest train you can find. Most G-class bullet trains depart from Shanghai Hongqiao, in Shanghai's west, and arrive at Suzhou North, a newly built station a ways outside the city. The overall journey time isn't long enough to justify the hassle of getting to these sparkling new suburban stations.

Suzhou

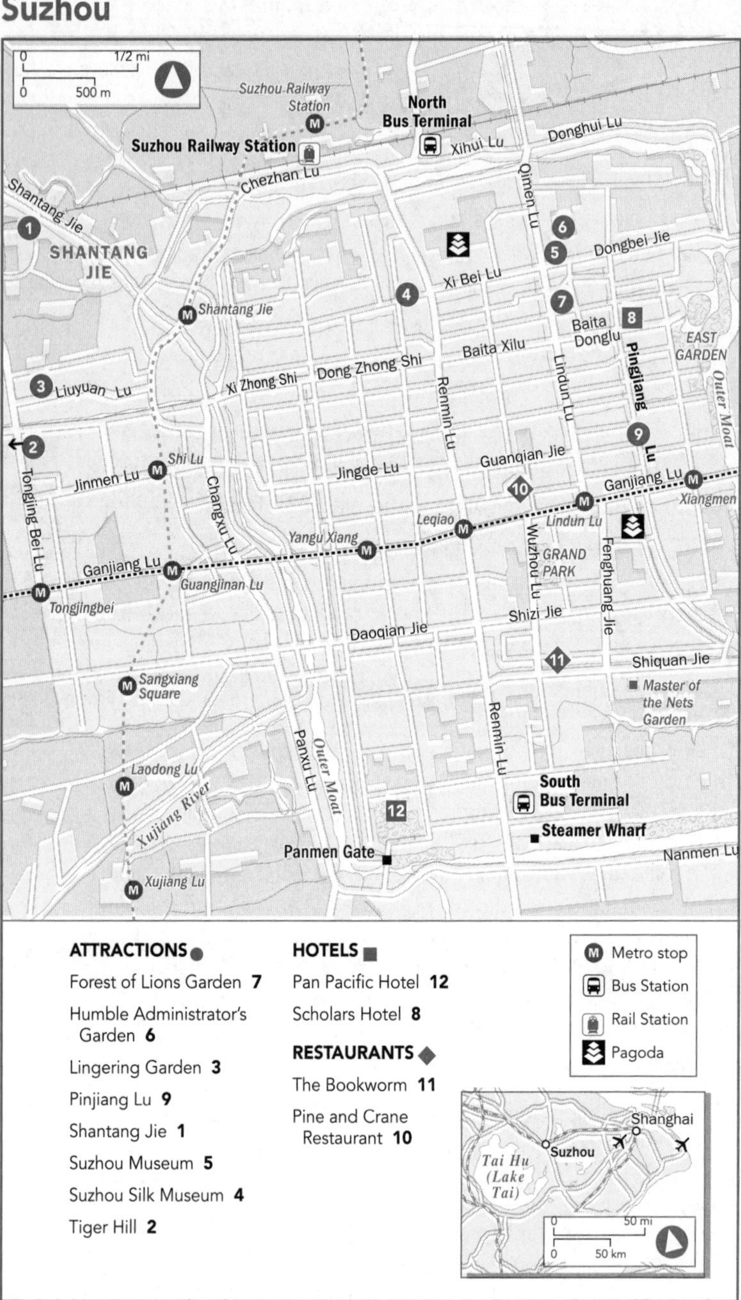
0 1/2 mi
0 500 m
Suzhou Railway Station
North Bus Terminal
Suzhou Railway Station
Xihui Lu
Donghui Lu
Chezhan Lu
Shantang Jie
SHANTANG JIE
Qimen Lu
Dongbei Jie
Xi Bei Lu
Shantang Jie
Baita Donglu
Baita Xilu
EAST GARDEN
Liuyuan Lu
Xi Zhong Shi
Dong Zhong Shi
Renmin Lu
Lindun Lu
Pingjiang Lu
Outer Moat
Shi Lu
Jinmen Lu
Changxu Lu
Jingde Lu
Guanqian Jie
Ganjiang Lu
Xiangmen
Lindun Lu
Leqiao
Yangu Xiang
Wuzhou Lu
GRAND PARK
Fenghuang Jie
Tongjing Bei Lu
Ganjiang Lu
Guangjinan Lu
Tongjingbei
Shizi Jie
Daoqian Jie
Shiquan Jie
Master of the Nets Garden
Sangxiang Square
Renmin Lu
Panxu Lu
Outer Moat
Laodong Lu
Xujiang River
South Bus Terminal
Steamer Wharf
Panmen Gate
Nanmen Lu
Xujiang Lu
ATTRACTIONS
Forest of Lions Garden 7
Humble Administrator's Garden 6
Lingering Garden 3
Pinjiang Lu 9
Shantang Jie 1
Suzhou Museum 5
Suzhou Silk Museum 4
Tiger Hill 2
HOTELS
Pan Pacific Hotel 12
Scholars Hotel 8
RESTAURANTS
The Bookworm 11
Pine and Crane Restaurant 10
Metro stop
Bus Station
Rail Station
Pagoda
Shanghai
Suzhou
Tai Hu (Lake Tai)
0 50 mi
0 50 km

Plenty of trains still run from Shanghai Railway Station to Suzhou's main station, both much nearer their respective city centers. Most of these take an hour (versus 30 min. on high-speed rail), but there are a handful of quick trains that depart from here too. Be careful you get on a train going to "Suzhou" rather than "Suzhou North," and don't get out at the "Suzhou Industrial Park" that comes just before the city proper. Fast-train tickets in a second-class seat will cost RMB39.5 and can be easily bought at the station on the day of travel, though you may have to line up (see p. 284 for more on buying train tickets). The last train back from Suzhou main to Shanghai main departs at 10:23pm.

Suzhou is also well connected by **bus** to Shanghai, but the train really is a no-brainer. Likewise, almost all Shanghai agents will have **tours** to Suzhou, but it's just as easy, a lot more fun, and a whole lot cheaper to see the town on your own.

Getting Around

At the time of writing, there were two **subway** lines in Suzhou. Line 1 runs east to west, cutting through the center of the ancient city, where there are four stops. Line 2 skirts the western fringe of the city but connects both railway stations. By the time you read this, Line 4 may well be open. This looks to be the most useful line, cutting north to south and running from Suzhou Railway Station down past, or close to, nearly all of central Suzhou's main sights. Additionally, **tourist buses** depart from close to the north exit of Suzhou Railway Station along five routes. **Rickshaws** are a popular means of exploring Suzhou city center and can be hired for specific journeys by the hour for leisurely exploration. **Taxis** are numerous and relatively easy to hail. The base fare is RMB13.

Exploring Suzhou

Central Suzhou, surrounded by remnants of a moat and canals linked to the Grand Canal, is a protected historic district, 3.5km (2¼ miles) across, in which no skyscrapers are allowed. More than 170 bridges arch over the 32km (20 miles) of slim waterways within the moated city. The poetic private gardens number about 70, with a dozen of the finest open to public view. No other Chinese city contains such a concentration of canals and gardens.

Classic Gardens

Suzhou's magnificent, and formerly private, gardens are small, exquisite jewels of landscaped art often choked with visitors—making a slow, meditative tour difficult. The designers of these gardens aimed to create the illusion of universal scale within a limited setting by borrowing from nature and integrating such elements as water, plants, rocks, and buildings. Poetry and calligraphy were added as the final touches. Listed below are some classic gardens worth visiting.

Forest of Lions Garden (Shizi Lin Yuan) ★★ GARDEN Built in 1342 by a Buddhist monk to honor his teacher and reportedly last owned (privately) by relatives of renowned American architect I. M. Pei, this large garden consists of four small lakes, a multitude of buildings, and big chunks of tortured rock that are supposed to resemble lions. Many of these oddly shaped rocks come from nearby Lake Tai (Tai Hu), where they were submerged for a very long time to achieve the desired shapes and effects. During the Song Dynasty (A.D. 960–1126), rock appreciation reached such extremes that the expense in hauling stones from the lake to the capital (then Kaifeng) is said to have bankrupted the empire. Containing the largest rocks and most elaborate rock gardens in Suzhou, the Forest of Lions Garden can be a bit ponderous, but then again, you won't see anything like this anywhere else. The garden is located at 23 Yuanlin Lu (✆ **0512/6727-2428**). It's open daily from 7:30am to 5:30pm; admission is RMB30 from April to October, RMB20 from November to March.

Humble Administrator's Garden (Zhuo Zheng) ★ GARDEN Usually interpreted as "Humble Administrator's Garden" but also translatable, tongue-in-cheek, as "Garden of the Stupid Officials," this is the largest of Suzhou's gardens, dating from 1513 and making complex use of the element of water. Linked by zigzag bridges, the maze of connected pools and islands seems endless. The creation of multiple vistas and the dividing of spaces into distinct segments are the garden artist's means of expanding the compressed spaces of the estate. As visitors stroll through, new spaces and vistas open up at every turn. This is probably the busiest of the gardens, and the crowds can dampen the enjoyment of the space. Located at 178 Dongbei Jie (✆ **0512/6751-0286**), the garden is open daily from 7:30am to 5:30pm; admission is RMB90 from April to October, RMB70 from November to March.

Lingering Garden (Liu Yuan) ★★ CLASSICAL GARDEN This garden in the northwest part of town is the setting for the finest chunk of Lake Tai rock in China, a 6m-high (20-ft.), 5-ton contorted castle of stone called Crown of Clouds Peak (Juyun Feng). Composed of four sections connected by a 700m-long (2,297-ft.) corridor, the Lingering Garden is also notable for its viewing pavilions, particularly its **Mandarin Duck Hall,** which is divided into two sides: an ornate southern chamber for men, and a plain northern chamber for women. Lingering Garden is located at 80 Liuyuan Lu (✆ **0512/6533-7940**). It's open daily from 8:30am to 6pm; admission is RMB55 from April to October, RMB45 from November to March.

Master of the Nets Garden (Wangshi Yuan) ★★★ GARDEN Considered to be the most perfect, and also smallest, of Suzhou's gardens, the Master of the Nets Garden is a masterpiece of landscape compression. Hidden at the end of a blind alley, its tiny grounds have been cleverly expanded by the placement of walls, screens, and pavilion halls, producing a maze that seems endless. The eastern sector of the garden consists of the residence of the former owner and his family. At the center of the garden is a small pond encircled by verandas, pavilions, and covered corridors, and traversed by two arched stone bridges. Strategically placed windows afford different views of bamboo, rock gardens, water, and inner courtyards, all helping to create an illusion of the universe in a garden. In the northwest part, don't miss the lavish **Hall for Keeping the Spring (Dianchun Yi),** the former owner's study furnished with lanterns and hanging scrolls. This was the model for the Astor Chinese

Garden Court and Ming Furniture Room in the Metropolitan Museum of Art in New York City. The Master of the Nets Garden is located at 11 Kuotao Xiang, off Shiquan Jie (✆ **0512/6529-3190**). It's open daily from 7:30am to 5:30pm; admission is RMB40 from April to October and RMB30 from November to March. In the summer months, the garden opens again between 7:30 and 10pm, when lights are switched on and evening performances of traditional music and dance are staged (RMB100).

Tiger Hill ★ PARK This multipurpose theme park can be garishly tacky in parts, but it's also home to some local historic sights, chief among them the remarkable leaning **Cloud Rock Pagoda (Yunyan Ta)** at the top of the hill. Now safely shored up by modern engineering, this leaning seven-story octagonal pagoda dating from A.D. 961 is thought to be sitting on top of the legendary grave of He Lu, the King of Wu during the Spring and Autumn period (770–464 B.C.) and Suzhou's city founder. He Lu was reportedly buried with his arsenal of 3,000 swords, his tomb guarded by a white tiger, which was said to have appeared 3 days after the king's death (hence the name of the hill).

Partway up Tiger Hill is a natural ledge of rocks, the **Ten Thousand People Rock (Wanren Shi),** where, according to legend, a rebel delivered an oratory so fiery that the rocks lined up to listen. Another version claims they represent He Lu's followers who were buried along with him, as was the custom at that time. A deep stone cleavage, the **Pool of Swords (Jian Chi),** runs along one side of it, reputedly the remnants of a pit dug by order of Qin Shihuang, the first emperor, who was searching for the 3,000 swords. Tiger Hill is located 3km (2 miles) northwest of the city at 8 Huqiu Shan (✆ **0512/6532-3488**). It's open daily from 7:30am to 6pm; admission is RMB80 from April to October and RMB60 from November to March.

WATER GATES & CANALS

The canals that crisscross the city center have not been well tended over the years and many have simply been built over. Perhaps the best place to have an extended stroll beside the water in central Suzhou is **Pinjiang Lu,** which runs between the Humble Administrator's Garden and Ganjing Dong Lu. Once a ragbag of steaming snack stores and knockoff vendors, it's been cleaned up in recent years and is now stacked with trendy cafes and boutiques along much of its 1km (½-mile) length. With willow trees lining the street and several arched bridges crossing the water, it's a picturesque stroll, though this hasn't gone unnoticed by the tourist masses who throng here at weekends. For those more interested in the scenery than in the food and shopping opportunities, try to arrive early. The after-dark atmosphere can also be charming if you don't mind the noise and bustle. There's a ticket office for **boat rides** toward the northern end.

In the northwest part of town, near the Lingering Garden, is **Shantang Jie,** chock-full of Suzhou's old houses, narrow alleyways, arched bridges, and canals. It too has come in for tourist development in recent years (even boasting its own subway stop) and is heavily commercialized in parts. Nevertheless, there's a certain charm to the architecture and ambience, and you can take a gondola ride here (RMB50 per person for 30 min. approx.).

MUSEUMS

Suzhou is synonymous not only with gardens and canals, but also with silk. Its silk fabrics have been among the most prized in China for centuries, and the art of silk embroidery is still practiced at the highest levels. The **Suzhou Silk Museum (Suzhou Sichou Bowuguan),** at 2001 Renmin Lu (✆ **0512/6753-6538**), just south of the railway station, takes visitors through the history of silk in China, with an interesting section on sericulture complete with silkworms, cocoons, and mulberry leaves. Weavers demonstrate on traditional looms. The museum is open daily from 9am to 5pm. Admission is free.

Opened in 2006, the **Suzhou Museum (Suzhou Bowuguan),** just west of the Humble Administrator's Garden at 204 Dongbie Jie (✆ **0512/6757-5666;** www.szmuseum.com), was the last design of U.S. architect I. M. Pei's career. It combines characteristics of a typical Suzhou garden with modern geometric designs, and is worth a visit both for the building and its well-laid-out collection of locally discovered cultural relics, including an exquisite Pearl Pillar of the Buddhist Shrine from the Northern Song Dynasty. The museum is open Tuesday to Sunday, 9am to 5pm (last admission 4pm). Again, admission is free.

Where to Stay & Eat

Most of the newest and most luxurious hotels are located outside the city moat. If you plan to spend the night in Suzhou, staying close to the central sights is heartily recommended. A traditional favorite for its quintessential Chinese garden setting is the former Sheraton Hotel and Towers, now the **Pan Pacific Suzhou,** 259 Xinshi Lu, near Pan Men in the southwest corner of the old city (www.panpacific.com/suzhou; ✆ **0512/6510-3388**). This five-star hotel receives rave reviews for its Chinese-style buildings, which blend seamlessly into the environment. If you want to be in the heart of the old town, try the **Scholars Hotel** at 60 Baita Dong Lu (pingjiangpalace.com; ✆ **0512/6770-6688**). It's a Chinese-managed hotel, but the rooms have a certain boutique charm, and the location, just west of Pingjiang Lu, is excellent.

Although hotel restaurants serve the most reliable fare and accept credit cards, Suzhou has a number of good restaurants. Many are located on **Taijian Nong,** also known as "Gourmet Street," near Guanqian Jie, one of Suzhou's main drags. Maybe the most famous local restaurant on this street is the 200-year-old **Pine and Crane Restaurant (Song He Lou)** at 72 Taijian Nong (✆ **0512/6727-2285;** daily 8am–9pm), which serves specialties such as squirrel-shaped Mandarin fish (*songshu guiyu*) and the exquisitely shredded pan-fried turnip cake (*luobosi subing*). The tourist street of **Pingjiang Lu** has a variety of restaurants and cafes, while **The Bookworm** at 77 Shiquan Jie (www.suzhoubookworm.com; ✆ **0512/6526-4720**) is a lovely bookstore-restaurant-cafe offering coffees, smoothies, and sandwiches to cure any homesickness.

TONGLI ★★

80km (49 miles) W of Shanghai

If post-development Suzhou fails to evoke the canal charm you were expecting, try **Tongli,** 20km (12 miles) southeast. It's one of the most interesting and easily navigable of the many water towns that developed centuries ago around the busy canal-based trading networks within the Yangtze Delta. It's also an easy day trip, either from Shanghai or nearby Suzhou. For information on other, similar options, see the "The Water Towns of Jiangnan" box.

Getting There

Buses depart from the **Shanghai Sightseeing Bus Center** at 8:30am, returning from Tongli at 4pm (90 min.; RMB130, including the standard RMB100 entrance to the old town). It's a lengthy walk from the drop-off point to the main gate of the old town, though shuttles run regularly (RMB5).

Tongli Bus Station is a 5-minute walk from the old town. Here you can pick up regular **buses** to Suzhou (50 min.; RMB8) and Shanghai (90 min.; RMB31). Tongli is close enough to Suzhou that **taxi** drivers should be willing to make the trip, though you may need to bargain a price. Expect offers in the region of RMB100.

Getting Around

Tongli is small and compact, compared to many water towns. Maps are available at the main ticket office. It's simple to make a loop of the town **on foot,** but six-person wooden **boats,** propelled by gondoliers, can be hired (RMB70 for 30 min. approx.).

Exploring Tongli

The main attraction in Tongli is the **Retreat and Reflection Garden (Tuisi Yuan)** ★, in the center of the old town. Built in 1886 by a dismissed court official, the garden contains the family's residences in the west, meeting and entertaining rooms in the center, and a small but cleverly designed landscaped garden in the east. The use of winding walkways with different-shaped windows, jutting pavilions, and a reflecting pond make the garden appear larger than it is. West of the garden are two of the town's better-preserved traditional residences. **Jiayin Tang,** built in the 1910s as the residence of a famous local scholar, Liu Yazi, has high white walls and doorways topped with upturned eaves. The highlight at **Chongben Tang,** also with four courtyards and three doorways, is the refined brick, stone, and wood carvings of propitious symbols such as cranes and vases. Connecting the two residences are three bridges (*qiao*) named after **peace** (*taiping*), **luck** (*jili*), and **glory** (*changqing*) respectively. It was the custom in the old days to carry a bride in her sedan chair over all three. Today, tourists can don proper wedding finery and also be carried across the bridges in an old-fashioned sedan chair. Tongli was once famed for housing the excellent **China Sex Culture Museum,** a private collection of carnally themed carvings and statuettes. It was previously housed in

Tongli

ATTRACTIONS ●
Luoxing Zhou 3

RESTAURANTS ◆
Nanyuan Chashe (Nanyuan Teahouse) 1
Xiangge Jiulou (Shanger Restaurant) 2

Information
Gondolier Pier
TKTS Ticket Office

Dongxi Jie
Tuisi Yuan (Retreat and Reflection Garden)
Xinzhen Jie
Zhongchuan Bei Lu
Dechun Bridge
Chongben Hall (Chongben Tang)
Jiayin Hall (Jiayin Tang)
Changqing Qiao (Glory Bridge)
Tai'an Bridge
Ming Qing Street (Ming Qing Jie)
Taiping Qiao (Peace Bridge)
Jili Qiao (Luck Bridge)
Ding Zi River
Shangyuan Gang
Gengle Hall (Gengle Tang)
TKTS
ENTRANCE
To Shanghai
To Suzhou

THE water towns OF JIANGNAN

The area known informally as **"Jiangnan"** (literally, "south of the river") encompasses parts of Shanghai and neighboring Jiangsu and Zhejiang provinces. The "river" in question is the mighty Yangtze, and this area was once the heart of China's economy, its matrix of waterways channeling goods toward Beijing via the Grand Canal. Many merchant villages sprung up along these routes, and some now survive as water towns (*shui zhen*). The largest and most famous of these are **Zhouzhuang** (www.zhouzhuang.com) and **Wuzhen** (www.wuzhen.com.cn). **Xitang** (www.xitang.com.cn) is also very popular, largely thanks to a single, flying visit by Tom Cruise a decade ago while filming "Mission Impossible 3." All three towns are served by daily buses from the **Shanghai Sightseeing Bus Terminal** at the Shanghai Stadium. However, mass tourism has taken hold, and you'll likely find yourself being carried along the lanes, over the humpback bridges, and down cobbled alleys by a never-ending stream of chattering tour groups. Perhaps the quietest (though hardly undiscovered) town is **Nanxun** (www.chinananxun.com), close to the city of Huzhou, but it's also the remotest and tricky to get to. If time is short, consider visiting either Qibao or Zhujiajiao as a half- or full-day excursion from Shanghai. They are both within Shanghai city limits, and unlike the other places mentioned here, free to enter. **Qibao** is the easiest of all, located a few steps away from the eponymous station on Line 9 of the Shanghai subway. There's only one single central canal, dissected by a cobbled street. In the northern section, there are souvenir and knickknack stores, while a food street occupies the southern half. Qibao also has one of the oldest churches in Shanghai, built in 1867. Though not spectacular, Qibao is still worth stopping by, especially if this is the only chance you'll get to see a water town. **Zhujiajiao** is more of a traditional water-town *destination*, a charming matrix of burbling brooks, arched bridges, and whitewashed houses. It's only a 30-minute ride on the tourist bus that departs the Shanghai Sightseeing Bus Terminal at 9am and returns at 3:45pm (RMB12 one-way). If you have time, staying the night is highly recommended. The local authorities put on musical performances after dark when the atmosphere is wonderfully romantic.

Shanghai's Bund Tourist Tunnel but was pushed out to Tongli. Awkwardness among local officialdom struck again in 2014, when it was exiled once more, this time to Hainan Island.

Where to Stay & Eat

It's possible to bed down for the night in one of Tongli's privately run waterside guesthouses. Expect to negotiate a price, and be sure to check out the room before you agree to stay. Staying over has definite benefits. The crowds thin out massively after dark, and the waterside night scenes are lovely. There are several small restaurants along **Ming Qing Jie** that serve basic peasant dishes at reasonable prices; a meal for two averages about RMB75. **Nanyuan Chashe,** located in a restored Qing-dynasty building, serves tea and local snacks. Local specialties include *zhuangyuan ti* (the Tongli version of braised pigs' trotters), *xiao xunyu* (small smoked fish), and *min bing* (a sweet glutinous rice pastry).

Hangzhou

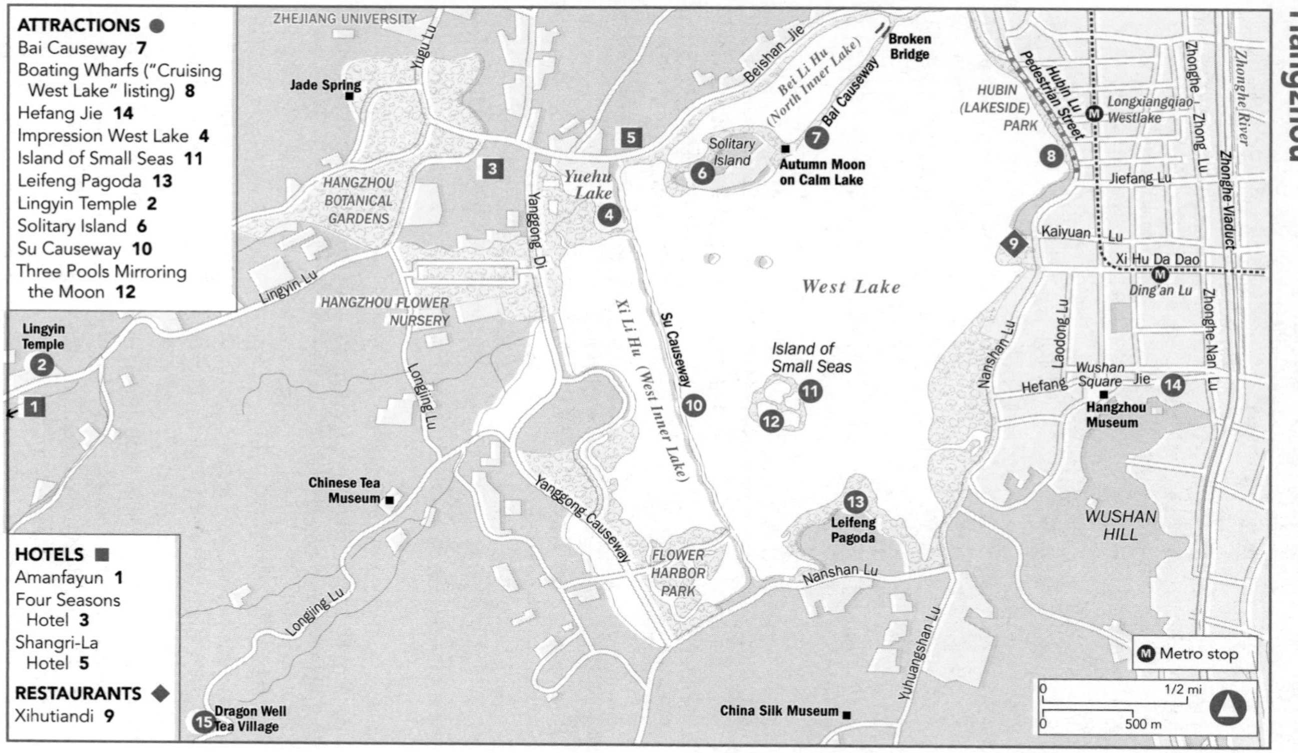
ATTRACTIONS ●
Bai Causeway 7
Boating Wharfs ("Cruising West Lake" listing) 8
Hefang Jie 14
Impression West Lake 4
Island of Small Seas 11
Leifeng Pagoda 13
Lingyin Temple 2
Solitary Island 6
Su Causeway 10
Three Pools Mirroring the Moon 12
HOTELS ■
Amanfayun 1
Four Seasons Hotel 3
Shangri-La Hotel 5
RESTAURANTS ◆
Xihutiandi 9
Metro stop
1/2 mi
500 m
ZHEJIANG UNIVERSITY
Yugu Lu
Jade Spring
Beishan Jie
Bei Li Hu (North Inner Lake)
Broken Bridge
Bai Causeway
Solitary Island
Autumn Moon on Calm Lake
HUBIN (LAKESIDE) PARK
Hubin Lu Pedestrian Street
Longxiangqiao-Westlake
Zhonghe Zhong Lu
Zhonghe River
Zhonghe Viaduct
Jiefang Lu
Kaiyuan Lu
Xi Hu Da Dao
Ding'an Lu
Zhonghe Nan Lu
HANGZHOU BOTANICAL GARDENS
Yuehu Lake
Yanggong Di
Lingyin Lu
HANGZHOU FLOWER NURSERY
West Lake
Xi Li Hu (West Inner Lake)
Su Causeway
Island of Small Seas
Nanshan Lu
Laodong Lu
Wushan Square
Hefang Jie
Hangzhou Museum
Lingyin Temple
Longjing Lu
Chinese Tea Museum
Yanggong Causeway
Leifeng Pagoda
WUSHAN HILL
FLOWER HARBOR PARK
Yuhuangshan Lu
Dragon Well Tea Village
China Silk Museum

HANGZHOU ★★★

185km (115 miles) SW of Shanghai

Seven centuries ago, Marco Polo pronounced Hangzhou "the finest, most splendid city in the world…where so many pleasures may be found that one fancies oneself to be in Paradise." Hangzhou's claim to paradise has long been centered on its famous **West Lake (Xi Hu),** surrounded on three sides by verdant hills. The islets and temples, pavilions and gardens, causeways and arched bridges of this small lake (about 5km/3 miles across and 14km/9 miles around) have constituted the supreme example of lakeside beauty in China ever since the Tang dynasty, when Hangzhou came into its own with the completion of the Grand Canal (Da Yunhe) in A.D. 609. Hangzhou reached its zenith during the Southern Song dynasty (A.D. 1127–1279), when it served as China's capital. In 2003, much to the horror of purists, West Lake was enlarged in the western section with an additional causeway along its new western shoreline. New sights, shops, and restaurants were added to the eastern and southern shores.

Getting There

Trains run at regular intervals throughout the day between Shanghai and Hangzhou. The vast majority now depart the **Shanghai Hongqiao Railway Station** (on Line 2 of the subway). Some still leave from the Shanghai South and Shanghai railway stations, but day-trippers will be wanting the fastest trains that travel the 185km (118-mile) route in as little as 45 minutes. These all depart from Hongqiao. Second-class seats are RMB73 each way. Most trains now arrive at the new **Hangzhou East Railway Station,** 8km (5 miles) northeast of West Lake. The old railway station is 2km (1¼ miles) due east of the lakeshore. Both are on Line 1 of the Hangzhou subway. The last train back to Shanghai departs at 10:25pm. All trains after 8:30pm leave from Hangzhou East Railway Station.

There are plenty of **buses** traveling between Shanghai and Hangzhou, but they are a lot less convenient than trains and take far longer. For those wanting to make a beeline to Hangzhou, a direct bus (RMB100) departs from Shanghai Pudong International Airport (✆ **021/6834-5743**) and runs between 8:40am and 8pm. The overall journey time is 3 hours, slightly longer than if you travel across the city by subway and jump on the next fast train, but infinitely more convenient. You're dropped near Wulin Square (Wulin Guangchang) in the center of the city.

Hangzhou also has an **airport** (www.hzairport.com) with an international terminal (Terminal A) that lies about a 30-minute drive from downtown. There are connections to Beijing and other Chinese cities, but not Shanghai (which is too close) or destinations in North America, Europe, or Australia.

Getting Around

The city surrounds the northern and eastern shores of West Lake, with green hills to the south and west. The lake is best explored on foot and by boat, while sights farther afield will require a taxi or bus (or a bicycle, if you are very fit). **Taxis** cost RMB11 for 3km (1¾ miles), then RMB2 per kilometer until 10km (6¼ miles) and RMB3 per kilometer after that. Air-conditioned **buses** cost RMB2, while tour buses with a Y-prefix cost RMB3 to RMB5. Bus no. K7 runs from the railway station to the Lingyin Temple via the northern shore of the lake at Beishan Lu, and bus no. Y1 makes a loop of the lake, stopping at various intervals. Hangzhou now has a **subway** system, easing the traffic on the often-clogged urban roads. There are three lines at the time of writing, with five more planned, though these are most useful for getting to and from the two railway stations (both on Line 1) rather than attractions. The closest station to the lake is the **Longxiang Qiao** station, on Line 1. Get out at Exit C and walk west for 5 minutes along Pinghai Lu to meet the eastern lakeshore. **Bikes** are great for making a loop of the lake (3 hr.) and can be rented from dozens of public rental points around the city. Despite the hassle, it's worth investing some time to apply for the Smart Card you'll need. There are four points within reach of the lake where this can be done. The easiest will probably be at the Hangzhou Bus IC Card Service Center at 20 Longxiang Lu (✆ **0571/8533-1122;** near Exit B of the **Longxiang Qiao** subway station). The others are: the main entrance of Orioles Singing in the Willows Park (Liulang Wenying) at 11 Nanshan Lu; the main entrance of Wushan Square (Wushan Guangchang) on Hefang Jie (near Yan'an Lu); and the main entrance of Youth Palace (Qingshaonian Gong) at Beishan Lu and Baochu Lu. You'll need to bring your passport and pay a RMB300 deposit, including RMB100 of stored value. These cards can be used to rent a bike from dozens of racks around the city. The first hour is free, with the charge going up by around RMB1 for every hour thereafter.

Visitor Information

Hangzhou has a tourist information hot line (✆ **0571/96123;** www.96123.com) and a network of tourist information points (including a branch at the West Lake Museum, and one near the ticketing point for the Lingyin Temple).

Exploring Hangzhou

WEST LAKE (XI HU)

Originally a shallow lagoon, West Lake gained its modern appearance in two mammoth projects—the first in the 11th century, the second in the 15th—which saw tens of thousands of laborers dredging and extending the lake to its current size. Strolling the lake's shores and causeways and visiting the tiny islands by tour boat should be at the heart of any visit to Hangzhou. A **Lakeshore Promenade ★★**—a combination walkway and roadway—encircles the lake, with the busiest parts along the eastern edge of the lake. The once-busy thoroughfare Hubin Lu has now become a pedestrian walkway, home to such outlets as Starbucks and Häagen-Dazs, while the area immediately to the south around Nanshan Lu and Xihu Da Dao is now known as **Xihutiandi** (West Lake Heaven and Earth), a miniature version of Shanghai's Xintiandi, right down to the *shikumen*-style (stone-frame) housing and with some of the exact same restaurants. Following are the top attractions around the lake:

BAI CAUSEWAY (BAI DI) ★★ WALKWAY Solitary Island is connected in the east to downtown Hangzhou by **Bai Di,** a man-made causeway providing one of the finest strolls around West Lake. Named after famous Tang dynasty poet Bai Juyi, who served as prefectural governor here in A.D. 822 to 824, the causeway runs east for half a mile, rejoining the north shore road at **Broken Bridge (Duan Qiao),** so named because when winter snows first melt, the bridge appears from a distance to be broken.

CRUISING WEST LAKE ★★ TOUR All along the lakeshore, but particularly on Hubin Lu near Gushan Dao (northwest corner of the lake), there are boats for rent, with choices ranging from 3m-long (10-ft.), heavy wooden rowboats (where you take the oars) to small junks propelled by the owner's single oar, to full-fledged ferries—flat-bottomed launches seating 20 under an awning. To tour the lake in a small junk costs around RMB120 for an hour. Larger passenger ferries sell tickets for RMB50, which includes entrance to the Island of Small Seas (below). Ticket booths are across the street from the Shangri-La Hotel on Beishan Jie to the north of the lake, and along the east side of the lake.

ISLAND OF SMALL SEAS (XIAO YING ZHOU) ★★ LANDMARK Make sure your boat docks on this island at the center of West Lake. The **Island of Small Seas** was formed during a silt-dredging operation in 1607. As a Chinese saying goes, this is "an island within a lake, a lake within an island." Its form is that of a wheel with four spokes, its bridges and dikes creating four enclosed lotus-laden ponds. The main route into the hub of this wheel is the **Bridge of Nine Turnings,** built in 1727. Occupying the center is the magnificent **Flower and Bird Pavilion,** an exceedingly graceful structure that is notable for its intricate wooden railings, lattices, and moon gates, though it only dates from 1959. It's open daily from 8am to 5pm; admission is RMB20 (included if you take a large passenger ferry to the island).

LEIFENG PAGODA (LEIFENG TA) ★ LANDMARK On the south bank of West Lake, this modern steel-and-copper pagoda affords some of the best panoramic views of the lake. Beneath the modern construction are the brick foundations of the original Buddhist pagoda built in A.D. 977. The bricks you see were part of an underground vault used to store precious Buddhist relics, including a rare woodcut sutra, which was found among the ruins. The pagoda and surrounding gardens are open daily from 7:30am to 9pm (to 5:30pm Dec–Mar); admission is RMB40.

SOLITARY ISLAND (GUSHAN DAO) ★ LANDMARK/PARK Situated just off the lake's northwest shore, this large island is accessible via the Xiling Bridge in the west and the Bai Causeway in the northeast. A roadway sweeps across the island, which is home to a number of minor sights, including **Zhongshan Park** (open daily sunrise–sunset; free admission), which was once part of the old Southern Song imperial palace built in 1252, though nothing remains of it. A climb to the top of the hill affords views of the lake to the south. Also here is Hangzhou's famous restaurant, **Lou Wai Lou,** and the large **Zhejiang Provincial Museum (Zhejiang Sheng Bowuguan), © 0571/8798-0281,** which contains the oldest grains of cultivated rice in the world (developed 7,000 years ago in a nearby village). The museum is open Monday from noon to 4pm and Tuesday through Sunday from 9am to 4pm; free admission.

SU CAUSEWAY (SU DI) ★★ WALKWAY The best view from the land of the Three Pools Mirroring the Moon (see below) is from the Su Causeway, the original great dike that connects the north and south shores along the western side of the lake (a third causeway added in 2003, the Yanggong Di, running parallel to the west, is primarily for vehicles and is not as scenic). Running nearly 3km (1¾ miles), Su Causeway, named for Hangzhou's poet-governor Su Dongpo (A.D. 1036–1101), is lined with weeping willows, peach trees, and shady nooks, and crosses six arched bridges. Near the southern tip is the **Flower Harbor Park (Huagang Yuan),** open 8am to 6pm with free admission, where there's a peony garden and ponds full of fat carp and goldfish.

THREE POOLS MIRRORING THE MOON (SAN TAN YINYUE) ★ Located just off the southern shore of the Island of Small Seas are three little water pagodas, each about 2m (6½ ft.) tall, that have "floated" like buoys on the surface of West Lake since 1621. Each pagoda has five openings. On evenings when the full moon shines on the lake, candles are placed inside. The effect is of four moons shimmering on the waters. Even by daylight, the three floating pagodas are quite striking.

OTHER ATTRACTIONS

Dragon Well Village (Longjing Wencha) ★ MUSEUM/SHOPPING West of West Lake is the village of **Longjing** (literally "Dragon Well"), the source of Hangzhou's famous Longjing tea**,** grown only on these hillsides and revered throughout China as a supreme vintage for its fine fragrance and smoothness. The best tea here is still picked and processed by hand. A popular stop near the village is the **Chinese Tea Museum (Zhongguo Chaye Bowuguan),** open daily from 8:30am to 4:30pm. Here, you can comb through the extensive displays of Chinese teas, pots, cups, and ceremonial tea implements. Admission is free.

Dragon Well Village itself, a few miles beyond the museum, is where much of the tea is grown and processed. Independent travelers are sometimes accosted by local farmers who will invite them into their homes, ply them with tea, and sell them a few pounds at inflated prices. This can actually be a good opportunity to buy this relatively expensive vintage at the source if you know how to bargain. The highest-grade **West Lake Longjing (Xi Hu Longjing)** retails in Hangzhou's stores for around RMB68 to RMB88 per 50 grams (2 oz.), so aim for a price well below that. It also helps if you are—or are with—a tea connoisseur, as vendors may sometimes try to pass off last year's vintage as the most recent. Caveat emptor!

Lingyin Temple (Lingyin Si) ★★ TEMPLE Located in the lush hills just west of West Lake, Lingyin Temple has been rebuilt a dozen times since its creation in A.D. 326. Don't expect to find much peace here, though, as the surrounding area seems to have been turned into one large amusement park, with prices to match. Entrance to the Lingyin Valley (open daily 7am–5:30pm) costs RMB100, while entrance to the temple itself is a separate RMB80. To get the most out of a visit, expect to spend the best part of the day here.

The main attraction on the way to the temple is a limestone cliff, called **Feilai Feng** (the "Peak That Flew from Afar"), so named because it resembles a holy mountain in India seemingly transported to China. The peak, nearly 150m (492 ft.) high, contains four caves and about 380 Buddhist rock carvings. The most famous carving is of a Laughing Buddha from the year A.D. 1000. Scholars have deemed these stone carvings the most important of their kind in southern China.

The present temple buildings go back decades rather than centuries. The Great Hall (Daxiong Baodian) contains a gigantic statue of Buddha carved in 1956 from 24 sections of camphor and gilded with nearly 3kg (6½ lb.) of gold—the largest sitting Buddha in China, and not a bad modern recreation.

If you want to get away from the crowds, farther west along the pathway past the main Lingyin Temple is the quiet and pretty **Temple of Goodness (Yongfu Si),** set amid groves of bamboo and willow. A climb to the Grand Hall at the top allows wonderful views of the surrounding hills and even glimpses of West Lake on a clear day. More exalted views are available at two other temples even higher up, **Taoguang Guanhai Si** and the 1,600-year-old **Lingshun Si,** which sits atop **North Peak Mountain (Beigao Feng)**. It's a fairly strenuous climb to the top, or you can take the cable car from behind the Lingyin Temple, though expect to line up for a ride.

Where to Stay & Eat

Most of the Western-branded hotels in Hangzhou are in the city, away from the lakeside. The **Shangri-la Hotel Hangzhou ★** (www.shangri-la.com; ✆ **0571/8797-7951**) is one of the first five-stars to make it to West Lake and has a great location at 78 Beishan Lu, just beside Solitary Island (Gushan Dao), but it's no longer the most luxurious hotel around. That honor probably belongs to the **Four Seasons Hangzhou ★★** (www.fourseasons.com/hangzhou; ✆ **0571/8829-8888**) at 5 Lingyin Lu. It's a sprawling, beautifully landscaped resort, well placed for exploring both the lake and the mountains, the latter rising up behind. Perhaps the loveliest, though most expensive resort, is **Amanfayun,** hidden away in the hills just west of Lingyin Temple ★★★ (www.amanresorts.com; ✆ **0571/8732-9999**). This is more a retreat than a tourist hotel. Private villas are designed as detox spa retreats, with TVs only available if you specifically request them, and low, moody lighting the order of the day.

For dining, **Lou Wai Lou ★★** (✆ **0571/8796-9023**; 30 Gushan Lu) is a Hangzhou institution. Though undoubtedly touristy, it has a great lakeside location on Solitary Island, and serves solid interpretations of all of

Hangzhou's signature dishes, including Beggar's Chicken (*Jiaohua Ji*) and West Lake Vinegar Fish (*Xi Hu Cuyu*), served in a sauce the color and consistency of molasses. There are international restaurants at **Xihutiandi** on the eastern shore of the lake, or a clutch of dumpling houses and family-run restaurants along **Gaoyin Jie,** one block north of the busy shopping street of **Hefang Jie**.

Hangzhou After Dark

If you're staying overnight in Hangzhou, the **Impression West Lake ★★** night show, 82 Beishan Lu (close to the Shangri-la Hotel Hangzhou; www.hzyxxh.com/en; ✆ **0571/8796-2222**), is a must-see. Performed on Yue Lake (a subsection of West Lake), it was choreographed by Zhang Yimou, the famed movie director who directed the opening ceremony for the Beijing Olympics. The show incorporates the natural landscape with stunning use of light and music, employing hundreds of local actors. The show keeps the natural surroundings intact with eco-friendly initiatives, including the audience seats perched above the lake, which retract into the water during the day. The hour-long show is performed every night at 7:45pm, and on Saturday there's also a second show at 9:15pm. Tickets come in a range of price categories but are generally very expensive. Ask your hotel to book you a seat.

NANJING ★

Jiangsu Province, 306km (189 miles) NW of Shanghai

Capital of the nation in the early years of the Ming (A.D. 1368–1644) and the first half of the 20th century, seat of the Heavenly Kingdom during the bloody Taiping Rebellion, and the site of one of history's most infamous massacres, this bustling city of eight million has a tumultuous past. It's often left off many China itineraries as, with one or two notable exceptions, it lacks visible reminders of its storied history. Suzhou and Hangzhou remain more scenic day-trip destinations, but history enthusiasts will like Nanjing more.

Getting There

Trains run at regular intervals throughout the day between Shanghai and Nanjing. The majority depart the **Shanghai Hongqiao Railway Station** (on Line 2 of the subway), while a handful still run from Shanghai's central railway station. Second-class seats are RMB134.5 each way. Most trains now arrive at **Nanjing South,** a newly built station on the fast-track to Beijing. The old railway station is closer to the middle of town. Both are on Line 1 of the subway. The last fast train back to Shanghai departs at 10:14pm, though slower sleeper trains run throughout the night.

Nanjing has its own airport, just under 50km (31 miles) southwest of the city, and daily **flights** connect to Beijing and Xi'an. However, if traveling from Shanghai, rail is the way to go. Nanjing has several **long-distance bus stations,** the main one located just west of the Nanjing Railway Station at 1 Jianning Lu. However, for day-trippers, train is the only option.

Nanjing

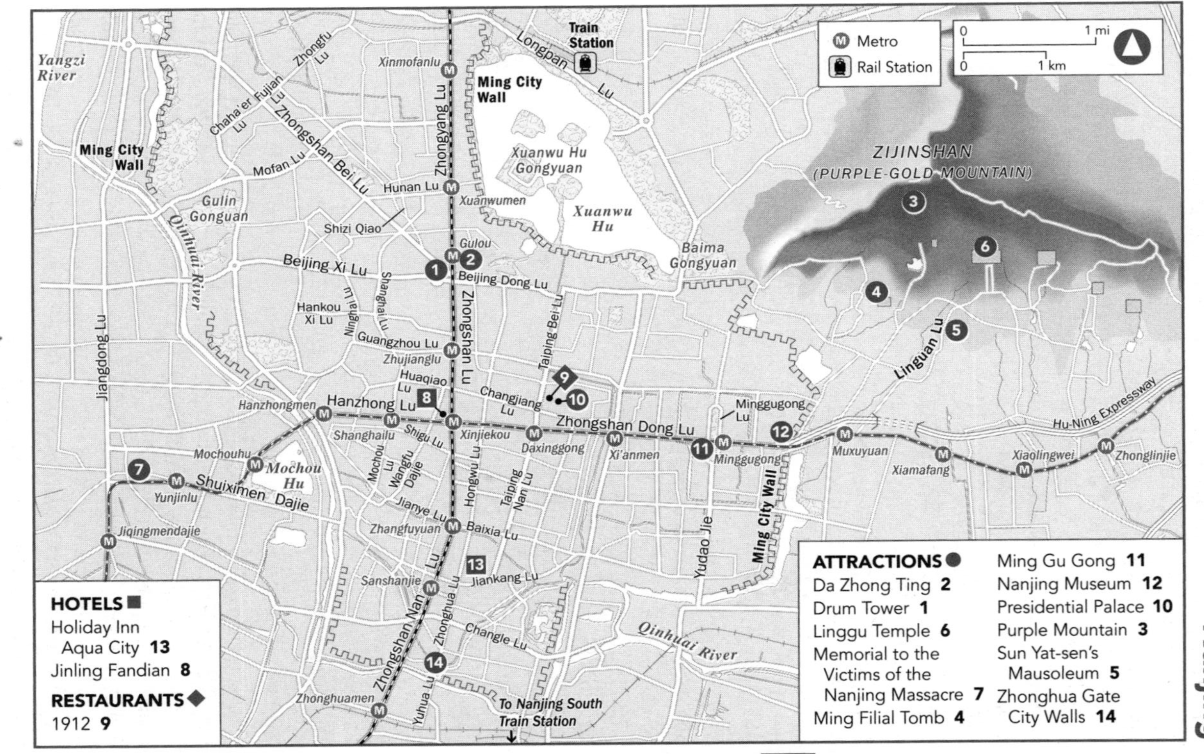
Metro
Rail Station
0 1 mi
0 1 km
Yangzi River
Ming City Wall
Train Station
Longpan Lu
Zhongfu Lu
Chaha'er Lu
Fujian Lu
Zhongshan Bei Lu
Xinmofanlu
Zhongyang Lu
Xuanwu Hu Gongyuan
Xuanwu Hu
Mofan Lu
Hunan Lu
Xuanwumen
Gulin Gonguan
Qinhuai River
Shizi Qiao
Gulou
Baima Gongyuan
ZIJINSHAN
(PURPLE-GOLD MOUNTAIN)
Beijing Xi Lu
Beijing Dong Lu
Ninghai Lu
Shanghai Lu
Hankou Xi Lu
Zhongshan Lu
Taiping Bei Lu
Jiangdong Lu
Guangzhou Lu
Zhujianglu
Huaqiao Lu
Linguan Lu
Changjiang Lu
Hanzhong Lu
Hanzhongmen
Minggugong Lu
Zhongshan Dong Lu
Hu-Ning Expressway
Shanghailu
Shigu Lu
Xinjiekou
Daxinggong
Xi'anmen
Minggugong
Muxuyuan
Xiamafang
Xiaolingwei
Zhonglinjie
Mochouhu
Mochou Hu
Mochou Lu
Wangfu Dajie
Hongwu Lu
Taiping Nan Lu
Shuiximen Dajie
Yunjinlu
Jianye Lu
Yudao Jie
Ming City Wall
Jiqingmendajie
Zhangfuyuan
Baixia Lu
Sanshanjie
Jiankang Lu
Zhongshan Nan Lu
Zhonghua Lu
Changle Lu
Qinhuai River
Zhonghuamen
Yuhua Lu
To Nanjing South Train Station
HOTELS
Holiday Inn Aqua City 13
Jinling Fandian 8
RESTAURANTS
1912 9
ATTRACTIONS
Da Zhong Ting 2
Drum Tower 1
Linggu Temple 6
Memorial to the Victims of the Nanjing Massacre 7
Ming Filial Tomb 4
Ming Gu Gong 11
Nanjing Museum 12
Presidential Palace 10
Purple Mountain 3
Sun Yat-sen's Mausoleum 5
Zhonghua Gate City Walls 14

Getting Around

Nanjing is a sprawling city not particularly conducive to walking, with sights scattered in different directions. The rate for **taxis** is RMB9 for 3km (2 miles), then RMB2.4 per kilometer. From 11pm to 6am, the price rises to RMB2.7 per kilometer after 3km. All taxi rides come with a RMB2 fuel surcharge. The **subway** is a fast and convenient way to get around town. There are currently four lines and two suburban subway routes (one that connects the airport). Lines 1 and 2 dissect the middle of the city and are the most useful for central attractions. Tickets are RMB2 to RMB4, depending on distance. **Buses** are a cheap way to get around Nanjing but difficult to use and not recommended.

Visitor Information

Nanjing has a bilingual magazine, "Map," which features information on wining, dining, and entertainment in the city in both English and Chinese. It's available in most of the top hotels and Western restaurants.

Exploring Nanjing

Sadly, Nanjing's Ming legacy can be found in only a few buildings and ruins today. In the center of town, the **Drum Tower (Gu Lou)** ★ was built in 1382 and contained a series of drums used to mark the night watches, welcome guests, and occasionally warn of approaching enemies (admission to grounds free, RMB5 to enter the second floor of tower and teahouse; subway: Gu Lou). Close by is a pavilion, **Dazhong Ting,** which houses a 25-ton bronze bell, cast in 1388. Toward the eastern part of town are the ruins of the first Ming dynasty imperial palace, the **Ming Gu Gong.** All that remains of the once massive palace, destroyed in the Taiping Rebellion, is the **Meridian Gate (Wu Men)** that once marked the front gate of the palace wall, five small marble bridges, and 12 large plinths that were once the foundation of another large gate. Sections of the Ming **city wall** are still visible here.

Memorial to the Victims of the Nanjing Massacre (Nanjing Datusha Jinianguan) ★★ MONUMENT/MUSEUM This memorial combines a number of graceful and stark outdoor monuments with an emotionally grueling museum covering the inhumanities perpetrated by occupying Japanese forces in 1937 and 1938. The somber atmosphere is horrifyingly explained in the series of photographs and video testimony. The site itself was an execution-and-mass-burial site during the invasion. The final room documents the reconciliation, however tenuous, between the Chinese and Japanese.

418 Shuiximen. Free admission. Tue–Sun 8:30am–4:30pm. Subway: Yunjin Lu.

Nanjing Museum (Nanjing Bowuguan) ★★ MUSEUM This excellent museum is worth at least an hour or two of your day in Nanjing and can be visited on the way to or from nearby Purple Mountain. The main hall is in the form of a temple and houses a reasonably engaging narration of Chinese history, from the prehistoric to the modern, while the new building to the left

THE TAIPING heavenly kingdom

During the mid-19th century, natural disasters, catastrophic floods and famines, aggressive incursions by Western colonial powers, and government neglect and corruption had all coalesced to create widespread unrest in China. It was in such a setting that the largest uprising in modern Chinese history occurred, the **Taiping Rebellion.**

The rebellion started in the mind of Hong Xiuquan (born Hong Huoxiu, 1814–64), a teacher and a farmer's son from Guangdong Province. After Hong failed his civil-service exams for the third time, he had a feverish dream of a bearded man and a younger man. Having been exposed to Christian-missionary material, Hong concluded these were the Holy Father and Jesus. Hong also kept seeing part of his own name, "Huo," in his Chinese version of the Bible, which he interpreted as another divine calling. He convinced himself that he was in fact Jesus' younger brother, and that his mission from his heavenly father was to "slash the demons"—the Manchu government and traditional Chinese folk religion. To this end, Hong formulated his own ideology, a mix of Christian ideals and Confucian utopianism. He soon amassed a large anti-Manchu, anti-establishment following in the south, and in 1851, led a group of 20,000 followers to establish the **Taiping Heavenly Kingdom,** with Hong himself as leader. Using their army and numerous ragtag peasant militias they mustered along the way, the Taipings swept up through south and central China and established themselves in Nanjing in 1853, renaming the city Tianjing (Heavenly Capital).

The Taipings preached a new order based on the equal distribution of land, equality between the sexes, monotheism, and the existence of small communities ruled by religious leadership. Save for the religious aspects, this was an order that prefigured the tenets of the Chinese Communist movement. Feudalism, slavery, concubinage, arranged marriages, opium-smoking, foot-binding, prostitution, idolatry, and alcohol were all to be abolished (at least in theory). While women under the Taiping were allowed a greater degree of freedom (there was even a Taiping army made up entirely of female troops), Taiping morals continued to stress obedience and chastity in women.

In the end, however, the Taipings were stymied by a combination of internecine struggles, corruption, defections, and flawed policies. However, the decade-long "project" only became doomed when Britain, the foremost colonial power of the time, decided to throw its weight behind a reconstituted Qing army. In theory, Taiping ideals and methods were closer to their own than those within the Qing court, but the British decided they would rather deal with the devil they knew than contend with the uncertainties of a fanatical Taiping force. The counterattack was brutal and merciless, and by the time the Chinese army succeeded in crushing the revolt, 14 years after it began, a reported 30 million lives had been lost. Some have put the figure as high as 100 million, which would make the rebellion the bloodiest conflict in human history. Hong Xiuquan himself died of illness in 1864, and his successor, his 14-year old son, was killed by Qing troops.

holds most of the artistic treasure. Standouts here include the **Lacquerware Hall,** with an exquisitely carved Qing dynasty throne; the **Jadeware Hall,** featuring an Eastern Han–dynasty jade burial-suit sewn together with silver from A.D. 200; and the **Fabric Embroidery Hall,** where visitors can view a demonstration of cloud-pattern brocade-weaving on an old-fashioned loom.

The basement level houses a nice folk-art section and earthenware from the Tang dynasty. The museum shop sells a wide selection of art and crafts.

321 Zhongshan Dong Lu. Free admission with passport. Daily 9am–5pm. Subway: Mingugong.

Presidential Palace (Zongtong Fu) ★ MUSEUM This palace has borne witness to most of the important events and personalities in Nanjing's modern history. It was the base of the Liangjiang Viceroy (a regional governor) during the Qing dynasty (1644–1911), as well as nerve-center for the Taiping Heavenly Kingdom (1853–64). It was where Sun Yat-sen held his inauguration as president on January 1, 1912, and ran his short-lived provisional government. And it was the seat of the Nationalist government on either side of the Japanese invasion (1927–37 and 1946–49). Though the palace site dates from the Ming dynasty, all today's buildings were built after 1870.

The palace has undergone a massive renovation in recent years and more areas have been opened up, with suspiciously new-looking fittings in places. In addition to the gleaming exhibition halls and relic sites, there are gardens and boardwalks to explore. In Xu Yuan, the garden on the western side of the compound, a stone boat is the only remaining original artifact from the days of the Taiping Heavenly Kingdom.

292 Changjiang Lu. RMB40. Daily 7:30am–5pm. Subway: Daxinggong.

Purple Mountain (Zijin Shan) ★ MAUSOLEUM/PARK/TEMPLE Covered with dense forests and dotted with the occasional lake, the mountain on the eastern edge of town got its name from the mountain's shales, which are said to have lent the place a mysterious purple glow at dawn and dusk. It's long been a retreat for locals seeking relief from Nanjing's infamous heat and is easily big enough to consume an entire day. There's a cable car, tourist trains, and lots of pleasant parkland. Of most interest to day-trippers will be the historic tombs and temples that dot the mountain's foothills. For RMB140, you can buy a combination ticket that will give you access to the three biggies (listed below), while a shuttle bus (RMB5) runs between these sights from morning until evening. If time is tight, head straight for **Sun Yat-sen's Mausoleum (Zhongshan Ling) ★★**, the magnificent mausoleum of Dr. Sun Yat-sen (aka "Sun Zhongshan"), widely revered as the founder of modern China (RMB80; daily 6:30am–6:30pm). The tomb itself is at the end of a long, steep set of stairs beginning with a memorial archway made of white Fujian marble and capped by blue glazed tiles. It has become a mecca for Chinese tourists seeking to pay their respects. On the way down, you'll be treated to a glorious view of downtown Nanjing. Make sure to get here early or late in the afternoon, as the place fills up like a zoo. The **Ming Filial Tomb (Ming Xiao Ling) ★** is the tomb of the founder of the Ming dynasty, Zhu Yuanzhang (1328–98), also known as the Hongwu emperor (RMB70; daily 6:30am–6:30pm). Zhu Yuanzhang was the only Ming emperor to be buried in Nanjing, and the tomb served as a model for the subsequent (and now more famous) Ming and Qing emperors' tombs in Beijing. Explanations of the tombs are in

THE NANJING massacre

On December 13, 1937, Japanese troops invaded Nanjing. What followed were the darkest six weeks of Nanjing's history, as over 300,000 Chinese were bayoneted, shot, burned, drowned, beheaded, and buried alive. The city was looted and torched, and corpses were thrown into the Yangzi River. Women suffered the most: During the first month of occupation, 20,000 cases of rape were thought to have taken place in the city. Many of those who survived were tortured.

During this time, a small number of Western businessmen and American missionaries, who stayed behind when their compatriots fled after the departing Chinese government, used their privileged status as foreign nationals to create a 3.9 sq. km (1½-sq.-mile) safety zone covering today's Hanzhong Lu in the south, Zhongshan Lu in the east, Shanxi Lu in the north, and Xikang Lu in the west. Around 250,000 Chinese found safe haven in 25 refugee camps inside it. The head of the safety zone was German businessman John Rabe, chosen in part because he was a Nazi. Often described as the Oskar Schindler of China, Rabe's initial determination to save his Siemens Chinese employees eventually took on a larger purpose as he even sheltered hundreds of Chinese women in his own backyard. There were countless individual moments of courage, too, as Chinese clawed their way out of mass graves, crawled to hospitals with bullet wounds, or sheltered their brethren at great risk to themselves.

Chinese only, but the area is more peaceful than Sun Yat-sen's mausoleum, and the architecture is stirring. Hidden amid the tall conifers east of Sun Yat-sen's Mausoleum is **Linggu Temple (Linggu Si)**. It's a beautiful-looking building, though the interiors now house ersatz waxworks of modern leaders (RMB35; daily 6:30am–6:30pm). Purple Mountain is best accessed from Xiamafang station on Line 2 of the subway. Shuttle buses run from here into the park itself.

Zhonghua Gate City Walls (Zhonghua Men Chengbao) ★★ MONUMENT Located in the southern part of town, this is the biggest and best-preserved of the city wall's original 13 gates. Built by the Hongwu emperor between 1366 and 1386, the wall, at 33km (20 miles), was the longest city wall in the world at the time, made of uniform bricks cemented with a mortar of lime, sorghum, and glutinous rice. Zhonghua Gate actually consists of four rows of gates, the first one 53m (173 ft.) long. Each gate entrance had a vertically sliding stone door lifted with a mechanical winch. Twenty-seven arched vaults inside the first gate could house up to 3,000 soldiers, who were set to ambush the enemy should the latter be so unfortunate as to be trapped within the gates. Climb to the top for some good views of the city, and to gaze at the kitschy fake guards. Along the way, watch for bricks that still bear the carvings of their maker and supervisor. In front of the walls, locals fly kites bought from vendors for RMB8.

Admission RMB35. Daily 8am–9:30pm. Subway: Zhonghuamen.

Where to Stay & Eat

The glut of upmarket hotels in Nanjing generally results in generous discounts. Despite being Chinese-managed, the **Jinling Fandian** has maintained its reputation since it opened in 1983 and has a great central location at 2 Hanzhong Lu (www.jinlinghotel.com; ✆ **025/8472-2888**). A solid low-priced alternative is the **Holiday Inn Nanjing Aqua City** at 1 Jiankang Lu (www.ihg.com; ✆ **020-3349-9520**), near the bustling shopping and dining streets around Confucius Temple as well as the Zhonghua Men city walls. There are several upmarket, modern restaurants in **1912,** a restaurant-and-bar district on the corner of Changjiang Lu and Taiping Bei Lu. 1912 has been constructed to create an "Old China" feel: gray stone, traditional roofs, and pedestrian walkways. It's touristy, for sure, but comfortable if you've had a long day, with Western standbys like KFC and Starbucks, and branches of popular Shanghai restaurants such as **Bellagio** and **South Beauty.** Other lively places to grab a late-night bite include **Shizi Qiao,** a popular pedestrian restaurant street off Hunan Lu, and the **Confucius Temple (Fuzi Miao)** area, close to the Sanshan Jie subway stop, which attracts swarms of people after dark.

PLANNING YOUR TRIP TO CHINA

This chapter provides a variety of planning tools, including information on how to get to China, how to get around, and the inside track on local resources.

It wasn't so long ago that foreigners were banned from visiting most of the Chinese mainland, had to use a completely separate currency, and had to struggle along with virtually nobody speaking a word of English. These days, traveling in China is much less of a challenge. If you can manage Paris without speaking French, you'll be okay in Beijing without having any Mandarin, not least because nobody will *expect* you to speak it. You can arrange various levels of assistance, either upon arrival or from home, but you can also travel independently just as freely as you would elsewhere. Flights are ticketless and easily booked online, train tickets can be couriered to your hotel for a few dollars, while hotel rooms can be snagged at a moment's notice through smartphone apps.

GETTING THERE

By Plane

The vast majority of Western visitors to China arrive by plane. Beijing Capital International Airport **(PEK)** and Shanghai Pudong International Airport **(PVG)** are the major mainland hubs for international flights, each served by a wide range of international and domestic carriers. Xi'an Xianyang International Airport **(XIY)** currently has no direct flights to North America, Europe, or Australia.

You should select your hub airport according to where you want to travel, and consider flying into one and out of another if that fits your itinerary and you can get a reasonable fare. Costs are often only slightly higher than if the ticket is booked as a traditional round-trip, and because China is so big, you may save nearly an entire day of your schedule. See Chapter 2 for some suggestions of how this might work.

There is no departure tax on either domestic or international flights, and all taxes and fees are included in ticket prices.

FROM NORTH AMERICA Among North American airlines, **Air Canada, American Airlines, Delta Airlines,** and **United Airlines** fly to Beijing and Shanghai. **Hawaiian Airlines** flies to Beijing only. **Air China** and **Hainan Airlines** fly directly to Beijing, while **China Eastern** flies directly to Shanghai. **Japan Airlines** and **All Nippon Airways** fly via Tokyo to Beijing and Shanghai. **Korean Air** and **Asiana Airlines** fly via Seoul to the same two cities.

FROM THE UNITED KINGDOM **British Airways** and **Virgin Atlantic** fly to Beijing and Shanghai, and **China Eastern** flights head directly to Shanghai. There are many creative routes flying via mainland Europe or the Persian Gulf States.

FROM AUSTRALIA & NEW ZEALAND **Air China** and **Qantas** have direct flights from Australia to Beijing and Shanghai. **China Eastern** flies directly to Shanghai. **Air New Zealand** offers direct flights from Auckland to Shanghai, but at the time of writing, there were no direct flights to Beijing. Connections can be made in Hong Kong or Singapore. There are indirect routes with **Singapore Airlines** via Singapore, **Philippine Airlines** via Manila, and **Garuda Indonesia** via Jakarta.

By Train

One train a day departs Hong Kong's Hung Hom Station for Beijing, and another separate service for Shanghai (see **www.it3.mtr.com.hk** for schedules and fares). From Moscow, trains travel via two different routes into China, one via Ulaanbaatar in Mongolia, the other crossing directly into China's northeast and traveling down to Beijing. Two trains per week make the journey from Hanoi in Vietnam to Beijing. See **www.seat61.com** for advice on all of these international train routes.

By Car & Bus

Neither Beijing, Shanghai, nor Xi'an has an international border remotely close to it, and entering China via car or bus is recommended only for the hardiest of adventurers.

By Boat

Beijing and Xi'an are inland cities, but Shanghai has two large ferry ports and it's a popular way to arrive, particularly for passengers traveling from Korea and Japan (see "Essentials" in Chapter 8). Liners often stop off at Shanghai as part of wider Asian cruises. Companies that run to China include **Cunard** (www.cunard.com), **P&O** (www.pocruises.com), **Princess** (www.princess.com), **Seabourn** (www.seabourn.com), and **Star** (www.starcruises.com).

GETTING AROUND

If you haven't got access to Google Maps (see "Top 10 Apps for China Travel" box), laying your hands on a map should be the first thing you do in a destination. These cost RMB3 to RMB6 from newspaper stalls or books (ask for a *ditu*), though most decent hotels can give you a free one. Ensure your map has Chinese characters. These will be useful when you want to show your destination to a taxi driver or bus conductor. Although building numbers are generally given in this book, they're of little use for directions. In Beijing, people generally navigate using street names and landmarks, while in Shanghai, they tend to use junctions.

By Plane

China's aviation industry has been on a seemingly inexorable rise in the last 20 years. Back in the 1990s, it was standard for every plane ticket to come slapped with an "Airport Construction Tax." Sure enough, hundreds of brand-new airports were subsequently built, and the work goes on. Beijing is due to have a second major international airport by 2018, and at the time of writing, 56 new airports are listed as "under construction."

The result is very crowded skies. With more and more Chinese being able to afford air travel, competition among airlines is fierce, and tickets are generally cheap and easy to buy. The only fly in the ointment for the aviation industry is the arrival of high-speed rail, a genuine alternative to air travel on some long-distance routes, particularly the Shanghai-to-Beijing line, where travel times are roughly comparable.

Booking domestic flights before you arrive in China is advisable if you will be traveling during peak season, or have limited time; however, on most routes, there is generally an oversupply of flights, and booking a ticket a few days before your journey is easily arranged. Most flights do not require a physical ticket to be issued: Your passport and a booking reference will almost always suffice. There are a number of good online booking sites, though the best for English-language customer service and payment flexibility is **Ctrip.com.** The days of having to ferret out an official "airline booking agent" in some musty Chinese-run four-star hotel are well and truly over.

By Train

The train is still the best way to travel in China for many reasons. Railway journeys tend to be more scenic than the endless highways, trains are more comfortable than even the best buses, and they also afford you the chance to wander around on what are often long, cross-continental journeys. Sleeper berths can be great fun, allowing you a chance to chat with the locals, avoid the cost of a hotel night, and spread out and relax as the country rolls by.

One slight downside to train travel is the stations. Older stations are generally conveniently located in city centers, but they are crowded and grubby. Meanwhile, the new breed of station, built specifically to cater to high-speed bullet trains, may be gleaming and spacious (some, like Shanghai Hongqiao, are bigger than the average international airport), but they tend to be located a long way outside the city center, cutting down the convenience factor when compared with air travel. On the upside, all bullet-train stations mentioned in

TOP 10 apps FOR CHINA TRAVEL

Packing a smartphone is not *essential* for travel in China, but it sure does help. Hotel and travel bookings, restaurant selections, language hiccups, and socializing are all now widely conducted online, and Wi-Fi coverage is ubiquitous. Install your apps *before* you leave. All Google services are currently blocked in China, including the Google Play app store. Which apps you choose to install will depend on whether you are able to read any Chinese. For travelers, the most vital app is probably **Didi Da Che.** It's a homegrown version of Uber and allows you to hail a cab wherever you may be. The problem is, not only is the app only in Chinese, you'll also need to speak Mandarin to use it effectively. The other super-useful Chinese-only app is **Dianping.** It's the TripAdvisor of Chinese restaurants, cafes, and bars. For those who can't claim the gift of the Chinese gab, there are several very useful English-language apps, available on both the Apple Store and the Google Play store.

1. **WeChat (Weixin)** Young Chinese do not exchange Twitter handles or make Facebook friends, they "WeChat." This homegrown take on WhatsApp is wildly popular and has an English version through which you can make free phone or video calls and send instant messages. If you want to stay in touch with folks you meet, get an ID as a matter of urgency.
2. **Ctrip** China's best travel-booking aggregator makes it simple to book hotel rooms, airline seats, and train tickets. It accepts payment using foreign credit cards.
3. **City Weekend** Only one in a crowded field of English-language expat magazines, "City Weekend" has the best mobile app, covering dining and nightlife in Beijing and Shanghai (and beyond).
4. **China Air Quality Index** China's increasingly toxic air pollution can ruin a day's touring. This app will

this book are now hooked up to urban subway networks, while security and embarkation-disembarkation times are still shorter than those at airports.

Even on a short China visit, taking at least one train journey is recommended to get a flavor for the country. Sometimes the train lines are attractions in their own right. The world's first commercial maglev (magnetic levitation) line travels between Shanghai and Pudong Airport at 431kmph (268 mph), a speed that has yet to be beaten anywhere on the network. The excitement and buzz that surrounded the very first high-speed rail link in China (which opened in 2009) has now turned to familiar complacency, at least among those who can afford the relatively high prices. But though carriages on these bullet trains are generally packed with humdrum commuter traffic, most have a **sightseeing area,** located immediately behind the driver, where passengers get to appreciate the tourist perks of high-speed rail with lots of extra window space.

The rate at which the high-speed network (*gaotie*) has been rolled out is nothing short of miraculous, and lines now extend across the eastern half of the country, with more to come by the time this book hits the shelves. A high-speed rail crash in Wenzhou in July 2011 left 32 dead and threatened further expansion, but that didn't stop the authorities, and following a few show-trials, it was help predict whether you need to pack a face-mask or just stay inside.

5. **Google Maps** Google's Chinese rival Baidu outdoes it in most things, but for maps, Google still wins. Building-accuracy is not as good as in Western countries, but for navigation, it's super-reliable. However, you'll need a VPN to use it (see no. 10).
6. **China Train** Currently only available on Apple, this is the app version of the excellent www.travelchinaguide.com site, which has great info on train times. The company also makes the useful **China Flights.** Try **China Train Booking** for an Android alternative.
7. **Explore Shanghai & Explore Beijing** Transportation maps of Beijing and Shanghai are both garishly colored and sometimes confusing tangles of subway lines and junctions. These apps help to plot a route home.
8. **Pleco** The king of Chinese dictionaries comes preloaded with two free dictionaries. Optical Character Recognition (OCR) can be purchased as an add-on. **Hanping** is a worthy alternative, but only if you use Android.
9. **Waygo Translator** The only paid-for app on the list instantly translates Chinese menus and signs into English using OCR and your smartphone's camera. It also works offline.
10. **A VPN** Having a Virtual Private Network (VPN) preinstalled on your phone is vital if you want to connect with family or friends back home via Facebook, Twitter, or any Google service. All are currently blocked in China via normal channels, but VPNs route around the "Great Firewall of China" by sending data via international servers. VPNs are provided by various companies and can be bought on short-term subscriptions. The authorities routinely crack down on the more popular apps, so search for the latest updates on this tiresome cat-and-mouse game before

business-as-usual. At the time of writing, not every line was seamlessly linked up, and Xi'an is as far as high-speed trains went in a westerly direction. Despite the prices (which are only marginally cheaper than air tickets), bullet trains are consistently packed. For more on the bullet trains and all aspects of rail travel in China, see this excellent roundup page: **www.seat61.com/China.htm**.

TYPES OF TRAINS For long-distance travel, opt for a C, D, G, or Z class train. C, D, and **G** trains are the new breed of high-speed (*gaosu*) intercity services, with G-class being the newest and fastest. **Z** *(zhida)* trains go directly between major cities but are not particularly fast. However, they are generally the best trains for overnight travel. **T** trains *(tekuai*—"express") come with high levels of accommodations and service. Staff in all of the above classes are uniformed and coiffed like flight attendants, willing and helpful. Avoid services with no letter prefix.

SEATING ARRANGEMENTS All high-speed trains (C, D, and G) have at least two seat classes: **Second-class** (*er deng*) carriages have only slightly more leg room than economy-class airline cabins. Seats are arranged in a 3–2 formation across the carriage, with the short-straw being the middle seat. If you're buying from an agent, ask to avoid this seat ("*bu yao zhong jian de zuo-wei*"). **First-class** (*yi deng*) carriages are more spacious, and seats are 5cm (2 in.) wider. There are only four seats in each row, arranged in a 2–2 formation. The vast majority of trains also have a **business class** (*te deng*) carriage where seats recline to horizontal. As the names imply, seat classifications map fairly well onto traditional aircraft cabins: Second-class bullet-train seats are comparable to economy seats on an aircraft, while first-class seats should be thought of as "premium economy." Business-class seats are as luxurious as they are in the air, though relatively cheaper; prices are only twice that of the second-class seats.

Long-distance Z-class trains have two kinds of sleeping berth. The **soft-sleeper** *(ruan wo)* carriage consists of lockable compartments, each containing four beds, the two upper beds slightly cheaper than the lower ones. There's a volume control for the PA system, and berths have individual reading lights. Modern trains also have individual TVs for each berth. A **hard sleeper** *(ying wo)* berth has couchettes, separated into groups of six by partitions, but open to the corridor. Berths are provided in columns of three and are cheaper as they get farther from the floor. The top berth has very little headroom and can be uncomfortably cramped, although it offers the most privacy. The bottom berth is the most spacious, but it also becomes public seating for the middle- and upper-berths during daylight hours, reducing its appeal. Hard-sleeper berths are quite acceptable for short overnight trips of 12 hours or so. For longer journeys of 24 hours or more, it's worth spending the extra for a soft sleeper.

More-modern trains have a mixture of Western (usually at the end of the soft-sleeper carriage) and Chinese squat toilets. Washbasins are found at the end of each carriage, and except on the highest-quality trains, there's cold water only (and this may sometimes run out).

Almost all trains also have a **hard-seat** class *(ying zuo),* which on many major routes is far from hard, although not the way to spend the night. **Soft seat** *(ruan zuo)* appears on daytime expresses only, is less crowded, and is now often in two-deck form, giving excellent views from the upper level.

TIMETABLES For individual train inquiries, **www.travelchinaguide.com** is the best resource. There is also an iPhone app that can be downloaded (see "Top 10 Apps for China travel" box).

TICKETS Train tickets used to be a nightmare to get hold of, with booking horizons of just a few days, a lack of information, and a paucity of authorized sellers leading to long and slow-moving lines at stations. Station queues can still be atrocious, both for length and for line-cutting, but now it's so much easier to avoid being part of the railway-station scrum in the first place thanks to online booking. Aside from last-minute emergencies, don't buy online then opt to collect from the station, as you'll need to arrive at the station very early and join the line you were trying so desperately to avoid. It's well worth paying a few dollars extra to have tickets couriered to you.

Online tickets can now be booked up to 60 days in advance. Those with Chinese credit cards and a decent knowledge of Mandarin can cut the middle-man out altogether at the official national rail site (www.12306.cn), but it won't be of much use to the majority of travelers. **Ctrip.com** and **chinahighlights.com** are both reliable sites that accept overseas credit cards, charging a few US dollars to courier tickets to your hotel (book **3 days in advance** to be sure this method works out). The latter is preferable, as its booking form allows passengers to request certain seats or avoid others. A slightly cheaper way to buy is to look out for in-town ticket offices (*shoupiaochu*), where tickets can be bought for a RMB5 commission. Other tour agents can also book, though expect to pay between RMB30 and RMB50 in commission (including delivery to your hotel). Agents within hotels may charge more. It's best to give agents a choice of trains and berth. You pay upfront, and you'll need to supply your full name and passport number. The exact ticket price, printed clearly on the ticket, will depend on the train and berth obtained.

In an effort to clamp down on the once-rampant black market dealing in train tickets, all tickets are now printed with the traveler's name and ID card number. Foreign travelers must submit their **passport** number. Ensure you give this correctly when you buy your ticket and have your passport on hand when you get to the station. Get either of these procedures wrong, and you won't be getting on your train. The downside to this new rule is that it's not possible for foreigners to use the many **automatic electronic ticket booths** installed at stations. These were originally designed with overseas travelers in mind—they have decent English-language menus—but they cannot accept foreign passports and so are useless in the face of the new regulations.

Station platforms only open a few minutes before the train's departure, but it's well worth getting to stations early. They can be huge places, difficult to navigate, with lines to pass through increasingly heavy security. Once you're on the train, attendants circulate to check tickets. On sleeper trains, the attendant will swap your ticket for a token with your berth number. Shortly before arrival, they will return to reexchange it, meaning you'll never miss your stop in China. Keep your ticket ready, as it will be checked again as you leave the station.

REFRESHMENTS C, D, G, and Z-class trains all have restaurant cars with counters where you can buy one of a choice of steaming TV-style dinners (*kuai can;* RMB25). These are usually dreadful, so it pays to prepare something in advance. Most stations have convenience stores; some have supermarkets and small bakeries. Ensure you load up before you get on the train, especially on long journeys. All is not lost if you do board empty-handed. All trains have attendants who push carts selling soft drinks, beer, mineral water, biscuits, and instant noodles.

COMFORT & SAFETY All seats on high-speed trains recline to varying degrees, though getting a rest is sometimes hard amid the chatter, snoring, and cries of passing attendants. Sleeping can sometimes be a challenge even in dedicated sleeping berths. Carrying a pair of earplugs is highly recommended.

Theft of personal belongings is a rare occurrence. Take sensible precautions as you would anywhere, and keep vital items (passport/money, and so on) close to you, but there's certainly no need for paranoia.

By Bus

China's highway system, nonexistent 25 years ago, is growing rapidly, and journey times by road between many cities have been dramatically cut to the point where, on some routes at least, buses are now faster than trains. Although many buses are battered, in some areas they offer a remarkable level of luxury—particularly on the East Coast. Some buses even have onboard toilets (although they may not work) and free bottled water.

Many bus stations now offer a variety of services. At the top end are *kongtiao* (air-conditioned), *gaosu* (high-speed, usually meaning that toll expressways are used), and *haohua* (luxury) buses, on which smoking is usually forbidden. These tickets are usually easy to obtain at the bus station, and prices are clearly displayed and written on the ticket. There are no extra charges for baggage, which in smaller and older buses is typically piled up on the cover over the engine next to the driver. It might be worth booking your ticket a day in advance on public holidays, but generally speaking, if you just turn up, you'll be on your way in under half an hour.

Buses usually depart punctually, pause at a checking station where the number of passengers is compared with the number of tickets sold in advance, then dither while empty seats are filled with groups waiting at the roadside who bargain for a lower fare.

Sleeper buses, although cheaper, should generally be avoided when an overnight train is an alternative. Usually they have three rows of two-tier berths, which are extremely narrow and do not recline fully. Sleeper buses are also a favorite haunt for pickpockets.

By Taxi

Up until recently, taxis were numerous and easy to hail on virtually any major city street-corner outside rush hour or periods of heavy rain. Not so now. The taxi industry is creaking in places, with fares kept artificially low by local governments against the backdrop of industry corruption, rising fuel costs, and extortionate car-loan fees. Drivers have one of the toughest urban jobs, working long hours on very thin margins, and there are signs that some may have given up trying. Those that are still in the game are employing new tactics, particularly since the arrival of taxi-booking smartphone apps such as **Didi Da Che** and **Uber** in 2014. These software platforms give drivers real-time information about nearby customers, including where they want to travel from and to, so it becomes all the easier to ignore you if you are waiting in an awkward location or want to travel to a nonlucrative destination. If you find dozens of taxis passing you by, this'll probably be the reason why. Uber does operate in Beijing and Shanghai, but like most tech in China, the Western brand lags far behind the domestic alternatives. Didi Da Che is the big beast, owned by Alibaba and Tencent, two of China's mightiest Internet firms. If you have a Chinese SIM card and can read and speak a little Chinese, it's an absolutely essential app to have on your phone. For most short-term visitors, it's not only *not useful*—it's actually made it much harder to find cabs.

For outward journeys, the best bet may be to ask your hotel concierge to help book or call a cab. For the return journey, things are trickier. If you are in a bar or restaurant, ask staff to help book you a cab before you leave. If you are already on the street and have no local friends to ask for help, walk away from the crowd and try to be patient. If you are totally stranded, head toward the nearest busy intersection or major hotel. If all else fails, try calling your hotel and asking them to use *their* smartphone app to book you a ride (lying about your *actual* destination if need be).

For more-planned, less-spontaneous, trips, try bargaining. This is less challenging than you might expect. For the reasons explained above, half- and full-day hires are very welcome by drivers. Start flagging down cabs the day before you want to travel, and negotiate an all-in price, using a pen and paper and the Chinese characters you should have had written down for you by your hotel receptionist. Avoid giving an exact kilometer distance, since if you overrun it, there may be attempts to renegotiate, even if the driver is at fault for taking a longer route. For the same reason, it's best to avoid being precise to the minute about a return time, but note that drivers sometimes have to be back in time to hand the car to the man who will drive it through the night. Be prepared to pay road tolls, and perhaps even to buy lunch for the driver (a culturally ingrained expectation among chauffeurs of all kinds). If you find a driver who is pleasant and helpful, take his mobile phone number and employ him on subsequent days and for any airport trips.

Chauffeur-driven car tours can be arranged at many four- and five-star hotels; however, the price will likely be three or four times what you'll pay by negotiating with a regular taxi driver. Branches of CITS and other travel agencies will also be happy to arrange cars for you, but again at a hugely marked-up price.

By Subway

China has undertaken a huge program of subway construction, and all the cities mentioned in this book now have their own metropolitan subway network. Specific details are given in the relevant chapters. Generally speaking, subway trains are cheap and convenient, and by far the best way to get around major cities. Shanghai and Beijing's subways now represent the largest- and second-largest networks in the world, respectively, and are still expanding. Shanghai's subway whisks tourists out to the suburban river town of Qibao and beyond, and by 2016, it may be possible to get all the way out to Beijing's once-remote Fragrant Hills on the new Western Suburban Line. Even in Xi'an, the fairly remote Terracotta Warriors will eventually be hooked up to the central network, though not in time for readers of this book, unfortunately.

TIPS FOR taking taxis AROUND TOWN

1. ***Never*** go with a driver who approaches you at an airport or major train station. Head directly to the official stand. Drivers who approach you are often *hei che*—illegal and meterless "black cabs."
2. Cabs waiting for business outside major tourist sights, especially those with drivers who call out to foreigners, should generally be avoided, as should cabs whose drivers ask you where you want to go even before you get in (this is particularly common in Xi'an). Flag down a passing cab, and most times, the precautions listed here will be unnecessary.
3. It's generally safe to go with taxis called by hotel doormen or at official stands outside hotels. If a taxi is parked outside a hotel, though, avoid getting in. Some unscrupulous drivers target hotels in order to take advantage of out-of-towners. If the driver is unwilling to use the meter, or demands to know where you want to go before you get in, look elsewhere.
4. Before you leave your hotel, ask the concierge to write down the name of your destination(s) and grab an official hotel business-card to show to the driver on your return journey. Few drivers speak more than a word or two of English and will not recognize the English name of your hotel when spoken.
5. Look to see if the supervision card, usually with a photo of the driver and a telephone number, is prominently displayed. If it isn't, you may have problems and you should choose another cab. It's not a crisis if the driver is obviously not the person in the photograph. Many cabs are subcontracted, sometimes legally, sometimes not, but a driver's use of the meter, and a display of *some* form of official ID, should be reassurance enough.
6. Can you clearly see the meter? If it's recessed behind the gear stick, partly hidden by the artfully folded face cloth on top, choose another cab.
7. Always make sure you see the meter reset. If you didn't actually see the flag pushed down, which shouldn't happen until you actually move off, then you may end up paying for the time the cab was in the line.
8. Have a map with you and look as if you know where you are going (even if you don't).
9. Rates per kilometer are usually clearly posted on the side of the cab. They vary widely from place to place, as well as by vehicle type. Base fares usually include the first 3km, and then the standard kilometer-rate begins. Rates do rise by 50% at a certain point. This is designed to compensate drivers for long one-way trips out of town. Most meters do this automatically, but some may be button-controlled. If you see the driver pushing buttons during the journey, try to see if the per-kilometer rate has increased (it will be displayed on the meter).
10. Pay what's on the meter, and don't tip—the driver will insist on giving change (although in some cities they will round up or down to the nearest Yuan). Always ask for a receipt (*fa piao*). Should you leave something in a cab, there's a remarkably high success rate at getting even valuable items back if the number on the receipt is called and the details on it provided.
11. Smile and be polite. Taxi drivers in China survive on wafer-thin margins, and it's a hard, difficult job. There are a few shysters in the industry, but most drivers are decent and honest and will appreciate your treating them as human beings.

Though nearly always busy (unbearably so at rush hour around busy hubs), subway trains are generally modern and spacious (Beijing's Line 1 and Line 2 are the notable exceptions). The only real downside is security. China is on anti-terrorism alert, and passengers must now submit all bags (no matter how small) to an airport-style scan before they enter the ticketed part of the station. It's normally a trifling inconvenience rather than a major hassle (the attention level of security staff suggest they're not exactly poring over every last object), but lines can build up at busier stations during weekends and rush hour.

By Car

Foreigners are allowed to drive in China, but they must first obtain a Chinese driver's license (International Licenses are not accepted). It's technically possible for a short-term visitor to obtain such a license, though the process is fraught, and that's even before you've headed out onto the gridlocked and often chaotic roads. Driving in China isn't recommended unless you are either extremely familiar with the terrain and planning on spending your entire trip outside of the major cities, or have a fondness for acute stress and frustration. However, if you are determined, there may be ways and means.

Terminal 3 of Beijing Capital International Airport has a Vehicle Management Station on the first floor (✆ **010/6453-0010;** daily 9am–6pm). In theory, there should be two officers staffing the desk who can speak English. For a RMB10 charge, they can help translate your home license and assist in filling out an application form (which requires Chinese to be written). For this, you'll also need two passport-style pictures (these can be obtained at the office for an additional charge) and a visa that lasts no longer than 90 days. You'll then be sent upstairs to the airport first-aid station to fill out further forms and have an eye test (an additional RMB10). Assuming all is successful, you'll then be given a crash course in road basics at the Vehicle Management Station before being issued your temporary license. You can then proceed to **Avis** (www.avis.com) or **Hertz** (www.hertz.com), both of which have offices within the airport (Avis is within the Beijing Airlines Traders Hotel, while Hertz is across in Terminal 2). They will likely need to see confirmation of your address, so have a receipt of your hotel booking handy.

The application process will be fairly intimidating for those not familiar with Mandarin, but not half as intimidating as being out on the road. In China, the law of the jungle prevails. You are almost guaranteed to be tailgated, cut off, blasted by foghorns, and surprised by drivers who emerge from junctions in front of you without bothering to look first. The best advice for motorists in China is to expect the unexpected, and to travel at much slower speeds than you may be used to back home. You may have no choice in this, as traffic in major cities is bad—very bad—and getting worse all the time.

For enthusiasts looking for a real driving expedition, contact **Nature Adventure Voyage Off-Road** (www.china-driving.com), which has many years experience organizing self-drive trips in China, and can arrange for you to drive your own car or a local rental vehicle.

VISAS

If China is your primary destination, you'll need a visa to enter the country. These must be acquired in advance. The most obvious place to get one is your nearest Chinese embassy or consulate, though Hong Kong allows visa-free travel for most citizens of most Western countries, and it's easy to get a mainland visa. A visa will usually expire if you haven't used it within 3 months of the date of issue, so don't apply too early.

To obtain a visa, your **passport** must have at least 6 months' validity and two blank pages remaining. Visa applications typically take 3 to 5 working days to process, although next-day visas are available for those applying in person and paying an additional fee (same-day visas are possible in emergencies). "L" tourist visas are valid for 30 days. Double- and multiple-entry tourist visas are also available at some consulates.

Many embassies and consulates (including all those in the United States) do not accept postal applications. In addition to the Washington, D.C., embassy, there are consulates in New York City, Chicago, Houston, San Francisco, and Los Angeles. If you're a U.S. citizen *not* living in or near one of these cities, you'll need to use an agent to make your application or face an expensive expedition.

Applying for a visa requires completion of an application form that can be downloaded from the consular websites or sent by mail. One passport photograph is required per applicant, and most consulates ask that "L" tourist visa applicants provide proof of return travel and accommodation bookings. Copies of online receipts are generally accepted. For those planning to wait until they arrive in China to make hotel bookings, go to **www.ctrip.com** and make some ghost bookings in your own name. Many hotels on the site do not require payment in advance or even credit card details, so documentation can be easily obtained, even if it turns out to be wildly inaccurate.

The visa fee depends on which passport you hold, not where you apply. For a single-entry visa processed in the standard 4 days, U.S citizens are charged US$140 (if applying from overseas, the price will be roughly the equivalent of US$140; visit **www.china-embassy.org**). New Zealanders are charged NZ$140 (visit **www.chinaembassy.org.nz**) for the same. Citizens of Canada, the U.K., and Australia are now all routed through one of the "Visa for China" service centers in those countries (visit **www.visaforchina.org**). Even if you live next door to the consulate, you'll still need to pay a service fee. For Canadians, it's now effectively C$142 (the price is the same for single- or double-entry visas). For Brits, the cost of a single-entry visa is now £66, while Australians must pay A$98.50. It's possible to apply by post at each of the Visa for China service centers, but an additional fee is levied. There may be supplementary fees for a fast-track service or additional entries.

Once you're inside China, visas can usually be extended for a maximum of 30 days at the Foreigners' Entry-Exit Department of the **Public Security Bureau (PSB)** in most major towns and cities. First extensions are usually granted easily. Again, visa-extension processing times and requirements vary from place to place, and while some PSBs will issue an extension on the spot, others will take up to 7 working days to process. A passport photo, complete application form (available from the PSB), and the hotel receipt for that night are usually required, and some PSBs will grant an extension only if you have less than a week (or sometimes only 3 days) left on your current visa. If you have trouble getting an extension, local agencies can sometimes help, although they will charge a hefty fee.

There are two ways to visit China without a visa, though they're only available to those stopping over en route to a third destination. The **24-hour visa exemption** is available in Shanghai and Beijing. Show your passport and onward flight ticket to a point *outside* mainland China (Hong Kong counts as a separate country in this sense, as it has its own border controls), and you should be allowed to explore for a few hours without requiring a visa. Your onward flight *must* be departing from the same airport within 24 hours of the moment you enter. The **72-hour visa-free transit** is available at Beijing, Xi'an, and Shanghai, and there are usually separate customs lines (or special-purpose booths) for travelers hoping to take advantage. Again, travelers must prove they have onward travel booked to a third country (i.e., are not merely returning to their home country). You must also have flown directly into that airport from your home country and have plans to fly directly out of China on the next leg of your journey. The major hitch is that you're prohibited from leaving the city, and you'll also need to register at a local police station once you are downtown.

ACCOMMODATION TIPS

When China reopened its doors to tourists in the early 1980s, hotel choices were very limited for foreigners, but these days, there are increasingly more options, and the only thing that is thin on the ground is character. At the upper end of the scale, **international chains** are keen to get their slice of the Chinese pie and are opening new joint-venture hotels around the country. In the major cities, you'll find the gamut of international chains, including Best Western, Crowne Plaza, Grand Hyatt, Hilton, Holiday Inn, Kempinski, Marco Polo, Marriott, Ramada, St. Regis, Shangri-La, Sheraton, and Sofitel, among others. In most joint-venture hotels, the buildings are Chinese-owned, and the foreign part of the venture is the management company, which provides senior management and trains the staff, tries to ensure conformity with its standards, does worldwide marketing, and generally provides up to 90% of what you'd expect from the same brand at home. **Chinese-owned chains** are also improving and expanding. However, while the exterior appearances of domestic and international five-stars may be similar, if you have the choice, go for the latter, as while prices will be comparable, service is almost always better. **Budget choices** are more limited, in part because hotels require licenses to receive foreign guests, and many cheapies don't have these. Saving the day, though, are a new breed of **business chain hotels** such as Jinjiang Inn and 7-Days Inn, which are sweeping the nation and offer inexpensive (usually under RMB220), functional, modern rooms, often with good locations near the city center.

In general, Chinese hotels receive almost no maintenance once they open. There are five-star hotels in Beijing that have gone a decade without proper redecoration or refurbishment. Foreign managements force the issue with building owners, but it's rare that standards are maintained. Thus **the best choice is almost always the newest**—teething troubles aside, most things will work, staff will be eager to please (if not quite sure how), rooms will be spotless, and rates will be easily bargained down, since few hotels spend any money on advertising their existence.

[FastFACTS] CHINA

ATMs/Banks It's possible to travel in China carrying nothing more than your home bank card. China now has four out of the five most valuable banks in the world, and they have become much more internationalized in recent years. It means that nearly all ATMs at major banks accept foreign cards (including those at airports), and the peculiarities of the banking system are such that exchange rates are usually reasonably good (and nearly always better than professional money-changers back home, who do not generally have a glut of Chinese renminbi and therefore offer poor rates to sell it to you in advance). The downside is that you may well be charged a fee at both ends of the transaction, but this can still be outweighed by the improved exchange rate you'll get. Put simply, if your card shows Cirrus, Maestro, MasterCard, Visa, or American Express, your card will nearly always work in ATMs belonging to one of the big beasts of Chinese banking: **Bank of China, Industrial and Commercial Bank of China (ICBC), China Construction Bank,** and the **Agricultural Bank of China.** In the event of any problems, look for the **Bank of China,** which is *the* most internationalized of the four. There are a number of smaller banks that may also be hooked up to international networks, but this is less of a given. ATMs are found throughout all major cities and nearly all offer a choice of English-language- or Chinese menus. Visa (**www.visa.com/atmlocator/index.jsp**) and MasterCard (**www.mastercard.com/global/atmlocations**) both have ATM locators on their sites. ATMs may have a maximum transaction limit. For debit cards, this may be as low as RMB2,000 to RMB3,000, but should be higher for credit cards. You are usually allowed a second transaction on the same day, though this will incur additional costs. Your own bank may have a withdrawal limit and lock cards that breach it. It pays to check this before you leave home. This will likely be calculated in your home currency. Finally, if you are planning to travel to China without any renminbi, be sure to check whether you need to apply for a six-digit PIN to use with ATMs in China. In case of emergencies, should you be asked for a six-digit PIN for a card that has only ever had a four-digit number, try adding two zeroes to the end.

Traveler's checks can be cashed at selected branches of the Bank of China and at foreign-exchange desks in hotels, but are no longer a common form of payment. US dollars, in contrast, may be exchanged at most branches of almost any Chinese bank, so even if you plan to bring checks, having a few US dollars (in good condition) for emergencies is a good idea.

International credit cards can be used at most good

hotels, restaurants, and some large tourist-oriented shops. Although Visa and MasterCard signs abound, it's possible that only the Chinese versions of the cards are accepted, so pack cash if you are going downmarket with your eating, drinking, shopping, or lodging.

Business Hours China has a highly entrepreneurial culture, and privately run shops, restaurants, and bars generally open early and close late every day of the week. Offices are generally open from 9am to 6pm but are closed Saturday and Sunday.

Customs In general, you can bring into China anything for personal use that you plan to take away with you when you leave, with the usual exceptions of firearms and drugs, or plant materials, animals, and foods from diseased areas. Other prohibitions include "printed matter, magnetic media, films, or photographs which are deemed to be detrimental to the political, economic, cultural, and moral interests of China," as the regulations put it. Large quantities of religious literature, overtly political materials, or books on Tibet or Xinjiang might cause you difficulties. There are no problems with cameras or video recorders, GPS equipment, laptops, or any other standard electronic equipment. Customs officers are for the most part easygoing, and foreign visitors are very rarely searched. Customs declaration forms have now vanished from all major points of entry, but if you are importing or exporting more than US$5,000, or RMB20,000 in cash, theoretically you should declare it. An official seal must be attached to any item created between 1795 and 1949 that is taken out of China; older items cannot be exported. You are highly unlikely to find any genuine antiques, so this is a moot point (and if the antiques dealer is genuine, then he'll certainly know all about how to get the seal). Cheap DVDs on sale in China are sure to be pirated and will be confiscated if found on your return. They're often poor-quality; it's not really worth the risk, especially in the low-cost streaming era.

Dentists Beijing and Shanghai have some excellent dental offices, but prices are generally high if you expect to be seen by an English-speaking practitioner. Ensure you have appropriate dental insurance and see individual chapters for specific details.

Disabled Travelers Although China has a large number of people with disabilities, provisions for the disabled are often poorly designed and implemented, and this can make travel difficult. The more developed, settled cities of Shanghai and Beijing have become *friendlier* to travelers of limited mobility, with hotels having increasing numbers of wheelchair accessible rooms, and elevators installed in subway stations. However, even in the capital, uneven paving, unavoidable steps, and heavy traffic are all hindrances, and it's easiest to travel in a specialist group or with those who are fully familiar with giving you whatever assistance you may need. **Tour Beijing** (www.tour-beijing.com/disability_travel) has a good reputation.

Doctors & Hospitals Advanced facilities staffed by foreign doctors are easily found in Beijing and Shanghai, with one or two international clinics also available in Xi'an. These are listed as appropriate in this book and can also be found in local expat magazines. Many **major hotels have doctors on staff** who will treat minor problems, and who will be aware of the best place to send foreigners for further treatment. For coughs, colds, and minor stomach upsets, local pharmacies generally stock a wide range of **over-the-counter medications** (including many that are prescription-only in the West), but you should make sure you understand the possible side-effects before taking anything. Many Chinese head straight for the local hospital at the first sign of a sniffle, but avoid this if you possibly can. Chinese hospitals are notorious for overmedicating (there are major profit incentives for doing so), and children, the elderly, and even healthy adults will generally find themselves hooked up to an antiviral drip within minutes of being seen. If you do need to go to a Chinese hospital outside of major cities, head to the biggest hospital in the nearest large town. Hospitals are usually numbered in order of size and seniority, so if in doubt, ask around for the "No. 1" hospital. Foreigners who do end up in provincial facilities often get special treatment, but you may not consider it special enough. Contact the **International Association for Medical Assistance to Travelers** (✆ **716/754-4883,** or **416/652-0137** in Canada; **www.iamat.org**) for tips on travel and health concerns in China, and for lists of local, English-speaking doctors. You can find listings of reliable medical clinics overseas at the **International Society of Travel Medicine (www.istm.org).**

Drinking Laws China has very liberal drinking laws, and alcohol is widely available. Theoretically you need to be over 18 to purchase alcohol, but this is seldom enforced. Alcohol can be bought in any convenience store, supermarket, restaurant, bar, hotel, or club, seven days a week, and may be drunk anywhere you feel like drinking it. If the shop is open 24 hours, then the alcohol is available 24 hours too. Closing times for bars and clubs vary according to demand, but typically it's all over by 3am. In the unlikely event you are driving, the previously lax attitude to drunk driving has been tightened up in recent years. A 2011 law specifies the legal limit at no more than **0.08% blood-alcohol.**

Electricity The electricity used in all parts of China is 220 volts, alternating current (AC), 50 cycles. Most devices from North America, therefore, cannot be used without a transformer. If you have 110V devices, your hotel may be able to supply a voltage converter. The most common outlet takes the North American two-flat-pin plug (but not the three-pin version, or those with one pin broader than the other). You may also come across outlets for the three-flat-pin (two pins at an angle) variety used in Australia, and less frequently, the two-round-pin plugs common in Europe. Most new or five-star hotels have outlets designed to take all three plugs. Adapters with two or three flat pins are available inexpensively in department stores, and good hotels can often provide them free of charge. Shaver sockets are common in bathrooms of hotels from three stars upward.

Embassies & Consulates Most countries maintain embassies in Beijing and consulates in Shanghai. See the relevant chapters for further information.

Emergencies ✆ **110** for the police, ✆ **119** for fire, or ✆ **120** for ambulance, although they may soon be merged. If in doubt, call ✆ **110.** Some English may be spoken, but it's best to have a Chinese speaker make the call if possible.

Family Travel Travel with kids is increasingly popular, and children are generally treated wonderfully by local people. This said, China presents certain challenges for families. Temperatures at either end of the extreme may be uncomfortable for children in high summer and deepest winter. Air pollution is serious across the country and may affect young lungs, especially asthmatics. Finally, using public transportation can be extremely stressful if you're clutching onto small children, due to the enormous crowds.

You should also ensure that there are plenty of fun things for the kids to do, and that hotels and restaurants are as kid-friendly as possible (many of the best have child-zones). Your biggest challenge may be the long journeys between destinations and the lack of familiar foods (unless your children have been brought up with Chinese food).

In better news, many travel expenses are discounted for kids. Children under 1.4m (4½ ft.) get 25% discounted tickets on sleeper trains, those under 11 travel half-price on planes, and many attractions also offer reduced rates.

Health Trips to the cities featured in this book will normally not require additional inoculations, but do ensure your standard inoculations, typically for **polio, diphtheria,** and **tetanus,** are up to date well in advance of a trip. No matter how good your pretrip health is, it's worth taking a basic **first-aid kit** and a selection of your preferred over-the-counter medicines with you. China has suffered from a number of major viral outbreaks in the last 15 years (**SARS** and **Avian Flu H7N9** were the biggies), but monitoring and government transparency have improved tremendously as a result. For the latest on a constantly changing situation, consult the **World Health Organization** (www.who.int) and the **Centers for Disease Control and Prevention** (www.cdc.gov).

Despite all the spitting and coughing, China is a health-obsessed nation (partly due to the appalling state of its government-managed health service), and fewer travelers suffer from bugs and stomach upsets in China than they do in the likes of India or Egypt. The chief risk here is from **air pollution,** which has become "beyond index" bad in recent years. Beijing and Xi'an both suffer terribly, though conditions in Shanghai seem to be deteriorating too. Those with chronic respiratory conditions should make sure they take adequate medication with them. Even those with previously clear lungs may find themselves coughing and spluttering through the haze, and face masks are now a common sight on city streets. To purchase one in China, head to your nearest pharmacy. There are branches of **Watson's** (a good Hong Kong brand) in each of the cities in this book.

Water should not be drunk from the tap, but is safe to drink after boiling. Bottled water may not be the pristine mineral water it claims to be but is safe, cheap and widely available from convenience stores.

Insurance Insurance is essential when traveling to China. Purchase travel insurance with air ambulance or scheduled airline repatriation built in. Be clear on the terms and conditions—is repatriation limited to life-threatening illnesses, for instance? If you do end up in the hospital in China, you may face a substantial bill, and you may not be allowed to leave until you pay it *in cash*. For insurance payouts, you'll need to claim the expense when you return home, so make sure you have adequate proof of payment.

Internet Access

Despite highly publicized monitoring of traffic and blocking of websites, China remains one of the easiest countries in the world in which to get online. Almost every hotel offers Wi-Fi coverage from room to lobby. Many do so for free. It tends to be only the upmarket, five-star hotels that attempt to charge an hourly, or daily, fee, though some now throw in free Wi-Fi with standard room rates. Free Wi-Fi has become the norm in cafes, bars, and restaurants, though you'll need to ask for the password (*wuxian mima*). Many city governments provide free Wi-Fi in public areas, but this will only be available if you have a China SIM card and register for the service. Ubiquitous Wi-Fi, alongside the popularity of the tablet and smartphone, means you're unlikely to need one of the dwindling number of **Internet bars.** These are dark, dingy, and smoky places mainly popular with serious Internet gamers (of which China has plenty).

As has been widely reported, China has a sophisticated system of Web filtering and blocking. Facebook, YouTube, and Twitter are blocked, as well as all sites run by Google (Gmail, Google Maps, and the Google Play app store included). In their place is a panoply of homegrown versions that work beautifully for locals but are next to useless for foreigners. It is still possible to access your favorite sites with the use of a VPN (Virtual Private Network). This is a paid-for application, installed onto your laptop, tablet, or phone, which attempts to trick the China filters by sending your request via anonymous international routers. Search for "China VPN" before you leave home, and take your pick from what is likely to be a large choice. There's no risk in using such services; it's not considered illicit. The main danger is that your VPN will simply stop working. VPNs are relatively easy for the authorities to block, and the most popular are occasionally put out of action. For most of the last decade, the authorities have been happy to let *some* people visit prohibited overseas sites on the basis that the vast majority have no interest in doing so, but Internet controls have tightened up under the presidency of Xi Jinping.

LGBT Travelers In 2001, legislation was relaxed to the tune that homosexuality is no longer considered a mental disorder in China. This was seen as a tacit declaration that homosexuality had been legalized, and while much of China is still in denial, there is now a growing gay scene. Big cities, particularly Beijing and Shanghai, have gay bars, clubs, saunas, and massage parlors. For more information, check out **www.utopia-asia.com**, publisher of the ***Utopia Guide to China,*** which has details of the gay scene in 50 of the country's cities.

Legal Aid If you get on the wrong side of the law in China, contact your consulate immediately.

Mail & Postage Sending mail from China to international destinations is remarkably reliable. Take the mail to post offices rather than using mailboxes. Some larger hotels have postal services on-site. It helps if mail has its country of destination written in Chinese characters (which hotel staff can help with), but this is not essential. Letters and cards written in red ink will occasionally be rejected. Overseas mail: **postcards** RMB4.50, **letters under 10g** RMB5.40, **letters under 20g** RMB6.50. EMS (**express parcels** under 500g): to the U.S.: RMB180–RMB240; to Europe RMB220–RMB280; to Australia RMB160–RMB210. **Normal parcels** up to 1kg (2¼ lb.): to the **U.S.** by air RMB102, by sea RMB20–RMB84; to the **U.K.** by air RMB142, by sea RMB22–RMB108; to **Australia** by air RMB135, by sea RMB15–RMB89. Letters and parcels can be registered for a small extra charge. Registration forms and Customs declaration forms are in Chinese and English.

Mobile Phones Virtually all modern mobile phones will work in China, though international roaming charges can be horrendously expensive. The most obvious option is to buy a "pay-as-you-go" local **SIM card** on arrival in China. These are available at airports and train stations, and you can buy top-up cards from the service-provider shops, as well as some news kiosks and post offices in larger cities. **China Mobile** tends to have the best coverage, but **China Unicom** is the other major alternative. SIM cards generally cost around RMB100 and include a limited amount of talk-time. Getting the shop that you buy the SIM from to install and activate it makes life easier. If you're going to be traveling extensively, bear in mind that calls will be cheapest in the "home zone" where you bought the SIM card, so if you have any choice about it, buy the SIM where you will be spending most of your time (or where you expect to make and receive the most calls).

It may be better value to ensure your SIM has a generous data allowance rather than talk time. Not only will this give you access to online maps, which are bound to be useful as you travel around, but there are also numerous apps that allow smartphone users to make voice and video calls through VoIP technology. If you don't opt to buy a local SIM, you'll be able to make calls wherever you have Wi-Fi, assuming you have a modern smartphone and a relevant app. The king of these is **WeChat.** It offers crystal-clear call quality in China and a variety of other useful functions (see "Top 10 Apps for China Travel" box, p. 282).

Money & Costs See "Money & Costs" box.

Packing Tips While there are a few important items to remember, generally speaking, the less you pack the better, especially if you're planning to take a lot of public transportation during your trip. Most items can be purchased easily (and more cheaply) in China than at home, and if you decide to take the items back with you, then they'll become mementos of your trip. Of course, China is a big country with a diverse climate range, so what you take will also depend on where you're going and when. Each of the three featured cities in this book gets very hot in the summer, while Beijing can be absolutely frigid in winter (though invariably dry). Taking clothes you can layer will give you the greatest flexibility, and a **raincoat, hat,** and **good sunglasses** will come in handy any time of year. Aside from the usual items you'd take on any trip, a few things that can be useful or difficult to get in China are: specific medicines; earplugs; travel bathplugs; and for women, moisturizer (it is difficult to purchase creams without whitener in China) and tampons (expensive and not always available). Finally, be aware that carrying **tissues** is vital as you travel around. They are not always installed in the places you might expect (public bathrooms and restaurants, for example), and you'll be expected to have your own. Tissues (*zhijin*) are easily bought in China, but make sure you never leave your hotel room without a packet.

Pharmacies Herbal and nonherbal remedies are widely available in mainland pharmacies. Pharmacies are also the most helpful source of anti-pollution **face masks.** See further information in individual destination chapters.

Police The **PSB (Public Security Bureau;** *gong'an ju*) is the primary security body in China. Police officers *(jingcha)* are best avoided unless absolutely necessary; few officers speak English, so they will likely feel the same about you. If you must see a police officer, approach your hotel for assistance first, and visit the PSB offices listed in this guide for dealing with visa extensions, since these are the most likely branches to have an English-speaker.

Safety China was long touted as one of Asia's safest destinations, but this is changing. Physical violence is still virtually unheard of, but petty theft and scams are on the rise. Be cautious about theft in the same places as anywhere else in the world—crowded markets, popular tourist sights, bus and railway stations, and airports. Take standard precautions against pickpockets (distribute your valuables around your person, wear a money belt inside your clothes, and avoid obvious displays of wealth). If you are a victim of theft, make a police report (go to the same addresses given for visa extensions in each city, where you are most likely to find an English-speaking police officer). But don't necessarily expect sympathy or action. The main purpose is to get a theft report to give to your insurers for compensation.

Visitors should be aware of various **scams** in areas of high tourist traffic, and be wary of Chinese who approach and speak in English: "Hello, friend! Welcome to China!" or similar. Those who want to practice their English and who suggest moving to some local haunt may leave you with a bill that has two zeros more on it than it should. Fake "art students" who approach you with a story about raising funds for a show overseas are another pest. In fact, they are merely enticing you into a shop where you will be lied to extravagantly about the authenticity and true cost of various paintings, which you will then be pressured into buying. If you have a local SIM, it's possible (though unlikely) you'll receive a random **telephone scam** call. This will involve somebody claiming to be a police officer suggesting you have flouted a local regulation and threatening arrest unless "bail money" is paid. Just hang up.

China has recently joined the list of nations on high terrorism alert. In 2014, there was an appalling coordinated knife attack at a railway station in the southwest, and in 2013, a car exploded on Tian'anmen Square in what the police described as a "suicide attack." The result is a huge number of uniformed guards and police officers at major tourist sites, and scanners—everywhere. All bags need to be scanned at railway stations, subway stations, and all notable tourist spots (museums included). Those looking like they come from China's largely Muslim northwest are likely to be frisked before they are allowed onto Tian'anmen Square. China remains a largely safe place, but check the latest travel

WHAT THINGS COST IN CHINA	US$	UK£	RMB
Taxi from the airport to downtown Beijing	21.00	13.00	130
Double room, moderate	97.00	61.00	600
Double room, inexpensive	56.00	36.00	350
Chinese meal for two, moderate	12.00	8.00	75
Bottle of beer in restaurant	1.29–2.41	0.82–1.54	8–15
Small bottle of water	0.24–0.48	0.15–0.31	1.50–3
Good cup of coffee	4.02–5.64	2.56–3.58	25–35
Admission to museums	Free	Free	Free
Admission to scenic areas	24.00–32.00	15.00–20.00	150–200

advice issued by your government before you set out. The U.S. State Department (**www.travel.state.gov**) and U.K. Foreign and Commonwealth Office (**www.gov.uk/foreign-travel-advice**) both have regularly updated sites.

Senior Travel While Chinese seniors receive discounted admissions to many attractions, these rarely apply to foreigners (although it's always worth having ID and asking). Some familiar foreign brand-name hotels may offer senior rates if you book in advance, although you'll usually beat those prices simply by showing up in person, if there are rooms available.

Smoking New laws passed in 2011 that deem smoking illegal in all enclosed public places have thus far had little effect. Although over a million Chinese die each year from smoking-related diseases, the health implications of smoking are not widely publicized, and the Chinese government remains the world's biggest cigarette manufacturer. On trains, smokers are generally sent to the spaces between the cars, but they won't bother to do so if no one protests. It's quite normal to dine amid a cloud of smoke, though some of the better restaurants do now have nonsmoking sections.

Student Travel Education is highly esteemed in China, and students are well received and often eligible for discounts at attractions, providing they have a valid **ISIC** (International Student Identity Card; www.isic.org).

Taxes Occasional taxes are added to hotel bills, but these are minor and usually included in the room rate. Service charges appear mostly in foreign-branded hotels, and range from 10% to 15%. The better restaurants may add an automatic service charge, but this is still quite rare, especially outside hotels. There is no departure tax for domestic or international flights. There are lesser taxes for international ferry departures at some ports.

Tipping Tipping is not expected and will likely be refused if offered. The Chinese do not tip, but those involved in the tourist trade are familiar with tipping and are unlikely to refuse it. If you are on an escorted tour, your leader may collect a kitty to be distributed as appropriate.

Toilets Street-level public toilets in China are common, many detectable by the nose before they are seen. These used to carry a nominal charge but are now free in most places. Toilet paper isn't provided but can often be purchased from an attendant at the entrance. In many cases, you merely squat over a trough, so it's generally best to use the standard Western equipment you'll find in your hotel room, at department stores, or in branches of foreign fast-food chains.

MONEY & COSTS

THE VALUE OF CHINESE RENMINBI VS. OTHER POPULAR CURRENCIES

1	AUD	CAD	EUR	NZD	GBP	USD
RMB	4.9	5.1	7	4.6	9.6	6.2

The chart shows how many renminbi you can get for one of six major international currencies. Conversions provided were correct at press time. However, rates fluctuate, so consult a currency-exchange website such as **www.xe.com** to check up-to-the-minute rates before departing.

11 THE CHINESE LANGUAGE

Mandarin Chinese is the national language of China, and it is spoken across the country. It's not as hard to learn as it might first appear, at least up to a basic level. Chinese grammar is considerably more straightforward than English. There are no genders, no definite articles ("the," "a," "an"), no plurals, and no need to conjugate verbs like you would in French or Spanish. **Pinyin** is the name of the official system of Romanization, and uses familiar "English" letters to guide pronunciation. It's wonderfully consistent, and aside from one or two left-field sounds (those featuring "r" and "ü" most obviously), most syllables have a near-identical equivalent in English. Practice a little, and there's no reason why you can't make simple words and sentences understood, even on your first trip to China.

The main barrier to this ambition is those pesky **tones.** Mandarin suffers from a real lack of possible sounds. The solution to this phonetic poverty is to multiply the available sounds by making them tonal—speaking them at different pitches. In Mandarin, there are four main tones, plus a "neutral" tone, and each syllable in a sentence must be said "correctly" for it to be quickly understood. For most native English speakers, stringing together entire sentences of fixed-tone sounds is an incredibly unnatural process, and you will not be mastering it on a two-week vacation. However, if you do get just one or two words "correct," conversational possibilities will open up. Mandarin is an incredibly context-dependent language, and lots of information that English speakers would find essential is routinely omitted. It means Chinese speakers are well used to hunting for clues in the linguistic undergrowth. Put another way, find yourself bargaining with a shopkeeper, and it won't matter if you say the number in the wrong tone.

The other main difficulty in learning Mandarin is the written script (this can accurately be called "Chinese," as the same script, give or take, is used for all the many different Chinese dialects that exist). Pinyin is really only used by young children and foreign learners of Chinese, so don't expect passersby to grasp something you've written in perfectly correct Pinyin, especially if it's out of context or the appropriate tones are not indicated.

It's well worth sampling a language by listening to a few example words or sentences on **Google Translate** (which shows you the Chinese characters, the Pinyin, and the relevant tones). Do this in advance of your trip, as the site is blocked in China. Also, if you have a smartphone, make sure you have a dictionary that can vocalize words (**Pleco** is a particular favorite. See p. 283).

English is not widely spoken anywhere in mainland China, though young people are often enthusiastic about practicing their skills with foreigners. The flip side is that nobody will expect you to speak Mandarin. If you can muster a word or two, you'll probably come in for some serious flattery.

A GUIDE TO PINYIN PRONUNCIATION

Letters in Pinyin mostly have the values any English speaker would expect, with the following exceptions:

c *ts* as in bi*ts*

q *ch* as in *ch*in, but much harder and more forward, made with tongue and teeth

r has no true equivalent in English, but the *r* of *r*eed is close, although the tip of the tongue should be curved to the top of the mouth, and (this is the tricky bit) the lips stay apart.

x also has no true equivalent. Try the *sh* of *sh*eep without curving the tongue and you'll be about there (the result is a sound where the "sh" is less *thick* than usual).

zh is a soft j, like the *dge* in ju*dge*

The **vowels** are pronounced roughly as follows. The main curveball here is the **e,** which is pronounced more like a "u" in English (see the example given):

a as in f*a*ther

e as in *err* (*leng* is pronounced as English "lung")

i is pronounced *ee* after most consonants, but after *c*, *ch*, *r*, *s*, *sh*, *z*, and *zh*, is a buzz at the front of the mouth behind closed teeth

o as in s*o*ng

u as in t*oo*

ü is the lips-pursed *u* of French t*u* and German *ü*. Confusingly, ***u*** after *j*, *x*, *q*, and *y* is always *ü*, but in these cases, the accent over *ü* does not appear.

ai sounds like *eye*

ao as in *ou*ch

ei as in h*ay*

ia as in *yak*
ian sounds like *yen*
iang sounds like *yang*
iu sounds like *you*
ou as in t*oe*
ua as in g*ua*va
ui sounds like *way*
uo sounds like *or,* but is more abrupt

Tones

The **First** tone is high and flat: –
The **Second** tone rises from a mid to high pitch: /
The **Third** tone falls to a low pitch before rising slightly: ˇ
The **Fourth** tone falls from a high to low pitch: \

Note that when two or more third-tone "ˇ" sounds follow one another, they should all, except the last, be pronounced as second-tone.

MANDARIN BARE ESSENTIALS

Greetings & Introductions

English	Pinyin	Chinese
Hello.	Nǐ hǎo.	你好
How are you?	Nǐ hǎo ma?	你好吗?
Fine. And you?	Wǒ hěn hǎo. Nǐ ne?	我很好，你呢?
I'm not too well/things aren't going well.	Bù hǎo.	不好
What is your name? (very polite)	Nín guì xìng?	您贵姓?
My (family) name is . . .	Wǒ xìng . . .	我姓 . . .
I'm known as (family, then given name).	Wǒ jiào . . .	我叫 . . .
I'm [American]	Wǒ shì [Měiguó] rén.	我是美国人
[Australian]	[Àodàlìyà]	澳大利亚人
[British]	[Yīngguó]	英国人
[Canadian]	[Jiānádà]	加拿大人
[Irish]	[Àiěrlán]	爱尔兰人
[New Zealander]	[Xīnxīlán]	新西兰人
I'm from [America].	Wǒ shì cóng [Měiguó] lái de.	我是从美国来的
Excuse me/I'm sorry.	Duìbùqǐ.	对不起
I don't understand.	Wǒ tīng bù dǒng.	我听不懂
Thank you.	Xièxie nǐ.	谢谢你
Yes (that's correct).	Duì.	对
No (that's not correct).	Bú duì.	不对
No (I don't want that).	Wǒ bú yào.	我不要
No (that's not acceptable).	Bù xíng.	不行

Basic Questions & Problems

English	Pinyin	Chinese
Excuse me/I'd like to ask	Qǐng wènyíxià	请问一下
Where is . . . ?	. . . zài nǎr?	. . . 在哪儿?
How much is . . . ?	. . .duōshǎo qián?	. . . 多少钱?
. . . this one?	Zhèi/Zhè ge . . .	这个 . . .
. . . that one?	Nèi/Nà ge . . .	那个 . . .
Do you have . . . ?	Nǐ yǒu méi yǒu . . . ?	你有没有 . . . ?
What time does/is . . .	. . . jǐ diǎn?	. . . 几点?
What time is it now?	Xiànzài jǐ diǎn?	现在几点?
When is . . . ?	. . . shénme shíhou?	. . .什么时候?
Why?	Wèishénme?	为什么?
Who?	Shéi?	谁?
Is that okay?	Xíng bù xíng?	行不行?
I'm feeling ill.	Wǒ shēng bìng le.	我生病了

Numbers

Familiar Arabic numerals appear on bank notes, most signs, taxi meters, and other places. Be particularly careful with *four* and *10,* which sound very alike—hold up fingers to make sure. Note, too, that *yī,* meaning "one," tends to change its tone all the time depending on what it precedes. Don't worry about this—once you've started talking about money, almost any kind of squeak for "one" will do. Finally note that "two" alters when being used with expressions of quantity.

English	Pinyin	Chinese
zero	líng	零
one	yī	一
two	èr	二
two (of them)	liǎng ge	两个
three	sān	三
four	sì	四
five	wǔ	五
six	liù	六
seven	qī	七
eight	bā	八
nine	jiǔ	九
10	shí	十
11	shí yī	十一
12	shí èr	十二
21	èr shí yī	二十一
22	èr shí èr	二十二

English	Pinyin	Chinese
51	wǔ shí yī	五十一
100	yì bǎi	一百
101	yì bǎi líng yī	一百零一
110	yì bǎi yī (shí)	一百一（十）
111	yì bǎi yī shí yī	一百一十一
1,000	yì qiān	一千
1,500	yì qiān wǔ (bǎi)	一千五百
5,678	wǔ qiān liù bǎi qī shí bāi	五千六百七十八
10,000	yí wàn	一万

Money

The renminbi (RMB), or "people's currency," is most simply rendered as the word *yuan*, but this is rarely used. Instead, the Chinese speak of "pieces of money," *kuài qián,* usually abbreviated just to *kuài.* Denominations less than one exist, but recent inflation means they are hardly ever referred to these days.

English	Pinyin	Chinese
RMB 0.1	yì máo qián	一毛钱
RMB 1	yí kuài qián	一块钱
RMB 2	liǎng kuài qián	两块钱
RMB 5.5	wǔ kuài wǔ	五块五
RMB 5,500	wǔ qiān wǔ bǎi kuài	五千五百块
Small change	língqián	零钱

Banking & Shopping

English	Pinyin	Chinese
I want to change money.	Wǒ xiǎng huàn qián.	我想换钱
credit card	Xìnyòngkǎ	信用卡
traveler's check	lǚxíng zhīpiào	旅行支票
department store	gòuwù zhōngxīn	购物中心
convenience store	xiǎomàibù	小卖部
market	shìchǎng	市场
May I have a look?	Wǒ Kànyíxia, hǎo ma?	我看一下，好吗？
I want to buy . . .	Wǒ xiǎng mǎi . . .	我想买 . . .
How many do you want?	Nǐ yào jǐ ge?	你要几个？
Two of them	liǎng ge	两个
Three of them	sān ge	三个
1 kilo	yì gōngjīn	一公斤
Half a kilo	yì jīn	一斤
1m	yì mǐ	一米
Too expensive!	Tài guì le!	太贵了
Do you have change?	Yǒu língqián ma?	有零钱吗?

Time

English	Pinyin	Chinese
morning	shàngwǔ	上午
afternoon	xiàwǔ	下午
evening	wǎnshang	晚上
8:20am	shàngwǔ bā diǎn èr shí fēn	上午八点二十分
9:30am	shàngwǔ jiǔ diǎn bàn	上午九点半
noon	zhōngwǔ	中午
4:15pm	xiàwǔ sì diǎn yí kè	下午四点一刻
midnight	wǔ yè	午夜
1 hour	yí ge xiǎoshí	一个小时
8 hours	bā ge xiǎoshí	八个小时
today	jīntiān	今天
yesterday	zuótiān	昨天
tomorrow	míngtiān	明天
Monday	Xīngqī yī	星期一
Tuesday	Xīngqī èr	星期二
Wednesday	Xīngqī sān	星期三
Thursday	Xīngqī sì	星期四
Friday	Xīngqī wǔ	星期五
Saturday	Xīngqī liù	星期六
Sunday	Xīngqī tiān	星期天

Transportation & Travel

English	Pinyin	Chinese
I want to take . . .	Wǒ xiǎng qù . . .	我想去乘 . . .
plane	fēijī	飞机
train	huǒchē	火车
bus	gōnggòng qìchē	公共汽车
long-distance bus	chángtú qìchē	长途汽车
taxi	chūzū chē	出租车
airport	fēijīchǎng	飞机场
stop or station (bus or train)	zhàn	站
(plane/train/bus) ticket	piào	票
luxury (bus, hotel rooms)	háohuá	豪华
high-speed (buses, expressways)	gāosù	高速
air-conditioned	kōngtiáo	空调
I want to go to . . .	Wǒ xiǎng qù . . .	我想去 . . .
When's the last bus?	Mòbānchē jīdiǎn kāi?	末班车几点开?

Navigation

English	Pinyin	Chinese
north	běi	北
south	nán	南
east	dōng	东
west	xī	西
central	zhōng	中
inside	neì	内
outside	waì	外中
I'm lost.	Wǒ diū le.	我迷路了
Turn left.	Zuǒ guǎi.	左拐
Turn right.	Yòu guǎi.	右拐
Go straight on.	Yìzhí zǒu.	一直走
junction	lùkǒu	路口
10km	shí gōnglǐ	十公里

Hotel

English	Pinyin	Chinese
How many days?	Zhù jǐ tiān?	住几天?
standard room (twin or double with private bathroom)	biāozhǔn jiān	标准间
passport	hùzhào	护照
deposit	yājīn	押金
I want to check out.	Wǒ tuì fáng.	我退房

Signs

Here's a list of common signs and notices to help you identify what you are looking for, from restaurants to condiments, and to help you choose the right door at the public toilets. These are the simplified characters in everyday use in China, but note that it's increasingly fashionable for larger businesses and for those with a long history to use more complicated traditional characters, so not all may match what's below. Also, very old restaurants and temples across China tend to write their signs from right to left.

English	Pinyin	Chinese
hotel	bīnguǎn	宾馆
	dàjiǔdiàn	大酒店
	jiǔdiàn	酒店
	fàndiàn	饭店
restaurant	fànguǎn	饭馆
	jiǔdiàn	酒店
	jiǔjiā	酒家
bar	jiǔbā	酒吧
Internet bar	wǎngbā	网吧

English	Pinyin	Chinese
cafe	kāfēiguǎn	咖啡馆
teahouse	cháguǎn	茶馆
department store	bǎihuò shāngdiàn	百货商店
shopping mall	gòuwù zhōngxīn	购物中心
market	shìchǎng	市场
bookstore	shūdiàn	书店
police (Public Security Bureau)	gōng'ānjú	公安局
Bank of China	Zhōngguó Yínháng	中国银行
public telephone	gōngyòng diànhuà	公用电话
public restroom	gōngyòng cèsuǒ	公用厕所
male	nán	男
female	nǚ	女
entrance	rùkǒu	入口
exit	chūkǒu	出口
bus stop/station	qìchē zhàn	汽车站
up (get on bus)	shang	上
down (get off bus)	xia	下
long-distance bus station	chángtú qìchē zhàn	长途汽车站
luxury	háohuá	豪华
highway	gāosù	高速公路
railway station	huǒchēzhàn	火车站
hard seat	yìng zuò	硬座
soft seat	ruǎn zuò	软座
hard sleeper	yìng wò	硬卧
soft sleeper	ruǎn wò	软卧
direct (through) train	zhídá	直达车
express train	tèkuài	特快
subway station	dìtiězhàn	地铁站
airport	fēijīchǎng	飞机场
dock/wharf	mǎtóu	码头
passenger terminal (bus, boat, and so on)	kèyùn zhàn	客运站
ticket hall	shòupiào tīng	售票厅
ticket office	shòupiào chù	售票处
left-luggage office	xíngli jìcún chù	行李寄存处
temple	sì	寺
or	miào	庙
museum	bówùguǎn	博物馆
memorial hall	jìniànguǎn	纪念馆
park	gōngyuán	公园
hospital	yīyuàn	医院
clinic	zhěnsuǒ	诊所
pharmacy	yàofáng/yàodiàn	药房/药店
travel agency	lǚxíngshè	旅行社

Index

See also Accommodations and Restaurant indexes, below.

General Index

A

Accommodations. ***See also*** **Accommodations Index**
- Beijing, 96–109
  - airport hotels, 110
  - Chaoyang District, 104–108
  - City Center & South Dongcheng, 98–102
  - Haidian District, 108–109
  - North Dongcheng (Gulou Area), 102–103
  - Xicheng District, 108
- best, 3–4
- Chengde, 140–141
- Hangzhou, 271
- Huashan, 182
- Luoyang, 189–190
- Nanjing, 278
- Shanghai, 226–238
  - airport hotels, 238
  - business motels, 235
  - the French Concession, 231–232
  - Hongkou & Zhabei, 234–236
  - Huangpu & the Old City, 227–231
  - Jing'an, 233–234
  - Pudong, 236–238
- Suzhou, 262
- tips on, 291–292
- Tongli, 265
- Xi'an, 162–168

Acrobatics
- Beijing, 126–127
- Shanghai, 253

Air travel, 279–281
- Beijing, 56–57
- Hangzhou, 267
- Luoyang, 183
- Nanjing, 272
- Shanghai, 192–193
- Xi'an, 143–144

Altar for Harvests (Xiannong Tan; Beijing), 87

Amilal (Beijing), 123

Ancestor Worshiping Temple (Fengxian Si; Luoyang), 185

Ancient Architecture Museum (Gudai Jianzhu Bowuguan; Beijing), 87

Ancient Coin Exhibition Hall (Gudai Qianbi Zhanlanguan; Beijing), 85

Ancient Han Tombs (Gumu Bowuguan; Luoyang), 186–187

Ancient Observatory (Gu Guanxiang Tai; Beijing), 77

Antique and Art City (Xi'an Shuyuanmen Guwan Yishu Cheng), 174–175

The Apartment (Shanghai), 253

Aperture Club (Guang Juan Julebu; Xi'an), 177–178

Apps for travel in China, 282–283

Architecture, 44–46

Art Deco, Shanghai, 207

The arts, 42–44

ATMs/banks, 292
- Beijing, 63
- Shanghai, 201
- Xi'an, 150

B

Ba Da Hutong (Beijing), 105

Bai Causeway (Bai Di; Hangzhou), 269

Baiyun Taoist Temple (Baiyun Guan; Shanghai), 211

Bank of Communications Building (Shanghai), 207

Banks and ATMs, 292
- Beijing, 63
- Shanghai, 201
- Xi'an, 150

Banpo Neolithic Village (Banpo Bowuguan; Xi'an), 161

Bar at Migas (Beijing), 123

Barbarossa (Shanghai), 251

Bar Rouge (Shanghai), 251

Bars and pubs
- Beijing, 122–125
- Shanghai, 251–252

Bei Feng (North Peak), 181

Beihai Park (Beihai Gongyuan; Beijing), 85

Beijing, 55–130
- accommodations, 96–109
  - airport hotels, 110
  - Chaoyang District, 104–108
  - City Center & South Dongcheng, 98–102
  - Haidian District, 108–109
  - North Dongcheng (Gulou Area), 102–103
  - Xicheng District, 108
- arriving in, 56–57
- day trips from, 131–141
  - Chengde, 137–141
  - The Great Wall, 131–136
  - the Ming Tombs, 136–137
- exploring, 65–96
  - around Central Dongcheng, 77–78
  - Central Dongcheng (Beijing), exploring, 65–77
  - North Dongcheng (Gulou Area), 79–83
  - South Dongcheng, 83–84
  - Xicheng, 85–88
- getting around, 60–62
- for kids, 128–130
- layout, 58–59
- neighborhoods in brief, 59–60
- nightlife, 121–130
- restaurants, 109–118
  - cafes and coffee shops, 119
  - Central Dongcheng, 111–114
  - Chaoyang District, 116–118
  - North Dongcheng (Gulou Area), 114–116
- shopping, 118–121
- visitor information, 57–58
- waterways, 84

Beijing Aquarium (Beijing Haiyangguan), 129

Beijing Art Museum (Wanshou Si), 92

Beijing Capital International Airport, 56–57

Beijing Concert Hall (Beijing Yinyue Ting), 128

Beijing National Stadium, 91

Beijing New Art Projects, 88

Beijing Opera (Jingju), 125–126

Beijing Planning Exhibition Hall (Beijing Guihua Bowyuguan), 74

Beijing Police Museum, 75

Belgian Bar (Xi'an), 177

Bell & Drum Towers (Xi'an), 154

Beverages, 49

Bibliotheca Zikawei (Shanghai), 218

Biking
- Beijing, 62
- Hangzhou, 268
- Xi'an, 2, 147

Bird, Flower, Fish, and Insect Market (Shanghai), 249

Books and maps
- Beijing, 64
- Shanghai, 202
- Xi'an, 150

British Consulate (Shanghai), 206

Broadway Mansions (Shanghai), 207

Brown Sugar (Shanghai), 252, 254

Buddhism, 30

The Bund (Waitan; Shanghai), exploring, 203

Bund Bull (Shanghai), 206

Bund History Museum (Shanghai), 206

Bund Sightseeing Tunnel (Shanghai), 255

Bund Sightseeing Tunnel (Waitan Guanguang Suidao; Shanghai), 206

Burlesque, Shanghai, 254

Business hours, 293

Bus travel, 286
Beijing, 57, 62
Hangzhou, 267, 268
Huashan, 181
Luoyang, 184
Shanghai, 193, 200
Suzhou, 259
Tongli, 263
Xi'an, 144, 147

C

Calendar of events, 53–54
Cang Long Feng (Green Dragon Ridge), 181
Cantonese food, 47
Capital Museum (Shoudu Bowuguan; Beijing), 87
Car travel, 289
Cathay Hotel (Shanghai), 203, 206
Cathay Theatre (Shanghai), 207
Cellphones, 296
Central Dongcheng (Beijing), 59
exploring, 65–77
restaurants, 111–114
Century Park (Shiji Gongyuan; Shanghai), 223
Chairman Mao's Mausoleum (Mao Zhuxi Jinian Guan; Beijing), 74
Chang Ling, 137
Chaoyang District (Beijing), 60
accommodations, 104–108
exploring, 88, 90–92
restaurants, 116–118
Chaoyang Park (Chaoyang Gongyuan; Beijing), 129
Chaoyang Theatre (Chaoyang Juchang; Beijing), 127
CHAR (Shanghai), 252
Chengde, 137–141
Children, families with, 294
Beijing attractions, 128
best for, 5
Shanghai, 254
suggested itinerary, 17–21
China Art Museum (Shanghai), 223–224
China Baptist Publishing Building (Shanghai), 206
China National Film Museum (Zhongguo Dianying Bowuguan; Beijing), 90
China Sex Culture Museum (Tongli), 263, 265
Chinese language, 300–307
Chinese New Year (Spring Festival), 50–51
Chinese opera, Shanghai, 254
Chinese Tea Museum (Zhongguo Chaye Bowuguan; Hangzhou), 270
Chongben Tang (Tongli), 263
Chopsticks, 47
City Walls (Cheng Qiang; Xi'an), 154–155
Climate, 51–52
Cloud 9 (Shanghai), 252
Cloud Rock Pagoda (Yunyan Ta; Suzhou), 261
Club JZ (Shanghai), 254
Confucianism, 30
Confucius Temple (Kong Miao; Beijing), 79
Confucius Temple (Wen Miao; Shanghai), 211–212
Constellation (Shanghai), 251
Consulates, Shanghai, 201–202
Cotton Club (Shanghai), 254
Cotton's (Shanghai), 251
Credit cards, 292–293
Cruise ships, Shanghai, 196, 280
Cultural Relics Exhibition Hall (Xi'an), 151
Customs House (Shanghai), 203
Customs regulations, 293
Cycling
Beijing, 62
Hangzhou, 268
Xi'an, 2, 147

D

Dajing Pavilion & Ancient City Wall (Dajing Ge; Shanghai), 212
Daming Palace (Daming Gong; Xi'an), 157
Damo's Cave (Damo Dong), 189
Dance clubs, Shanghai, 253
Dazhalan (Beijing), 87
Dino Beach (Shanghai), 256
Disabled travelers, 293
D-Mall (Shanghai), 248
Doctors and dentists, 293–294
Beijing, 63
Shanghai, 201
Xi'an, 150
Dongcheng (Beijing), 59
exploring
Central Dongcheng, 65–77
around Central Dongcheng, 77–78
North Dongcheng (Gulou Area), 79–83
South Dongcheng, 83–84
Donghuamen Night Market (Beijing), 111
Dongtai Lu Antiques Market (Shanghai), 249
Dongyue Temple (Dongyue Miao; Beijing), 90–91
Dragon Boat Festival, 54
Dragon Well Village (Longjing Wencha; Hangzhou), 270
DR Bar (Shanghai), 252
Drinking laws, 294
Drum & Bell Towers (Gu Lou/ Zhong Lou; Beijing), 79, 82
Drum Tower (Gu Lou; Nanjing), 274
Drum Tower (Xi'an), 154
Duolun Lu Culture Street (Shanghai), 221–222

E

Eating, 46–49
Eid al-Fitr, 54
Eight Outer Temples (Wai Ba Miao; Chengde), 139
Electricity, 294
El Nido (Beijing), 123
El Ocho (Shanghai), 252
Embassies, 63
Emergencies, 294
Emperor Jingdi's Mausoleum (Han Yangling; Xi'an), 161–162
ERA: Intersection of Time (Shanghai), 253

F

Fairmont Peace Hotel (Shanghai), 207
Families with children, 294
Beijing attractions, 128
best for, 5
Shanghai, 254
suggested itinerary, 17–21
Fayuan Temple (Fayuan Si; Beijing), 87–88
Feilai Feng (Hangzhou), 271
Five Dragon Pavilion (Beijing), 85–86
Flower and Bird Pavilion (Hangzhou), 269
Flower Harbor Park (Huagang Yuan; Hangzhou), 270
Food and cuisine, 46–49
The Forbidden City (Gu Gong; Beijing), 65, 68–71
Forbidden City Concert Hall (Beijing), 128
Foreign Languages Bookstore (Beijing), 64
Forest of Lions Garden (Shizi LIn YuAn; Suzhou), 259–260
Forest of Steles Museum (Beilin Bowuguan; Xi'an), 155–156, 176
Forest of Stupas (Ta Lin), 189
Former Residence of Lao She (Lao She Jinian Guan; Beijing), 77–78
Former Residence of Sun Yat-sen (Shanghai), 217
Formula One Racing, 54
Fragrant Hills Park (Xiangshan Gongyuan; Beijing), 93–94
The French Concession (Shanghai), 2, 198
accommodations, 231–232
bars and lounges, 251–252
exploring, 213, 216–219
shopping, 248
Fuxing Park (Fuxing Gongyuan; Shanghai), 198, 213, 255
Fuyou Antiques Market (Shanghai), 249

G

Gaojia Dayuan (Xi'an), 173
Great Bell Temple (Da Zhong Si; Beijing), 92–93
Great Hall of the People (Renmin Dahui Tang; Beijing), 74–75
Great Leap Brewing (Beijing), 124
Great Mosque (Da Qingzhen Si; Xi'an), 156
Great Tang All Day Mall (Da Tang Bu Ye Cheng; Xi'an), 160
The Great Wall, 2, 15, 24, 131–136
Great Wild Goose Pagoda (Da Yan Ta; Xi'an), 158, 160
Green Dragon Ridge (Cang Long Feng), 181
Gubei Water Town (Gubei Shui Zhen), 135
Gulou area (Beijing), 123

H

Haidian District (Beijing), 60
  accommodations, 108–109
  exploring, 92–96
Hall for Keeping the Spring (Dianchun Yi; Suzhou), 260–261
Hall of Eminent Favors (Ling'en Dian), 137
Hall of Heralding Spring (Dian Chun Tang; Shanghai), 209
Han City Fashion and Accessories Market (Shanghai), 250
Hangzhou, 10–11, 25, 267–272
Hanyuan Palace (Hanyuan Gong; Xi'an), 157
Happy Magic Watercube Waterpark (Beijing), 130
Happy Valley Amusement Park (Beijing Huanle Gu; Beijing), 130
Health, 294–295
Hengshan Road Community Church (Shanghai), 213, 216
Hiking, The Great Wall, 135
History of China, 27–42
Holidays, 50–51, 53
Hong Kong and Shanghai Bank, 203
Hong Kong Shopping Center (Shanghai), 248
Hongkou and Zhabei districts (Shanghai), 198
  accommodations, 234
  exploring, 221
Hongqiao Airport (Shanghai), 193
Hongqiao International Airport (Shanghai), 192
Hongqiao Market (Hongqiao Jimao Shichang; Beijing), 121
Hotels. *See also* Accommodations Index
  Beijing, 96–109
    airport hotels, 110
    Chaoyang District, 104–108
    City Center & South Dongcheng, 98–102
    Haidian District, 108–109
    North Dongcheng (Gulou Area), 102–103
    Xicheng District, 108
  best, 3–4
  Chengde, 140–141
  Hangzhou, 271
  Huashan, 182
  Luoyang, 189–190
  Nanjing, 278
  Shanghai, 226–238
    airport hotels, 238
    business motels, 235
    the French Concession, 231–232
    Hongkou & Zhabei, 234–236
    Huangpu & the Old City, 227–231
    Jing'an, 233–234
    Pudong, 236–238
  Suzhou, 262
  tips on, 291–292
  Tongli, 265
  Xi'an, 162–168
House of Blues and Jazz (Shanghai), 254
Huajue Xiang (Xi'an), 175
Huangpu District (Shanghai), 197–198
  accommodations, 227–231
  exploring, 203–209
  restaurants, 239–240
Huangpu Park (Shanghai), 206
Huangpu River (Huangpu Jiang), cruises, 223
Huashan, 16, 24, 179–182
Huguang Guild Hall (Huguang Huiguan Xilou; Beijing), 126
Humble Administrator's Garden (Zhuo Zheng; Suzhou), 260
Hutong, 97

I

Imperial College (Guozijian; Beijing), 79
Imperial Mountain Retreat (Bishu Shanzhuang; Chengde), 138, 139
Impression West Lake (Hangzhou), 272
Insurance, 295
InterContinental Ruijin (Shanghai), 217
International Artists Factory (Shanghai), 216
Internet and Wi-Fi, 295–296
  Beijing, 63
  Shanghai, 202
Island of Small Seas (Xiao Ying Zhou; Hangzhou), 269
Itineraries, suggested, 8–26

J

Jade Buddha Temple (Yufo Si; Shanghai), 219–220
Jade on 36 (Shanghai), 252
Jian-ghu Bar (Beijing), 127
Jiangnan, water towns of, 265
Jiankou, The Great Wall at, 136
Jiayin Tang (Tongli), 263
Jing'an District (Shanghai), 198
  accommodations, 233–234
  exploring, 219–221
  restaurants, 244–245
  shopping, 248
Jing'an Park (Jing'an Gongyuan; Shanghai), 220
Jing'an Sculpture Park (Shanghai), 254–255
Jing'an Temple (Jing'an Si; Shanghai), 220
Jingshan Park (Jingshan Gongyuan; Beijing), 71
Jinjiang Amusement Park (Shanghai), 256
Jinmao Tower (Shanghai), 224–225
Jinshanling section of the Great Wall, 135
Juanqinzhai (Beijing), 68
Junji Peak (Junji Feng), 188

K

Kommune (Shanghai), 252
Kunming Lake (Kunming Hu; Beijing), 94–95

L

Labor Day, 54
Lama Temple (Yonghegong; Beijing), 82
LAN Club (Beijing), 124
Lantern Festival, 53
Lao She, Former Residence of (Beijing), 77–78
Lao She Teahouse (Lao She Chaguan; Beijing), 127
League of Leftist Writers Museum (Shanghai), 222
Legation Quarter (Dongjiaomin Xiang; Beijing), 75
Leifeng Pagoda (Leifeng Ta; Hangzhou), 269
LGBT travelers, 296
Lilong (Shanghai), 219
Lingering Garden (Liu Yuan; Suzhou), 260
Linggu Temple (Linggu Si; Nanjing), 277
Lingshun Si (Hangzhou), 271
Lingyin Temple (Lingyin Si; Hangzhou), 271
Liyuan Theater (Liyuan Juchang; Beijing), 126
Longhua Temple (Longhua Si; Shanghai), 218
Longmen Grottoes (Longmen Shiku; Luoyang), 183–187
Lotus Flower Cave (Lianhua Dong; Luoyang), 185
Luoyang, 183–190
Luoyang Museum (Luoyang Bowuguan), 187

Lu Xun Park and Memorial Hall (Lu Xun Gongyuan/Lu Xun Jinianguan; Shanghai), 222
Lu Xun's Former Residence (Shanghai), 222

M

M20 (Shanghai), 221
M50 (Shanghai), 220–221
M97 (Shanghai), 221
Mai Bar (Beijing), 124
Mail and post offices, 296
- Beijing, 64
- Shanghai, 202
- Xi'an, 150

Malls, Beijing, 120
Mandarin Duck Hall (Suzhou), 260
Mandarin Oriental Blaze (Beijing), 109
Mansion Hotel (Shanghai), 217
MAO Livehouse (Beijing), 127–128
Maps and books
- Beijing, 64
- Shanghai, 202
- Xi'an, 150

Markets, Beijing, 120–121
Master of the Nets Garden (Wangshi Yuan; Suzhou), 260–261
May Day, 51
Medical Prescription Cave (Yaofang Dong; Luoyang), 186
Mediocre Art Salon (Xi'an), 176
Mei Lanfang Grand Theatre (Mei Lanfang Da Juyuan; Beijing), 126
Memorial to the Victims of the Nanjing Massacre (Nanjing Datusha Jinianguan), 274
Meridian Gate (Wu Men; Nanjing), 274
Meteorological Signal Tower (Shanghai), 206
Mid-Autumn Festival, 54
Ming City Wall Park (Ming Chengqiang Gongyuan; Beijing), 78
Ming Filial Tomb (Ming Xiao Ling; Nanjing), 276
Ming Gu Gong (Nanjing), 274
The Ming Tombs, 136–137
Mobile phones, 296
Moller Mansion (Shanghai), 217
Money and costs, 299
Monument to the People's Heroes (Renmin Yingxiong Jinian Bei; Beijing), 73
Monument to the People's Heroes (Shanghai), 206
Muse (Shanghai), 253
Museum of Contemporary Art (Shanghai Dangdai Yishuguan), 208
Museum of Modern Art (Shanghai), 221
The Muslim Quarter (Xi'an), 156–157
Mutianyu, 132, 134–135

N

Nanjing, 272–278
Nanjing Dong Lu (Shanghai), 247
Nanjing Lu Pedestrian Mall (Shanghai), 247
Nanjing Massacre (1937), 277
Nanjing Museum (Nanjing Bowuguan), 274–276
Nanjing Road (Nanjing Dong Lu; Shanghai), 207
Nan Luogu Xiang (Beijing), 83
Nanxun, 265
National Centre for the Performing Arts (Guojia Da Juyuan; Beijing), 75–76
National Day, 51, 54
National Museum of China (Beijing), 76, 77
Natural History Museum (Shanghai), 221
Near Wall Bar (Xi'an), 177
Nightlife
- Beijing, 121–130
  - bars, pubs and clubs, 122–125
  - performing arts, 125–130
- Hangzhou, 272
- Shanghai, 250–254
- Xi'an, 176–178

Night market
- Beijing, 111
- Chengde, 141

1933 (Shanghai), 221
North Dongcheng (Gulou Area; Beijing)
- accommodations, 102–103
- exploring, 79–83
- restaurants, 114–116

North Peak (Bei Feng), 181
North Peak Mountain (Beigao Feng; Hangzhou), 271

O

The Old City (Shanghai), 198
- accommodations, 227–231
- exploring, 209–213

Old Jazz Bar (Shanghai), 254
Old Summer Palace (Yuanmingyuan; Beijing), 94
Old Sun Cave (Guyang Dong; Luoyang), 186
Olympic Forest Park (Beijing), 91
Olympic Park (Aolinpike Gongyuan; Beijing), 91–92
Olympic Park Observation Tower (Beijing), 91–92, 129
On The Road (Zai Lu Shang Jiu Ba; Xi'an), 177
Oriental Pearl TV Tower (Shanghai), 3, 225
The Original Works Artists' Studio (Shanghai), 216
Ox Street Mosque (Niu Jie Qingzhen Si; Beijing), 88

P

Packing tips, 296–297
Pairet, Paul, 240
Palace of Righteousness (Zheng Gong; Chengde), 139
Panjiayuan Flea Market (Panjiayuan Jiuhuo Shichang; Beijing), 121
Park Hotel (Shanghai), 207
Paulaner's (Shanghai), 251
Peach Garden Mosque (Xiao Taoyuan Qingzhensi; Shanghai), 212
The Pearl (Shanghai), 254
Pearl Market (Beijing), 121
Peony Festival (Luoyang), 183, 187, 189
People's Square (Renmin Guangchang; Shanghai), 207–208
Pharmacies, 297
- Beijing, 64
- Shanghai, 202

Pinjiang Lu (Suzhou), 261
Piying, 173
Police, 297
Pollution, 50, 52–53
Poly Theater (Baoli Dasha Guoji Juyuan), 128
Pool of Swords (Jian Chi; Suzhou), 261
Post office
- Beijing, 64
- Shanghai, 202
- Xi'an, 150

Potala Temple (Putuozongcheng Zhi Miao; Chengde), 139
Power Station of Art (Shanghai), 212–213
Presidential Palace (Zongtong Fu; Nanjing), 276
Prince Gong's Mansion (Gong Wangfu Huayuan; Beijing), 86
Propaganda Poster Art Center (Shanghai), 216
Pudong (Shanghai), 198
- accommodations, 236–238
- exploring, 223
- restaurant, 246

Pudong International Airport (Shanghai), 192–193
Pureland (Shanghai), 248
Purple Mountain (Zijin Shan; Nanjing), 276–277
Puyou Temple (Puyou Si; Chengde), "Silk Road," 140

Q

Q Bar (Beijing), 124–125
Qian Men (Beijing), 76–77
Qibao, 265
Qin Shihuang's Mausoleum (Xi'an), 154
Qipu Lu (Shanghai), 250

R

Restaurants, 2. *See also* Restaurants Index
Beijing, 109–118
cafes and coffee shops, 119
Central Dongcheng, 111–114
Chaoyang District, 116–118
North Dongcheng (Gulou Area), 114–116
best, 3
Hangzhou, 271–272
Luoyang, 190
Nanjing, 278
Shanghai, 238–246
the French Concession, 240–243
Huangpu, 239–240
Jing'an District, 244–245
Pudong, 246
Western-run chains, 246
Suzhou, 262
Tongli, 265
Xi'an, 168–173
Retreat and Reflection Garden (Tui Si Yuan; Tongli), 263
Ritan Park (Ritan Gongyuan; Beijing), 92
Riverside Promenade (Binjiang Da Dao; Shanghai), 225
Riverside Promenade Walk (Shanghai), 206–207

S

Safety, 297
St. Francis Xavier's Church (Sheng Fangjige Shawulüe Tang; Shanghai), 212
St. Ignatius Cathedral (Xujiahui Tianzhutang; Shanghai), 218–219
St. Joseph's Cathedral (Dong Tang; Beijing), 78
Sanhuang Palace (Sanhuang Xinggong), 188
Sanlitun (Beijing), 122
Sanxue Jie (Xi'an), 176
Sasha's (Shanghai), 252
Seasons, 50–51
Senior travel, 298
798 Art Zone (Qijiuba Yishuqu; Beijing), 88, 90
789 Nanjing Lu (Shanghai), 252
Shaanxi History Museum (Shanxi Lishi Bowuguan; Xi'an), 160–161
Shanghai, 191–256
accommodations, 226–238
airport hotels, 238
business motels, 235
the French Concession, 231–232
Hongkou & Zhabei, 234–236
Huangpu & the Old City, 227–231
Jing'an, 233–234
Pudong, 236–238
arriving in, 192–193, 196
day trips from, 257–278
Hangzhou, 267–272
Nanjing, 272–278
Suzhou, 257–262
Tongli, 263–265
exploring, 202–226
Hongkou & Zhabei, 221–223
Huangpu District, 203–209
Jing'an District, 219–221
The Old City and nearby, 209–213
Pudong, 223–226
getting around, 198–201
for kids, 254–256
layout, 196–197
neighborhoods in brief, 197–198
nightlife, 250–254
restaurants, 238–246
shopping, 246–250
street food, 244
suggested itineraries, 10, 20–21, 25–26
visitor information, 196
Shanghai Art Museum (Shanghai Meishuguan), 208
Shanghai Arts and Crafts Museum, 217
Shanghai Brewery, 251–252
Shanghai Centre Theater (Shanghai Shangcheng Juyuan), 253
Shanghai Changfeng Ocean World, 256
Shanghai Club, 203
Shanghai Disney Resort, 255
Shanghai Insiders, 219
Shanghai International Cruise Terminal, 196
Shanghai Jewish Refugees Museum, 222–223
Shanghai Municipal History Museum (Shanghai Shi Lishi Chenlieguan), 225–226
Shanghai Museum (Shanghai Bowuguan), 208–209
Shanghai Ocean Aquarium, 255
Shanghai Rowing Club, 206
Shanghai Science and Technology Museum, 255
Shanghai Tower, 224
Shanghai Urban Planning Exhibition Center (Shanghai Chengshi Guihua Zhanshiguan), 209
Shanghai Wild Animal Park, 255
Shanghai Wild Insect Kingdom, 255
Shanghai World Financial Center (Shanghai Huanqiu Jinrong Zhongxin), 226
Shanghai Zoo, 256
Shantang Jie (Suzhou), 261
Shanxi Grand Opera House (Shanxi Gewu Da Xiyuan; Xi'an), 178
Shaolin Martial Arts Training Center (Shaolin Wushu Guan), 189
Shaolin Suodao, 188
Shaolin Temple (Shaolin Si; Songshan), 187–189
Shaoshishan, 188
The Shelter (Shanghai), 253
Shikumen Open House Museum (Shanghai), 217–218
Shiliupu Marina (Shiliupu Matou; Shanghai), 223
Shopping
Beijing, 118–121
Shanghai, 246–250
Xi'an, 173–176
Shuyuanmen (Xi'an), 174
Sichuan cooking, 48
Silk Market (Xiushui Fuzhuang Shichang; Beijing), 121
Simatai, 135–136
Site of the 1st Congress of the Chinese Communist Party (Shanghai), 216
Small Wild Goose Pagoda (Xiao Yan Ta; Xi'an), 157
Smoking, 298
Solitary Island (Gushan Dao; Hangzhou), 269–270
Songshan, 25, 187, 188, 231
Song Shan Diaoqiao, 188
Song Shan Shaolin Suodao, 188
Songyang Suodao, 188
Songyue Temple Pagoda, 188
Songzhuang, 88, 90
Soong Ching-ling's Former Residence (Shanghai), 217
South Bund Soft Material Spinning Market (Shanghai), 250
South Dongcheng, exploring, 83–84
South Dongcheng (Beijing), accommodations, 98–102
South Gate (Nan Men; Xi'an), 155
Spas, Beijing, 104
Spirit Way (Shen Dao), 136
Spring Festival, 53
Spring Festival (Chinese New Year), 50–51
Starbucks (Beijing), 119
The Star Live (Beijing), 128
Stone Room Cave (Shiku Dong; Luoyang), 186
Street food
Beijing, 111
Shanghai, 244
Xi'an, 168
Student travel, 298
Subway, 287, 289
Beijing, 60–61
Hangzhou, 268
Nanjing, 274
Shanghai, 193, 198–199

Suzhou, 259
Xi'an, 146
Su Causeway (Su Di; Hangzhou), 270
Summer Palace (Yiheyuan; Beijing), 94–96
Sun Yat-sen, Former Residence of, 217
Sun Yat-sen's Mausoleum (Zhongshan Ling; Nanjing), 276
Suzhou, 17, 257–262
Suzhou Museum (Suzhou Bowuguan), 262
Suzhou Silk Museum (Suzhou Sichou Bowuguan), 262

T

Taikang Lu (Tianzifang; Shanghai), 216
Taiping Heavenly Kingdom, 275
Taiping Rebellion, 275
Taishishan, 187, 188
Tang Dynasty (Tang Yue Gong; Xi'an), 178
Tang Paradise (Da Tang Fu Rong Yuan; Xi'an), 161
Tang Western Market (Xi'an), 175
Taoguang Guanhai Si (Hangzhou), 271
Taoism, 30
Taxes, 298
Shanghai, 202
Taxis, 286–288
Beijing, 61
Chengde, 139
The Great Wall, 134
Hangzhou, 268
Luoyang, 184
Nanjing, 274
Shanghai, 193, 199–200
Xi'an, 146–147
Teahouse of Prince Gong's Mansion (Gong Wang Fu Chaguan; Beijing), 126
Teahouse theater, Beijing, 127
Temperatures, average, 52
Temple Bar (Beijing), 125, 127
Temple of Distant Peace (Anyuan Miao; Chengde), 140
Temple of Goodness (Yongfu Si; Hangzhou), 271
Temple of Happiness and Longevity (Xumifushou Miao; Chengde), 140
The Temple of Heaven (Tian Tan; Beijing), 83
Temple of the Eight Immortals (Ba Xian An; Xi'an), 158
Temple of the Eight Immortals Antiques Market (Xi'an), 175
Temple of Universal Joy (Pule Si; Chengde), 140
The Temple of Universal Peace (Puning Si; Chengde), 140
Ten Thousand Buddha Cave (Wan Fo Dong; Luoyang), 185
Ten Thousand People Rock (Wanren Shi; Suzhou), 261
Terracotta Warriors (Bingmayong; Xi'an), 150–151, 154
Terracotta Warriors (Xi'an), 2
Thousand Buddha Hall (Qian Fo Dian), 189
Three Binyang Caves (Binyang San Dong; Luoyang), 185
Three Pools Mirroring The Moon (San Tan Yinyue; Hangzhou), 270
Tian'anmen (Gate of Heavenly Peace; Beijing), 71–72
Tian'anmen Square (Tian'anmen Guangchang; Beijing), 2–3, 73–74
Tiandi Theater (Beijing), 127
Tianqiao Acrobatics Theatre (Tianqiao Zaiji Juchang; Beijing), 127
Tianzifang (Shanghai), 252
Tiger Hill (Suzhou), 261
Tipping, 298
TMSK (Shanghai), 252
Toilets, 298
Tomb-Sweeping Festival, 54
Tongli, 16–17, 263–265
Toy City (Hongqiao Tianle Wanju Shichang; Beijing), 121
Train travel, 280, 281–286
Beijing, 57
Chengde, 138
Hangzhou, 267
Huashan, 181
Luoyang, 183
Nanjing, 272
Shanghai, 193, 196
Suzhou, 257, 259
Xi'an, 144
Twin Villas (Shanghai), 217

U

Underground Palace, 137
Unico (Shanghai), 251
Union Church (Shanghai), 206
Union Insurance Company Building (Shanghai), 203

V

Visas and visa extensions, 290–291
Beijing, 64
Shanghai, 202
Xi'an, 150
Visitor information
Beijing, 57–58
Hangzhou, 268
Nanjing, 274
Shanghai, 196
Xi'an, 144–145
VPN (Virtual Private Network), 283

W

Waibaidu Bridge (Shanghai), 206
Wangcheng Park (Wangcheng Gongyuan; Luoyang), 187
Wangfujing Bookstore (Beijing), 64
Wangfujing Dajie (Beijing), 119–120
Water, drinking, 295
Weather, 50–52
Beijing, 64
Shanghai, 202
Wenshu Hall (Wenshu Dian), 189
West Lake (Xi Hu), 267, 268–269
West Peak (Xi Feng), 181–182
White Cloud Temple (Baiyun Guan; Beijing), 96
White Dagoba Temple (Baita Si; Beijing), 86–87
White Horse Temple (Baima Si; Luoyang), 186
Workers' Cultural Palace (Laodong Renmin Wenhua Gong; Beijing), 72–73
Wudaokou area (Beijing), 122
Wudaoying Hutong (Beijing), 127
Wusong Kou Passenger Terminal (Shanghai), 196
Wuzhen, 265

X

Xi'an, 142–178
accommodations, 162–168
arriving in, 143–144
cuisine, 169
day trips from, 179–190
Huashan, 179–182
Luoyang, 183–190
exploring, 150–162
getting around, 146–147
itineraries, 15–16, 20, 24
layout, 145
neighborhoods in brief, 145–146
nightlife, 176–178
restaurants, 168–173
shopping, 173–176
visitor information, 144–145
Xi'an Insiders (near Xi'an), 183
Xi'an Museum (Xi'an Bowuguan), 157–158
Xi'an Xianyang International Airport, 143
Xi Cang Market (Xi'an), 176
Xicheng (Beijing), exploring, 85–88
Xicheng District (Beijing), 59–60
accommodations, 108
Xi Feng (West Peak), 181–182
Xihutiandi (Hangzhou), 268–269
Xintiandi (Shanghai), 216–218
Xitang, 265
Xiu (Beijing), 125
Xujiahui (Shanghai), 213

Y

***Yaodong* (cave dwellings), 183**
Yifu Theatre (Shanghai), 254
Yu Garden (Yu Yuan; Shanghai), 209

Yugong Yishan (Beijing), 128
Yuyuan Bazaar (Yuyuan Shangcheng; Shanghai), 209, 211, 248

Z

Zapata's (Shanghai), 252
Zhao Ling, 137
Zhejiang Provincial Museum (Zhejiang Sheng Bowuguan; Hangzhou), 270
Zhonghua Gate City Walls (Zhonghua Men Chengbao; Nanjing), 277
Zhongshan Dong Yi Lu Walk (Shanghai), 203, 206
Zhongshan Park (Hangzhou), 269–270
Zhou Enlai's Former Residence (Shanghai), 217
Zhouzhuang, 265
Zhujiajiao, 265
Zhuque Gate (Xi'an), 155
Zoo Bar (Xi'an), 177

Accommodations

A.hotel (Beijing), 106–107
Aman at Summer Palace (Beijing), 108–109
Amanfayun (Hangzhou), 271
Andaz Xintiandi Shanghai (Shanghai), 231
Bamboo Garden Hotel (Zhu Yuan Binguan; Beijing), 102–103
Bijiayi Kuaijie Jiudian (Huashan), 182
Central Hotel (Shanghai), 230
Christian's Hotel (Luoyang), 190
Citadines Central Xi'an, 164
CITIC Hotel Beijing Airport (Beijing), 110
Conrad Hotel (Beijing), 104
Courtyard 7 (Beijing), 103
Days Inn Forbidden City (Beijing), 101–102
Dazhong Airport Hotel (Shanghai), 238
Double Happiness Courtyard Hotel (Beijing), 100
Du Ge Hotel (Beijing), 102
East Hotel (Beijing), 107
East Peak Hotel (Dong Feng Binguan; Huashan), 182
The Emperor Beijing Forbidden City, 101
Fairmont Peace Hotel (Shanghai), 227–228
Four Seasons (Beijing), 104–105
Four Seasons Beijing, 110
Four Seasons Hangzhou, 271
Fraser Residence Shanghai, 232
Grace Hotel (Beijing), 107
Grand Hyatt Shanghai, 236
Grand Mercure Shanghai Central (Shanghai), 235
Grand Noble (Xi'an), 164
Grand Park Xi'an, 166
Gran Melia (Xi'an), 167
Green Tree Inn (Shanghai), 235
Han's Royal Garden (Beijing), 102
Hilton Beijing Wangfujing (Beijing), 98
Hilton Hotel (Beijing), 110
Hilton Xi'an, 163
Holiday Inn Express Beijing Dongzhimen, 107–108
Holiday Inn Express Luoyang City Center, 189–190
Holiday Inn Nanjing Aqua City, 278
Hotel Indigo (Shanghai), 228
Howard Johnson Hongqiao Airport Hotel, 238
Huashan Kezhan, 182
The Hulu Hotel (Beijing), 101
Hyatt on the Bund (Shanghai), 234
Jano's Backpackers (Xi'an), 165
Jinjiang Metropolo Hotel Classiq Off Bund (Shanghai), 229–230
Jinji-ang Star (Shanghai), 235
Jinling Fandian (Nanjing), 278
Kevin's Old House (Shanghai), 233
Langham Hotel (Shanghai), 231
Longemont Hotel (Shanghai), 233
Mandarin Oriental Pudong (Shanghai), 236
Mansion Hotel (Shanghai), 231–232
Melody Hotel (Xi'an), 165
Mercure (Xi'an), 165
North Peak Hotel (Bei Feng Fandian; Huashan), 182
Opposite House (Beijing), 105–106
The Orchid (Beijing), 103
Pan Pacific Suzhou (Suzhou), 262
Park Hyatt Beijing, 106
Park Hyatt Shanghai, 237
Peking International Youth Hostel, 103
The Peninsula Hotel (Shanghai), 228
Pentahotel (Shanghai), 234
Pudong Shangri-La (Shanghai), 237
The Puli Hotel & Spa (Shanghai), 233
Puning Hotel (Puning Si Shangketang Da Jiudian; Chengde), 140
Qi Wang Lou Hotel (Chengde), 140–141
Raffles Beijing, 99–100
Ramada Plaza Pudong Airport (Shanghai), 238
Red Lantern House (Beijing), 108
Red Wall Garden Hotel (Beijing), 100–101
Regal International East Asia Hotel (Shanghai), 232
Ritz-Carlton Pudong (Shanghai), 237–238
The Rosewood (Beijing), 106
Salvo Hotel (Shanghai), 230–231
Scholars Hotel (Suzhou), 262
Shanghai International Airport Hotel, 238
Shanghai SOHO International Youth Hostel, 235–236
Shangri-la Hotel Hangzhou, 271
Sofitel Renmin Square (Xi'an), 163–164
Super Motel 168 (Shanghai), 235
Traders Upper East Hotel (Beijing), 110
URBN Hotel (Shanghai), 234
Waldorf Astoria (Shanghai), 229
The Waterhouse at South Bund (Shanghai), 229
Westin Xi'an, 167
Wyndham Grand (Xi'an), 167–168
Xi'an Garden Hotel (Xi'an), 168
Xi'an Green Forest Hotel (Xi'an), 166
Xiangzimen International Youth Hostel (Xi'an), 165–166
Yoyo Hotel (Beijing), 108

Restaurants

Bao Luo (Shanghai), 241
Bellagio (Beijing), 116
Black Sesame Kitchen (Beijing), 114
Blue Frog (Shanghai), 246
The Bookworm (Beijing), 119
The Bookworm (Song He Lou; Suzhou), 262
Cafe Zarah (Beijing), 119
Capital M (Beijing), 111–112
Capo (Shanghai), 239
Charmant (Shanghai), 242
Chuan Ban (Beijing), 113
Crescent Moon (Beijing), 113–114
Crystal Jade Restaurant (Shanghai), 241
Dadong Roast Duck (Beijing), 116
Dali Courtyard (Beijing), 115
De Fa Chang (Xi'an), 170
Ding Ding Xiang (Xi'an), 170
Din Tai Fung (Beijing), 117–118
Din Tai Fung (iAPM Mall; Shanghai), 242–243
Di Shui Dong (Shanghai), 242
Duck de Chine (Beijing), 112
Duo (Xi'an), 170
8-1/2 Otto e Mezzo Bombana (Shanghai), 239
881 South Beauty (Qiao Jiang Nan; Shanghai), 244
Element Fresh (Shanghai), 246
Fanji Lazhi Roudian (Xi'an), 171
Franck (Shanghai), 240
Fu 1088 (Shanghai), 244–245
Ginger (Shanghai), 241
Guyi Hunan (Shanghai), 245
Hai by Goga (Shanghai), 241–242
Hatsune (Beijing), 116–117
Isola del Nord (Xi'an), 171
Jade on 36 (Shanghai), 246

Jia San Guantang Baozi (Xi'an), 171
Kabb (Shanghai), 246
King's Joy (Beijing), 114
Lao Sun Jia (Xi'an), 172
Lao Wan (Xi'an), 172
Lei Garden (Beijing), 112–113
Lost Heaven (Beijing), 113
Lou Wai Lou (Hangzhou), 271–272
Luoyang Peony Hotel (Luoyang Mudan Da Jiudian), 190
Mr. Shi's Dumplings (Beijing), 115–116
Mr and Mrs Bund (Shanghai), 239–240
Najia Xiaoguan (Beijing), 118
Nanyuan Chashe (Tongli), 265
Noodle King (Biang Biang Mian), 172
Old Luoyang Noodle House (Lao Luoyang Mianguan), 190
Pin Chuan (Shanghai), 243
Pine and Crane Restaurant (Song He Lou; Suzhou), 262
Qin Tang Fu (Beijing), 117
Sake Manzo (Beijing), 117
Shanxi 13 (Shan Shi San; Xi'an), 173
Sichuan Citizen (Shanghai), 243
Southern Barbarian (Shanghai), 243
Susu (Beijing), 115
Taijian Nong (Suzhou), 262
Tang Dynasty (Tang Yue Gong; Xi'an), 173
Temple Restaurant Beijing, 112
Ultraviolet (Shanghai), 240
Vegetarian Lifestyle (Shanghai), 245
Wagas (Shanghai), 246
Xin Qianlong Da Jiudian (Chengde), 141